A Few Kind Words About Hate

A Few Kind Words About Hate

The Dark Side of Family Life and the Bible

Una Stannard

GermainBooks

GermainBooks
970 Garden Way
Ashland, OR 97520

SAN 2015986

ISBN: 0-914142-00-3

Library of Congress Control Number: 2006925927

For all abused children of the world

May this book help alleviate their plight

Table of Contents

Preface

A *Few Kind Words About Hate* is an important and shocking book, shocking because it presents convincing proof that nearly all of us have been damaged either by the inability of our parents to truly accept and love us, or—far more often than you would imagine—by their outright cruelty, be it conscious or unconscious. This wide-ranging, remarkable book gives one the feeling of visiting a dark foreign land—the land of our childhood—one with which we were intimately familiar long ago but had mostly forgotten. It brings to life the emotions of our childhood with uncanny, disturbing accuracy. It is distressing to revisit those long-forgotten, devastating early incidents we gladly obliterated from memory, but it is also healing. When we reexperience the realities of our childhood, we free ouselves of much of its suffering, which most of us have suppressed and carry as an unecessary burden throughout our entire lives.

The reader might still ask: "Why should I suffer through all that again?" Another answer is this: those who fail to deal with the now-forgotten wounds inflicted by their parents are destined to inflict similar (or opposite) wounds on their own children, without realizing they are doing so. The book shows how small incidents, long forgotten, damaged our self-image. Once we confront our own childhood wounds, we can avoid hurting our children in similar ways (it is common for parents to do so). Even if our children are now adults, it will help us understand and help them. The book also shows us why we don't want the painful new awareness it offers, why we must pay an emotional price to achieve it, and why the stakes in our becoming aware are so enormous for us and for succeeding generations.

There is another reason it is worth revisiting our forgotten childhood wounds, our mute grief over not being helped and loved at times when we most needed it, and our helpless rage at the injustices inflicted by our parents, often unintentionally. As children, these wounds were much too painful to bear; we wiped them from our consciousness. But this anesthesia of forgetfulness, which we still require to numb our pain, also dulls our ability to love, to feel the excitement of being alive, and to grieve when we are hurt; it blocks our natural urge to live fully, to expand and grow. By struggling to feel our childhood suffering again, we cancel the anesthesia that has fogged our emotions for our whole life; feeling our old pain makes us aware of our aliveness, shows us we can experience emotions that we didn't realize we had lost. Grief and suffering are part of our emotional spectrum; blocking these feelings also diminishes our ability to feel love, happiness and the exhilaration of living fully.

This book is titled *A Few Kind Words About Hate* because it is a compassionate study of the way most of us unconsciously carry around a load of buried hate—much of it for ourselves. The author helps free us from hidden hate by bringing it into the open, showing how it originated and what keeps it festering—with lots of surprises. She describes many aspects of our love-hate relationship with our parents few of us have had the courage to face. Readers will be surprised at how liberating it is to read this guide to the long-hidden emotions of our childhood.

Una Stannard is a poet with a mischievous sense of fun. She rakes the harmful practices of the Church and the family with the grapeshot of truth and keen observation. She delivers a magnificent lecture on how the cruelties of family life, big and small, have created the violent, cynical world in which we live. This lecture begins with a survey of the cruelty and violence of God as portrayed in the Bible. It shows that this Biblical cruelty and violence are a precise reflection of those same qualities that are rampant in family life. The book is an astonishing assembly of autobiography, wit, scientific facts, legal data, social commentary, analysis of family dynamics, history, and a travelogue through the inner workings of the mind. It shows how childhood abuse and neglect—emotional and physical—make us believe in a cruel God and callously ignore the violence of our families and culture.

Most of the book is concerned with the effect of family life on children, how children are subtly taught they are bad, how they are mistreated and disrespected—either subtly or overtly. Here are the "family values" listed in the titles of five chapters: Fear, Hate, Kissing the Rod, Guilt, and Religion. These may sound extreme, but when the curtain is drawn on the realities of family life, as it is here, one finds many of these feelings—as the book demonstrates with many examples.

It is not possible to adequately summarize this engaging, wide-ranging book. Attempting to do so would be tiresome, whereas it itself is disturbing, fascinating, often witty and hilarious. Read it and see for yourself.

—John Backus, Sc.D.
Publisher, GermainBooks

About the Author

Una Stannard was born Barbara Garlitz and was known as Barbara Una Stannard for most of her life. She held a PhD from Harvard and was for a time an assistant professor at the University of California in Berkeley. She delighted in being alive, in relationships, and in helping others. Stannard was married and lived with her husband in San Francisco. An avid scholar, she was an original thinker whose writings were ahead of her time. She is the author of the feminist novel *The New Pamela* (Ballantine Books & Sphere Books, Ltd., 1969), *Married Women v. Husbands' Names* (GermainBooks, 1973), a discussion of the legal issues for a married woman who wished to keep her own name (these were difficult ones at the time), and *Mrs Man* (GermainBooks, 1977), a scholarly yet witty feminist book describing the plight of wives throughout history. (*Publisher's Weekly* gave it a good review.) She also published many articles, among them, "The Male Maternal Instinct" (*Transaction*, 1970), "Clothing and sexuality" (*Sexual Behavior*, 1971) and "The Mask of Beauty" (*Woman in Sexist Society*, 1971). Una Stannard died unexpectedly in 2004.

Stannard had been working on the present book for seven years at the time of her death. She had planned to include one or two more chapters. She is the author of a children's book that GermainBooks plans to publish after the present volume. Stannard was a poet with a large catalogue of poems, unpublished, probably because they are unfashionably clear and full of her disturbing insights into the human condition.

Chapter 1   My Introduction To Hate

After a twentieth century filled with wars: two world wars and many smaller ones, after holocausts and ethnic and religious slaughters, nuclear bombs, car bombs, school shootings, road rage and on and on and on, and after the twenty-first century started out with terrorists using airplanes as bombs, how dare I say a few kind words about hate?

I never meant to. I wouldn't have thought much about hate if my own had stayed buried the way it's supposed to, which it would have if, ironically, I hadn't taken the "love drug," MDMA, popularly known as Ecstasy. I took it because my relationship with my husband had reached such a low, I was willing to try anything, and a friend assured us that MDMA produced a life-transforming love. But that's not why I took it. Marriage had made me cynical about love. When I used the word, which I rarely did, it had quotes around it to make clear that I was speaking of that alleged, that mythic thing called 'love'. I took the drug because my husband intended to and I didn't want to be left out.

To encourage us, our friend revealed that Ecstasy, especially the first time, released you from your ordinary busy head into a bliss you didn't know existed, which was why it got the name Ecstasy. My husband was released into bliss. I wasn't, so it turned out that, after all, I was left out. I was set free from my ordinary busy head, but not into ecstasy.

About forty minutes after I took the drug, as I lay in a dark room, eyes closed, a bright blue sky flashed on inside my head that in a mini-second changed into a wide screen of blackness—or was it a blackboard?—on which appeared in large chalked letters: YOU ARE EVIL. You'd think that damning judgment would have shocked me. It didn't. I accepted it as a truth I'd always known, and when "You Are Evil" dissolved into an embryo, I also knew with a sureness I'd never experienced before that I was the embryo, and that even then I was frightened of my mother. I didn't know why, nor did I wonder why, perhaps because Ecstasy's soothing hand was on my brow and stayed there during the two hours I lay on my bed literally speechless (I couldn't open my mouth), taking in the terrible truth that hate had ruled my life, that I'd despised or envied most of the people I'd known, that my acts of kindness had selfish motives, that my wit was a weapon, that my deepest goal in life was to triumph over my older sister, that behind my shyness was a hanging judge, that … . Why go on? Everyone I later met who'd taken Ecstasy had realized they were "all love." I'd learned I was "all hate."

When I reported my trip to the friend who'd introduced me to the drug, she was horrified and ordered me never to mention it to the friends we had in common, whom she was urging to take the "love drug" so they could form a loving community. I refused to be silent because, as I said to her, I thought my trip was better than a bliss out, that learning that hate had ruled my life was a great gift, the gift of self-knowledge.

Thus on February 9, 1986, in the late middle of my life, did an illegal chemical start me on a journey into myself that quickly revealed I'd had another life. I don't mean a past life; I mean my childhood, which I thought I'd remembered in great detail. I had, and I hadn't remembered only the good times; I knew I'd been mostly unhappy, but I'd totally blanked out the atrocities. Ecstasy having led me to the gates of my hell, I started to meditate and slowly discovered a childhood so savage—strangling, punching, starvation, broken ribs and much more—that my mind at first refused to accept it. With every new memory, I'd say, "I don't believe it. I'm making it all up." How could such atrocities have happened and I'd forgotten them?

My forgotten childhood was not the only mystery that astonished me. Hamlet was right: "there are more things in heaven and earth" than I'd thought possible. During meditation only fragments from my horrific childhood surfaced. To try to get more than fragments, I used a device I call, "letting my hand write." I'm a writer and to get first drafts I dismiss the conscious part of my mind and let my hand be the conduit for I know not what. "Letting my hand write" worked. It dredged up many shocking memories, but also something that was, for me, far more shocking. When I transcribed what my hand had written onto the computer, I noticed that where I should have written "I," I'd often written "you." Puzzled, I changed the "you's" to "I's" until honesty told me to change nothing. I was soon compelled to face that something—what?, coming from where?—was addressing me!

I was appalled, incredulous. Such things were not supposed to happen to rational people, especially to someone with a PhD. And yet, not only was something writing through my hand, an inner voice had begun speaking to me, a voice that knew about my abuse, gave me advice and was a fount of wisdom and compassion, a voice I eventually named my "Kind Force" because it was kind. For a long time, I didn't tell anyone about it except my husband, sure my friends would think I was crazy. I didn't know I'd tapped into what's called an inner guide or self-helper, a mysterious phenomenon I'd then never heard of.

It took me years to accept the reality of my Kind Force. Like a baby bird, my mouth accepted the food dropped into it and ignored the source. The child who'd been so cruelly hurt couldn't take in that a beneficent force was helping her, especially a force that was invisible. Besides, I didn't want to be blackballed from the Reason & Science Club, in which I'd been a member in good standing all my adult life. But not to face facts, even invisible ones, is not scientific. Scientists were forced to believe in the reality of quarks, though they can't be seen. I was eventually forced to believe in the reality of the invisible Kind Force that changed my life.

Acknowledging its reality was so embarrassing that when I began this book, I didn't mention it. I couldn't continue that dishonesty. Scholars must cite their sources, so I must cite my Kind Force, a voice that told me truths not only about myself but general truths about love, hate, fear, family life, truths that made me suspect that all original knowledge is a gift from a mysterious realm that lies beyond what we regard as the real world. I hope my 'source' will give authority to what I say. It's the hope of a coward, for I'm sure what I say will make many of you angry, so angry that I'm offering you an alternate target to punch—my invisible Kind Force not material me.

Of course, most readers will decide that my knowledge is no mysterious gift, that the savage abuse of my childhood, like the fist my mother punched into my cheek, jellied my brain. Others may get so angry they'll insist that devilish Ecstasy dredged up false memories from my childhood, or they'll wish my mother's assaults had finished me off. They may think their anger is righteous. It isn't. It's trying to keep them safe, keep them from remembering the bad things that happened to them in childhood. For believe it or not, if you'd been brought up in a loving family, you wouldn't get angry. You'd be a living Bodhisattva filled with compassion, like Jesus or Mother Teresa or Kuan Yin, who has thousands of arms, which she sorely needs to comfort the billions of children crying loudly or silently (the ones too scared to cry out loud) in this vale of tears that families create.

To create more compassion in the world, we have to stop being like Fundamentalists and Sentimentalists, who treat the family as a holy icon. That icon has to be smashed if the world is to become a loving place. Truth is what smashes sacred beliefs, most of which turn out to be lies we were trained to think were true. One of the sacred beliefs is that families are loving institutions. *Schindler's List,* Steven Spielberg's movie about the German holocaust, was shown on television on February 21, 1997. In an afterword, Spielberg said that we have to search for the source of hatred. I'm sure that it didn't cross his mind that you don't have to search far, that the source is in the home. Do I hear howls of protest? Let me quote George Bernard Shaw: "Make any statement that is so true that it has been staring us in the face all our lives, and the whole world will rise up and passionately contradict you."

Fannie Lou Hamer, the black woman who worked for civil rights in scary Mississippi in the 1960s, said, "Whether I want to do it or not, I got to. This is my calling. This is my mission." I too feel I have a mission, the mission my Kind Force (on the wings of Ecstasy) imposed on me: to write about the hatred family life generates in children. I wish it wasn't my mission. Like everyone else, I want to be liked and what I have to say is far more than politically incorrect; it's super dynamite, an H-bomb, guaranteed to infuriate. So, I'm giving you fair warning. It might be wise to drop this book into the garbage can, like the mothers all over the world who drop unwanted babies into dumpsters. The severely rejected baby in me will understand.

Chapter 2   **The Heart Of Hate**

When David Livingstone walked into the African jungle and Robert Peary set sail for the North Pole, they had a rough idea of what they hoped to find. When I set out on my inner journey, so did I. Ecstasy having opened me to the world within my mind, I meditated twice a day, often for forty minutes, hoping that it would do for me what I'd read it did for others: eventually elevate me to a place of peace and bliss. It didn't. Meditation took me where the drug had. For years I found myself in the convoluted fissures and ravines of my brain, trekking through a country that has largely been unmapped

The Terra Incognita Of Hate

I used to be a scholar, which is a kind of explorer. Exploring my mind was very different. No calm dredging facts out of books. I was the book that was laid open, forced to undergo surgery without anesthesia. I was like Prometheus, who was chained to a rock while an eagle tore at his liver, except the eagle of my awareness tore at my memory, exposing the bloody horrors of my childhood and their consequences, like my mother's punch in the face, which didn't damage just my cheek. My cheek healed, but the hate she punched into me became a part of me. I thus painfully, reluctantly became a scholar of hate, knowledge I feel obliged to share, for my hate, though it bears my identifying marks, is as universal as fingerprints. I'm not Frankenstein's monster, though for a long time I thought I was. I'm a representative of humankind. Homo sapiens, Man, the wise, should have been named, Homo qui odit, Man, the hater. No other species hates the way humans do, a phenomenon that needs exploration.

"All Gaul is divided into three parts," said Julius Caesar. "All hate is divided into two parts," says the world, which crudely separates hate from anger, anger being sometimes justified and hate never. But hate is fall out from anger. Anger leaps up and when it can't express itself it hunkers down and stagnates into hate. Fresh anger, anger not fouled with hate festering from the past, is so rare I prefer to use hate as the generic term for a family of feelings.

Arabs had over two hundred words for the color brown because of their intimacy with the camels they lived with. Forced to become intimate with hate, I became able to see various kinds, and I don't mean animosity, rage, hostility, ill will, rancor, resentment, which are fairly similar states. Hate can be as different as life and death. For there's a hate that sparkles like champagne and bubbles us with renewed life, and also a dark red hate that has sat too long on the grape skins and eats holes in our system and vomits blood into the world.

Hate is maligned because we're afraid of it. We shouldn't be. Hate should be a friend, for when we let it out of its shrouded cage, we see it's not a roaring beast but a hurt, frightened child who needs to be held and comforted, needs to be loved. Becoming able to love that hate-filled child isn't easy. We have to get off the dope we've been fed, especially at Christmas, that love jingles like bells in every heart. That sweet lie is confected by the same media that entertains us on TV with actors being fake-killed in front of our eyes. If we didn't enjoy the killing, it wouldn't be there: advertisers wouldn't make money. We also watch the real stuff. In 2003 we were glued to snuff films, films showing us real killing as the war in Iraq went endlessly on.

America started that war, allegedly to exterminate the despot Saddam Hussein and fight terrorism. But Saddam had once been a child who was cruelly scorned and abandoned by his mother, a child who forever sought revenge. Despotism, terrorism is hate let loose, the hate in the heart of frightened, unloved children, hate that has so much power because it comes from a stronger force.

Prometheus was chained to a rock for giving fire to mankind, a source of good as well as evil. The good news about hate is that it's not, like hydrogen or helium, an irreducible element; it's a derivative emotion. It derives from love, love gone wrong. Hate is a reaction to not being loved. In the heart of hate is always the puzzled, angry cry—"Godamn you, why didn't you love me?" Only because love is its source can I say a few kind words about hate. Only because hate is a mushroom cloud that once was love *must* I say a few kind words about hate.

Chapter 3   **Holy Hate**

Early in the twentieth century when Margaret Sanger campaigned for birth control, she dared to use in public words like penis and vagina, which were then regarded as so obscene that the New York Society for the Suppression of Vice broke up her meetings, the United States Post Office banned her newsletter and she was sent to jail for violating the laws of decency. The culture now permits us to use "penis" and "vagina" in public, but to say "I'm full of hate" in public is to violate the laws of decency.

Hate is the four-letter word the world is more afraid of than fuck. During the many generations when it was taboo to say fuck in polite society, fuck had the glamour of the vicious. Even today among those who disapprove of dirty words, it still has glamour. "Fuck" is sexy. But to say, "I'm full of hate" is not sexy. I've done it and seen a flash of red in people's eyes. It was as if I'd transmogrified into Count Dracula with his bloody mouth and pointy eye teeth. People let out a silent shriek. I'd spoken the unspeakable. In the early eighteenth century, Alexander Pope said of fashionable preachers that they "never mention Hell to ears polite." Even in the twenty-first century, you'd better not say out loud that you're filled with hate. Your listeners turn into fundamentalist preachers and consign you to Hell, as the culture says they should.

"Thou shalt not hate thy brother in thy heart" said Jesus. "May I be free from anger," prayed Buddhists. Never let your "angry passions rise," Isaac Watts told children in his 1715 poem "Against Quarreling and Fighting." Even former President Clinton in June 1997, when he gave a speech at his daughter's high school graduation, advised her class not to waste a day "trapped by hatred." Good people are not supposed to hate. "Ain't no such thing as I can hate anybody and hope to see God's face," said the civil rights worker, Fannie Lou Hamer. Believers in God are certain they'll go straight to hell if they hate, and unbelievers are equally certain that it's immoral to hate. "Perhaps a Hitler," they say, "but ordinarily, I don't hate. Sure, sometimes I get angry, justifiably angry, but hate, No. Vile hate groups hate, but not me."

Because my first Ecstasy trip pushed my face in my hate, I couldn't deny I was a hater, and when I began my journey into myself, I was so ashamed of monstrous, hate-filled me, I thought death should be my punishment. I had an image of my body, like Bonny and Clyde's when they're shot to death in the movie, jumping and dancing from the barrage of bullets riddling them. I was sure my journey would be a process of draining away the putrid pus of hate. That's not what happened.

As my journey progressed and a fair number of ghastly memories surfaced from my childhood, I understood why it had taken me until late middle age to gain the strength to remember. But far more important, the startling notion that I had a good reason to be filled with hate began to seep into my consciousness. Not long afterward, when I was sitting in my car waiting for a red light to change, out of my mouth screamed the word, "Filth!" involuntarily. And I yelled it several times.

I'd later remember that my mother used to yell "Filth!" at me, but on that day I thought I was yelling "Filth!" at her. Since many of the memories that surfaced were about her appalling treatment, I felt no guilt. On the contrary, an exhilarating surge of fury and indignation filled my being, so that a few days later a miracle happened. During a long walk, I found myself moving lightly, energetically, buoyed up by the joy of being alive. I'd never before walked like that. I thought of Jesus walking on the water, then felt it was blasphemous to compare evil me with him. I dared to hope, though, that my joy was a reward for somehow having become less evil. In a profound sense it was. I didn't know it then, but a little self-love had penetrated the self-hatred I'd always lived with and, as love always does, it buoyed me up. I did float along.

I then recalled some unusual words I'd read about anger. They were in Beryl Markham's *West with the Night* (1942), the section in which she described the birth of a colt. Just before it was born, Markham rested her head against the mare's belly and felt the colt already struggling, "demanding," as she put it, "the right to freedom and growth." Will it, she asked, "be strong and stubborn enough to snap the tethers of nothingness ... ?" "Will it have the *anger* to feed and to grow and to demand its needs?"

Only when I'd begun the hard labor of letting my memories be born out of my unconscious, only when "Filth!" sprang from my mouth and I experienced the joy of healthy hate, did I understand Markham's words. For I was feeling the flicker of healthy hate I'd felt as baby before it was submerged by fear, the baby who, if she'd been able to talk, should have yelled at her mother: "Get away from me! Don't you dare hurt me!" That baby's long overdue hate, was enabling me "to snap the tethers of my nothingness" and demand "the right to freedom and growth."

That cry, "Filth!" was at long last my lion's roar. That's what I called it right away — "my lion's roar" — and I went to the zoo several times to hear the lions roaring. I'd stand inside the large resounding room and wait for the lions to come inside for their raw meat, wait to hear their expansive roars, and I'd softly roar with them, as if I too were an animal marking out the boundaries of my vastness, my roaring statement to the world: "I am here, magnificently here in my space and don't tamper with me. I defy you."

You can't roar at mistreatment when you think you don't matter. I was beginning to believe I did matter. I was getting back what had been frightened out of me when I was a baby, what Rousseau called, "the fire of childhood," getting back enough fire to know that "NO ONE SHOULD HAVE DONE THIS TO ME!" I later called that kind of hate "holy hate," and it was the right word for the lion's roar that filled me with a new sense of energetic life.

I relate this story at the beginning of the book to convince you that it *is* possible to say a few kind words about hate, that hate *can* be holy, can be healing, like the mold that becomes penicillin.

Holy hate is not the hate we're used to. It's not the hate that bursts into wars, into guns, into bombs; it doesn't slap, punch, kick, knife, kill. It's not the cruel words that we hurl at others and that our inner critic hisses at us. It's not the hate that has been ravaging the world from the beginning of human history. Holy hate is almost out of this world; it's rarer than blue diamonds.

Chapter 4   **Unholy Hate**

I called the last chapter "Holy Hate" because when I finally registered that my mother shouldn't have mistreated me, an exhilarating surge of fury, indignation and power flooded my being and began to heal me. I also called it "Holy Hate" to contrast it with the Holy Bible, a book also known as the Good Book, but where hate is more common than the stones that were God's favorite instrument of death, a book whose pages are bloody with killing, torture and vengeance, with hate that doesn't heal, that increases and multiplies—unholy hate.

Why I Studied the Bible

I know what I say is true, and I'm astonished that I do. I know because I finally studied the Bible, I who was born an atheist. At least, when I was a child, religion affected me the way looking at *National Geographic* did—how odd that Ubangi women wore rings that stretched their necks to an enormous length. Religion was for me what it would be for the proverbial alien from Mars—a strange practice of the natives.

When I was a scholar, I consulted the Bible to check references, though once, having chanced upon, "The race is not to the swift, nor the battle to the strong," I was impressed and read Ecclesiastes, where I was surprised to find this hedonistic advice: "A man hath no better thing under the sun than to eat, and to drink, and to be merry." But I was soon confused by contrary advice—that to "fear God and keep his commandments ... is the whole duty of man." I also read the Book of Job, felt the same confusion, and gave up on the Bible, though I continued to think that reading the whole Bible should be part of everyone's education. But I didn't get past the first few chapters of Genesis in the secondhand King James Bible I bought when I was in college, nor did I get any further when in middle age I bought The New English Bible, hoping that because it was in modern English I'd read it through. Nor did *Freethought Today*, the newsletter of the Freedom from Religion Foundation, get me to read the Bible. The Biblical atrocities that were often quoted for their readers' delectation made reading the Bible, like watching violent TV, seem a bad use of time.

I did read part of the New Testament after I was on my inner journey and came under the influence of the Pathwork, 258 lectures that had been channeled by an entity who called himself the Guide, which contained much psychological wisdom and advocated the path I'd intuitively taken—opening up to all my feelings, no matter how shameful or painful. Because Christianity was the foundation of the Pathwork, I read the four Gospels. I wasn't impressed, I was mostly bored until I read Christ's promise that after he died, he'd dwell in mankind as an

"Advocate," and "Spirit of Truth" (John 14:16-17). That gave me pause, a shocked pause. For, as I told you in the first chapter, soon after I began my inner journey, I became aware of a personal advocate in my own mind who was always telling me truths. Could what I'd called my Kind Force be Christ dwelling in me? Was Christianity true after all?

That's why I occasionally went to a church and sat through the service. But I felt no closeness to Christ or God. The rituals turned me off, especially people eating a cracker alleged to be the body of Christ. I also found the hymns dispiriting, unlike the classical religious music I became interested in at the beginning of my journey. I'll always fondly remember the first time I heard Mozart's *Vespers* and was transported to a universe I hadn't known existed, a universe of kindness I wanted to stay in forever; I played it over and over, my personal, spiritual lullaby. I became devoted to classical religious music, and when I heard Handel's "I Know that My Redeemer Liveth," atheist me had to admit that she longed for a redeemer to rescue her from her misery.

Because of that desire and because I'd been told that the chorus at San Francisco's Glide Memorial Church was marvelous and that the church was unlike any other, I went to a Sunday service. The moment I walked into the hall where the chorus was singing with joyous exuberance I knew what I'd been told was true. But not because the chorus sang well. Love filled the room. I knew it was love, though I'd never before felt it's presence.

Tears came to my eyes. I should have let them flow, but exposure to such a heavy dose of love was too much for me. I took a deep breath and looked around at the people packing the hall, all ages, all colors, poor and rich, gay and straight, singing along with the chorus and rhythmically clapping. I was so taken out of my usual self that I actually sang along with everyone else, though in a whisper and without clapping, and yet for the first time in my life I felt a closeness to others that lifted me into an exalted mood that lasted even during a speech about banning guns given by a local politician honored that day. I was eager to hear the Reverend Cecil Williams' sermon, sure it would be an emanation of the loving spirit that pervaded his church.

Because of the politician's speech, The Reverend Williams had time only for a few words, which turned out to be an admonition not to commit the standard litany of sins, the first one being that we shouldn't hate. My exaltation fizzled away. I was an alien again. I'd hoped when I felt the love in the room that a hater like me could be loved too, especially since the church had a program for people who'd been abused when they were children. But the Reverend Cecil Williams apparently didn't know that hate could sometimes be holy. Like everyone else, he'd categorically said, "Thou shalt not hate."

I didn't go back to Glide, but I continued to read books about different religions — Buddhism, Sufism, Hinduism. I even read born-again Christian books by Catherine Marshall and Chuck Colson, which didn't help me find God either. Books about near-death experiences helped more. They made God, or rather, a Light that was total love, seem real, but not for long. My atheism always flowed back like the tide. Nor did Buddhist meditation in its various forms give me the spiritual bliss others experienced. I ended up disheartened and envious, convinced that I was missing a gene or that hate-filled me was too wicked to feel God's love. Then one evening on TV I chanced upon Father Thomas Keating speaking about Centering Prayer, practically guaranteeing that anyone who meditated his way would ultimately feel God's love. Under his influence, I started meditating again, and for months, twice a week at seven in the morning, I went to a church to join a Centering Prayer group, but I experienced nothing but the usual chat in my head. Indirectly, though, something did happen.

When buying Keating's book about Centering Prayer at a Christian bookstore, my eyes had fallen on a card that said, "God is forever loving you." Though ashamed that atheist me wanted to buy it, I did and almost immediately found myself repeating, "God is always loving me." I'd changed "forever" to "always" and "you" to "me" because I so wanted God to love me in all ways. Whereas my mother had given me the Good Housekeeping Seal of Disapproval, I wanted God's total approval and, to my amazement, the constant repetition of "God is always loving me," did make me feel loved. After about three months, though, the feeling of being loved, like the rapture of an affair, faded away.

Whatever I did, my cynicism reasserted itself, cynicism that triumphed and ended my dalliance with religion when I read the Ten Commandments for the first time. Years before at a Halloween party a man dressed as an Old Testament figure blew a shofar (a trumpet made from a ram's horn) and declared that the Ten Commandments were the most important civilizing force in history, that they'd taught the world the basics of morality. I shrugged, assuming that what he said was true, for I knew that "Thou Shalt not kill" or steal were two of the commandments. I had no interest in reading the other "Thou shalt nots," nor would I have except that in the course of writing this book it crossed my mind that the prohibition against hate was probably so widespread and accepted because "thou shalt not hate" was one of the Ten Commandments.

The Ten Commandments

When I decided I should read the Ten Commandments, I didn't know where they were. A dictionary directed me to two places, and I chose the first. When I was flipping through the New English Bible to

Exodus, chapter 20, I got the hunch that since the prohibition against hate was so strong, "thou shalt not hate" would turn out to be the first commandment. My hunch was wrong. I quickly scanned through the rest, but among "Thou shalt not kill," "Thou shalt not commit adultery," "Thou shalt not covet thy neighbor's wife," there was no "Thou shalt not hate." I was so surprised that it wasn't a commandment, I reread the ten, this time slowly.

That's when the character of God began to astonish me. The Ten Commandments, I discovered, was not a mere list of ethical precepts. The six "thou shalt nots" were a short appendix to the lengthy first four commandments, which introduced me to a God I found shocking.

Ignorant me had thought "Thou shalt not hate" must be a commandment, probably the first. Shocked me discovered that in the first two commandments God revealed that he was a hater, and proud of it. "Thou shalt have no other gods before me," he declared because "I, the Lord thy God, am a jealous God." My mouth literally opened when I took that in, for jealousy is more than the anguish of finding out that someone you thought loved you loves another; it's hating that person because he or she does. If the Ten Commandments was one of the great civilizing forces in history, why was God proudly proclaiming his jealousy? I remembered being disturbed years before by a line in the famous Psalm 23 ("The Lord is my shepherd") that said God would "spread a table before me in the presence of my enemies." Why, I'd wondered, would a good God help someone make his enemies jealous? Like everyone else in my generation, I'd heard that God was love, but when I read the Ten Commandments I discovered a God who wasn't loving, a God whose besetting sin was jealousy.

After God demanded that his chosen people love no other God, he said that if they did love another, he'd think of them as among those "who hate me," and not only punish them but their children and their children's children "to the third and fourth generations." That sounded to me like childish tit for tat—if you hate me, I'll hate you back. But God was serious; he immediately said the same thing in another way, that he'd be merciful only to those who loved him exclusively and did whatever else he told them to do—obey every one of his commandments, never use his name disrespectfully and, because he'd made the world in six days and rested on the seventh, also rested on the seventh day. But his chosen people could rest only from their daily labor; their day of rest must be wholly devoted to worshiping him.

I soon called God "Jealous," the name he called himself. I'm not kidding. Once when he was telling his chosen people what he often told them, that they must not worship any other God, his reason simply was: "for the Lord, whose name is Jealous, is a jealous God" (Exodus 34:14). My "name is Jealous"! God actually, incredibly, called himself

Jealous as if jealousy was nothing to be ashamed of. And God was unashamed. He talked about his jealousy frankly and forced his chosen people to behave so he'd never feel jealous. Not only must they not love anyone else, they had to love him "with all [their] heart and soul and strength" (Deuteronomy 6:4-6). Since jealous people can't bear to have a rival mentioned, jealous God forbade his chosen people even to speak the name of other Gods (Exodus 23:13). So jealous was God that if his chosen people violated the day that was supposed to be devoted to his worship by merely gathering a few "sticks ... they must be put to death" (Numbers 15:32-36).

Just as God was unashamed of his jealousy, he was unashamed of the violence he'd commit if the people he'd chosen to be his "special possession" (Deuteronomy 26:17) aroused his jealousy. He liked to boast that a "fire [would be] kindled" by his jealous rage that would devour "earth and its harvest" (Deuteronomy 32:22). "A mighty blow from Almighty God" awaited those who forgot he was the only God (Isaiah 13:6). The Lord "will rip them up like a wild beast" (Hosea 13:3-8). But God was a wild beast when it came to love: all who "bent the knee to Baal [another God]," whose "lips have ... kissed him" will die (1 Kings 19:18). God was no better than a jealous husband who kills his rival when he finds him kissing his wife.

The Killer God

The book of Kings and Hosea I just quoted from are well into the Bible. I was galloping through it. I couldn't believe what I was reading. I don't mean the obvious myths. I mean God's character. My stunned disbelief kept me reading on and on as more and more bombshells exploded. They were bombshells to me because this was the God who'd been praised to the skies and worshiped for centuries.

I soon changed his name from "Jealous" to the God of Wrath. For jealousy was not his chief sin. Rage was, uncontrolled rage. Whenever he got in a rage for any reason, he acted out, usually by killing. He adored killing—animals and humans, singly and en masse.

Like many serial killers, God started out killing animals. A mountain of animals must have been sacrificed to appease his wrath, animals that had to be without a blemish and be slaughtered in the precise way God ordered. Twice a day God had to be fed the blood of a perfect ram, one ram at dawn and another at twilight (Exodus 29:38-42). The blood of other animals had to be put into a basin and thrown on his altar (Exodus 24:6-7), and yet more animals had to be burnt on his altar because he found the smell of burning flesh "a soothing odor" (Exodus 29:18). Perhaps because the smell anticipated dinner; perhaps because it covered up the stench of putrefying blood.

God's bloody gluttony disgusted me, but when I read that he demanded the sacrifice of first-born sons, I was horrified. "You shall give me your first-born sons. You shall do the same with your oxen and your sheep" (Exodus 22:29). In several other passages in the Old Testament God demanded the sacrifice of first-born sons, but he elsewhere ordered that an animal be sacrificed in place of a newborn (Exodus 34:19-20). I later learned that the Bible is not in chronological order and that the passages ordering human sacrifices were early and that, unlike other Gods, the God of Wrath put an end to human sacrifice. Some scholars believe that the story of God ordering Abraham to sacrifice Isaac, then rescinding the order, marks the end of human sacrifice among the Israelites.

Perhaps so, but though God stopped ritual human sacrifice, he went on killing humans who broke his commandments, which were not ten but (so say those who counted them) an incredible 613! And God did not hand out a death sentence only for major crimes. Simply reviling your mother and father meant death (Exodus 21:17), and priests who didn't wear linen drawers under their robes "to cover their private parts" when they were in God's holy tabernacle would "incur guilt and die" (Exodus 28:42-43). God instantly killed Uzzah for preventing the Ark of the Covenant from tipping over. Why? Because in order to save the Ark, he had to touch it, and one of God's commandments was that no one must touch the Ark (2 Samuel 6:6-7). Other poor souls who displeased God dropped dead on the spot or were eaten by lions or bitten by poisonous snakes. God's killing was capricious. He overlooked David's many grave sins but had a pack of little boys who jeered at Elisha's bald head mauled by bears (2 Kings 2:23-25).

God had no special love for children. He urged the slaughter of children in war. When he ordered the Israelites to conquer a country, he'd often say "spare no one; put them all to death, men and women, children and babes in arms" (I Samuel 15:3). Utterly destroy "the little ones" along with everyone else, he commanded (Deuteronomy 2:34). Indeed, one of the pleasures of war was to "dash [babes] against the rock" (Psalms 137:9).

The God of Wrath enjoyed war so much he constantly encouraged the Israelites to fight by promising to help them. I will "send my terror before you" so your enemies will be thrown into confusion, he said. His very own "angel" would lead them to the Amorites, the Hittites and other tribes, and "I will bring an end to them" (Exodus 23:20-27). God didn't just enjoy slaughtering the enemy. He equally enjoyed slaughtering his own people. I will "bring war in vengeance upon you," God told the sinful Israelites, so that "instead of meat you shall eat your sons and your daughters" (Leviticus 26:25,29).

"Let my wrath burn hot against them" so I "may put an end to them," God raged to Moses when he discovered that some of the

Israelites had made a golden calf in honor of Baal. Moses talked God out of killing them. And God didn't kill them himself; instead, he made Moses his hit man. "These are the words of the Lord," explained Moses when he ordered the tribe of Levites to arm themselves and "each of you kill his brother, his friend, his neighbor." The remaining Levites killed about 3,000 of the Baal worshipers, and Moses praised them for turning against their sons and brothers and thus bringing "a blessing" upon themselves, for by killing them they'd consecrated themselves to the Lord (Exodus 32:10-29). They and God, like initiates in the Mafia, had become blood brothers.

Though Moses consecrated himself to the Lord completely, God showed him no mercy when he later failed to follow an order exactly. Not long before the Israelites were to enter the Promised Land, they needed water, and God told Moses to speak to a rock and it would produce water. Instead, Moses struck the rock. For that act of disobedience, God exacted the ultimate punishment; he told Moses he would not receive the reward he'd looked forward to for many years — he could not enter the Promised Land. The hexed Moses soon obediently lay down and died.

God was not always cruel. Some of his commandments were kind and fair. He ordered the Israelites not to "put an obstruction in the way of the blind," not to delay paying a hired man his wages, and to use accurate scales and weights (Leviticus 19:14, 13, 36). God also ordered the Israelites to leave the gleanings of the harvest to the poor and aliens, to whom they must be especially considerate since they too had been aliens in Egypt. Neither should they "ill-treat any widow or fatherless child." But no sooner did God command kindness than he warned his people that if he learned someone hadn't been kind, "my anger will be roused and I will kill you with the sword" (Exodus 22:21-24), and yet three lines later God insisted, "I am full of compassion."

God at times described himself as forgiving, and yet when Eve got Adam to eat a forbidden apple, God told both of them that not only would they die but every one who'd ever be born. God's lust for killing was too intense to be satisfied by having people die one by one. Mass destruction turned him on. After deciding that the people he'd created were corrupt, God caused a huge flood and drowned every creature on earth except Noah, his family and the animals in the Ark (Genesis 6-8). God then promised he'd never use a flood to "lay waste the earth" (Genesis 9:11), but he laid waste the earth and its people in other ways. Enraged by the evil in the cities of Sodom and Gommorah, he rained down fire and brimstone (sulfur) on both the guilty and innocent, despite his promise to Abraham to kill only the guilty. No promise could keep the God of Wrath from abstaining from the pleasures of wholesale slaughter. He looked forward to judgment day, the "great day of the

Lord," to quote the Prophet Zephaniah, when, except for the few who were saved, God would again kill everyone on earth, when "blood shall be spilt like dust and ... bowels like dung" (1:4,17).

Until that great day, the Lord satisfied his appetite for blood and guts in his usual ways. The last book in the Old Testament is the prophecy of Malachi, who warned priests that because they defiled God's altar by sacrificing blemished animals, God was going to "cut off" their arms and "fling offal" in their faces (2:1-14). Thus would God punish his priests for breaking a rule! I was glad to be done with the bloody God of the Old Testament and looked forward to being washed clean in the New.

Hate Triumphant

I wasn't washed clean in The New Testament, which surprised me. Jesus did deliver messages very different from those of the God of Wrath. He advocated forgiveness not revenge, mercy not the death penalty. He dared disobey the commandment not to work on the Sabbath, and he broke Mosaic Law by preventing an adulteress from being stoned to death. Whereas God was always threatening and punishing his people, Jesus spent most of his time healing their physical and mental suffering. God had ordered warriors to destroy "the little ones," but Jesus declared children to be of the kingdom of heaven. God demanded that his people build him a Holy Ark made of the finest wood, cloth and leather and decorated with gold and jewels (Exodus 25-28; 35-40), but Jesus was poor, homeless and rode on an ass.

Nevertheless, in the New Testament the God of Wrath became a stronger presence than Jesus, who at times sounded like His Wrathship. His message of forgiveness forgotten, Jesus prophesied an old-fashioned Last Judgment when God's few chosen ones would go to heaven and the wicked would burn eternally in Hell (Matthew 24, Mark 13 and Luke 21). And Jesus, his message of forgiveness again forgotten, warned that God would "torture" anyone who didn't forgive his brother (Matthew 18:32-34). That reminded me of the God of Wrath commanding the Israelites to be kind or he'd kill them "with the sword" (Exodus 22:21-24). When Jesus said that "God's wrath rests upon" anyone who disobeyed the son of God, meaning him (John 3:36), he might as well have been the God of Wrath ranting.

The disciples of Jesus could also speak like the God of Wrath. When people in a Samaritan village refused to put Jesus up for the night, John and James asked him, "Lord, may we call down fire from heaven to burn them up?" (Luke 9:51-65). The early Christians could similarly manifest their old God's wrath. When Ananias and his wife Sapphira withheld some of the money they'd got for selling their property from the

Christian community, they dropped dead, as if the God of Wrath was again decking those who deviated from his rules (Acts 5:1-12).

A new Christian blinded a sorcerer who tried to mislead a prospective Christian (Acts 13:4-12). That man was Paul, who was acting the way he used to. Born a Jew, he'd spent his early career as a righteous killer of those who worshiped God's new rival, Jesus. He stopped his God-ordained killing only when, on the road to Damascus, he had a vision of Jesus, which convinced him that he, himself, now "possessed the mind of Christ" (1 Corinthians 2:16). Yet Paul too in many of his letters to the early Christian communities, sounded like the God of Wrath. "Am I to come to you with a rod in my hand," he asked the Corinthians, "or in love and a gentle spirit?" (1 Corinthians 4:20-21). "When I come this time," he later warned them, "I will show no leniency" (2 Corinthians 13:3).

Paul was not much inclined to leniency. He looked forward to the coming "fury of retribution" (Romans 2:8) when God would pay every man for his "wickedness" (Romans 1:18). Paul reminded the early Christians that when the Israelites had fornicated with Moabite women, God brought on a plague that killed 23,000 of them and predicted that, if they set their desires on evil things, they too would be "destroyed by the destroyer" (1 Corinthians 10:10). They would deserve the punishment, for God was not "unjust ... to bring retribution upon us" (Romans 3:5-6). Paul may have sounded like Jesus when he told the Romans, "Do not seek revenge," but the reason they needn't seek revenge was that they could count on "divine retribution" (Romans 12:19).

In these passages and many similar ones we're back in the world of the Old Testament, and when we read the last book of the New Testament, the Revelation of John, it's as if Jesus had never lived. We're again wading waist deep in blood, for "the great day of the Lord" prophesied by Zephaniah—the Last Judgment—had arrived. John insisted that his Revelation was "a message from Christ," but the Jesus who forgave those who crucified him was not the Christ who poured forth this vengeful, sadistic tirade. It was a message from the same God whose "spirit ... suddenly seized" Samson, whereupon "he killed thirty men" (Judges 14:19)—the God of Wrath.

In the Revelation of John, the God of Wrath was back as of yore, his "eyes" flaming "like fire," "a sharp two-edged sword" coming out of his mouth (1:14, 16), "the marks of slaughter upon him" (5:6), ready once more to punish all who hadn't made him their only God and followed his every commandment because, as God had said over and over in the Old Testament and which he repeated in the Revelation of John, "all whom I love, I reprove and discipline" (3:19).

Revelation is indeed a book of "discipline" that would excite sadists and masochists beyond their wildest dreams of inflicting or receiving pain. Of its twenty-two chapters, all but two recount slaughter after slaughter by God and his henchmen, who are given the power to destroy the world. The following are a few samples from this insane-with-rage killing orgy:

A pale horse named Death will kill one quarter of the earth "by sword, and by famine, by pestilence and wild beasts" (6:8). Then angels will hurl down hail and fire mixed with blood so that a third of the trees and grass would burn. Many people will be tormented by locusts that have the sting of scorpions, and in their agony will long to die. But the sufferers will not have a quick release; to increase God's pleasure, they must suffer for five months (9:5-6).

The slaughter gets worse. Four angels with squadrons of cavalry that number "two hundred millions" (9:15-16) will kill a third of mankind. Other people will drown in blood when an angel of the Lord gathers all the grapes on earth, throws them in "the great winepress of God's wrath" and turns the wine into blood that will flow across two hundred miles and rise to the height of horses' bridles (14:19-20). God's wrath is not yet sated. Seven angels will be given "seven golden bowls full of the wrath of God" (15:7-8) and pour them on the earth, so that people develop "foul malignant sores" and seas and rivers turn to blood.

When, after many similar orgies, world-wide destruction is complete, an angel, to celebrate God's "just" victory (19:2), will call birds to "God's great supper" where they will gorge on "the flesh of all men, slave and free, great and small" (19:17-19; 20:10). Hitler didn't invent holocausts; God preceded him by thousands of years, and on a scale that far surpassed him. The blood bath of "The Revelation of John" is a proper finale to the blood bath of much of the Bible. Hollywood couldn't have done it better.

I'm Not the Only One

The Bible has such a great reputation for holiness that many people may think I haven't seen God straight, that I've seen him through the distorted lenses of my own hate, or that I cited rare and exceptional instances of his bad behavior. I'm not the only one who's been appalled. The Hebrew Prophets were so disgusted with the insanely jealous, unjust, merciless, unforgiving, terrifying, vengeful, blood-guzzling, war-mad God of Wrath that they tried, as we would say today, to give him a better spin. Amos and Jeremiah were certain that God really abhorred animal sacrifice, and they and other Prophets were sure that God loathed war, that what he really wanted was to create a world in which "nation shall not lift sword against nation nor ever again be trained for war" (Hosea 2:18-13; Isaiah 2:4). Jeremiah even told the Israelites that God wanted peace so much that they should surrender to the warring king of Babylon without a fight (27:12-14).

The God of Wrath a pacifist? That was Jeremiah's belief not God's, but he and the other Prophets prefaced their words with the phrase, "the Lord saith," although the God they were allegedly quoting was saying the opposite of what he normally said. Did they comprehend they were putting their own ideals into God's mouth?, ideals of justice, forgiveness and peace so advanced they haven't yet been realized.

Perhaps the Prophets put a different spin on God because they couldn't face what the God they worshiped was like. Others did see God without ideals clouding their vision. In the first and second centuries, many Greeks and Romans were horrified by the God of the Jews who ruled by terror. Marcion, a second-century Christian, was so repelled by him that he founded a rival church that rejected the whole Old Testament. The Gnostics too repudiated the "The God of Israel ... as a king ... implacable in his resentment, meanly jealous ... and confining his partial providence to a single people." I'm quoting Edward Gibbon who, in the first volume of *The Decline and Fall of the Roman Empire* (1776), also remarked on the bloody murders, executions and massacres that "stain almost every page of the Jewish annals." About twenty years later, Thomas Paine in *The Age of Reason* (1794-95) also denounced the Bible, for its "cruel and tortuous executions," its "unrelenting vindictiveness" and for being the history of a people "addicted ... to cruelty and revenge." Contrary to popular belief, Paine didn't rail against the Bible because he was an atheist. He was shocked by the Bible because he believed in a beneficent God. That was one reason he was sure the Bible was not the word of God but more likely "the word of a demon."

Paine's denunciation of the Bible and that of his predecessors didn't influence me. I came to my God-damning conclusions on my own. I did learn from the newsletters of the Freedom from Religion Foundation about some of God's atrocities, but not until I read the Bible myself, page after page of the Old and New Testament, did the extent of his violence hit me with full force or the character of God become real to me. Other denunciations of the Bible, I was ignorant of. I'd never heard of Marcion, and the Gnostics were hardly more than a name to me. I'd known that Gibbon had cast a scornful eye on the Bible, but I didn't look up what he'd written until I'd read the Old Testament myself. Nor had Paine been a role model because I hadn't known he'd written about the Bible. This chapter was well under way when, thumbing through a book of quotations, I saw a section on the Bible and read a quotation from *The Age of Reason*. My eyes lit up and that day I tracked down a copy in a second-hand bookstore. Great was my delight to discover that Thomas Paine, that champion of common sense, felt as strongly as I did. I was later pleased to learn that Gandhi also couldn't stomach the Old Testament. He told William Shirer that he was "offended by all the violence, the lust for revenge and punishment" and "eye for an eye" justice (Gandhi: *A Memoir*, 1979).

Paine said that if people would read the Bible as if it were simply a book, not God's holy words, reason would make them come to the same conclusions he had. Without knowing what Paine had said, I'd done that, and I, who'd been searching for God, found a God who hated far more than I'd thought anyone could hate, a God whose rage races like a wildfire through the pages of the Bible, a God whose lust for killing made the Bible a slaughterhouse, a God who didn't even pretend to wear royal robes but nakedly dripped blood.

Thank God, I studied the Bible! I wrote that automatically, thanking a God I didn't believe in, especially not the God of Wrath who, if he'd existed, would have stomped on me the way BIG FOOT came down and flattened the tiny man at the beginning of the Monty Python shows. Thanks to what then—to my ignorance—made me think that "thou shalt not hate" must be one of the Ten Commandments. Otherwise, presumptuous me would have thought I was the chief of haters and written a book about hate that omitted to pay proper tribute to the biggest hater of them all.

Chapter 5   **The Bad Book**

The Problem

In March 1998, two Arkansas boys, one thirteen and one eleven, opened fire on their schoolmates and teachers, killing five and wounding ten. The thirteen-year-old, Mitchell Johnson, had become a Christian a few months before, and when he was in jail he asked his mother to bring him a Bible. Perhaps, hoping to find God's words for him in his plight, he did what many people do and with half-shut eyes opened the Bible and placed a finger on a verse. The odds are great that he put his finger on an act of violence, like God ordering the Israelites to "put to the sword" Og, King of Bashan "with his sons and all his people, until there was no survivor left" (Numbers 21:35). Considering his situation, Mitchell may have shaken his head, wondering, "How come God was always telling people to go out and kill and that was okay? How come, even without an order from God, David would go raid a tribe and kill everyone and God didn't punish him? God rewarded him—he made him a king. Hadn't he, Mitchell, acted like David? And like God too?, who killed practically every time he got angry. So why shouldn't he kill when he got angry? How come God and David were praised for killing but he was put in jail like a criminal? It wasn't fair."

It wasn't fair. Why should Mitchell Johnson have been punished when he'd done only what God and many heroes in the Bible did again and again?

Soon after I read the Ten Commandments, I renamed God, "Jealous," but as I continued to read the Bible, I changed it to the "God of Wrath." I also began calling the Good Book the Bad Book. I did because I was genuinely shocked by its immorality. When Luther became sufficiently outraged by the corruptions of the Catholic Church, he nailed ninety-five articles of indictment on the church door. What follows are six (out of many) lessons taught in the Bible, which, as Thomas Paine said have "served to corrupt and brutalize mankind."

Killing Is A Virtue

"Thou shalt not kill," said God, but he couldn't have meant it because he committed or sanctioned thousand upon thousands of murders. In regard to killing, God had a bad case of what George Orwell called "doublethink," which the dictionary defines as "thought marked by the acceptance of gross contradictions and falsehoods." The Gideon Society has been putting Bibles on the bedside tables of hotels since 1899, but travelers' morals would be more improved by reading a murder mystery. At least at the end the killer gets caught, whereas God always gets away with murder. And so did the Israelites whenever, on God's orders, they stoned to death those who broke certain commandments. The Old Testament is as full of God-ordained slaughters as fruit in a fruitcake, and the New Testament ends with the Christ-ordained slaughters in The Revelation of John. The Bible sanctions so much killing that I wondered why God made "Thou shalt not kill" one of his commandments. If he'd been honest, he would have said, "Thou shalt not kill, except when I, the Lord thy God, tell you to, for to kill in my name is holy." That may be why so many assassins say that God told them to do it.

Governments, when they kill, model themselves on God. They declare murder a crime and yet have ordered untold thousands of young people to murder in wars, for which the best murderers get medals. Some wars may be necessary, but though Governments declare murdering a fellow citizen a crime, they murder them themselves, almost always cruelly, perhaps to let the government and the people enjoy the psychological pleasures of murder. A placard at the jail where a serial killer was about to be executed in 1979 read: "Good Morning Ted Bundy. I'm going to kill you," expressing the same pleasure in an anticipated murder that Bundy must have felt as he stalked his victims, the pleasure that God felt when he told his sinful chosen people he was going to devour them like a "panther" or a "lion."

Vengeance Is A Virtue

Whenever God's "anger pours out like a stream of fire," he "takes vengeance on his adversaries," said the Prophet Nahum, who did not disapprove; he celebrated God's vengeance. Over and over he called "The Lord ... good," for letting loose his power and fury (Nahum 1:2-11). The Israelites, following their Lord's example, also thought vengeance was good. The vast majority of the 150 Psalms were unashamed prayers for vengeance. In Psalm 18, for example, the psalmist thanked God in advance that he'd soon be setting his "foot on my enemies' necks" when, "like mud in the streets will I trample on them." "O God, who grantest me vengeance ... I will ... sing psalms to thy name."

God wished his enemies ill, and the Israelites followed suit: "May his line be doomed to extinction" said Psalm 109:13, repeating one of God's common curses. "I am full of the anger of the Lord, I cannot hold it in," raved Jeremiah (6:11), having learned from God it was good to act out rage. Since Jeremiah didn't have God's power, he begged God to help him, to see to it that "screams of terror ring out from [the] houses" of the sinful Israelites (18:22). Again influenced by God's example, the Israelites took pleasure in gloating over their enemies. "The Lord is on my side ... and I shall gloat over my enemies," said a Psalm (118:7)—to cite only one of many examples of the God-approved joys of gloating.

However, Proverb 24 tells us not to gloat when your enemy falls or "the Lord will see and be displeased with you," a moral improvement, except that the proverb ends by saying that if you do gloat, God "will cease to be angry with him [your enemy]." In other words, if you do gloat, God, the master revenger, won't continue to be angry at your enemy and finish him off for you. But Proverb 24 is exceptional; the Bible usually taught the Israelites that they didn't have to be mealy-mouthed about gloating, that they could gloat openly. Nor did God withhold the pleasures of gloating from the Christians; on Judgment Day they could look forward to the greatest gloating fest of all. Thomas Aquinas, who was made a saint, said that the greatest pleasure in the afterlife, next to contemplating God, would be watching the torture of the eternally damned. Or, as a contemporary Wisconsin Catholic exulted, "They're going to burn in hell and we get to watch" (*Freethought Today*, April 1998).

The common curse, "Goddamn you," exists because we learn from the Bible that God might damn someone for us. When a pack of boys jeered at Elisha's bald head, he "cursed them in the name of the Lord," and the Lord heard him and sent "two she-bears ... out of a wood and mauled forty-two of them" (2 Kings 2:23-25). When we say, "Goddamn you," we forget that it's a cry for vengeance, that there's a pause after God, then a request that God oblige us as he did Elisha by becoming our hit man.

Jealousy Is Love

Smitten by love at first sight, God singled out the Israelites to be his one and only, and expected, nay demanded, that he be their one and only in return. What's worse, because he'd chosen them to love, he expected them to go on loving him no matter how badly he treated them. "For you alone have I cared among all nations of the world; therefore will I punish you for all your iniquities" (Amos 3:2). The poor Israelites, they hadn't asked to be chosen, and yet they were put in love-chains by God, who freed them from slavery in Egypt yet treated them like slaves. If they made him jealous (by worshiping another God), God would beat them up, even kill them, all the time protesting his great love. Like a battering husband, like an O J Simpson, God preferred to see his "special possession" dead rather than loving another. God confused insane possessiveness with love and by his example taught us it was good.

Religious Intolerance Is A Virtue

Having decided that he was "the greatest of all Gods" (Exodus 18:11), God ordered his chosen people to exterminate those who didn't bow down and worship him, which they did in abundance, and with his blessing. Following their precedent, Christians fought the Crusades and many other 'holy' wars to force everyone to worship their "greatest of all

Gods," Christ. God said it was okay to kill someone of a different religion because *his* religion was the only true one. To this day, Catholics remain certain that only *their* faith leads to salvation. Christ "is the one mediator between God and humanity," pronounced Pope John Paul II (*Crossing the Threshold of Hope*, 1994). For thousands of years the Bible has taught us not only that "My religion is better than yours," but that persecuting and slaughtering those of a different religion is one of the highest virtues. For thousands of years millions of people have honored a book that advocated the most violent kind of religious intolerance.

Blind Obedience Is A Virtue

Because Eve and Adam didn't follow one of God's orders, they were put on death row. What had they done that merited the death penalty not only for them but for their descendants to the umpteenth generation? They ate fruit from a tree that made them, as God said, like him, "knowing good and evil" (Genesis 3:22). Lowly humans, the Bible teaches us, aren't supposed to be like God and know good from evil; they're supposed to be programmed robots.

Was it right for Abraham to obey without a protest when God ordered him to sacrifice his son? And should Isaac, more willingly than a lamb, have submitted to his own slaughter? At the last minute, God rescinded his order, but he didn't tell Abraham that the lesson he should learn was that one shouldn't obey wicked orders. On the contrary, he praised Abraham for being a "God-fearing man" (Genesis 22:12). If an angel of God hadn't stopped Abraham from slitting his son's throat and Abraham had been charged with murder, he would have said, "I was just obeying orders." That's what the Nazis said at their trials, and they spoke the truth. Obediently, they'd done what they'd been told to do by Hitler, one of the government authorities that the New Testament teaches us we must obey because, as Paul explained, " there is no authority but by act of God," that, therefore, authorities are God's agents and have the right to punish you, even kill you for an offense (Romans 13:1-6). Paul was reflecting the totally obsequious attitude toward officials in his time, one that most people still feel toward their bosses, which most bosses, like God, still feel is the right attitude.

Punishments Make Us Good

Parents may urge their children to read the Bible because they hope the example of God killing for the smallest offense will scare them into being good. That may also be why preachers who thunder hell and damnation at their congregations advise them to mend their ways by studying the Bible: like God, the preachers are sure that threats and punishments work. They forget that most of the Israelites, despite God's frequent punishments, kept on sinning.

God's goal was laudable. He barraged his chosen people with Thou Shalt Nots and constantly punished them so they would rise above the norm of the times—not steal, not give false weights, not chase after whores, not be callous to the poor. Some Israelites did rise to God's standards, but most of them didn't. The Prophets railed on and on about the Israelites' sins—that they "grow rich and grand," "refuse to do justice" to the poor, that they steal, murder, commit adultery and act like cruel tyrants (Jeremiah 5:28, 22:17). What to do about it? The Prophets could only urge God to punish his chosen people even more savagely.

Scholars who study fairy tales report that giants are almost always stupid. The Giant in the Bible is no exception. Despite all evidence to the contrary, God continued to believe that his threats and punishment would make his chosen people good. Jesus preached compassion and forgiveness, yet the New Testament ends with God at the Last Judgment inventing crueler and crueler punishments to inflict on sinners. If Armageddon should arrive and the world be demolished, would it finally penetrate God's thick head that his threats and punishments hadn't produced goodness? I doubt it. If God is the God of the Bible, he'd be as pig-headed as we are, who, influenced by the Good Book, go on warning people that if they don't "Just say no" to sin, they'll be punished. Nevertheless, all the sins that the prophets railed against are still marching on. Indeed, by the closing years of the twentieth century, America was building more and more prisons to accommodate the 1.8 million men and women who were living proof that God's formula for goodness doesn't work.

Why?

Why do we worship a God who adored killing animals and drinking their blood?, whose greatest pleasure was war?, who practiced genocide?, who approved of the wartime sports of raping women and looting? Why do we worship a God who killed for a trifle and exploded with rage when things didn't go his way? Why do we worship a God who thought that returning hate with hate—vengeance—was a virtue, and that it was right to wipe out those of a different religion? Why do we worship a God who ruled by fear and demanded unquestioning obedience? Why do we worship a God who didn't know the difference between love and jealousy?

It's not as if God hid his faults. He commits his crimes in plain sight, but we react as if we didn't see them. Though God constantly urged his people to go to war, we call him a loving God. The Revelation of John is an orgy of mass murders but, instead of being nauseated, we believe what we're told, that we're receiving a holy message from Christ. We accept God's order to Abraham to kill his son as passively as Isaac did and don't question God's morality. We call one of the most violent books ever written a Book of Love and think our children will become good by reading it. Why don't we see that in most ways the Bible is no better than the Romans' brutal games and the murders we watch on TV and in movies? Why, instead of banning the Bible, do we, to quote a hymn, "Sing the praise and glory of God"?, a God who was worse than Hitler. Why such moral blindness?

Nowadays, we may be blind to God's character because few people read the Bible. On February 4, 1998 *The New York Times* ran an article on the mass killing of unarmed civilians in Africa. The reporter said that Liberia, which had been slaughtering unarmed civilians for eight years, had originated that style of fighting. I was taken aback. For if the reporter had read the Bible, he would have known that the Liberians hadn't started anything new, that they slaughtered pretty much the way the ancient Israelites used to. "Spare no one; put them all to death," ordered God, "men and women, children and babes in arms" (I Samuel 15:3). Similarly, Michael Karpin and Ina Friedman, in *Murder in the Name of God* (1998), accused Orthodox Israeli rabbis of causing the assassination of Yitzhak Rabin by claiming that God ordered the Israelites to kill those who opposed his beliefs. If they'd read the Bible, they would have known that the Rabbis didn't distort ancient Jewish concepts, that the Lord over and over ordered the murder of those who didn't follow the precepts of his religion.

Perhaps we can't see the Bible straight because we've been told so often that God is good and loving that, like dissidents who undergo 'reeducation' in China, we put on Holy Spectacles when we read the Bible to make sure we see only what we're supposed to. Or, perhaps, since God so often said that his wrath was good and his killing admirable, we've been conditioned to think of rage and killing the way God does.

Thomas Paine said that we can't see the Bible straight because of another kind of conditioning, that of the Church, which for centuries maintained that the Bible was the words of the Supreme Being Himself. Humans do tend to accept uncritically what authorities say. For decades people read Freud and Jung as if their words were the not-to-be-questioned truths of Gods. So why shouldn't people have accepted as sacred what the Greatest Authority in the Universe said in his own holy book? But the Bible may have become sacred in part because people had no choice; they had to believe it, or else.

Chapter 6   **The Sacred Book**

On Sunday November 22, 1998 on NBC News I learned it was Bible Week, that it had been celebrated for sixty years, but that now the American Civil Liberties Union wanted it banned. I'm sure they did because church and state are supposed to be separate, not because (to quote Gibbon again) murders, executions and massacres "stain almost every page of the Jewish annals," and the last book of the New Testament is a Niagara Falls of blood. NBC News didn't mention the violence in the Bible, nor God's rage, jealousy and lust for vengeance. NBC wouldn't have dared say one bad word about the Bible. Copies of it, leather bound with "The Holy Bible" embossed in gold on the cover, were shown in close-ups. They treated the Bible as sacred.

What Is Sacred?

Considering its violence and immorality, how could the Bible be regarded as sacred? But what is sacred? I'd never asked myself what it meant, so I looked it up in the dictionary and found that (among other things) sacred means "worthy of religious veneration," "made or declared holy." And, I learned from history, that the Bible had had to be "declared holy" before it became sacred. Just as the Church elevated human beings to sainthood, the Church elevated a human book (bible used to simply mean a book) into The Holy Bible, the sacred words of God.

Just as it takes the Catholic Church many years to make someone a saint, it took people many years to sanctify the Bible. At first only what the Prophets wrote was thought to have been "impelled by the Holy Spirit" and therefore "the words of God" (2 Peter 1:20-21). The whole of the Old Testament wasn't regarded as "the words of God" until some time after the birth of Jesus and it was not until about 150 years after Jesus' death that the Gospels achieved sacred status. It took longer for the rest of the New Testament, but eventually the Church declared that the whole Bible had been written down from God's dictation, which made it Holy Scriptures, which meant that it could contain "no falsehood anywhere," as Thomas Aquinas argued in the 1260s. For how could a falsehood be in the Bible if God was its author?

In 1564 when Church leaders met at Trent, they officially decreed that the entire Bible was the sacred words of God. At the same time they decreed that anyone who didn't believe the Bible was sacred would be anathematized. Anathematize means to be put under a curse for deviant behavior and be subject to correction, which meant torture, imprisonment, excommunication, and/or execution. The Church, like military dictators, controlled its subjects by force.

Church officials became as "terrible and fearful" as the God of Wrath. To deny the literal truth of the Bible often meant being burned at the stake, death by fire having been chosen because it was thought to be the most painful way to die. In 1600 Giordano Bruno was burned at the stake for suggesting (among other heresies) that the universe was infinite, a view that made him accursed because it questioned the finite world God described in Genesis. Since God also said that on the fourth day of creation he hung up the sun in the vault of heaven to light the stationary earth below, when Galileo in 1632 published a book demonstrating that the earth revolved around the sun, the Church ordered all copies burned and threatened him with torture and imprisonment. Galileo was afraid of torture and did believe in God, so he recanted. I "abjure, curse, and detest these heresies," he wrote to convince the church fathers he was sincere. He wasn't. His consolation during the eight years he spent under house arrest was that whatever the Church decreed, the fact was that "*I pur si muove,*" the earth moved, not the sun.

As the centuries passed, questioning the infallibility of the Bible was not a death sentence, though it could mean imprisonment. The English publisher of Thomas Paine's *The Age of Reason* (1794-95) was found guilty of blasphemy and imprisoned, the book was suppressed and anyone who read or discussed it could be prosecuted by the clergy. Paine was hanged in effigy and, despite or because of his belief in a benign God, not the God of Wrath, he was damned as an infidel for the rest of his life.

Paine was part of a movement that was trying to break down belief in the literal truth of the Bible. A goliath of a job. The power of the Church continued to be enormous. Whenever scientists made discoveries that disagreed with the Bible, the Church was likely to draw its anathema gun. Well into the twentieth century, various churches declared that the Bible came straight from the mouth of God and that anyone who thought otherwise would go to hell.

"I believe the Bible as it is," William Jennings Bryan proudly said on July 21, 1925. He was prosecuting John Scopes who'd broken a Tennessee law by teaching the evolutionary theory of creation. For Bryan and the jury that convicted Scopes, the Bible meant exactly what it said, that God created the adult Adam out of dust and the adult Eve from one of Adam's ribs, and God damn the scientists and anyone else who said that human beings evolved from apes. Fundamentalists continue to argue that the Genesis story of the creation of the universe is as scientific as the discoveries of geologists and physicists and should be taught in schools as an alternative theory of creation, a movement that gained such strength that many science teachers were frightened into silence. In 1998, the National Academy of Sciences wrote a guidebook to encourage and help educators teach evolution, but in August 1999 the Kansas Board of Education voted to remove evolution from the required subjects taught in schools.

In the late twentieth century, belief in the old-time religion became so strong that parents wanted to introduce their children to the Bible at the earliest possible age. In April 1996 when a publisher issued *Baby's First Bible*, it had explosive sales, and sales of children's Bibles and storybooks based on the Bible increased and multiplied. I learned that information from a long article in the October 13, 1997 *Publishers Weekly* on "Sacred Texts," whose first two sections were called, "The Bible Still Matters" and "It's Still the Good Book." It is. When the magazine asked book buyers the standard question, "What one book would you want if you were stranded on a desert island?" the most common answer was "The Bible." In his 1997 bestseller, *The Bible Code*, Michael Drosnin told of feeding the Bible into a computer and discovering a hidden code that predicted, among many other events, the Holocaust, the Gulf War, the assassinations of Lincoln and Kennedy and the end of the world (2002). An executive at Simon & Schuster, the book's publisher, had been certain the book would be a bestseller because, she said, "People long to believe—that God, or some spiritual being beyond our ken, does exist and actually wrote the Bible."

Did God actually write the Bible? Hundreds of thousands of people who believe in God are sure he did. Why not? The God who created the universe could surely do a small thing like write the Bible. Besides, we've all had inspirations that come from a source beyond our conscious mind. Roman writers, like Ovid and Cicero, explained them as "seeds of the divine mind sown in man," and Quakers as "the still small voice" of God speaking to man. That God personally handed Moses the carved-in stone Commandments or that an angel handed Joseph Smith golden tablets inscribed with the Book of Mormon may not be credible, but why not accept that God himself was channeled by those who wrote down the Bible?

I can't and for one simple reason. If the Bible had been taken down from God's dictation, why did he describe himself as wildly jealous, as gloating over his enemies, as filled with rage and lusting to kill? For me, the strongest argument that God didn't write the Bible is that he painted such an unflattering picture of himself.

Perhaps God was so far gone in his iniquity that he didn't realize that jealousy and rage were not divine, and most people have only praise for his conduct. For example, in the century before Jesus was born, Rabbi Hillel summed up the *Torah* (the first five books of the Old Testament) as saying, "What you don't want men to do to you, don't do to them." But when I read God's many threats to his chosen people—that the fire of his wrath or plagues or wars would destroy them if they didn't obey him— the message I received from the *Torah* was: "Do what I say or else!" The God I encountered in the Bible constantly did to others what he wouldn't want done to himself. Hillel did what the Prophets had done when they said that God really loathed animal sacrifice and didn't want men to fight wars. Hillel invested the God of the Israelites with his own wisdom and humanity, which Jesus changed to "Do unto others what you would have them do unto you."

Rabbi Hillel was able to say what he thought God said because the Rabbis who studied the Old Testament felt free to 'improve' it. Even when they believed that every word was sacred because it came from God, they could always draw different meanings from the same words and make God say what *they* thought. Unlike Galileo, who could believe that the earth moves around the sun only in the privacy of his own mind, Rabbis had a forum. Their commentaries on the Old Testament are collected in the many volumes of the *Talmud*. The Jews thus gave themselves a way to soften the fearful God of Wrath, to be open to new ideas, to change with the times, just as scientific theories change when new facts are discovered.

Christianity didn't take that path. For most of its history it shut the door on change. In the mid seventeenth century, Archbishop James Ussher wrote what became the definitive history of the world, a history that began with God creating the world as he did in Genesis, which Ussher said happened in 4004 BC. His dates were printed in the English Bible well into the twentieth century. Christians had to accept as true not only the Genesis story of the creation of the universe, but stories that nowadays appear only in tabloids—that a girl had a baby but remained a virgin, that priests can turn wine and bread into the blood and body of a man who died long ago, and that One God can turn into three Gods. Faith became believing the impossible. As Byron in *Don Juan* (1823) joked about the Trinity: "I devoutly wish the three were four, On purpose so I can believe more."

The Bible became sacred because for hundreds of years people were too scared of being killed or severely punished to read it with their minds turned on. When I decided to write this exposé of the God of Wrath and damn the Bible as a bad book, I had a fantasy of being waylaid by a Christian fundamentalist with an Uzi who'd say as he pulled the trigger, "Blessed be the name of the Lord." My fear was a legacy from the time when it *was* worth your life to question anything in the Bible.

Gospel Untruths

In most American courts, witnesses are required to put their right hand on the Bible and swear "to tell the truth, the whole truth and nothing but the truth, so help me God." And yet the Bible they swear on celebrates a God who wasn't interested in discovering the truth, but only in having his every word accepted as true, a God whose violence, jealousy and vengeance were ways of not seeing the truth. The Bible does contain some lasting truths, but considering its bulk, not many, even in the Gospels. The belief that the four Gospels (Matthew, Mark, Luke and John) are a repository of truths about Christianity is so widespread that we say, "It's the Gospel truth" to assure someone we're not lying. We shouldn't.

In the first place, the Gospels are a corrupt text. As D.C. Parker in *The Living Text of the Gospels* (1997) pointed out, even after the Gospels were officially declared sacred, the scribes who copied them would change one Gospel to make it agree with another and made so many alterations and adaptations of a passage that scholars often have no idea what the original text was.

The Gospels are corrupt in a more important way; they're an altered account of what was remembered of the life and sayings of Jesus. It took me a long time to discover that. As I told you in Chapter 4, I read the Gospels before I read the whole Bible and didn't question their accounts of Jesus. Only after I read the Bible from Genesis on did I realize when I got to the New Testament that the God of the Old Testament was rearing his wrathful head there too, so much so that at times Jesus sounded as punishing and unforgiving as God did. That upset and puzzled me. Why was Jesus, who'd come to give the world good news, repeating the God of Wrath's bad news? Knowing nothing of the history of the Gospels, I decided that Jesus, like the rest of us, was capable of having contradictory beliefs. Later slow-witted me 'remembered' that Jesus was born into a Jewish culture and would have studied the Old Testament and been influenced by the God of Wrath. But I remained puzzled because wasn't Jesus supposed to be different from the Jews? Why would we have Christianity if Jesus hadn't been different?

Much of my puzzlement would have been cleared up if I'd known that, although the Gospels appear first in the New Testament, they were not written first. They were written after Paul's letters to the early Christians, letters Paul wrote without reading the Gospels, for they were written after he died. Paul's Holy Book had been the Old Testament, which he seemed to know by heart. No wonder that the God of Wrath was a large presence in the New Testament, especially since Paul had been so devoted to the God of Wrath that he'd traveled around killing those who desecrated the one and only God by worshiping another God, the new one called Christ.

After his conversion to Christianity, Paul's violent temperament was softened. In a famous passage in 1 Corinthians 13, Paul described love as "not quick to take offense," as keeping "no score of wrongs," and not gloating "over other men's sins." But though Paul could be eloquent on the power of love, he was more interested in power. He wouldn't have understood the Jesus who, when his disciples were disputing which one of them was the greatest, set a child among them and said, "the least among you all—he is the greatest" (Luke 9:46-48). Paul wanted Jesus to be "the greatest." He wrote about a Jesus of "everlasting power and deity" (Romans 1:20), a Jesus who'd be "enthroned" at God's "right hand," "supreme head to the church," bearing a title higher than that of any sovereign who had ever lived or would live (Ephesians 1:20-23). Just as the Romans eagerly conferred absolute power on a leader and made him an Emperor, Paul, a Roman citizen, turned Jesus into the greatest Emperor of all. It was Paul who gave Jesus the title "the Savior," a title that was given to Gods in other religions and to Roman Emperors who, when they ascended the throne, became divine Saviors, as Paul said Jesus became when he ascended his throne in heaven.

Those who put the New Testament together wanted readers to think of Jesus the way Paul did, with a halo around him; they wanted readers to learn right away that Jesus was a Very Important Person, not a nobody carpenter from Nazareth. The first words we read when we open the New Testament are, "A table of the descent of Jesus Christ." The Gospel According to Matthew was put first in the New Testament because it begins with a lengthy genealogy tracing Jesus' lineage back to men like Abraham and King David. The fact is that no one knows who his ancestors were, but in the Old Testament the Prophets had predicted that the longed-for Messiah would come from a royal line, so 'proof' was extracted from the Old Testament. Important people were supposed to have important forebears. The Buddha, who lived about 500 years before Jesus, was also said to have come from a royal line, the *Sakya* line.

Ancient peoples, though, could trace their descent back to the most august ancestor possible—God. That was not an ego-boost. It amazed me when I read Herodotus that he had no doubt whatsoever that someone could be the son of a God. Alexander the Great's mother was convinced he was the son of Zeus. Roman emperors who declared themselves divine not only believed it, so did the Senators and the populace. "August Caesar, Son of a God," said Virgil in the *Aeneid*, and he believed it. Similarly, right after the account of the noble descent of Jesus, we learn that he, like Roman emperors, was also the Son of God.

Zeus used to fly down as a swan or a shower of gold and impregnate mortal women who always had sons, and God begat in a similar way and also had sons. In the Old Testament, God, having promised Abraham that Sarah, though ninety-years old, would bear a son, "visited Sarah ... and "did unto Sarah as he had spoken. For Sarah conceived, and bare Abraham a son in his old age" (Genesis 21:1-2). We don't know what form God assumed when he caused Sarah to conceive, but he visited Mary as a Holy Spirit and she too had a son.

When Jesus was born, however, religious officials and the populace didn't know that God's Holy Spirit had sired him. For if they had, Jesus wouldn't have lived a life of obscurity for many years. The Christmas stories we celebrate—Jesus' divine conception, his birth in a manger where the Magi bring the new Messiah gifts — were put into the Gospels to turn a man into a God. The early Christians were imitating the Romans, who had to proclaim their emperors Gods in order to worship them. Jesus had to be the son of God for an additional reason — to fulfill a divine purpose. He "will save his people from their sins," announced God on the first page of the first Gospel, as if God had known before Jesus' birth that Jesus would die on the cross to atone for mankind's sins. In the Old Testament God had always said that he foreordained history, but in regard to Jesus, God was not the one with the foreknowledge: Paul was.

"Christ," said Paul, "gave himself up on your behalf as an offering and sacrifice whose fragrance is pleasing to God" (Ephesians 5:1-2). "Fragrance" reminded me of God ordering animals to be burned on his altar because he liked the "soothing odor" (Exodus 29:18). I was right to be reminded of the sacrifice of animals because Paul, unable to give up the Hebrew belief that only by the shedding of blood are "our sins ... forgiven" (Ephesians 1:7), turned Jesus into an animal, the lamb without a blemish traditionally sacrificed and eaten at Passover. But the real Jesus wasn't a sacrificial lamb; he was the human son of God being sacrificed. "In Christ ... our sins are forgiven through the shedding of his blood" (Ephesians 1:7), said Paul, as if God had reverted to the time when, like his hated rival Baal, child sacrifice had been central to his worship. But God hadn't reverted to barbarism, Paul had.

Jesus probably wouldn't have approved of the bloody role he was to assume in Christianity. When he was alive, he'd stopped believing that blood sacrifice was necessary for the forgiveness of sins. At least, he twice quoted the Prophet Hosea, who said that God really wanted mercy not animal sacrifice (Matthew 9:13; 12:7) and he'd had his sins forgiven by confession and baptism in water, an Essene rite of purification that John the Baptist used. According to the Gospels, though, Jesus said at the Last Supper that at future Passovers the bread and wine they ate and drank would be a remembrance of his blood sacrifice. "This is my blood, the blood of the covenant, shed for many," he said in Mark (14:24), and in Matthew we find, "for the forgiveness of sins" (26:28-29). But would Jesus have suggested that Jews drink even symbolic blood when they were forbidden to eat blood (their meat had to be drained of blood before cooking)?

At the time the Gospels were being written, the Eucharist, eating the body and blood of Christ, had become a ritual in the suppers the new Christians shared. But the New Christians may not have been obeying Jesus' orders; they may have been imitating the much more popular religions of the period in which devotees symbolically ate the flesh and blood of Mithra, Dionysus and other Gods. Perhaps the new Christians wanted to attract converts from these religions by adopting a ritual that would let them continue eating the flesh and blood of a God, the new God, Christ.

I've led you a little way into the maze of scholarship on this disputed point to give you a sense of the difficulties scholars have in determining what Jesus said and what he didn't.

Another point disputed by scholars is whether or not Jesus preached the sermon about the Last Judgment in which he predicted he'd appear in glory. Many scholars think that mini-apocalypse was not forecast by Jesus, and not only because it reeks of the God of Wrath's vengeance. Scholars ask if the still-living Jesus, who didn't yet know he'd be crucified, would picture himself appearing in glory after his death? They also ask if Jesus, who'd limited his ministry to Jews, would say that "before the end [of the world] the Gospel must be proclaimed to all nations" (Mark 13:10-11). It was Paul, not Jesus, who thought that Christianity must be preached to the Gentiles, a mission to which he devoted his life. In addition, both Mark and Luke have Christ say that anyone who wished to be his follower must "take up his cross" (Mark 8:34; Luke 9:23), a phrase that wouldn't be used by Jesus *before* his crucifixion but by early Christians.

If Jesus didn't make this prophesy, why is it in the Gospels? If Jesus didn't say that he was shedding his blood for the forgiveness of sins, why is it in the Gospels? So readers would think Jesus believed what Paul did. Since the Gospels were written after Paul's letters to the new Christians, the authors of the Gospels were able to put Paul's beliefs into Jesus' mouth. They thus concealed that it was Paul not Jesus who'd laid down many of Christianity's fundamental tenets, including the cornerstone of the future Church — that without Christ's blood sacrifice mankind could not be redeemed from their sins. The more I studied the New Testament, the more I was sure that Christianity should have been called Paulianity.

Paul would have disagreed. Because he'd been touched by the Holy Spirit on the road to Damascus, he thought that Christ lived in him (Galations 2:20-21), so that whatever he preached, he received "through a revelation of Jesus Christ" (Galations 1:11-12). Perhaps, but the Prophets had also said, "the Lord saieth," when they expressed opinions that were opposite to those of the God of Wrath. Paul was the first of many people who were sure they knew what Jesus really thought, but as the first and because his words were put into the mouth of Jesus, Paul had the greatest influence.

Later Christians also put their beliefs in Jesus' mouth. For example, in Matthew (16:17) Jesus is reported as saying to Peter, "On this rock, I will build my Church," a statement apparently giving authority to Peter to found the Christian Church. However, most scholars agree that Jesus had had no thoughts of founding a church since he expected the world to end soon, that the passage was added to the Gospels to give divine authority to the already established Church. In Matthew (28:19) the resurrected Jesus is also reported as saying that the Church should "go forth" and "baptize men everywhere in the name of the Father and the Son and the Holy Spirit," thus making the uninformed reader of the Gospels think that Jesus believed in the Trinity, which didn't begin to become part of Church doctrine until long after he died.

Who knows how many scribes also felt free to put their finger in the Gospel pie and add their plum? Why not? The text they copied hadn't been an honest record of Jesus in the first place. It had been composed by men who'd never known him, who had necessarily learned about him from others. Peter, who had known Jesus, is supposed to have been the source for Mark, the first Gospel written, but no one can vouch for other sources or even the accuracy of what Peter remembered since the information was gathered years after Jesus died. But whatever the accuracy of their sources, the goal of the authors of the Gospels was not to give the world an accurate record of the words of Jesus. Their goal was to present a Jesus who was religiously correct, to make him conform to the beliefs held by Paul and the early Christians. Most scholars agree that not much of what Jesus said survives in the Gospels.

How to decide what Jesus actually said? "The Sabbath was made for man, and not man for the Sabbath," and "He who is without sin, let him cast the first stone" have resonated in the hearts of almost everyone, except Jewish, Christian and Muslim fundamentalists who adhere strictly to commandments and are the first to cast stones at those who don't. But most people have been drawn to the Jesus who wasn't like the God of Wrath, the Jesus who could break rules, who thought for himself and was compassionate.

One was Thomas Jefferson, who felt that Jesus had developed "the most sublime and benevolent code of morals which has ever been offered to mankind." In an 1813 letter to John Adams, he said that to have this code of morals handy he'd gone through the New Testament and cut out the authentic words of Jesus and pasted them into a book of forty-six pages, not a difficult task for Jefferson, who thought Jesus' words were "as easily distinguishable as diamonds in a dunghill."

We're so used to the New Testament being treated as sacred that to hear it called a dunghill shocks us. Jefferson must have been greatly offended to call it a dunghill. So am I. And not because God came down like Zeus and impregnated Mary with his Holy Spirit, and not because Jesus was given a phony noble ancestry, and not because eating the body and blood of Jesus is a reversion to human sacrifice and cannibalism, and not because most people after death were consigned to everlasting torture in Hell. I'm offended by the New Testament because it perpetrated a fraud on the public. It promoted as new a religion that was fundamentally old, a religion that had little to do with its supposed founder.

When I read the Gospels, I trusted I'd be reading the truths of Jesus. I didn't expect to find the God of Wrath's beliefs or Paul's, or those of the early Christian communities, or the authors of the Gospels or the scribes who copied them or doctrines of the established Church, with sprinkles of Jesus on top. When I took in that much of what Jesus said he did not say, that others put their own or old beliefs into his mouth, I felt conned, and I had been. The Gospels misrepresented Jesus by pretending he said what he didn't say. It's an ancient example of the practice of disreputable lawyers, critics and politicians who quote people in ways that make them seem to believe what they don't. Paul, the authors of the Gospels, and those who put the New Testament together were far more interested in creating a Christian myth than in telling the truth about Jesus. Gandhi said that God is truth. Why should a document that's riddled with lies be venerated as sacred?

The God of Wrath's Alias

When Paul expressed his views, he thought Jesus was speaking through him. Like the many others who followed him—those who said that Jesus was a strict Orthodox Jew, a pure Aryan, a Buddhist, a feminist, a homosexual—Paul was unaware that he'd recreated Jesus in his own image. It was Paul, not Jesus, who couldn't imagine a world without a supreme God, the "master whose slaves [the rest of us] must be" (Colossians 3:24).

In recounting the history of the Egyptians, Herodotus said that after they were freed from "the kingship of the priest of Hephaestus, they could not live a day without a king." The earliest Christians at first lived a communal life, but soon they too couldn't live without a king. Like Paul, most people couldn't conceive of a society without a powerful leader on the throne, his iron scepter ready at hand, a belief that eventually led to the hierarchies of priests that pyramided up to the Pope in the Catholic Church, which wanted to create a world Christendom in which everyone would be a slave to the new master, Christ, and to his earthly agents (priests).

The world needed to stop submitting to fearful authorities, needed to abandon the master-slave paradigm the God of Wrath stood for. Marcion, a second-century Christian, had been so appalled by the God of Wrath he'd totally rejected the Old Testament, which was included in the Bible because few people could imagine life without a God of Wrath in charge. The Church developed the doctrine of the Trinity in part to keep the God of Wrath the chief God and consign Jesus, though declared to be of the same divine substance, to second place. The world wasn't ready to worship a God who advocated love and forgiveness. The Israelites had wanted their Messiah to be a warrior who'd free Israel from Roman rule and restore the glory days when David was king and the Israelites were a mighty nation. They wanted their Messiah to be a better General than the God of Wrath, who'd, alas, lead his people into many battles they'd lost, and who'd let them be conquered by the Babylonians, Assyrians,

Greeks and Romans. The Israelites didn't want a Jesus; they wanted an Alexander the Great, who'd help them conquer the world.

Christians were pacifists for some 300 years (no soldier could become a Christian), and yet the John who wrote Revelation had already turned Jesus into a warrior with "a sharp two-edged sword" coming out of his mouth (1:16) and "the marks of slaughter upon him" (5:6). It was as if those who chose to end the New Testament with Revelation were repudiating what Jesus stood for. For John made Jesus a bigger mass-murderer than the God of Wrath and said he was "destined to rule all nations with an iron rod" (12:4-5), although Jesus hadn't ruled with an iron rod. The iron rod was the police truncheon the God of Wrath relied on. The Christ in The Revelation of John who acts like the God of Wrath was the old God with a new name. "Christ" became the God of Wrath's alias.

Jesus is often called Christ in the Gospels although he didn't acquire the title "the Christ" (Greek for messiah) until after his crucifixion. But it was right that the new religion got a name that had nothing to do with Jesus because the God they called Christ was so obviously the God of Wrath. The Christ who was invoked to insure victory in battle was the fire-breathing God of Wrath smelted into a cross. In 312 when the Emperor Constantine was at the Milvian Bridge hoping to conquer Rome, he said he saw in the sky a pillar of light in the form of a cross, and the words, "In This Sign Conquer," which meant to him that Christ would bring him victory. His soldiers, betting on the Emperor's God, painted a cross on their shields, and the magic worked. Constantine did conquer Rome and, understandably, converted to Christianity, for Christ was indeed a great God, a God after his own heart.

"In the sign of the Cross conquer," slaughtering for the greater glory of Christ, became the rallying cry of the Crusades. Bernard of Clairvaux, whose rousing sermons began the Second Crusade in 1146, told the crusaders that they should demonstrate their love of Christ by killing as many infidels as they could. When the Christian Church conquered pagan communities and forced them to worship Christ, they were displacing many brutal pagan Gods with their own, Almighty killer-God. When Christianity triumphed in the western world, the Church became an international God of Wrath, a master who ruled with a rod of iron and felt free to kill anyone who disagreed with its doctrines or believed in other Gods. The Church became the raging maniac of the Old Testament concealed behind a mask of Christ. Children were often buried in the foundation of new buildings to give them strength. I sometimes picture the crucified Jesus buried in the foundation of the Vatican.

Generations have worshiped the warrior God of the Bible, whose endless slaughters conditioned them to regard war as a God-like pursuit. When, later in his life, Ivan the Terrible (1530-1584) became religious, he didn't stop fighting wars or curb his cruelty: he used to plan his tortures during Mass. He instinctively knew that the real God wasn't Jesus but the God who'd said, "Let the high praises of God be on their lips and a two-edged sword in their hand" (Psalm 149). It was the God of Wrath who inspired the 1866 hymn, "Onward Christian Soldiers marching as to war, with the cross of Jesus going on before."

In 1912 Mark Twain wrote a war prayer—"Oh Lord, our God, help us to tear their soldiers to bloody shreds"—but didn't dare publish it while he was alive. Why not? Twain was merely repeating what God often said in the Bible, that he or his angels would help soldiers tear his enemies to bloody shreds. Twain was saying what generals often said to their soldiers before a battle: "God be with you," which meant they hoped God would protect them while they killed more soldiers than the other side did.

The English poet, Siegfried Sassoon, began the first World War eager to fight in defense of liberty, then discovered that the slaughter was actually about "aggression and conquest." Convinced that the soldiers had been duped, he thought the war should be settled by negotiations. He expressed his anti-war views in a letter published in the London *Times* on July 31, 1917, a letter that led to his almost being tried for treason. Sassoon *was* a traitor, not only to England but to God. According to the Bible, to believe that war is madness is to repudiate God.

Few have repudiated him. The chaplain at Pearl Harbor who on December 7, 1941 said, "Praise the Lord and pass the ammunition," was a Christian who worshiped the God of Wrath, as were those who erected a large stone cross with a bronze sword fixed to it as a World War II memorial in front of St Paul's Anglican Church in Toronto, Canada. The chaplains in Vietnam who, via the radio, blessed the bombs on airplane carriers, were also Christians whose God was the God of Wrath. Contemporary Christians, though they may ally themselves with a God of Love and Peace, threaten, punish and wage wars like the God of Wrath. They even pray to God before they play football games, as if, like Christians about to wage war, they wanted God to be on their side and help them defeat the enemy (the opposing team).

The common opinion is that Jesus came to the world to teach love and forgiveness. If the New Testament had delivered only that message, perhaps the world would have become a better place. As things are, we need a Second Coming. The new religion that was called Christianity was given to the world over 2000 years ago, a religion that became widely influential, and yet it hasn't immunized us from the black death of hate and violence that has always plagued humans. The world we live in is a world of hate and violence because the God of Wrath, despite Jesus, is our God. The Bible remains sacred because we still worship that God. If you don't believe me, read the newspapers.

Chapter 7   The Newspaper Bible

Why I Studied the Newspapers

I used to rarely read newspapers, so when I heard Thoreau's remark that if you've read one newspaper you've read them all, I felt justified. I did keep up with some of what was going on in the world, and what I gleaned from TV or the radio was enough for me. And yet, at seven o'clock one morning I found myself at a café reading the whole first section of the San Francisco Chronicle. I was at the café because I'd lain awake since four and wanted a change of scene; I'd bought a newspaper for a reason I'll explain.

Three weeks before, I'd begun a form of body therapy called craniosacral osteopathy and the doctor's hands had felt rigid tissue in my right cheek and left butt, stiff memorials, like gravestones, of some of the blows of my childhood. Years before I'd remembered the incidents, but I hadn't known my body still preserved each one like a mummy. Not until the kind hands of the doctor began to soften the tissues did I discover that hate was locked in them, hate that only then began to release.

That I was filled with hate, I'd known since I began my inner journey, hate that I'd felt again and again, hate I thought I'd pretty much dealt with. I was astounded and dismayed that more hate was in me, hate that ignited raging scenarios in my head, which early one morning wouldn't let me sleep.

That helpless raging, which had gone on for three weeks, was happening at the same time as I was studying the Bible. That's why on the morning of July 31, 1997 as hate-filled me approached the café and my eyes glanced at a newspaper stand, the headline—"SUICIDE ATTACK RIPS ISRAEL"—made me think of the Israelites' many attacks on their enemies in the Old Testament, so I bought a paper.

At first I ignored the story about Israel; I'd learned about it on TV the night before. I read an item of local news also on the front page, to the left of the headline. Willie Brown, the mayor of San Francisco, was furious because at a rally demanding their rights, some bicyclists had blocked traffic and committed mayhem. The Mayor wanted them sent to jail, their bicycles confiscated. Only by being punished to the full extent of the law, he raged, would these "lawless, insurrectionist types" learn to respect others' rights. Willie Brown was letting the fire of his wrath pour from his mouth and, I felt sure, a part of him would have liked to smite the bicyclists with a two-edged sword. Willie Brown, I now understood because I'd read the Bible, often acted like "The King of kings and Lord of lords" (Revelation 19:16).

I then turned to the headline story about Israel. In a Jerusalem market two Palestinian suicide bombers had blown themselves up, killing thirteen Israelis and wounding about 170 others. I didn't read it through. Even when I'd seen the carnage on TV, I hadn't paid much attention. I'd become inured to the constant bombings in Israel. (On page 11, the newspaper listed the fourteen bombings that had occurred since the 1993 Oslo peace accords.) On page 8 I learned that the prime minister of Israel, Benjamin Netanyahu, was considering a military strike on the Palestinians, who, in their turn, would seek vengeance just as God did in the Bible.

I returned to the front page, where I read about a man soon to be executed for a rape and murder he said he didn't commit. The evidence of his innocence was so strong that the United States Court of Appeals granted him an emergency hearing to consider a stay of execution. The governor of California was opposed to a stay. Politicians in America know that the public strongly believe in the Old Testament's, "an eye for an eye," and far prefer to cast stones than turn the other cheek.

On page 3 was more news about the 1996 bombing of a building in Saudi Arabia where United States Air Force personnel had been housed, nineteen of whom had been killed and more than 500 injured. The United States suspected that Iran was behind the terrorist attack, and a Saudi Arabian had agreed to give the FBI information about an Iranian connection. But he'd suddenly announced he knew nothing. I didn't blame him for backing off. Iran was run by despots who, like the God of Wrath, thought that anyone who opposed them ought to be killed.

Members of the Rio de Janeiro police force were also acting like despots. I read on page 8 that they'd been caught in a video "extorting money, beating people with a billy club, shooting two people and killing one in a Sao Paulo slum." They'd been trained under a military dictatorship and continued to be under the jurisdiction of lenient military courts. They therefore felt free to break the law and continue their old sadistic pleasures, like the Christ in The Revelation of John acting like the God of Wrath in the Old Testament.

On page 9 I learned that a man who'd headed another dictatorship, Pol Pot of Cambodia, in a show trial by the Khmer Rouge, had been put under house arrest for life. A mild sentence for a man who, between 1975 and 1979, had exterminated almost two million Cambodians by execution, torture, overwork, disease and starvation, carrying on the tradition of the wholesale slaughterer in the Bible.

On the same page was a long account of the current slaughter in the long war in Sudan, where southern militia forces were destroying villages and crops, stealing flocks of goats and sheep, killing people and selling thousands of women and children into slavery. I shook my head in amazement. Here I was, reading about a massacre like those in the

Bible, when the Israelites, on God's orders, would kill "all the men," capture the "women and their dependents" and carry off "their beasts, their flocks and their property" (Numbers 31:1-12). I felt that if a slide of the Sudanese war could be put on top of a slide of the Biblical war, they'd match.

This was my God of Wrath harvest from the newspaper of July 31, 1997, and an ample harvest I thought it was, especially since the twelve-page first section of the paper was half ads. Had that day been exceptional? If Thoreau were right and newspapers recounted similar news over and over, would the God of Wrath be as large a presence on other days? I started to read newspapers (local ones and occasionally The New York Times and Los Angeles Times). I had a reason now. I wasn't displacing the stream of chat in my head with newspaper chat, I was on the trail of the God of Wrath.

I've often noticed that when I get interested in a subject, information about it constantly pops up. It isn't magic. I merely pay attention to what previously I hadn't been interested in, and until I read the Bible, I'd been unaware of the God of Wrath. But when I began reading newspapers (which I did from July 31 to December 31, 1997), I discovered that God wasn't dead, that his Wrathship was alive and acting out virtually everywhere on the planet earth.

The Living Bible

On July 31 the newspaper had carried a story about Pol Pot, the former dictator of Cambodia, who'd slaughtered like the God of Wrath. On September 8, the newspaper announced the death of another corrupt dictator, one who'd consciously modeled himself on the God of Wrath. He was Mobutu Sese Seko who, the paper said, had changed his name from Joseph-Desire Mobutu to one that meant, "The all-powerful warrior who, because of his inflexible will to win, will go from conquest to conquest leaving fire in his wake." "The all-powerful warrior … leaving fire in his wake" had not only created a name embodying traits of the God of Wrath, his long, bloody rule over Zaire revealed that he'd absorbed many lessons in ruthlessness from the Old Testament. He'd also learned to hide his rage for power behind a mask of Christ. The newspapers he controlled called him Messiah, compared his mother to the Virgin Mary, and on the television stations he ran, showed him descending from clouds, like Christ in the Gospels and The Revelation of John.

"The all-powerful warrior … leaving fire in his wake" having died, he must have been greeted by the God of Wrath and, when the fire streaming from both of them had spent its force, I can hear God say, "Welcome, *landsman*," a Yiddish word (pronounced lonts-mon) that means "someone who comes from the same hometown," or, loosely, "my kind of person."

God would then have taken Mobuto to meet other dead *landsmen*, like Stalin, who was back in the news in August because of the discovery north of St Petersburg of a two-and-a-half acre grave that contained the "shattered skulls and twisted skeletons" of 9,111 political prisoners executed by Stalin's secret police in 1937. The mass burial reminded me of an incident in the Old Testament when Moses' leadership was questioned and God punished the rebels by splitting the earth open, which swallowed them, their wives, sons and dependents, whereupon "the earth closed over them, and they vanished from the assembly" (Numbers 16:31-33). It may be human nature to hide the evidence of a crime, but Christian dictators could have learned how to "disappear" many corpses by reading the Bible, just as people learn to make bombs from terrorist handbooks.

The holy book of the Muslims also advocates terrorism. "When ye encounter the unbelievers, strike off their heads, until ye have made a great slaughter among them," says the Koran (XLVII), and the Armed Islamic Group of Algeria (known as the GIA) proudly announced their obedience to God in the September 27 paper: "We are that band, with God's permission, who kill and slaughter, and we will remain so until ... the word of God is raised high." During my newspaper watch, the GIAs slaughtered mightily for God. The August 30 newspaper reported that they'd massacred 300 people in a village, and on September 24, 200 more in a suburb. Using machine guns, firebombs, knives and iron bars, they slit throats, cut off heads, tossed children from terraces, disemboweled pregnant women and burned down houses. They dragged off young girls and raped them before slitting their throats, sparing only the pretty ones, whom they took to their mountain hideaways to serve as sex slaves. On July 31 I'd been astonished by the similarities between the Sudanese war and the wars in the Bible and, except for the difference in some weapons, the GIA also might have been ancient Israelites, killing all the men, smashing children's heads on rocks, murdering every woman who was not a virgin, sparing only the virgins for their own use (Numbers 31:17-19) and ripping "open all the pregnant women" (2 Kings 15:16).

The GIA were one of many terrorist groups. On September 24 the newspaper ran a story about the "Nasty Little War Dragging On In Brazzaville," where only "ten percent of the city's 800,000 residents" remained, driven out by the Cobras, young men well-supplied with "beer, morale and AK-47 machine guns." "Drunk and drugged teenagers" were also the main fighting forces in the long civil war in Liberia, which the August 4 newspaper said had killed 200,000 people, and on November 17, I read that Egyptian Islamic militants were continuing their five-year-old guerilla war by gunning down, then slitting the throats of dozens of tourists at Luxor. The latest massacre by the Tamil Tigers, ethnic separatists in Sri Lanka, had meanwhile been reported on October 17.

Before I began reading newspapers, I'd been aware that the Hutus and Tutsis of Rwanda had for some time literally been at each others' throats, and on September 23 the newspaper reported that the Tutsis had massacred 2000 Hutu refugees, and on October 16 that they'd killed more of them. Other mutual slaughterers, the warring groups in the former Yugoslavia, were in the news again on September 5 when the paper ran a long story about the torture and executions that had previously taken place in Croatia—the cries and screams echoing in villages, the women raped before they were killed, the homes looted, from which Serbs stole "tens of thousands of dollars." The paper ran this old news because it might become new news. For despite peace agreements, the August 4 paper had reported that Bosnian Croats, "fortified with beer and clubs," were preventing Muslims from returning to their villages. The Israelis and Palestinians also couldn't stop their feuding. On September 4 the newspaper reported another suicide bombing in Israel.

And so the massacres went on and on, until the last half of December when, like a Christmas bonus, blood flowed as if, as in The Revelation of John, God had emptied more bloody bowls of his wrath on the world. On the 15th and 23rd the papers reported that Tutsis had again attacked Hutus in a refugee camp, committing their routine atrocities, like splitting a little girl's head open with a machete. More carnage was reported on the 24th, this time in Chiapas, Mexico, where long-standing violence between the Zapatistas and the Institutional Revolutionary Party had climaxed when gunmen with combat rifles stormed into a village church and mowed down forty-five peasants. The warring sects in Ireland also chose the Christmas season to spill more blood when on December 27, as a protest against recent peace talks, Catholic terrorists in a high-security prison managed to shoot to death "King Rat," the leading Protestant terrorist. And on the last day of 1997, the newspaper reported that the dictator of Iraq, Saddam Hussein, had recently ordered the execution of "hundreds if not thousands" of men who'd been in jail for insulting his regime or belonging to an opposition political party.

It was hard to decide whether Saddam Hussein, known as the Butcher of Baghdad, deserved the blood prize or the Armed Islamic Group in Algeria who, a few days before Ramadan, increased their holy slaughtering. On December 31 the paper said that during the previous ten days they'd slaughtered more than 300 men, women and children by again slitting throats, hacking bodies to pieces, shooting and beheading, sparing only the young females whom they kidnapped. The newspaper estimated that during their almost six-year holy war they'd killed 110,000 people.

In 1776 in *The Decline and Fall of the Roman Empire*, Gibbon remarked on the bloody murders, executions and massacres that "stain almost every page of the Jewish annals," and as I plodded through the news from the last day of July to the last day of December, I discovered that bloody massacres were also staining "almost every page" of the newspapers. There were so many massacres that it crossed my mind that, in addition to the Sports Section, newspapers should have a Massacre Section.

The Massacre Section would be thick, for the massacres of one warring nation or group against another were not the only ones. Besides the usual rapes, murders and police violence, personal mini-massacres went on and on. On September 16 I read about a South Carolina man who, enraged because he'd been fired from his job, returned gun in hand and shot some people dead, as did two other angry employees—one in California and the other in Wisconsin—both on the same day (December 20). And three teenagers, one in Mississippi (October 1) another in Kentucky (December 1) and a third in Arkansas (December 15), who'd felt "pushed around" or had "had enough," went to school with guns and also proclaimed like the Lord, "Vengeance is mine."

During the period I read the newspapers, Theodore Kaczynski, known as the Unabomber, went on trial after spending eighteen years sending mail bombs to selected people, which killed three and maimed others. Terry Nichols was also tried and found guilty of helping Timothy McVeigh blow up the Federal building in Oklahoma City, which had killed 168 people and wounded 500. Nichols, unlike McVeigh, was not sentenced to death, which so enraged some people that the jury forewoman received three bomb threats, her callers undoubtedly unaware that they were coming from the same wrathful place as McVeigh and Nichols.

The Virginia Military Institute was also coming from the same wrathful place. On August 21 the newspaper ran a story about the Institute's "Rat Line," its famous program of "ritualized abuse," during which upperclassman were permitted to abuse freshmen, who must submit no matter how harsh the discipline. In other words, the upperclassmen were permitted to act like God, to let loose their wrath and commit violence without fear of retribution.

United States' senators, I learned, had the same freedom. On September 13 the newspaper reported that Senator Jesse Helms, to keep William Weld's nomination as ambassador to Mexico from being considered by the Senate, wielded an "iron gavel," which he again and again banged down to silence fellow senators who pleaded for fairness or who tried to raise a point of parliamentary procedure. Senator Richard Lugar, second in command on the Foreign Relations Committee, sighed afterward that, "sometimes democracy does not work very well." But democracy was not at work; Helms had reverted to Biblical despotism, an accepted fact of Congressional life that gives committee chairmen the right to exercise their power with no restraint, a power that Helms admitted he wanted to uphold, the omnipotent power of the God of Wrath.

Helms, though he hated Communism, would have liked to impose his wrathful will the way Communist leaders do. The August 26 newspaper ran a long article about the Chinese government's anti-crime campaign, called "Strike Hard." Those communal Gods of Wrath, as if wielding God's rod of iron, executed 4,367 Chinese citizens in 1996, many for petty offenses: two men were executed for stealing a car, another for "vandalizing strips of electric cable," and one sick soul "for sticking thorns and needles into the buttocks of female cyclists."

In God of Wrath governments, as in the Bible, every rule, no matter how petty, must be obeyed. A September 16 newspaper reported that Pakistan's Department for Promoting Virtue and Preventing Vice, commonly known as the religious police, were making sure that men grew their beards so that the hair protrudes "out of a fist clasped at the base of the chin," a rule like one in Leviticus (19:28), which ordered Israelites not to "shave the edge of [their] beards." The November 19 paper reported that in Afghanistan, the Taliban had recently imposed an extreme form of Islamic rule. Not only were people severely beaten for infractions of rules, but new rules forbade women from going to school, working, or getting medical care. The rules could not be questioned, for the Taliban authorities thought they came from Allah, which reminded me of the Bible, where God, after uttering a commandment, would often say, "I am the Lord," which meant, "Do what I say and never question it because I am God."

"I am the Lord. Do what I say and never question it" has always been the motto of Gods of Wrath at home. In the Bible, many proverbs urged parents to beat their sons, though to "be careful not to flog [them] to death" (Proverbs 19:18). Cases of parents who impose Biblical discipline on their children and who actually do beat them to death are from time to time reported in the Newspaper Bible.

On November 17 the paper told of a Brooklyn, New York, couple who'd broken the arm of their four-year-old and beaten his five-year-old brother so hard that "belt marks" were on his body. Perhaps, because of the intervention of Children's Services, they and their three siblings won't be beaten to death in the mini-Buchenwald their parents created. A two-year-old in Greeley, Colorado wasn't so lucky. He was beaten to death with "wooden spoons and a rubber spatula." On September 23 the newspaper reported that his mother had confessed that the child, who'd been adopted from a Russian orphanage, had "violent rages" and, afraid he'd "harm her or her other child," she'd "lost it."

Another woman who "lost it" made international news. She was a young woman from England, working as an au pair in America, who on October 30, was convicted of killing an eight-month-old baby by violently shaking him and slamming his head against a hard object. The defense had argued that the baby had really died from a fall he'd had three weeks before when he'd hit his head. The jury didn't believe that and neither did some doctors. The November 17 newspaper reported that San Diego pediatricians had analyzed the cases of ninety-five children who'd died of similar injuries and concluded that since the baby had a two-and-a-half-inch skull fracture, it would not have gone unnoticed for three weeks. They were sure that the day the au pair phoned 911 and told the police she might have been "a little rough" with the baby was the day she'd slammed his head against a hard object.

Not only does medical evidence support the doctors' claim, so does the Bible where, as we've seen, a favorite way of killing babies was to "dash them against the rock" (Psalm 137:9). The Biblical way remains common. On September 23 the newspaper reported that a Tutsi, during an attack on the Hutus, grabbed a boy by his feet and swung his head against a tree trunk until he was dead, and on November 21 that a Georgia father, enraged because his wife had left him, abducted their six-month-old son, held him "by his ankles and slammed his head on the pavement."

Light in the Darkness of the Newspaper Bible

The news in the papers was not all bad news. Just as there's some genuine love in the Bible, there was love in the Newspaper Bible, in fact more love than in the Bible. For example, on October 1, the newspaper reported that the National Conference of Catholic Bishops had issued a document maintaining that, although God says that homosexuality is immoral, he nevertheless "loves every person as a unique individual" and so should we. On the same day, the newspaper also reported that the Roman Catholic Church in France had made a "Declaration of Repentance" to the Jewish people for the Church's complicity with the Nazis during World War II, and asked "forgiveness from God and from men" for not immediately speaking up and protecting the Jews.

I was also pleased to discover in the Newspaper Bible that the public was more and more following the advice of Jesus to "never despise one of these little ones." Whereas the God of Wrath had had no objection to using children as slaves, the October 1 paper reported that Congress was expected to ban the import of products made by the fifteen million indentured child laborers, some of whom were sold by their parents into slavery as early as four. Whereas in Biblical times, having sex with children wasn't a crime, the October 6 newspaper reported that in the Philippines a law had been passed that made rape of a minor punishable by death. And whereas the Bible encouraged parents to beat their children severely, the Newspaper Bible gave a fair amount of space to parents or caregivers who were punished for beating children. In fact, on October 9 the newspaper reported that an Arizona couple who'd been observed on a plane "forcefully and inappropriately" slapping and verbally abusing their newly adopted Russian daughters were arrested when the plane landed. To arrest parents for slapping a child or calling it names would have outraged the God of Wrath, as I'm sure it outraged many living God-of-Wrath parents.

In Our Own Image

On December 31, 1997, the day the newspaper reported that Saddam Hussein had started the New Year right by executing "hundreds if not thousands" of prisoners who'd opposed his regime, I decided to start the New Year right too: I would stop reading newspapers. I should have stopped months before because I'd soon learned that Thoreau was right; if you've read one newspaper you, more or less, had read them all. The same old wars and atrocities were repeating themselves in the papers just as they did in the Bible, which taught me something else, that each daily newspaper was an episode in an ancient serial. The bloody footprints of the God of Wrath in the Bible were continuing their trek through the local newspapers.

New Year's resolutions are rarely kept and I didn't keep mine. I didn't stop reading newspapers. I'd got hooked, which was why I hadn't stopped sooner and why I kept indulging my habit: two or three times a week I'd buy a paper. I couldn't resist because I got a high from seeing I was right, that the God of Wrath was a living presence in the world.

I was glad I hadn't stopped reading newspapers when I read an item in the January 17, 1998 newspaper that began — "In a sermon charged with hatred and rage, Iran's spiritual leader, Ayatollah Ali Khamenei ..." and burst out laughing. Imagine calling a leader "spiritual" and describe him as filled with hatred and rage! But why not? We're used to it. A God "charged with hatred and rage" has been the spiritual leader of most of the world for more than two thousand years.

I'd smile whenever I remembered those words about Khamenei until, almost a year later, I was struck with a thunderbolt — that the bloody footprints of the God of Wrath continue their trek through the newspapers not because a God charged with hatred and rage is a living presence in the world but because the bloody footprints aren't God's.

Paine said that the Bible "has served to corrupt and brutalize mankind." When I was writing the chapter, "The Bad Book," I agreed with him. For when the Bible was held in awe and studied diligently, the God of Wrath had to have been a role model. But after I studied the newspapers and saw the similarities between the Newspaper Bible and the Bible, I no longer wholly blamed the Bible. The Bible has not "served to corrupt and brutalize mankind"; the Bible reflects a corrupt and brutal mankind.

Why did it take me so long to understand what to me is now screamingly obvious?, that when God in Genesis said he made man in his own image, he was telling the truth. The fundamental reason why the Bible is not a sacred book is that it was written by God-of-Wrath us. We too solve our problems the way he did, chiefly by hate—by verbal and physical violence, by yelling, slaps, fist fights, murders, massacres, wars, and by inventing weapons that have become more and more lethal. We might argue that sinful man, not God, invented the weapons, but the God we get to know in the Bible would have happily mowed down thousands with Uzis and A-K 47s and launched missiles with nuclear warheads on Sodom and Gommorah. Nor would the God in The Revelation of John have thought twice about destroying the world with hydrogen bombs.

But God had nothing to do with that Revelation of mankind's destructive imagination. John, a man filled with hate, wrote it. Humans created God in their own image. Humans invented guns and bombs. Humans have been the wrathful Lords of the world. But we can no more see that we're haters than that the God of Wrath is a hater, which was why when God said he created man in his own image, we were sure he was paying us a compliment.

Instead of becoming conscious of our hate, mankind launched it into outer space, into a jealous, vengeful, bloodthirsty God of Wrath, a God whom we, with fear and trembling, bow down and worship. When I was a child I regarded religion as a strange practice of the natives, comparable to Ubangi women elongating their necks with rings. Religion, I discovered, is far stranger than fashions. As I was studying the Bible, I was more and more struck by the paradox that the same culture that brands hate as a sin, deifies hate in its religion. We worship a God who's a gigantic blowup of human hate and we can't see that it's our own hate.

That God is a gigantic blowup of human hate, we won't be able to comprehend as long as we "dwell in the House of the Lord" (Psalm 23) or (to quote the dictionary), as long as we believe that God is the "perfect, omnipotent, omniscient originator and ruler of the universe," and that God is good.

By some sleight of mind, we don't see that God is jealous, cruel, vindictive, and a warmonger. He's a blowhard, too. In children's books, we find drawings of heads with puffed cheeks and lips pursed, blowing with all their might. They represent the wind that can huff and puff and blow our house down. The wind in children's books is like the invisible God in the Bible, huffing and puffing up storms, hurricanes and tornados that wreak havoc, for which he's not ashamed, nor for any other catastrophe he conjures up; he boasts about them.

That Thomas Paine should have thought such a God a "demon" is not surprising. And God, as if he anticipated the criticism, explains again and again that he creates disasters because he has no other option, that to maintain law and order, he must punish his people for their sins. Just as a father tells a child he has to beat him because he's bad, God tells his people he has to administer disasters. Floods, earthquakes, volcanic eruptions, crop failures, plagues, wars wouldn't exist, God says, if his people had been good and obeyed his commandments. When the Israelites were defeated in a battle, as they often were, God would say that the Assyrians (or some other enemy) had been the instruments of his wrath. In other words, that if the Israelites had been good, God wouldn't have arranged for the Assyrians to conquer them.

But God didn't tell his people that the Assyrians were the instrument of his wrath until *after* they were defeated. God doesn't predict specific disasters; only after a disaster does he say he foreordained it. He has to postdate his predictions; for if they turned out to be wrong, he wouldn't be omniscient, a God who rules a planet where nothing happens by chance, where everything is predestined — past, present and future.

And yet God wasn't the know-it-all he claimed to be. Otherwise the Bible he wrote wouldn't be a storehouse of outdated beliefs. Instead of saying that he'd created the world in six days, he would have told us what actually happened. Then physicists wouldn't still be racking their brains figuring out theories of the origin of the universe. If he'd told us the truth instead of saying he created Homo sapiens from dust and a rib, Darwin wouldn't have had to take a long journey to the Galapagos Islands, and paleoanthropologists wouldn't still be patiently digging up bones trying to discover how humans evolved from apes.

Of course, Christian fundamentalists insist that God did tell us the facts about the origin of the universe and of humans. But if they fully believed that God told us the whole truth and nothing but the truth in his Bible, they'd also be pressuring schools to stop teaching that the earth is round and revolves around the sun. They'd demand that schools teach that God, on the fourth day of creation, hung up the sun in the vault of heaven to shine on a world that was flat and had four corners.

They'd also demand that children be taught the facts of life exactly as they're found in the Bible, where in the Old Testament we hear only about the "seed" of Abraham and other men, and in the New Testament that Jesus was created solely from God's Holy Spirit. Not a word is said about Jesus' genetic inheritance from his mother. Our all-knowing God turns out to be as ignorant as Zeus, who believed that his 'shower of gold' was all that was required to make a woman pregnant, and as ignorant as Allah, the God of the Muslims, who told his people that he'd created each of them out of a single drop of semen. Not until the late 1870s, when scientists proved that women also had 'seed,' did we finally learn that women were as essential as men in the formation of new life. If our God had been truly omniscient, we wouldn't have had to wait for this information; the facts would already have been in the Bible.

Christian fundamentalists are like Jewish friends of mine who, to prove God knew everything ahead of time, insist that he forbade his people from eating pork because he knew it could cause trichinosis, and that he required males to be circumcised because he knew of its health values. But Herodotus tells us that the ancient Egyptians also refused to eat pork and practiced circumcision. Since the Israelites were slaves in Egypt for 400 years, the commandments not to eat pork and to be circumcised may not be examples of God's superior wisdom but the legalization of old customs, especially since other tribes besides the Hebrews and the Egyptians didn't eat pork, and cutting off foreskins was a widespread primitive rite of passage. Besides, it turned out that God was wrong about circumcision; in the late twentieth century we finally began to learn that it's physically and psychologically harmful.

If God had known everything, the Israelites wouldn't have thought they were the first people to worship the one true God. God would have told them that other tribes, long before the Israelites, had worshiped a one God who lived up in the sky and watched over them, who punished them when they did wrong and to whom they prayed for mercy or to get what they wanted. If God had known everything, he would have told Moses when he handed him the Ten Commandments that they weren't a ground-breaking code of ethics; he would have given credit where credit was due, told his people, for example, that the Egyptians had had similar "thou shalt nots," and that about a thousand years before he put together his Commandments, Hammurabi, King of Babylonia, had developed a code of 282 laws, a lot of them like his own, and some of them equally cruel. For example, in Hammurabi's code we find that "If a man strikes his father, his hand shall be cut off," and in the Bible God says that if a wife, when trying to protect her husband from a man he's fighting with, "catches hold of the man's genitals, you shall cut off her hand" (Deuteronomy 25:11).

The Prophets Isaiah and Jeremiah dreamed of a kinder world, especially a world without war. But if God had wanted peace, since he was all-powerful, he would have stopped wars. Instead, he saw nothing wrong with premeditated mass killing. In Rome there was a Temple of Avenging Mars. A Temple could have been built for the Avenging God of the Bible.

Thomas Paine accused the Israelites of fighting with an "exulting ferocity" that distinguished them "above all others on the face of the known earth for barbarity and wickedness." Paine was wrong. The ancient Israelites were by no means the most barbaric tribe "on the face of the known earth." The Assyrians were far more vicious, though it's hard to choose. Alexander the Great and his armies reveled in the gore of wholesale slaughter as they conquered the whole known world. All soldiers fought with an "exulting ferocity," which the God who said he was holier than all other Gods never objected to. On the contrary, as I've pointed out, he urged his soldiers to rip open the bellies of pregnant women, smash babies heads against rocks and loot everything in sight.

God in the Bible was not the "perfect, omnipotent, omniscient originator and ruler of the universe." He was like the despots of ancient times, like the kings in Egypt, Crete, Mesopotamia and Persia, who relished killing, and craved absolute power, which they felt was their right because they imagined they were Gods or demi-Gods, and who also, like God in the Bible, ruled by fear. "Great is the Lord … he is more to be feared than all gods," boasted David (1 Chronicles 16:25-27), but his God was no more frightening than other despots. They were all terrifying, all inhumane, and proud of it.

When I was discussing whether or not God wrote the Bible, I suggested that if he had dictated it, he wouldn't have painted such an unflattering picture of himself. It's more likely though, that God was so barbaric he didn't know that jealousy, rage and warmongering were wrong. Or, to put it another way: God didn't know it was wrong because most people in ancient times didn't know it was wrong. The Almighty God who proudly takes center stage in the Bible was an ignorant, crude, savage, opinionated, boasting charlatan, so blind to his faults he rarely bothered to pretend to be better than he was. God in the Bible acts like a Mafiosi godfather, not like a Jesus or Gandhi. To me, it's the greatest Wonder of the World that millions of people for thousands of years have worshiped him.

"God's in His Heaven, All's Right with the World"

To say that God was as cruel as the despots who lived in ancient times and as ignorant as everyone else, shocks and offends believers, who don't want their perfect, all-powerful, all-knowing God knocked off his heavenly pedestal. For all to be right in the world, as Robert Browning put it in the nineteenth century, we have to believe we're dwelling in the House of the Lord, and will dwell in it forever.

Even atheist-me discovered that I too dwelt in the House of the Lord. That awful day I was walking along the street so angry at my mother I thought my head would burst when a huge pine cone whacked down onto the sidewalk, missing my head (I felt the rush of air) by less than an inch. My instant reaction was to thank God that he hadn't brained me for dishonoring my mother. At that moment, I wasn't an atheist. I was reacting as if a punishing, all-powerful God did rule the world. I know I was dwelling "in the House of the Lord" because I felt only relief; I didn't register that Almighty God had missed his mark—me.

A tornado is sometimes called a "finger of God." In April 1998 a finger of God flattened towns in Alabama. On ABC News, a five-year-old asked his mother why God brought the tornado. He asked her because he hadn't yet absorbed the doublethink required to live comfortably in the House of the Lord. His mother had, so she told her son that God "didn't bring the tornado, baby. He saved us." "God showed us his grace," said another survivor interviewed on TV.

But what about the people who didn't survive? Why didn't God show them his grace? The woman who said, "God showed us his grace" in her secret heart knew the answer. In the Bible God said over and over that if we were good and obeyed him, we would prosper, but if we were bad and didn't obey him, "it will be his delight to destroy and extermi-nate [us]" (Deuteronomy 28:63). We believe that. "God sees you when we're bad or good, so be good for goodness sake," warns Santa Claus in "Santa Claus is Coming to Town." You'd better be good because if you're not "The Goblins'll get you." That's part of the refrain of a nine-teenth-century children's poem (James Whitcomb Riley's, "Little Orphant Annie") about a boy who refused to say his prayers. One night when he went to bed, his parents heard him holler and rushed upstairs, but he was nowhere to be found. All that was left of him were his pants and jacket. The goblins who got that bad boy were God's agents, and the bad boy knew as he was 'disappeared' that he'd got what was coming to him.

That childish system of justice pervades our lives: if I'm good, God will be good to me. If I'm bad, he'll punish me. When a hurricane destroys our home, when we get hurt in an accident or develop cancer, our gut reaction is that God did it to us because we deserved it. "Do good, O Lord, to those who are good … but those who turn aside into crooked ways, may the Lord destroy them" (Psalm 125:4-5).

But what if we're sure we haven't done anything bad? Those who dwell in the house of the Lord often, like Job, ask why God lets bad things happen to good people. Again and again in the Psalms the Israelites asked God that question. "Give me justice, O Lord," they demanded, "for I have lived my life without reproach" (Psalms 26:1). And yet, for all their protests, indignation and fury, the Israelites could not damn God when he was unjust. He was too fearsome: "O Lord, do not condemn me in thy anger, do not punish me in thy fury. Be merciful to me, O Lord, for I am weak" (Psalms 6:1-2). Since they were weak and God was all-powerful, no matter how cruel and unfair God was, it was safer to blame themselves, to decide: "How good it is for me to have been punished" (Psalm 119:71). Before Moses lay down and died, as God ordered him to, he delivered this eulogy: "Great is our God ... all his ways are just, a faithful God, who does no wrong, righteous and true is He" (Deuteronomy 32:3-4). As Paul argued, the mere fact that God was "judge" of the world made him just (Romans 3:5-6). Therefore, when God brings "retribution upon us," we should accept his judgment.

Those who have a less childish system of justice and live in the House of the Lord, accept God's judgments in a more sophisticated way. They deal with the problem of why some people die in a tornado and others don't by explaining that since God foreordains everything, he never takes people before their time. Therefore, it was God's plan for the people who died to die in that tornado on that day. Others answer the question with less certainty but with full acceptance: "The Lord giveth and the Lord taketh away," or "God's will be done." "God had his reasons," said a woman whose husband had been murdered.

"God's in his heaven, all's right with the world" even when things go wrong. For who are we, lowly humans, to dare question what God does? He moves in mysterious ways. No matter how unjust an affliction seems—when our child dies, when we're paralyzed in an accident—someday we'll discover that God did the right thing, that he gave us that trial to strengthen us. God always knows what's best. "I know that God will do what's right for me," said a man in prison who was coming up for a parole hearing, a belief that sustained him when he wasn't paroled. When we don't get a job we desperately want, we resign ourselves by thinking that "God had something else in mind for me." A boxer after losing a fight said, "It was God's will that it didn't go my way." God answers every prayer, though sometimes it's a no.

A woman who was kidnapped asked God why he'd let that terrible thing happen to her; she felt betrayed and abandoned by him. As the days passed and her kidnapper raped her, she abandoned God. But when she was safe again, she was sure God had delivered her and kept her alive for a reason. She then felt guilty for having abandoned God, who, she decided, had, after all, not abandoned her (Debbie Morris,

Forgiving Dead Man Walking, 1998). When someone escapes death in an accident, we say, "God saved her," but when someone dies in an accident, we don't say, "God killed her." That would make God a murderer, a thought we mustn't even think or God might kill us. "God exists. God is finally punishing him," said a man when he learned that the dictator of his country was at last overthrown and would stand trial. For that man and for most believers, God wouldn't be God if he wasn't just, at least ultimately just, so mankind invented that huge high security prison called hell in which God metes out punishments that fit earthly crimes. "Oh what a tangled web we weave, When first we practice to believe" (to parody Walter Scott).

In this world of frequent injustice, of sickness, accidents, earthquakes, cruelty and war, what we most want is to go on believing in God. Some inmates at Auschwitz put God on trial and found him guilty, but most of us can't do that. When we cry out, "God, why hast thou forsaken me?" we want to be told that he really hasn't. When an atrocity happens, we want the same God who presumably caused it to console us. In March 1998, after children were gunned down in a schoolyard in Jonesboro, Arkansas, a minister assured their parents that "God will comfort you." When a father angrily asked a priest, "Where was God when my son was murdered?" the priest, after telling him that we can't understand God's ways, assured him that God is always with us and that we should try to feel his ever present love. Many people do feel it. "He walks with me and He talks with Me and He tells me I am His own"; God holds me in his "everlasting arms"; "Take my hand, precious Lord"; God is always there in my time of need — to quote or echo hymns.

We can't bear to feel that God is helpless to help us. We need a God who'll hear our cries when we're in danger and, we hope, save us, a God to whom we can pray when we're in trouble, whom we can ask for what we want, who, when we have to make a decision, will tell us what to do, a God who has a place for each of us and a task on earth that he wants us to do, and who, when he takes us up to heaven, will tell us our lives were worthwhile, that we were his true and faithful servants.

I understand the need for such comforts; I've often longed for them. I even understand the comfort that fundamentalists feel who rest on the literal words of the Bible. Why puzzle out what's true and what isn't? If God said he created the world in six days, he did, and that's an end to it. God made the rules once and for all, and all we have to do is obey them. Fundamentalists turn into Gods of Wrath when people disagree with them because their belief system has been threatened. They don't want to ask existential questions about the meaning of life. They want the security that comes from obedience, from surrendering totally to God's will.

"Surely goodness and mercy shall follow me all the days of my life, and I will dwell in the House of the Lord forever," says Psalm 23 because we want to dwell in God's house forever, a simple world of just rewards and punishments administered by a God who watches over us and tells us what's right and wrong and always does what's best for us (though we may not think so at first), a God who, when we put our hand on the Bible and swear to tell the truth, will know if we lie and punish us because he is the "perfect, omnipotent, omniscient originator and ruler of the universe."

We rarely ask why a God who knows everything lets so many people who commit perjury in court get away with it. We rarely ask why our omnipotent God doesn't prevent natural disasters and the many human holocausts that have bloodied the earth. Our need to feel loved and taken care of is so great that we're willing to think of natural disasters and human cruelty as God's punishments for our sins. God has to be out there. Otherwise we'd be, to use A E Housman's words, "a stranger and afraid in a world I never made." We fear that if we step out of "the House of the Lord," we'd step into empty space. So we stay in our safe-house.

In a poor section of Paris, I saw a building so old that huge wooden buttresses had to prop it up. The Bible is like that building. We prop it up with interpretations that change the meaning of a text so we can think it says what we want it to say. Like the Prophets, we put a different spin on the bloody God of Wrath so we can go on worshiping him. We entangle ourselves in inconsistent beliefs and shut down our minds so we don't ask uncomfortable questions. We dismiss unpleasant facts about the character of God, like Jon Levenson, a professor of Jewish studies at Harvard Divinity School, who said in an article on "Raising Spiritual Children," that we should teach children that "The only hero in the Bible is God. Everyone else has flaws and failures" (Newsweek, December 7, 1998). And this of a God who relished animal sacrifice, who rejected the crippled and deformed as unclean, who condoned slavery and soldiers capturing women in war to use as sex slaves, who saw nothing wrong in stoning people to death and never advanced beyond "an eye for an eye" justice.

In a 1972 case (Furman v Georgia) the death penalty was declared cruel and unusual punishment as measured against "evolving standards of decency." Standards of decency cannot evolve in the Bible, and yet we continue to regard it as an everlasting monument of Eternal Truths, not a relic of an ignorant and barbarous age that has kept our emotions and even our intellect imprisoned in the ignorant and barbarous times in which it was written. Like that ancient building in Paris, it should be torn down. But we keep propping it up.

Paine thought that by writing an exposé of the Bible, he would tear it down and thus "tranquilize the minds of millions" by freeing them of their fear of an unjust God and letting them get to know a God who was akin to "everything that is tender, sympathizing and benevolent in the heart of man." Paine was wrong. His belief in a benign God damned him as an atheist. The real God in the eighteenth century was the God of Wrath. He still is. We now say that God is Love, but if we believed it, we wouldn't honor the hate-filled Bible. We continue to honor the Bible, and Americans, after two world wars and one of the bloodiest holocausts, put "In God We Trust" on their money. They did because the world we live in and the God we say rules it, are extensions of the Houses of the Lord we were raised in.

Chapter 9 **Our Father Who Aren't In Heaven**

The Goddess Athena, when she first appears in Greek mythology, emerged from the head of Zeus fully grown and fully armed, a fierce and ruthless warrior. Similarly, the Judeo-Christian God comes on stage in the Bible as if to the triumphant strains of Wagner's "Ride of the Valkyries," fully grown and fearsome, power radiating from his invisible presence.

When despots claimed they were Gods, they wanted their subjects to think of them as if they too, like Athena, had always been full-grown and had always worn the armor of a fierce and ruthless warrior. That humans created such Gods reveals our wish that we'd never been unarmed and vulnerable, that we hadn't been born helpless babies. It's a way of denying the history of our childhood, which often, even in the twenty-first century, is like past history, a time when children endured the cruelty of the despots who totally controlled their lives, the despots who had the right to kill them at birth, sacrifice them to Gods, swaddle them so tightly they couldn't move, drug them with gin and opium to keep them quiet, mutilate their genitals, rape them, sodomize them, set them to work at hard labor or as prostitutes at the earliest possible age, abandon them as freely as Hansel and Gretel were 'lost' in the woods, sell them into slavery and beat them as often and as severely as they wished.

Always

Next to the right to kill infants at birth, the most sacred right of parents was their not-to-be-interfered-with right to slap, spank, punch, thrash, switch, whip, belt, cane, paddle and flog their children. "Spare the rod and spoil the child," was engraved on the lintel of most homes. We think that proverb is in the Bible, but it's an old English one that derived from a Latin proverb, and repeats advice that was repeated at least nine times in the book of Proverbs. For example, "A father who spares the rod hates his son, but one who loves him beats him" (13:24). The common wisdom was that if you loved your child and wanted him to become a good adult, you had to beat him. Therefore, the "rod of correction" (Proverbs 22:15) was regularly applied. The Russian writer, Maxim Gorky, born in 1868, was often beaten with sadistic glee by his maternal grandfather. To console him, his maternal grandmother told him that his dead father had also been beaten, and once "so unmercifully that the neighbors took the child away and hid him." Whereupon little Maxim asked, "Do they always beat children?" to which his grandmother quietly answered, "Always."

The age when it was thought wise to begin to beat a child could be very young. One American mother thought that four-months old was not too soon. "Logan and I," she wrote to a friend in April 1866, "had our first regular battle to-day, and he came off the conqueror ... I whipped him till he was actually black and blue, and until I *could not* whip him any more, and he never gave up one single inch." His mother whipped him, she said, because he was "greedy," "given to fits of temper" and "a gorilla for screaming," four-month-old sins that whippings were supposed to cure.

This mother was no drunken woman in the slums. She was Hannah Whittall Smith, an educated, generally kind woman, who'd been brought up by peace-loving Quakers. She recounted the beating in a letter to an old friend, obviously without shame and, according to the wisdom of her time, she had no reason to be ashamed. Beating children was regarded as a religious duty because it saved their souls. Susanna Wesley, the mother of John Wesley (one of the founders of Methodism), proudly said that after her children "turned a year old (and some before) they were taught to fear the rod and to cry softly."

Sinners in the Hands of an Angry God

John Wesley was born in 1703, the same year as the American theologian, Jonathan Edwards, who was also beaten by his mother in infancy. When he was in his late thirties, Edwards preached a sermon that became famous, one of the most violent hell-fire and damnation sermons ever written, "Sinners in the Hands of an Angry God." His sermon is also one of the most repetitious ever written. Over and over Edwards warned his congregation that "the black clouds of God's wrath" are "now hanging directly over your heads," that "the bow of God's wrath is bent, and ... nothing but the mere pleasure of God ... keeps the arrow ... from being drunk with your blood," that "at any moment" God could open his hand and cast you into hell, which meant that some people sitting right in front of him in the meetinghouse "in health, quiet and secure ... before tomorrow morning" could be in hell where they deserved to be, for human hearts were so corrupt people ought to be "abominable in [God's] eyes," they ought to be hated by him, held "in the utmost contempt" and sent to hell.

When I was reading "Sinners in the Hands of an Angry God," I often shook my head, amazed that Edwards was eulogizing God's wrath. I felt superior to Edwards, certain that when I'd read the Bible, I'd reacted to the God of Wrath the way one should, with revulsion and horror. I was unaware that my indignation was purely intellectual, that a part of me, like Edwards, was on God's side and felt his wrath was just.

I made that discovery the next day when I woke up tired, so tired that as I worked at my computer I kept nodding off. I had to lie down and nap but woke unrefreshed and remained tired. When I went out (I had a dentist's appointment or I wouldn't have gone out), I literally dragged myself through the streets. I was so tired that after I dragged myself home, I lay on the sofa and fell into a heavy sleep, from which I awoke more tired, and now freezing. When my heaviest bathrobe couldn't warm me up, I was sure I was coming down with the flu, though it felt worse than any flu I'd had. All evening I lay on the sofa in a stupor, sweating and feverish. I felt so sick that I said an eternal goodbye to my husband. He smiled in disbelief, but I knew I was dying. In bed, I was glad to be dying; I didn't want to wake in the morning and have to face another day of misery.

I woke up well, bursting with energy. I hadn't had the flu. What had afflicted me? I didn't figure it out until, as I was taking notes on "Sinners in the Hands of an Angry God," I found I'd stopped. I was staring blankly ahead, 'seeing' the baby I was in her crib, lying as usual in diarrhea, the result of the foul, sour milk her mother fed her, the baby who was icy cold because she had on only a diaper and undershirt and the window was wide open to let in the freezing winter air, the baby who, despite the cold, would often break into sweats from the fevers that plagued her, the baby who stiffened with fear when her mother entered the room. For she knew a hand would come down and smack her, or that a diaper pin would be stuck into her, or her chest squeezed until a rib broke, that her foul diaper would be rubbed on her face as her mother yelled "Filth!" at her.

The memories I had that morning were not new. I'd remembered them long before, but they'd been cool, intellectual memories. Once, though they'd almost turned into feelings. I'd heard a news report about a baby who'd been found dead in her crib, hidden under a blanket, a baby whose existence had been concealed from the caseworker who visited to make sure the mother was treating her children well. That baby's suffering haunted me for a while, then passed away. Not until I read "Sinners in the Hands of an Angry God" did my memories deconstruct into the misery of the anguished baby I'd been. My memories turned into feelings because in his sermon Edwards raged at his congregation with the same fury as his mother when she'd beaten him, fury that reminded the baby in me of her mother's fury when she'd attacked her. I partly turned into that baby, who was almost always sick and who escaped from her misery by dropping into a trance-like sleep from which she hoped never to wake, the baby who was so sick she wanted to sleep forever, permanently out of her misery, the baby who, to retain her sanity, constructed a just world by agreeing with the God who'd judged her to be so evil that she deserved to be punished every day of her life. I had to relive being that guilt-ridden baby in the crib before I understood why as an adult I accepted every blow of fate as my just deserts. My first reaction when in my fifties I broke a wrist was to smile, a reaction that puzzled me. No more.

I'll always be grateful to "Sinners in the Hands of an Angry God" for hurling me back into the hands of my angry God. If I hadn't relived my early agony, if the stone wall of my intellect hadn't been blasted into raw feelings, I wouldn't have understood at a gut level why Edwards and millions of others have accepted the God of Wrath in the Bible without a protest. They'd been acquainted with that God since birth.

When Edwards preached that in hell God will "have no compassion upon you, he will not … in the least lighten his hand; there shall be no moderation or mercy … he will have no regard to your welfare, nor be at all careful lest you should suffer too much," God wasn't God in the Bible. God was the mother who beat him when he was an infant, who did not "lighten [her] hand," who had shown him no mercy, who had not been "at all careful lest [he] should suffer too much," the God who was angry with him "every day and every night," the absolute sovereign from whom there was no "defense" and "at whose rebuke the earth trembles." "Take this and this, you damned sinners," Edwards lashed out at his congregation, delivering the sermon his mother by her actions delivered to him.

When Edwards preached "Sinners in the Hands of an Angry God," he was preaching to the child alive in the members of his congregation who'd also grown up in households where they were at the mercy of a God whose "wrath was too quick for" them, so that "suddenly destruction" could "come upon" them at any moment, a God from whose hands there was no "deliverance." Edwards was preaching to a congregation who'd also created a just world by deciding they deserved every beating. They were like the Psalmists who would plead with God not to punish them in his fury, but who would always decide, "How good it is for me to have been punished" (Psalm 119:71).

A parent who beats children becomes their terrifying God of Wrath. Every blow beats into their minds as well as their bodies the judgment of the God of Wrath whose possessions they are — that they're irredeemable sinners who ought to be cast into hell. If beatings had not already created the same wrathful God in the minds of the members of Edwards' congregation and the same self-damning philosophy, they would have stood up in that meetinghouse outraged at Edwards or convinced he'd gone mad, and a part of him was mad, driven mad by the angry God who'd beat him. Those who listened to Edwards submitted to his rhetorical lashes because the beatings they'd endured had also driven them out of their right mind.

Manus

On an impulse, I counted the number of times the word 'hand' appeared in "Sinners in the Hands of an Angry God." Twenty-three (if you include "hands" in the title). I couldn't decide if that number was significantly large, but that Edwards chose the "hands" of God as his theme was significant. "Manus," a Roman legal term signifying the father's supreme authority, is Latin for "hand," the human instrument of power as teeth are for many animals.

In the Bible, God's hands terrify. "With a strong **hand** and an out-stretched arm, and with terrible power" I'll "fight against you in burning rage and great fury," said Jeremiah, speaking as if he were God (21:5; 32:21). "His **hand** is stretched out still," God's "anger has not turned back," said Isaiah over and over in a long poem warning the Israelites what God was going to do to sinful them (Isaiah 9, 10). Sinners "shall fear and tremble when they see the Lord of Hosts raise his **hand** against them, as raise it he will" (Isaiah 19:16).

In a moving passage in the New Testament (Hebrews 12:5-14), we get a glimpse of the fear and trembling children felt when the Gods of their household raised a hand against them. The passage, whose purpose was to give New Christians courage when they were persecuted, quotes the Old Testament proverb (3:11-12), "Whom the Lord loves he corrects, just as a father does," and explains that if a father didn't use "the rod," his son would not lead "an honest life." "Discipline, no doubt, is never pleasant; at times it seems painful," the passage continues, but it was necessary when we were children, and we can learn from it now. When we're beaten by non-Christians we can do what we did when we were beaten in childhood: "stiffen your drooping arms and shaking knees, and keep your steps from wavering" so "the disabled limb will not be put out of joint, but regain its former powers." Proverb 19, when it warned parents to be careful not to flog their son to death, wasn't exaggerating. Parents beat their children mercilessly.

"God strikes with an iron hand," said a seventeenth-century proverb because the hands of parents felt like iron to children. Christians used to speak of waiting for "the dreadful day of judgment," like the days of their childhood when they'd waited for the hand of their living God to smite them. ("Smite" occurs 325 times in the Old Testament.) Hell was supposed to come after death, but for the vast majority of children hell was in their homes. The myth of hell is not a myth; hell has been real for billions of children. Some twentieth-century children who killed the parents who regularly and savagely beat and raped them have described jail as heaven: it was the first time in their lives they'd felt safe. They were in jail because they'd broken one of mankind's most ancient laws, that parents can hit a child, but the child can't repay in kind. "If a man strike his father, his hand shall be cut off," said one of the ancient laws of Hammurabi, but the hand of the father who strikes a child is not cut off.

Where was God?

"God is a hate-filled person bent on judging and condemning you, and identifying you as an evil thing," said a man at the incest survivor meetings I went to. They were Twelve Step meetings and almost all of us hated Step Three, which told us we should "turn our will and our lives over to God." "Why should we surrender to a God who did nothing when we were beaten and raped?" we asked. "Where was he? Up in Heaven indifferently or sadistically watching?"

The people at these meetings had been severely abused, but children whose beatings were mild, or who were merely rejected or screamed at, see God as a God of Wrath too. In her "Introduction" to *A History of God* (1993), Karen Armstrong confessed that when she was a child she was afraid of God, the "stern taskmaster," the vengeful, "hideous deity" who spied out every violation of his rules.

A character in Henry Fielding's *Tom Jones* (1749) points a finger upward and says, "There's one above from whom you can conceal nothing." Children at first think the one above is Mother/Father. In an article on "Raising Spiritual Children" in the December 7, 1998 *Newsweek*, a four-year-old is quoted as asking if God is Dad. Only as we grow older, does the "one above" from whom we can conceal nothing become God in heaven, Armstrong's spying, vengeful deity, whom we soon forget was once our parents. Although we may later define God as love, or an inner light, or as the remote Overseer and Sustainer of the universe, or as an ethical ideal or an embodiment of compassion, our various concepts of God have one thing in common: they're reactions against our first God, the God of Wrath, who remains our earliest and strongest concept of God, the one who lives on in the unconscious of most of us.

In 1882 Nietzsche boldly announced that God was dead. He was wrong. God is not dead. The Bible continues to be a bestseller because every child who's smacked and/or beaten, raped, devalued, rejected— and that includes most of us—recreates the God of Wrath. Catholic priests thought that once a child got into their confirmation classes the Church would control their minds for life. They were naive. Long before a child learns the first catechism, they've already been indoctrinated in the fundamentals of what the Church teaches. Catholic children find it easy to believe in the three-headed God of the Trinity, because they've already learned to worship a real two-headed God, the Twinity, those huge creatures who towered over them and did whatever they wanted to them.

The God of Wrath is familiar to almost all of us before we go to Church or read the Bible, and not only because the heavy hand of our real God smote us for our offenses. God set up 613 commandments that had to be obeyed because parents created many rules that had to be obeyed. In the world of the Bible, God, who is above reproach, is always

punishing people for their sins because in the world of home parents
were always punishing those born sinners. God punishes without fear
of retribution because parents did. God says, "all whom I love, I reprove
and discipline" because parents told children that they reprimanded and
hit them because they loved them. The Biblical God never learned that
threats and punishments didn't make his people good because parents
have never learned.

God's words are law because parents words were law. God's words
are sacred because the words of parents were sacred: children thought
their parents knew everything and that everything they said was true.
God in the Bible is always right and just because parents maintained that
whatever they did was right and just. Disobedience is the cardinal sin in
the Bible because it was at home. The Bible ordered anyone who reviled
his father and his mother to be put to death because woe to the child who
dared criticize its parents.

God is omnipotent because parents were all-powerful. Raw power is
the meat and drink of God in the Bible because raw power was the meat
and drink of parents. God gets away with unrestrained rage because parents did. God is an absolute authority to whom we must submit because
parents were absolute authorities to whom we had to submit. Because
parents handed down judgments from which there was no appeal, God
in the Bible does.

Psalm 111 says that "the fear of the Lord is the beginning of wisdom"
because children learned early that it was wise to fear their parents. The
god-fearing man is constantly praised in the Bible because when he was
a child he was constantly afraid of his parents. Because parents knew no
other way to control their children except by fear, neither does God, who
once told the Israelites that he would "pursue them" with a naked sword
and fill them with so much "fear that, when a leaf flutters behind them in
the wind, they shall run as if it were the sword behind them" (Leviticus
26:1-39). We live with that frightening God breathing down our necks,
unable to stop believing that he exists. We can't begin to escape that God
until we stop running, turn around and see who God is.

Jesus asked us to pray to "Our Father who art in heaven," unaware
that our Father was not in heaven. "Where was God when I was being
abused?" we would ask at incest survivor meetings. HeShe was at home
doing the abusing. Fortunately for me, in late middle age I at last remembered that my mother had tortured me, which eventually helped me
understand the human origin of the God of Wrath. But recognition of my
original, wrathful God was only the first step toward release. I couldn't
have escaped from my mother's power over me without the Kind Force
that was replacing the Cruel Force who'd once controlled my life.

In the first chapter I told you about that Kind Force, the inner voice I
began to hear who knew about my abuse and whose wisdom and advice

helped me heal. The day after I read "Sinners in the Hands of an Angry God" and relived some of my early agony, my Kind Force again helped me. In bed that night, sweating, miserable, I was unable to escape from my suffering by falling asleep. I lay there wanting to die, when I found myself repeating, "I am good. I deserve the best" and, I said it over and over. My Kind Force had given me an antidote to the lie mother had taught me that I was bad, evil. As I repeated that I was good, that I didn't deserve to be punished, my misery faded away. My Kind Force had assured me many times before of my fundamental goodness, but, thanks to Edwards' sermon, which had hurled me into the fiery flames of my infancy, I managed to become one with that baby's suffering and experienced a bit of the self-compassion I still find so difficult to feel, self-love that for a while released me from the hands of my angry God. I fell asleep with a smile on my face. That's why I woke up the next morning bursting with energy, the flu I thought I'd had, gone.

Jonathan Edwards couldn't get over his conviction that God had deservedly damned him because he didn't know his mother had been the God who'd first damned him. He was haunted by the idea that God's almighty will throbbed through the universe because he didn't know his mother's will had throbbed through his childhood universe. Because he didn't know that his mother's beatings had created his concept of God, Edwards' was condemned to worship a God who couldn't love him, not for long. In his *Personal Narrative*, he recalled the times he did experience God's love, but mostly he wrote of his yearning to be in heaven, the "world of love," where he could freely express his love to Christ and be loved in return. He was virtually certain, though, he wouldn't get to heaven. "The bottomless depths of secret corruption in [his] heart" meant that God would have to send him to hell. For only if he became perfect could God love him and send him to heaven, and he despaired of that, just as he must have despaired when he was a child that he would ever become perfect enough for his mother to love him.

The Bible is family life writ large, a revelation of the sickness of family life. A Cruel Force not a Kind Force pervades both, a Cruel Force that more often than not still dominates and demands submission. That power imbalance was, perhaps, inevitable. We're born tiny and totally dependent on parents who can do with us as they please; we're born weak and helpless and our parents are strong and powerful.

That original inequality spreads out of the home like black oil spreading across an ocean, creating the model of low and high, weak and strong, superior/inferior, master/subject that has shaped the way we relate to people and therefore shaped religion, government and the structure of society.

Chapter 10   **Created Unequal**

In 1776 the American colonies informed the British Empire that they would no longer endure tyranny. They declared their independence, and their intention to establish a nation unlike any other, one based on the proposition that "all men are created equal."

Looking Down On
The trouble with the proposition that "all men are created equal" is that it goes against human nature, or seems to. In democracies citizens may be equal under the law, but in daily life, they're not. Some people are very much "more equal than others," as George Orwell perceived. They are because we don't want to be equals; we want to be better than the next guy. "We all behold with envious eyes," said Jonathan Swift, "our *equal* raised above our *size*," so "let me have the highest post, suppose it but an inch at most" ("On the Death of Dr Swift," 1731). God saw nothing wrong with that desire. He promised his chosen people he'd raise them "high above all the nations." "You shall be always at the top and never at the bottom" (Deuteronomy, 26:18-19; 28:13).

And yet, even when we get to the top, when we've attained the "highest post" possible, we want to be higher. The ancient Egyptian king, Rameses II, had sixty-six foot statues of himself erected throughout his kingdom. Twentieth-century dictators, like Hitler, Stalin and Saddam Hussein, had statues of themselves and their enormously enlarged pictures in high places everywhere. Dictators crave the ultimate high: they want to look down on everyone, like God.

Jewish children were taught that God sees everything and will "punish the wicked for all eternity." But they already know it. Whatever their religion, race, or creed, children, from the earliest age, learn to fear the God who looks down on them from on high. Parents may tell them that God is up in heaven, but children know better. When I was a child, I was sure my mother could see everything I did, even inside my head, so I'd better not lie or have bad thoughts, especially about her.

Dictators want to be up so high because once they were down so low. By posting their statues and portraits in high places, dictators become the God of everyone's childhood, reducing their subjects to frightened children who are sure that everything bad they do will be seen and punished. Dictators invented the secret police to get multiple eyes that, hopefully, could spy out every wrongdoing. In dictatorships, we're back in the family, a small child again looked down on by judgmental, punishing Gods.

George Orwell wouldn't have conceived of a Big Brother who's always watching us if he hadn't once been a child. Swift wouldn't have conceived of *Gulliver's Travels* if he hadn't been born a Lilliputian into a family of Brobdingnagians.

A Different Species—Children

Swift made the Lilliputians (the little people) a different species from the Brobdingnagians (the big people) because children think they're a different species. When little children are with adults, their eyes light up when another child enters the room. "Ah," they seem to be thinking, "one of my own kind, one of the little people." It was self-evident to Thomas Jefferson that "all men are created equal," but it's not self-evident to children. They think they're unequal, permanently unequal. Babies don't know about growth. For them, parents have always been big.

Parents tell children that one day they'll be big too, but for children the present is all there is. In the everlasting now in which they live, they're permanent midgets in a world of huge beings who, unlike them, have hair on parts of their bodies, jumbo 'wee-wees', bags of flesh drooping from their chests, hands like shovels and enormous, rock heads. We created extraterrestrials who are undersized because when we were little we thought we were aliens from another sphere who'd landed on a planet of Giants. The first Giants were the mighty beings who could pick babies up as if they weighed nothing, raise them a mile above the ground to hug and kiss or to smash against a wall, Giants whose size and strength made their wishes law and punishment their right.

When Giants cry, children are shocked and amazed; they don't think Giants have feelings like theirs. Parents don't think children are like them either. They think they're a different, inferior species. The phrase to "look down on" goes back to the time when parents from their great height looked down on children and judged them beneath them not only in size but in essence.

Until fairly recently in virtually all societies children were despised. John Locke, in his *Essay Concerning Human Understanding* (1690), compared children to "idiots, savages, and the grossly illiterate." Jews said newborns were "shapen in iniquity" (Psalm 51). Though Jesus announced that children were "of the kingdom of Heaven," he need not have bothered; the Old Testament view of original human nature prevailed in Western thought. For century after century Christians proclaimed that the "whole nature" of children "is a seed of sin." I'm quoting John Calvin (1509-1564), whose view predominated for over 200 more years.

For a few decades in the nineteenth century, the belief that children were sinners changed. "Heaven lies about us in our infancy," a line from Wordsworth's Immortality Ode (written between 1802 and 1804) was quoted or echoed endlessly and lovingly throughout the century. Even ministers, many of them, used "Heaven lies about us in our infancy" as a text for sermons. But by the end of the century, Wordsworth's "Trailing clouds of glory do we come from God" was replaced by the theory that since the embryo in its development repeats the history of the race, children are born savages, savagery that in the twentieth century was attributed to the 'killer' genes passed down in our DNA from chimpanzees. Influenced by nineteenth-century child worship, many people in the twentieth century said that children were born innocent, a sentiment that vaporized when a child committed violence. In April 1996, an ABC News story about a six-year-old who almost beat a baby to death was captioned, "Killer Instinct?"

I've given you this brief sketch of mankind's low opinion of children to explain why small doesn't refer only to physical size. If parents, instead of regarding children as inferiors, animals, idiots, sinners and savages had thought of them as important, intelligent, good and loving, 'small,' 'little' and related words wouldn't have taken on secondary, disparaging meanings. According to *The American Heritage Dictionary*, 'little' and 'small' in addition to meaning small in size, mean "unimportant, trivial," "of minor status." To be low, besides meaning having little height, also means to be "base," to violate "standards of decency or morality." To be belittled is to become little again, downgraded to a runt, a pipsqueak, small fry.

Small men have it rough in our culture. Men are supposed to be the superior sex, that is, to be 'above' women; therefore to be small like a child is, by that fact alone, to be inferior. Because of their handicap, short men don't rise to the heights as often as tall men. A 1998 survey revealed that ninety percent of executives were tall. Therefore, when a successful short man makes it into *Time* and *Newsweek*, the magazines feel obliged to reveal his embarrassing height just as they reveal that someone is Jewish or in a wheelchair. What a wonder! Mr Cabinet Member is a pint-sized five foot five. Because of that shortcoming, the media often suggest a compensatory trait to explain a short man's high status. On May 26, 1997 a CNN reporter described Judge Matsch (who presided at the trial of the man who bombed the Federal Building in Oklahoma), as "small in stature but a commanding presence."

A Different Species — Parents

No matter what their height, parents, to their children, have a commanding presence. Children look up to parents, and not only because they're taller, but because they think they're a superior species. Why shouldn't they? Not only do parents' heads reach to the sky, they stand upright, walk on two feet and come and go as they please. They do whatever they want, get whatever they want, make sounds that have meaning. Besides, they know everything and have enormous strength. The child's initial awe of parents would have been harmless if parents had looked down on infants and also felt awe, awe at a new existence teeming with life. Some parents did and do, but the vast majority didn't and still don't.

A friend recalled looking down at her month-old daughter and feeling a surge of power; she knew she could do anything to her daughter and her daughter would have to submit. She was disturbed by the feeling and didn't understand where it came from. She didn't know that her mother had felt the same surge, and her mother's mother, and so on back in time. Most parents don't consciously feel the power surge and few who do are disturbed by it. On the contrary. They find their empowerment intoxicating. They're no longer a looked-down-upon child but someone who's looked up to. The position they began life with is reversed. When men and women become parents, they begin their transformation into the all-knowing, all-powerful Gods who, having performed the feat of creating new life, have acquired subjects they totally control. The first Gods were the monarchs who ruled the home.

A Different Species — *Übermensch*

"The King is dead, long live the king," people would shout when a king died. They were like the ancient Egyptians described by Herodotus who, after they were freed from the rule of a priest, "could not live a day without a king." For most of history mankind has been unable to live without kings because we begin life ruled by parents at home. The system seemed so natural and right, we created Gods who ruled over us like parents. Our addiction to parent substitutes didn't stop there.

God in Genesis first created an inferior species called animals, then a separate, superior species — humans — to have dominion over them. Similarly, humans created a superior species to have dominion over them. Just as, by a psychological ruse called a ritual, we elevate an ordinary man into a Pope, country after country waved a magic wand over certain men and women and, lo and behold, there, decked out in satin, lace and sparkling jewels, stood the aristocrats, whose descendants, as they drive by in golden coaches, the British still cheer.

In the nineteenth century, Nietzsche dreamed of a world of *Übermensch* without realizing that a race of Supermen already existed, the aristocrats, who were accepted as different and superior to others as naively as children accepted parents as different and superior to them. In ancient times, kings and despots and important people like Caesar were believed to be the sons of Gods, a belief that lingered on. Not until 1946 did Emperor Hirohito of Japan disavow that he was a direct descendant of the Sun Goddess. At the beginning of the twenty-first century, the king of Thailand (formerly Siam) believed he was semi-divine and so did his subjects.

In Greek mythology Gods were said to have special blood in their veins, a rarified fluid called "ichor," and in the early nineteenth century, kings and their descendants began to call their blood "blue blood." The blood Royal, since it originally came from the God who'd sired their ancestors, made aristocrats morally superior to commoners. A "villain," now means a wicked person, but it used to mean a "villein," a feudal serf who, because of his inferior blood couldn't help being a lowlife. Serfs, because of their bad blood, were biologically villainous. Aristocrats, because of their divine blood, were biologically virtuous — courageous, generous, honest, natural ladies and gentlemen.

To retain their divinity, aristocrats had to keep their blood pure. Egyptian royalty often practiced incest so their divine blood would remain untainted. It was a sin for the Israelites to contaminate their blood, blood of the chosen people, by marrying those who hadn't been chosen by God. For aristocrats to intermarry with the "vulgar" would pollute their bloodlines, make their descendents mongrels, no longer purebreds, unlike the pedigreed dogs and horses they raised. Aristocrat means the best *aristos* in power *kratos* because those who could trace their descent back to God had the divine right to rule.

God's Caste System

When the American revolutionaries declared that the "Creator" had made all men equal, they were doing more than defy George III. For if "all men" really were "created equal," "virtue and ability," as Thomas Paine declared, were not hereditary, which meant that the Americans were also committing blasphemy, defying the caste system that God himself had created, a system succinctly described in an 1849 hymn:

> The rich man in his castle,
> The poor man at his gate,
> God made them high or lowly,
> And ordered their estate.

That hymn ("All Things Bright and Beautiful" by Cecil Frances Alexander) remained in the Anglican hymnal until 1963 because people continued to believe that God had created order in the world by making the upper class superior to the lower classes who, to keep the world orderly and peaceful, must not strive to rise above their God-given lowly stations. In nineteenth-century Ireland, the lady of many upper class houses would throw the menu from a gallery down to the servants in the kitchen, who knew their place and were content to remain below stairs. Nicholas II of Russia lost status among peasants when he treated the low class Rasputin as almost an equal. The peasants wanted their Czar, their divine authority, to stand on a dais above them, not step down to their level. In 1912 when the Titanic sank and passengers were struggling to get into life boats, people in steerage made way for the upper class, who took their

privileged treatment as natural, an acknowledgment of their innate superiority.

When Gulliver traveled to the land of the Houyhnhnms and came
upon a pack of "abominable" animals, it took him a long time before he
could let it sink in that those naked, hairy, disgusting brutes were of the
same species as he was. He was then grateful that his clothes had disguised him. Aristocrats assumed the trappings of a higher species and
for century after century the world went along with their pretense.

From time to time though, people did manage to see that the Emperor
had no clothes. "When Adam delved [dug] and Eve span [spun], Who
was then the gentleman?" was the war cry in the Peasant's Rebellion of
1381. All men were once equal, said Rousseau in *On the Origin of the
Inequality Between Men* (1754). Mankind, he argued, divided itself into the
oppressors and the oppressed only when some men acquired much more
property than others and enacted laws that kept them rich and those with
little property poor. In the nineteenth century, Karl Marx also thought
that private property had created the ruling class.

There's much truth in that theory, but Rousseau and Marx didn't dig
deep enough into the human archeological site. Long before mankind
developed property, they developed an institution in which the laws of
inequality, of the oppressor and the oppressed, were established. That
institution was the family, in which parents had the right to beat, yell
at and command their children to make them do what they were told, a
right that created the first oppressors and oppressed. God didn't establish a caste system, our first Gods did, a system that in infancy created the
further delusion, that to lord it over others is the highest good, a mind set
that still pervades our psychology, customs, language and institutions.

Bigger is Better

Having been brought up as inferiors, we long to be superiors, to
become high-and-mighty, words that were linked because height and
power were combined in parents. Family life makes us long to sit on
the high end of the seesaw so we can look down on others who have to
look up to us. We want to be the ones in high command, no longer in the
infantry (from *infans*, Latin for little child). The higher we get, the better
we feel we are. To be a "Sir" is better than to be a plain "Mr." A Duke
is better than a Count, a General better than a Colonel. It's best to be the
Pope, and better to be an Archbishop than a Bishop, a full professor than
an associate professor. Our different ranks are like the fake rabbits that
spur greyhounds on to be winners.

We want to be winners because we were losers at home. We go wild
with joy when our team wins because we've become the big, triumphant
ones. But, alas, only temporarily. How we wish we could be permanently up there with the stars, an international celebrity chased by paparazzi,

whose job wouldn't exist if we didn't have a lust for status. Americans, despite their democracy, kowtow to the Pope and visiting royals, and create their own royals — the Kennedys and Pop Stars — and envy the Rich and Famous. No one wants to be low man on the totem pole; we want to be on top of the world, have our picture taken on the highest peak of Mount Everest. I sometimes think that we had to erect bigger and bigger buildings until they scraped the sky because we were imprinted with the idea that bigger is better at an age when we were lowest in the scheme of things.

Because bigger was better at home, people of high status make themselves bigger. Judges sit on high benches. Preachers deliver God's message from pulpits, which were sometimes so high above the congregation that the preacher had to walk up many steps to get there. Lecturers stand on platforms not only so they can be seen and heard better but to signify that, like parents, they know more than the ones below.

Kings and other potentates further increased their height by wearing crowns. The Pope wears a triple crown, bishops tall double-pointed hats called miters. Buddhist holy men sometimes wear crowns and sit on thrones, as do some gurus. When the cult leader, James Jones, moved his followers to Guyana, he had them build him a throne. Frank Lloyd Wright and his second wife sat on a dais when they entertained at home to make clear who was the big shot, the big daddy, the top banana.

When monarchs and religious officials sat on their thrones, they made themselves even bigger by requiring those beneath them to make themselves smaller. Their subjects (which means 'to throw under') had to kneel so they became small like children, or lower — they often had to kiss the king's feet. Some had to get as low as you can get. Buddhist devotees prostrate themselves (often hundreds of times) before their guru or a statue of the Buddha. Catholic religious lie prostrate on the floor in submission and adoration before their Christ. God in the Bible preferred soldiers who assumed the lowest position. To choose the men who were to help Gideon conquer the Midianites, God ordered 10,000 potential soldiers to go to the water and drink. The 9,700 who kneeled and cupped the water in their hands were dismissed. God chose the 300 who lay down and lapped the water with their "tongue like a dog" (Judges 7:5). The military still demands dog-like subservience from their recruits, the abject subservience parents used to demand from children.

'Prostrate' comes from the Latin, to throw oneself flat; we have many other words that originally meant to literally put oneself down before an authority. We kowtow (from the Chinese, to knock the head on the ground); we grovel (from Old Norse, to face downward); we genuflect and curtsy (bend the knees). If we're Arabs we salaam, bow low while placing our right hand on our forehead. We lick boots; we bow and scrape; we cringe and cower; we stoop. From that position, we can't look someone in the eye, which subjects and slaves were not allowed to do. They had to lower their eyes in the presence of their king or master to acknowledge their unequal status, go back to the time when their eyes weren't on the same level as their parents' eyes.

Members of some primitive tribes had to crawl on the earth as they approached their King. God promised the Israelites that their enemies would one day "bow to the earth before you and lick the dust from your feet" (Isaiah 49:23). Swift remembered that passage when he had Gulliver say that in the country of Laputa an audience with the King was called having "the honor to 'lick the dust before his footstool'," which was meant literally: Gulliver had to snake on his belly to the throne while licking the floor. We may regard that posture as demeaning because in infancy we crawled or moved on our bellies on the dusty floor on which Brobdingnagians walked far above us, which may also be why we speak of worshiping the ground someone walks on.

If we hadn't been children who had to appease the mighty beings we lived with, the world wouldn't have many words that mean "I am helpless and you are powerful," therefore "I am your humble servant," your flunky, lackey, toady, slavey, lickspittle, doormat, ass-kisser. Yet, even when it becomes almost second nature to be a servile, submissive, obsequious flatterer, in our hearts we want to climb up a beanstalk and cut a giant down to size; we want to be Davids who deck Goliaths; we want to transform from Caspar Milquetoasts to Supermen. I knew a two-year-old who watched the TV series, *The Incredible Hulk* (in which the hero bulked into a super-muscleman), with ferocious longing.

We sympathize with underdogs because we identify with them, that is, until we get power and, having got out from under and onto a high horse, want only underdogs around us. We can bear no equal near our throne. Bosses want us to Yes-Sir them. Workers who get uppity, who get ideas above their station, must be reduced to proper size. Upstarts are no more allowed outside the home than they were in the home. A vice-president must not upstage the president. Big sisters and brothers lord it over kid sisters and brothers, often for life, as most parents continue to lord it over their adult children. Few adults visit Mom and Dad without feeling "this high" (palm held a couple of feet from the floor). When we meet someone new, we sniff each other out to establish rank. At cocktail parties, the first exchange usually is, "What do you do?" and we sigh with relief when we learn our status is higher, that I'm an assistant professor and *she* only teaches high school.

We proudly display our symbols of superiority, our Oscars, Emmys, trophies and blue ribbons. We hang our Olympic medals around our necks. Generals and Admirals sport gold braid, epaulets and campaign ribbons on their uniforms. The Chief Justice of the United States Supreme Court, William Rehnquist, to make instantly clear that he was the top justice, had gold bands sewn on the sleeves of his robe. We blazon a phony coat of arms on a pocket of our blazers to hint at a pedigree. The Duchess of Windsor, denied royal status, wore tall white plumes as a headdress to declare her preeminence, so that she'd literally jut out above others (the original meaning of "eminence"). How she longed to be a "Highness," a title that says without disguise that bigger does mean better.

Who Rules Britannia?

"Rule Britannia, Britannia rule the waves." "Never, never, never" did Britons want to be slaves. We all have that anthem singing in our heads — our longing "never, never, never" to be slaves again. That universal desire exists because we're born into monarchies and treated like slaves who, perforce, aimed to please, but were secret rebels who longed to overthrow the tyrants and become tyrants ourselves.

"Violence is bred by inequality," said Gandhi, who didn't know it begins in families, where children have to rebel against parents to get power and freedom. The violence innate in the dominant-submissive paradigm that families create made inevitable the infinite number of wars of conquest and rebellions against oppressors that have scorched the Earth. Britain and other nations have tried to rule the waves, but their success was never permanent because the nations they conquered sooner or later rebelled. Only one nation has always ruled the waves — the smallest but most influential in the world — the family.

"Nothing appears more surprising to those who consider human affairs with a philosophical eye, than the easiness with which the many are governed by the few," said David Hume ("Of the First Principles of Government," 1741). Hume wouldn't have found that fact surprising if he'd considered that all children have to surrender to the almighty parents who first govern them.

"Totalitarianism began, and totalitarianism still begins in the nursery," said the educator, A S Neill (*Summerhill*, 1960). It's been so difficult to rid the world of totalitarianism because the paradigm of domination and submission controls an area of our brains as if it had been hard-wired into a computer.

Chapter 11   **Inner Whisperings**

Dannion Brinkley had a near-death experience that made him able to tune into what others were thinking. In *At Peace in the Light* (1995), he tells of being in a parking lot at a supermarket and hearing person after person "pick themselves apart," tell themselves they were ugly, overweight, dumb, bad and had "done wrong things."

Brinkley was tuning in to that internal Simon Legree who lashes us for every fault, whose perfectionist standards give us no peace, the harsh taskmaster who shouts "Stupid!" when we make a mistake, the mocker who sneers, "I knew you couldn't do it" when we fail, the judge who gavels down, "Ugly!" when we look in the mirror. People with Tourette's syndrome, suddenly and against their will, find themselves cursing. Similarly, against our will, up pops a tyrannical voice in our head cursing us out.

That tyrannical voice is ancient. About 500 years before the Christian era, the religious leader known as the Buddha was plagued by what he called "inner whisperings," a voice that would tell him he shouldn't be doing this or that or be thinking whatever he was thinking. "You're not really enlightened," the voice would say. "You have a long way to go yet." The Buddha thought the malign whisperings were one of the temporary delusions of human minds, dark clouds floating across the brightness of our true mind. He therefore advised his followers to remain undisturbed no matter what the whisperings, to give them a label and calmly float them away. The Buddha labeled his, "Mara," and whenever he heard the criticizing and judgments, he'd say, "I know you, Mara," and they'd disappear, but only for a while. He had to endure Mara's tongue-lashings until he died.

The Buddha thought that malign whisperings were among the already existing thought forms humans can tune into. Nowadays, when geneticists are looking for the cause of all our ills in this or that gene, perhaps they'll find the inner critic "thought form" in a gene. I doubt it. I also doubt that the inner critic is the voice of our conscience. How could it be since it damns many things as wrong that aren't wrong, and has no compassion? It's solely a hanging judge.

The Buddhist, Gavin Harrison, experienced the single-minded malice of his inner whisperings as soon as he began to meditate. In *In the Lap of the Buddha* (1994), he said that "The Voice criticized if "I ate too much or too little." "If I walked too much or too little, or not at all, there was a judgment. It was incredible. ... The Voice was there, criticizing all the time." "The Voice" was the label that Harrison, following the Buddha's advice, gave to these unrelenting attacks. But saying "The Voice" didn't float the malign whisperings away, perhaps because when ever he said "The Voice," it was with a deep, gruff tone. He didn't know why.

He didn't discover why until he dreamed he was with the man who'd sodomized him when he was an infant. He'd never been able to remember who he was, and didn't recognize him in the dream until the man spoke and out came the deep, gruff voice he'd used to label his malign whisperings, a voice that so frightened him, he woke up.

In the mid nineties I was in a modern art gallery, scornfully walking away from a massive twisted metal sculpture, when "Stupid!" "Clumsy fool!" "Ugly kid!" began shouting in a male voice. I looked back, realizing that walking by had triggered a recording in the sculpture. Unfortunately, I didn't write down the name of the artist, but in an 1998 art show I saw Joan Dulla's miniature sculpture of a child's tricycle with chain bracelets attached that said, "Can't You do Anything Right?," "You're not good enough," "Shame on you," "I'm sorry you were ever born," and other words that "Forever Hurt You," to cite the title. These sculptures made public the verbal brickbats that are flung at children in millions of homes: the father of Michael Jackson used to call him "Nuthin," as if it were his name; on a TV program about troubled children, one adolescent said that his father always called him "Trash"; Ronald Reagan's nickname for his son Michael was the Yiddish insult, "schmuck." It's the rare child who grows up without having been called "Stupid," or told that he or she is not as smart or as good-looking as a sister or brother. Most of us die with these emotional punches still ricocheting inside our heads.

The Silent Sound Track

When Dannion Brinkley overheard people telling themselves they were ugly, dumb or bad parents, he may not have realized that what he overheard was rarely heard by the people themselves. I didn't hear my critic carping at me until (shortly after my inner journey began) I started daily meditation and became more conscious of what was going on inside my head. Since I'd not heard of inner critics, I called mine the Mocker, which I didn't realize was always there. I discovered that much later, the day I decided to write down its denunciations and found myself writing on and on and knew that I was transcribing a diatribe that never stopped.

People who are addicted to drugs know they're taking drugs. We don't know that the inner critic is an IV constantly dripping hate into our emotional bloodstream. In Hannah Green's *I Never Promised You A Rose Garden* (1964), the teenager who goes mad presses lighted cigarettes into her arm and feels no pain. We become so inured to the inner critic's unkind cuts that we don't feel them stabbing us. On the few occasions when we do hear them, for example, when "Clumsy!" pops up after a typo, we brush the epithet aside like a pesky fly. Even when women look in the mirror and hear "Ugly!" they quickly look away and think of other things.

The twentieth-century guru, Gurjdieff, never tired of saying that we're asleep and have to wake up. He didn't explain that one reason we stay asleep is to shut out that cruel voice. Our ears are always tuned into the inner critic, but to avoid hearing it we fill our heads with personal chat, or with the chat on TV and the radio, or we read newspapers, magazines, do crossword puzzles, phone a friend, resort to the thousands of ways we've invented to create the white noise that covers up our internal damnation.

Brain Cancer

When children chant at other children, "Sticks and stones may break my bones but words can never hurt me," it's bravado. They're pretending that being called "Fatty" or "Skinny Pickle" didn't get to them. It did get to them; feelings are more easily bruised than bodies, and the constant criticism of the inner critic doesn't harden us to putdowns. It keeps our bad feelings about ourselves alive and kicking. God daily created manna for the Israelites to eat in the desert; the inner critic daily creates our despised identity. Much truer than Descartes' "I think, therefore I am" is, "I am what my thoughts tell me I am."

The Gospel of John starts: "In the beginning was the Word," the Word that was God who created the universe. The Word that creates our personal universe can imprint our minds at our very beginning. I acquired mine in the womb. I told you in the first chapter that after I took the drug Ecstasy, I saw a blackboard on which was chalked in huge letters, "You are evil," followed by a picture of embryo-me. It took me more than a year to understand the meaning of the two images, that "You are evil" was the first message I received from my mother, her curse when she learned she was having yet another damn child. Perhaps she meant only that I was an evil to her, but I took it to mean that I was evil. Thus, when I was about an inch old, did my mother's Word damn me. Thus, when I was about an inch old, did the ancient bell of original sin begin tolling in my head. I never had to ask for whom the bell tolled; I knew it was tolling for Evil Me, Evil Me, Evil Me.

Not until thirteen years after I had that vision, when I was writing the above paragraph, did it dawn on me that "You are evil" was chalked on a blackboard to let me know it could be erased. I was so long in getting that hopeful message because "You are evil" had been the judgment of my first God. In the months we spend in the womb we're contained in the Great Creator of our life, a life that's sustained not only with nutrients for our growing body but for our growing awareness. When our One God, our Mother, utters a judgment of our worth, it becomes The Truth about us, as if it were part of our DNA.

Most of us scoff at the idea that preborns can be aware of their mothers' feelings toward them. We scoff because it's new information. For thousands of years, fetuses and infants were thought to be not only physically retarded but mentally and emotionally retarded — mindless, feelingless blobs. Typical was the philosopher Thomas Reid who in his *Inquiry into the Human Mind* (1764) referred to the "darkness of infancy, which is equal to that of idiots." Well into the twentieth century scientists would have agreed. They knew so little about the growth of the brain they falsely reasoned that since myelin (the insulating sheath around nerves) develops late and since higher brain functions are not fully developed at birth that preborns and newborns were semi-vegetables. Scientists later discovered that myelination was irrelevant, that the spinal cord acts as a primitive brain and that the brainstem has clusters of receptors, which means, as thousands of experiments have proved, that fetuses are "wired" to taste, smell, hear, even remember. For example, fetuses can remember music they heard in the womb.

Fetuses also mirror their mother's emotions. The mechanism by which this happens is sometimes called sculpting, the shaping of the billions of nerve cells by everything preborns experience or don't experience. For example, when a mother is seriously depressed, the nerve cells in the left frontal region of the fetus's brain, which regulate feelings of happiness, excitement and interest, are not sufficiently stimulated so that the baby is more likely to be sad, aggressive and have trouble sleeping. A massive amount of scientific evidence has also proved that when preborns, infants and young children are repeatedly exposed to physical and emotional abuse the lower centers of the brain seem to be permanently damaged, with the result that the babies are likely to become violent.

But most of us who are mistreated — beaten, rejected, belittled — don't become outwardly violent. When my mother branded my embryonic awareness with "You are evil," she didn't turn me into a bully. Only three times in my life have I hit anyone. Twice in childhood and once as an adult, when I threw a plastic cup at my husband, which missed. I reacted to my mother's cruelty not by beating others up but by beating myself up. I don't mean that I hurt myself. I, like virtually everyone and whether or not they act out their violence, developed an inner bully.

Here is a sample of mine. In 1996, the day after I finished teaching a course, I was depressed and let my hand write, and from it flowed: "Who are you to have given that course? You don't know enough. You talked too much. You were blowing your own filthy horn. You're nothing. You should stay in a closet, be dead. I order you to be dead. You beat everyone up with your superiority. You do, you know. No one likes you, you're too superior. Act like the schmuck you really are." The message I first received in the womb had become the mold into which I cast myself, the matrix of the malign inner world I daily, hourly recreated. I'm not alone. The inner critic sits in every one's mind spitting out its black ink like an octopus. It's a brain cancer we all suffer from, the worst mental disease humans acquire.

Instinct makes birds fly south in winter and fish swim back to where they were born in order to breed. Humans are said to be the least programmed of animals, and when they're conceived, their programming is minimal, but not for long. All babies soon become French, Eskimo, Japanese, which is necessary, but at the same time as they're picking up the culture of their country, they're picking up what's not necessary, an inner critic.

The Christian healer, Agnes Sanford, had a vision in which Christ took her to a marble temple in ancient Sparta to see a boy being sacrificed on an altar. "Now," said Christ to her, "you have seen the very worst thing that can happen upon the planet earth" (*Sealed Orders*, 1972). I disagree. Sacrificing children is not "the very worst thing that can happen on planet earth." The terror and pain of a child who's sacrificed lasts a short while. The worst thing that happens to children is to acquire an inner critic, whose denunciations last a lifetime.

In Franz Kafka's *The Penal Colony*, condemned convicts are strapped into a machine that etches the name of their crime into their flesh deeper and deeper until the culprit drops out of the machine dead. That machine could be a symbol of the inner critic, which etches its condemnations into our brain until we drop dead. It's the oldest instrument for self-torture ever invented. No more potent form of mind control exists.

Original Critics

In medieval times people believed the devil was real. In the late twentieth century a few people again suggested that the devil was at work on planet Earth. The devil has always been at work, for he's not a slick fellow with cloven hoofs in a red body suit who comes up from hell to torment us. The devil is in our head, on the hell channel we're always tuned into, whose everlasting message is that we're bad beyond redemption. "Public opinion is a weak tyrant compared with our own private opinion," said Thoreau, who most likely didn't understand that our low opinion of ourselves is transmitted by the unkind words and deeds of our parents. Few people say they believe in original sin, but if you have an inner critic, you are a believer. Your original critics—your parents—live on in you, constantly telling you you're a sinner. We should all put "Inc" after our names, signifying that we've incorporated a personal inner critic who carries on the degrading practices of the family firm.

When Gavin Harrison during meditation unwittingly used the deep gruff voice of the man who'd abused him, he revealed that his outer abuser had become his inner abuser. Our abusive, angry, domineering inner critic continues to do unto us what our parents did. Our inner critic is a martinet who fusses about petty matters because Mom/Dad did. It assumes the right to yell at us because Mom/Dad did. It's constantly on our case because Mom/Dad were. It acts as if it's all-powerful because Mom/Dad were all-powerful. It's hate-filled jibes are often disguised as concern for our welfare because often Mom/Dad's were.

The inner parent can't help itself; it has to follow the parental program; it's a robot, fundamentally stupid because it can't learn. If a parent labeled us stupid, it continues to call us stupid no matter what we accomplish. My mother labeled me a cretin, and my two older sisters gladly followed suit. That I got all A's in school (except for arithmetic), that I got a PhD, never changed their minds. When I was teaching English at a university, my actress sister asked me if I'd ever happened to hear of a Greek play called *Oedipus Rex*! Instead of indignantly telling her how stupid she was to ask, I mumbled that I had heard of it. I wasn't merely being polite; I was playing the cretin role I'd been cast in, which really wasn't a role: I still believed my mother's lie that I was a cretin. A seven-year-old who was told by her older brothers when they were teaching her how to ride a bicycle, "You're so damn clumsy!" at the age of twenty-five still heard that judgment whenever she attempted to learn a new sport.

Let someone criticize us, and we're floored, knocked down to childhood. Whether or not we manage to stand up for ourselves and talk back, the one who criticized us has been turned into our infallible parents. We took the criticism personally because it confirmed our low opinion of ourselves.

The Inner Twins

We continue to think we're stupid or ugly or "no good" because we're not merely the inner parent. The inner critic doesn't know that. When it cracks the parental whip, it thinks it's the parent. It's able to because the inner critic, in its role as parent, blanks out the victim it once was. Nevertheless, the victim is there. It has to be. A judge needs a criminal to condemn. Nazis needed Jews. The eagle eyes of dictators posted on walls need subjects to look down on. Master and slave are codependent. The one couldn't exist without the other. The inner critic lashes the victim and doesn't know it's also the victim, that it's conjoined twins, parent and child playing out their sado-masochistic dramas in a theater in the skull, repeat performances of the dramas of domination and submission enacted at home.

We submit to the harsh discipline of the inner critic for the same reason we submitted to parental discipline—because we're still the child who thought its parents were telling the truth when they said we were bad, ugly, stupid, beliefs that so damage our faith in ourselves that we think we ought to surrender to parents and let them run our lives. The child-self may surrender and become a goody-goody, but its obedience is always a mask concealing the would-be rebel, for whom freedom means being the 'naughty' child our parents thought they'd got rid of.

As children, we rebel much more often against our parents than we do when they become our inner parent. For the child in us remains a programmed robot who can't learn, who still believes the 'bad' news it was taught at home. If the child in us didn't have the same attitude toward itself as its parents did, the inner parent would have no power.

The child's submission gives the inner parent more and more power and, as the master becomes more ruthless, the slave becomes more docile. The master and slave in the inner critic are equally corrupt. The master excretes hate and the child eats the shit. The hate of the master and the self-hate of the child are in league together because they have the same goal; they want us to become 'good'. The inner parent yells louder because its harshness never makes the child good, and the child accepts the punishment because it still wants to be good, so Mom/Dad will love it.

Children feel afraid, angry and hurt when parents criticize them. The inner parent's putdowns constantly regenerate those old feelings, which keep us emotionally children. How can we be adults when something within us treats us like a child and we react like a child? Our Ego, wearing a crown and holding a scepter, sits on its throne, imagining it's in charge, unaware it's a figurehead, that behind the scenes internalized parents continue to run its life.

The Inner Critic Gone Mad

In *The Quiet Room* (1994), a personal account of schizophrenia, Lori Schiller said that her "Voices" would tell her that she was fat and ugly, that everyone hated her, that she was a bitch, rubbish, junk, nothing, a piece of shit. "The Voices" also commented negatively on everything she did or didn't do. Lori's voices were similar to Gavin Harrison's and mine and thine; the favorite curses of everyone's inner critic are: "You're ugly," "You're stupid, "You're no good," "You're a piece of shit."

But the voices schizophrenics hear are more intense than the voice of the inner critic. They're the inner critic gone mad. Schizophrenics lose the ability to control it. Whereas non-schizophrenics manage to be deaf to their inner critic most of the time, only by an enormous act of will and for a short while could Lori suppress her Voices, which were not "inner whisperings." She was certain they were outside her, shouting their denunciations for everyone to hear and telling the whole world that she deserved to go to hell for her badness, a hell her schizophrenia made visible. For example, amid smoke and fire she saw red and orange devils cut off men's balls and rape women, who screamed while the devils laughed. Lori thought the hells she saw were "worse than the worst horror movie" she'd ever seen. But they were no worse than the horrors in the Revelation of John, Dante's Inferno, and the paintings of hell by Hieronymous Bosch.

Those were produced by presumably sane people. Having an inner critic in residence, a team of master and slave, inevitably creates hells in our mind, venues in which masters punish and slaves are punished, inner fantasies that besides being written down, painted and filmed, become the living hell we call war, where a superior power tries to reduce as many people as possible to victims.

Our hellish religion was modeled on the inner critic. Our Biblical God is an invisible judge who's often mad, like the invisible demons that thundered at Lori that she was a vile sinner who deserved to be tortured, killed, go to hell. The God of Wrath is the outer expression of the dominant half of the inner critic, a God who wouldn't be God if he didn't have his chosen people to kick around. The God of Wrath couldn't have been a judgmental, merciless father if his children, in fear and trembling, hadn't submitted to his many punishments. We've clung to that cruel God the way young children cling to a parent after a beating, the way the child within us clings to its inner parent.

To love someone who hits and reviles us is crazy-making. To have a voice within that's always telling us we're bad, a judgment we accept, is, as far as I'm concerned, a certificate of our madness, the madness that makes us worship our vindictive God, who is no more God than are the people in insane asylums who think they're God. The 'Gods' in insane asylums have delusions of grandeur for the same reason the God of Wrath and the rest of us do: because we want to be as powerful as our powerful parents were, because we want to escape from the child in us who once "made himself nothing, assuming the nature of a slave," to quote Paul on Christ's alleged relationship to God (Philippians 2:6-8).

Everyone who acquires an inner critic is partly mad and, like Lori, we don't know we are; Lori denied she was crazy for years. When Lori's Voices yelled at her, she reacted as if demons outside her were telling her the truth. When our inner critic yells at us, though we know it's inside us, we too react as if a Know-It-All outside us was telling us a harsh truth. But most of the time we're unconscious of our inner critic, which is not a total blessing. It does keeps us from going mad, but our unawareness keeps our madness going.

Lori began to regain her sanity when she realized that the hate-filled Voices she thought were outside her head weren't real, that they'd once been the putdowns her parents had directed at her, putdowns that the chemistry of schizophrenia brewed into damnations. Though we're only partially mad, to regain our sanity we too have to face that our inner critic was once outside us, that its criticisms have their root in parental criticisms, criticisms we continue to think are the truth because we still react to them as if we were children. Unless we grow up and face reality, that mad pair—the frightening domineering parent and the frightened sub-missive child—will remain locked in a wrestling hold inside our head.

I suspect that many more people have climbed Mount Everest than have broken free of the inner critic's grip. We don't break free because the truth about family life frightens us. Gavin Harrison didn't recognize the face of his abuser in his dream, and most people in my incest sur-vivor group who dreamed about their abusers blanked out their faces. They couldn't bear to see that "My own Dad raped me!" "My own Mom sucked on my penis!"

In the Bible, the sight of God can make a person die of terror. Perhaps we made God invisible because we didn't want to see that the Gods who created us male and female in their own image were the almighty par-ents who mistreated us. We become sane when we're able to look our Gorgons in the face without terror turning us into stone.

The Buddha should have advised his followers to pay attention to their inner whisperings, to try to discover their source. By saying they were temporary delusions of the mind, clouds that could be floated away, he didn't confer a benefit on mankind. He was going along with the human need to remain unconscious of the suffering we endure when we're growing up. But, according to the Buddha legend, he grew up in a palace where he never saw or experienced suffering, an impossibility in real life. Home is where we experience our first and most lasting suf-fering. We've paid a heavy price for not becoming conscious of it: our emotional intelligence has been badly impaired. But few of us are aware we're retarded; we live in purdah, behind the veils of what we've labeled, "Home, sweet home."

Chapter 12   **False Memories**

Almost at the beginning of Lori Schiller's *The Quiet Room* (right after she described the onset of her schizophrenia), she made a sensational confession—that when she was a child she beat the family dog to death. "I kept hitting him, and hitting him," she said, "and didn't stop until he was dead." Lori was haunted by her crime; year after year she was racked by guilt.

After she got schizophrenia, Lori revealed her guilty secret to her family, who assured her her memory was false. It couldn't be true, they pointed out, since the dog she said she killed was a black mongrel, and the only dog they'd owned when she was a child was a gray miniature schnauzer who, after a long life, was put to death by a vet. They assured her that her memory was a ghastly fantasy generated by schizophrenia. After the drug clozapine subdued Lori's Voices, her "dark images" slowly faded and she realized that she couldn't have killed the dog for another reason: her childhood had been not merely without the "abuse and rage" that would make a child kill a dog but "exceptionally happy," "filled with love and comfort, fun and friendship."

It had been. Reading about Lori's childhood and adolescence was like flipping through a family album of Norman Rockwell snapshots. I sighed with envy, like the incest survivors at the meetings I went to, who would rail against the fate that had dropped them into a house of horrors not into the Brady Bunch family they'd watched on TV when they were children.

Lori's family was a lot like the Brady Bunch. Her parents were kind, concerned, generous, encouraging. Lori's best friend envied the close relationship she had with her mother, father and brothers. Her brother Mark remembered Lori (before schizophrenia) as "perfect," as smart and popular, a great dancer and writer, and with a great sense of humor too, a "star" whom her parents lost no opportunity to show off to their friends. "I so much wanted mommy and daddy to be proud of me," had been Lori's hope when she was a child, and she'd succeeded.

But being "perfect Lori" had a downside. Wanting to keep her parents proud of her, she didn't tell them when, at seventeen, the Voices began tormenting her. Nor did she tell them when the Voices got more constant and intense in college and when, in New York on her first job, they were ordering her to kill herself. Her parents didn't find out that something was wrong with her until, sure she could fly, she tried to jump out a window and was taken to a hospital.

Lori refused to face that she was mentally ill and her parents had the same reluctance. Her mother didn't want to take in that "the old Lori everyone knew and loved" was no more. Her father, though a clinical psychologist, insisted that Lori was merely having adolescent problems. "This mustn't come to light," he said when she was first hospitalized, and got her out of the psychiatric unit as quickly as if he were bailing her out of jail. Lori wanted to believe as much as her father that trying to jump out a window was an adolescent prank that had gone too far. A contrite, apologetic Lori said that she'd momentarily "flipped out," that, like a naughty child, she'd done "something wrong."

Lori again did "something wrong"—she again tried to kill herself, was again hospitalized and continued to have to be readmitted. But her parents, instead of facing that she had a mental disease, got angry at her. When they saw her hands, wounded from punching walls and windows, they'd yell at her. Once when Lori was in a halfway house and, obeying her Voices, tore her arms up with rose thorns, her mother got so angry that for a while, said Lori, "she refused to visit me."

Lori was angrier at herself than her parents were. She was "constantly caught up in a storm of self-hatred." Her Voices told her over and over what she didn't have to be told—that she'd become a loser, that her mother was ashamed of her, that her parents were no longer proud of her, that, though they loved her, they hated her too and wished she'd disappear from their lives, die.

Lori felt that way although her parents visited her almost every day and brought her food, new clothes, gifts. She would eagerly look forward to their visits, but as soon as they arrived she was caught up in "a whirl-wind of violent emotions." Having become fat, she found it difficult to be around her slim, beautiful mother, who found it difficult to be around her. During the half-hour visits, her mother would often retreat to the smoking room, and Lori would feel despair because she was no longer the ideal daughter of her mother's dreams. When she told her father that she'd been out of control the day before, he never asked what happened; he'd say that that was yesterday and today she was fine.

Still wanting them "to be proud of her," she struggled to maintain control during their visits. But she couldn't keep up the chit-chat for long. A "fire" of hate would build up inside that burst into open rage. "I hate you," she'd scream at her mother. "Get the fuck out of here," she'd scream at her father and yell at both of them to "Get away!" She "couldn't breathe." She was sure she'd "explode into a million pieces," and as soon as her parents left, she ranted and shrieked, helplessly watching her "raging brain" as it created fantasies of her parents being killed in an accident as they drove home, "blown to pieces in a plane crash," of herself stabbing them, shooting them, burning down their house when they were asleep.

Anger was an early symptom of Lori's schizophrenia. The friend with whom she shared an apartment noticed with astonishment that Lori would say cruel things to visitors. Soon after Lori was hospitalized, a social worker told her parents that, though Lori worshiped them, inside she was very angry at them, and that not accepting Lori's condition was harming her. Her parents disagreed. They thought it helped Lori that they were upbeat and refused to believe her disease was incurable. During visits, they couldn't help silently pressuring her to play the game of let's pretend Lori is normal.

Lori knew that having to be "on stage" during their visits was the reason she blew up at them. But the rage she expressed hadn't been created by schizophrenia; it released a rage that had been so close to consciousness in childhood that she'd had the fantasy of violently killing the dog, a fantasy so real she was positive it was true and felt guilty for years. The Lori who wrote the book sensed her fantasy was important because she revealed it near the beginning of the book, and as if it were true, not the false memory she then knew it was.

Yet what reason did the child Lori have to be in a rage? She hadn't been beaten, raped, screamed at; she hadn't been ignored or devalued; she hadn't had to live in fear. Her parents had been kind, attentive, indulgent. Compared with most childhoods, hers was a piece of cake with frosting on top. So why did she imagine herself walking into the kitchen one afternoon, seeing the dog chained to a door and being seized with such a fury that she beat it to death?, a fury so intense that every detail of the dog's destruction was etched in her memory—his barking "hysterically" when she first hit him, his foaming "at the mouth," "one of his legs" collapsing, his body writhing on the floor in "horrible spasms," blood oozing "from his ears and mouth."

Her graphic recall makes it seem as if Lori were remembering a real event, yet the dog she beat to death wasn't the purebred schnauzer her family owned but a "medium-sized black mongrel." Why did she make the change? Perhaps because the dog Lori imagined she'd killed was a stand-in for herself, not "perfect Lori," not a purebred, but a mongrel, and a black one. Black can be a symbol for evil in our culture, and when Lori developed schizophrenia, her Voices were always telling her she was so bad she deserved to die and be punished horribly in hell. She once sat in a church and promised God to "never be evil again."

What evil was she guilty of? Was it being filled with a rage so great that she felt she was a mad dog who ought to be kept chained in the kitchen, ought to be killed so her badness wouldn't get loose? But in her fantasy, she said that seeing the dog tied up, unable to escape, unable to move far in any direction triggered the fury that made her get one of her father's golf clubs and beat the dog to death.

That she chose to kill the dog with her father's golf club may be a clue because for Lori he didn't use a club only on the green; at home he used the club of demanding perfection from his children. Lori and her two younger brothers were expected to take the hardest courses at school and to get all A's. Unlike other children, they were not allowed to "goof off." In their spare time, they had to take up a sport, participate in school activities, join clubs. Even at meals, they were drilled in perfect table manners. The goal was, after getting into the 'right' college, to become like the rich, successful people in Scarsdale, New York. When Lori was able to take in that her Voices reflected some of her own rage, she didn't have a fantasy of killing a dog, she had "a grisly fantasy" of killing and mutilating the father who'd clubbed her to death with his perfection- ism, a fantasy that, she said, "nearly overpowered me with its gruesome detail." Was it worse than the gruesome details of killing the dog?

When Lori had schizophrenia, she would listen over and over to the then popular song, "Easy," which was about everyone wanting you to be what they wanted you to be and hating that you had to fake it. Lori wanted to be free of that pressure; she wanted to cut the tethers that made her unable to move far in any direction. When she came home from the hospital on weekends, she refused to go to the country club, which was the center of her parents' social life. She knew she didn't "fit in anymore," that her parents' friends would glance at her and look away because she had a shameful disease, had put on over fifty pounds, was no longer the pretty, smart, bubbly, out-going winner that both she and her parents had been proud of. Lori wanted to be free of her parents' values, but she'd been so obedience-trained that she couldn't escape from wanting to make her parents proud of her; she couldn't help feeling as ashamed as they were that she no longer belonged to the country club set, that she, who was supposed to have been perfect, had turned out to be a mongrel.

Lori's brother Mark, who wrote a chapter of her book, also suffered from having to be perfect. But it wasn't his father's high standards that made him feel not "good enough"; it was their embodiment in Lori. Three years younger than Lori, he grew up convinced he couldn't com- pare to "perfect Lori." Though his parents always praised his accom- plishments, he felt that it was Lori they delighted in, that it was Lori who got all the attention. In high school he felt suicidal, the way Lori did when she got schizophrenia; he too didn't want to live because he was "a real loser, a real failure." Mark saved himself by what he called "running away from home," going to a college that Scarsdale considered third-rate and moving to another city where he was known for himself, not as his father's son or Lori's brother, getting away so he could discover who he was and be happy being who he was.

After Lori got schizophrenia, her father felt so guilty for having pressured his children to always do "the hardest thing possible" that he urged his youngest child to take the "easiest classes" in high school, even remedial ones. But her father's perfectionism didn't cause Lori's schizophrenia. She would have become a schizophrenic no matter how she was brought up. Her father's perfectionism, though, may have affected the violence of her Voices, which were as loud, ferocious and overwhelming as her father's demands must have seemed to the child Lori. "I was never good enough for the rude chanting demons in my head," said Lori because as a child she'd never felt good enough. How could she feel good enough when she feared she might not live up to her father's standards? How could she feel good enough when she was certain that if she didn't live up to them, she'd lose his love?, a feeling that made her hate him, want to kill him. But how awful she was to have those evil feelings toward someone who was so good to her, someone she loved! That tangle of hate, love and guilt not only made her kill black mongrel Lori in her childhood fantasy, but kept making her try to kill herself when she got schizophrenia.

Her conflicting feelings toward her father may not have been the only reason Lori was in torment when she was a child. A first child, Lori was caught up in an intense relationship with her mother, which also made her feel chained, unable to move far in any direction.

In one of the chapters she wrote for the book, Lori's mother revealed that she'd had an unhappy childhood. Her own mother (who'd been a mild schizophrenic) had rarely hugged her or told her she loved her. She'd scream at her that she'd never wanted children, that she was the cause of her unhappiness, that she was "too loud," "too fat," that she didn't "stand up straight." When she was a child, Lori's mother dreamed of having "a little daughter" whom she could hold in her arms, sing to, "dress" "cuddle" "play with," to whom she could give all the love she hadn't got when she was a child. Overjoyed when her first child was a girl, she spent "every waking moment" with her. When Lori was a baby, her mother said she made her her doll. When she got older, Lori became her "playmate," then her "friend," "confidante," "soul mate." They would go to museums in New York City, "dressed alike in red and white checked blouses and wire-rimmed sunglasses," and eat "foot-long hotdogs and chocolate milk shakes" and laugh at "people's outfits" on the train home. "She was the childhood I never had," Lori's mother confessed.

The actress, Joan Crawford, behaved the same way when she adopted a daughter, whom at first she even called Joan. Crawford too always kept her baby with her, sang her lullabies, rocked her to sleep, gave her everything she wanted. When her daughter was a little older, for a short while she made her a buddy, a friend; they became a couple, the relationship like a marriage. Crawford, like Lori's mother, also made her daughter feel she was "the best, the most beautiful, the smartest, quickest, most special child on the face of the earth," until, unlike Lori's mother, Crawford became cruel. (Christina Crawford, *Mommie Dearest*, 1978).

Mothers often transfer to their children their own yearning to be born again and this time have everything perfect. Their desire can be so great they transmit it to the fetus. People who have relived uterine life sometimes report that they knew as fetuses that their job was to fill their mothers' needs. A man I met at a workshop bitterly complained that his mother had forced him to lead the life she would have led if she'd been male. "She treated me as if we were the same person," he said, which was how Lori's mother treated her: "She was the childhood I never had."

When she was being treated for schizophrenia, Lori asked her supervisory therapist, Dr Jane Doller, to assign her a female as a regular therapist. A part of her knew she had to deal with her feelings toward her mother, but the moment she saw Dr Fischer she was so "terrified" she ran away. Later, when she was able tolerate her presence, Lori still felt she had to protect herself "against whatever she was trying to do to me." Lori felt she needed protection because Dr Fischer looked like her mother; both of whom, said Lori, were "slender," "beautiful," with "dark curly hair" and "successful." For Lori, Dr Fischer was her mother, the mother she'd identified with when she was a child and still wanted to be like.

But the perfect being she should have been was buried under schizophrenia and the fat she'd gained, so that Lori was sure Dr Fischer saw her the way she was sure her mother did, as "disgusting," a "tub of lard" whom she wanted to kill, which gave Lori an overwhelming desire to kill Dr Fischer. But to Lori's horror, her fear and hatred of Dr Fischer changed to passionate love. She couldn't help filling her journal with "lovesick yearnings," which frightened her by their perversity. She'd wanted to trust Dr Fischer, but instead she felt "invaded, taken over. I felt I didn't know who I was and didn't know who she was." Lori was feeling the pull of love and hate, of sensuality and fear that babies feel when they fuse, melt, become one with a parent. Compelled to live out the ideal childhood her mother had wanted and to become the winner her father demanded, Lori hardly knew where she began and her parents ended. Swept up in the needs and aspirations of her parents, Lori felt she had to became an extension of them.

Lori was greatly helped in finding out who *she* was by Dr Jane Doller, her chief therapist. When Lori first saw Dr Fischer, she'd been terrified. Not so with Dr Doller, whom Lori liked from the beginning. She looked like "the Pillsbury Dough Girl, all pudgy and squeezable." Everything about her, her voice, her manner was soft and relaxed. She was unlike the therapists and staff who'd lorded it over her, who, when she was crying, had told her to stop the self-pity, who'd insisted that she could control herself if she chose to. Dr Doller, however, knew that it was Lori's "genuine distress" that made control at times impossible.

In her very first session with Dr Doller, Lori felt so safe that she let down her guard and did what she'd never done before, she said out loud what her Voices were saying, which was "Come to hell with me, Dr Doller." Lori waited to be punished, but Dr Doller calmly kept on talking and listening. Lori's Voices then told her that Dr Doller was a "witch," but something inside Lori, what she called "the real, well side of me" told her the Voices were lying, that "this was a woman I could trust."

Dr Doller was the first person Lori could wholly trust. Her parents' love had been conditional on her being the child they wanted her to be. Dr Doller accepted Lori as she was. Though Lori was grossly overweight and a schizophrenic filled with rage, Dr Doller never judged her and was "never repulsed." When Lori revealed her detailed plan to kill and muti-late her father, Dr Doller's response was a smiling, "You can do better than that." To Lori's astonishment, Dr Doller "always seemed to like me." More than that. Dr Doller empathized with her. The day her beloved Dr Fischer permanently left the hospital, Lori, racked with agony, cried out her pain and loss to Dr Doller who, Lori noticed, "had tears in her eyes too."

It was Dr Doller's total acceptance of her that gave Lori the strength to face that her demonic Voices were expressions of her own rage, to learn that we sometimes hate those we love, that it was therefore all right to use a punching bag to punch out her family. When Lori was having sexual feelings for Dr Fischer, Dr Doller told her not to be ashamed, that all feelings were good because they give us a chance to find out about ourselves. In her childhood fantasy, Lori beat the black, bad part of her-self to death. When she got schizophrenia, she kept trying to kill herself to get rid of her badness. Dr Doller's acceptance of her just as she was taught Lori to accept herself as she was, hate and all. The tension, Lori said, poured out of her body: "Dr Doller had taken all the badness in me and turned it into good."

Not long after her badness "turned into good," Lori began taking a new drug, clozapine, and her head slowly cleared, her Voices got softer. On April 20, 1989, she wrote in her diary, "I want to live." She wrote it over and over. She filled a page with, "I want to live." Six days later, on her thirtieth birthday, she wrote, "HAPPY BIRTHDAY, ME". Lori was celebrating the birth of a "Me" who was not her mother, who was not "perfect Lori." The "I" Lori had wanted to kill was the "I" who'd been enmeshed with her parents, the "I" who felt guilty for hating them. The "I" who wanted to live was the unique Lori, the real Lori, the Lori she was discovering.

Happy Families

Lori said that her childhood had been "exceptionally happy," "filled with love and comfort, fun and friendship," which was true. It was also true that she didn't beat the family dog to death. And yet, her belief that her childhood had been without the "abuse and rage" that would make a child kill a dog wasn't true, for her fantasy revealed how great her rage was and pointed at its cause. Lori's memories of her childhood as "exceptionally happy" were true, but so was her rage at having to fulfill her mother's needs and her father's expectations.

"All happy families are alike," the first words of Tolstoy's *Anna Karenina*, summon up for Americans Norman Rockwell illustrations of family celebrations at Thanksgiving and Christmas. But Tolstoy too was lighting a candle at the holy icon of "happy families," as if the unhappy families he wrote about in his fiction, the one he came from, and the one he and his wife created were exceptions to the happy norm. People in my incest survivor group wished they'd been born in a Brady Bunch family because they believed the TV family was real, as did the millions of viewers who would write to the program and ask, "Why can't *my* family be like the Bradys?"

Their families couldn't be like the Bradys because happy families are largely a mirage, the hocus pocus that books, TV, movies and ads regularly conjure up to screen us from seeing what families are actually like. Just as mankind has developed thousands of distractions to keep us unaware of the constant putdowns of our inner critic, so have we developed myths about happy family life and false memories of happy childhoods. We don't want to register the unhappiness that goes on behind the front door of home. Like that trio of monkeys, we cover our ears and eyes and seal our lips.

Nowadays we like to speak and write about a phenomenon called "the dysfunctional family," the "dys" (meaning bad) allowing us to think that bad families are exceptions to the functional norm, whereas the truth is that functional families are the exceptions to the dysfunctional norm. "The world according to Norman Rockwell," said Shana Alexander is "the only world" that "millions of ... Americans, most of them perhaps, ever allow themselves to see" (*Nutcracker*, 1985). Most of us want the harsh realities of family life to stay hidden behind the Norman RockWALL. Even more than we want a photograph of us to show us in the best light, we want to see our family in the best light.

Before schizophrenia, Lori saw her family in a glorious light, and on the surface she had a happy family. Her parents did love her the best way they knew how. But a force within every child sees the truth. Lori knew her mother was using her to have the happy childhood she'd been denied and that her father was a bullying football coach demanding that she get out there and win. Lori sensed that the 'real Lori' wasn't being allowed to live, that her individuality had been disrespected. Her brother Mark, subjected to some of the same family pressures, went to a college far from home, then moved to another city and returned only for short visits. Lori, subjected to greater pressure than Mark, was more trapped and her only release was rage, which her childhood fantasy of

killing the family dog revealed. When schizophrenia loosened her control, her rage surfaced, but the chances are almost one-hundred percent
that if Lori hadn't had schizophrenia, she would have led a conventional
life, like that of her parents, reasonably happy, productive and essentially
a good person, at times angry, but unaware of the rage smoldering in her
underground.

What struck me about Lori's story was that a child doesn't need to
be in a terrible family to be filled with hate. Beneath the surface of what
seem to be happy families, problems similar to Lori's are filling children
with justifiable anger, anger they rarely know they have. Almost all of us
let our sleeping mad dogs lie, or rather, we think we do.

Chapter 13   **Mr Hyde**

Dr Jekyll and Mr Hyde

When Robert Louis Stevenson's *The Strange Case of Dr Jekyll and Mr Hyde* was published in 1886, it was an instant best-seller. It not only remained popular, it became a classic. When I read it in college, I couldn't understand why; I found it boring, trite. But when I was writing about hate, I decided I should reread it. A story about a conventional doctor who had a brute filled with rage hidden within him, might be grist for my mill.

The old paperback I got at a bookstore had the conventional horror-story boogeyman on its cover. The whites of Mr Hyde's eyes were green and a fang protruded from his crooked, toothy smile. Below his Halloween mask of a face were huge hands, one holding a thick, gnarled cane like a weapon. The cover might have been an ad for a Hollywood monster movie. The book turned out to be almost as bad. It reminded me of the "awful warning" literature that used to be written for children, like the James Whitcomb Riley poem about the boy who refused to say his prayers and was 'disappeared' by God's goblins. Stevenson's hell and damnation story has a moral almost as simplistic. The serious, respectable, handsome Dr Jekyll, a man of fifty, who'd been "wild when he was young" drinks a magic potion so he can guiltlessly indulge in his old "irregularities." Stevenson doesn't name the "irregularities," but they were obviously drinking and womanizing. The Mr Hyde in Dr Jekyll soon becomes more and more cruel, writes blasphemy in holy books and finally kills. When Jekyll kills himself to destroy the Mr Hyde in him, the reader knows he's going straight to hell.

The religion that Stevenson had been taught as a child was still deeply imprinted in his brain cells. His nurse, a fanatical Calvinist, used to read the little boy hell and damnation tracts that so frightened him he'd lie awake, afraid to fall asleep. He had good reason to be afraid, for he was sick a lot, and since sickness was God's punishment for sin, if he died in his sleep, he might find himself in hell, which was where he did find himself when he managed to fall asleep. He would wake hysterical from nightmares of hell. A child who suffers from insomnia is a frightened child, and Stevenson was so afraid that when he talked about the future he always added, "If I am spared," as if God could grab the bad boy at any moment and drop him into hell. His favorite game was playing 'preacher'. He was still preaching the old-time religion in Dr Jekyll and Mr Hyde.

Stevenson wrote the story when he was thirty-five. What had happened to the rebellious young man who'd been a bohemian in college?, who'd worn a velvet smoking jacket and long hair, hung out in bars and brothels and consorted with thieves and other lowlifes, the young man who'd finally refused to follow his father's profession (engineer) or become a lawyer but had insisted on being a writer and had married a divorced woman, the young man who'd become an atheist and withstood the wrath of his father. When his father read Dr Jekyll, he could easily have thought that his renegade son had seen the light.

Stevenson didn't think he'd written a religious tract. He thought he'd written about man's dual nature, about the constant war between the better self and the "second and worse" self, which Stevenson called both Satan and the "brute that slept within," echoing ministers who often described man as part devil and part animal. What may have been new was that Stevenson, influenced by Darwin's theory that mankind had evolved from apes, gave Mr Hyde some of the physical features of a monkey. His walk is light and swinging, he can jump like a monkey and his hands are "lean, corded, knuckly" and covered with thick "swart" hair.

Mr Hyde is also much more the size of a monkey than a man. That startled me when I reread the book. The Mr Hydes in movies were large, gross, lumbering, but Stevenson's Mr Hyde wasn't. I'd completely forgotten that when Dr Jekyll drank the magic brew, he shrank; he shrank a lot. Mr Hyde, Stevenson often said, was "a very small gentleman," "particularly small," "dwarfish." When he wore Dr Jekyll's clothes, they were "enormously too large" for him.

I'm sure that Stevenson shrank Mr Hyde to suggest man's monkey origins, and yet I began to wonder if, by making Hyde childlike in size, Stevenson could have been saying something new about evil. Stevenson got the idea for Dr Jekyll and Mr Hyde from a nightmare, from the unconscious, which contains original knowledge, unlike the conscious mind, which is a conglomeration of beliefs current in one's time. Stevenson knew that he got his most creative ideas from the unconscious, from what he called the "Brownies," so that it may be that the "transcendental medicine" Dr Jekyll drinks shrinks him almost to the size of a child to express a truth that Stevenson's unconscious mind knew: that the origin of evil is not Satan lurking within man or the ghost of our brute ancestors but had something to do with childhood.

In Dr Jekyll's personal confession of his descent to ruin, he said of Mr Hyde: "That child of Hell had nothing human; nothing lived in him but fear and hatred," which "raged within him like a tempest." His imagination brimmed "with images of terror," his "soul" boiled "with causeless hatreds." Could Stevenson have been remembering the tormented psyche of his childhood created by the religious tracts his nurse read to him? Could the rage that seethed within Mr Hyde's soul have been hatred of his nurse for constantly terrifying him? Could it also have been Stevenson's rage at the father who wanted to totally control his life?

Mr Hyde's sudden eruptions of rage are the only evil that comes alive in the book. The first instance is his encounter with a girl about eight or ten who, running down a street, runs into Mr Hyde and falls down. Instead of helping her up, he "trampled calmly over the child's body and left her screaming on the ground." Later, on a night the moon was full, Mr Hyde is again walking the streets and chances upon an old "gentleman with white hair" who has an air of "innocent and old-world kindness." He no sooner asks Hyde for directions than Hyde breaks out "in a great flame of anger," stamped his foot, brandished his heavy, gnarled cane, and clubbed the old man "to earth." After trampling on him, Hyde hails down "a storm of blows," so violent that the man's bones are "audibly shattered" and his body "jumped upon the roadway." "With a transport of glee," Dr Jekyll later recalled, he "mauled the unresisting body, tasting delights from every blow."

Stevenson never murdered anyone. The murder was a fantasy, whose gruesome details reminded me of Lori Schiller's fantasy of killing the family dog, of "hitting him and hitting him," though he foamed "at the mouth" and writhed on the floor, of continuing to hit him until he lay dead, blood oozing "from his ears and mouth." The dog Lori clubbed to death in her childhood fantasy was both herself and the father whose perfectionist demands kept her on too tight a leash. When she got schizophrenia and could face her feelings without disguise, Lori had a "grisly fantasy" of killing and mutilating not a dog but her father.

The man Stevenson killed in his story may also have been his father. Not long after Dr Jekyll described Mr Hyde's delight as each blow hit the old man, he mentioned "the days of my childhood, when I had walked with my father's hand," the father who, like the man Hyde killed, was "high in public estimation." Moreover, Dr Jekyll, when he turned into Mr Hyde, once destroyed a painting of his father.

Below the surface of Stevenson's trite tale of sin and damnation, could he have been saying that the seemingly causeless rage that flames up in humans has its roots in childhood? Was that the unconscious reason he made Mr Hyde almost the size of a child? I don't know, but I do know that when Stevenson, writing as Mr Hyde, mauled a stand-in for his father, "tasting delights from every blow," he was tasting delights enjoyed by virtually all children.

"Lizzie Borden Took an Axe"

In January 1998 when then President Clinton swore that he had not had sex with that Lewinsky woman, no one believed him and dirty jokes about Clinton's sexual habits sprang up all over the country. Similarly, in June 1893 when Lizzie Borden was acquitted of killing her father and stepmother, an anonymous jingle swept through America that registered the public's conviction that, though a jury had pronounced her innocent, she damn well was guilty:

> Lizzie Borden took an axe
> And gave her mother forty whacks;
> When she saw what she had done
> She gave her father forty-one!

People, especially children, love that jingle, which was created and survives because it taps into a desire that springs up early in the hearts of most of us—to kill our parents and get away with it. The public was sure Lizzie Borden was guilty because of their own guilty secret.

Lori Schiller concocted what she called "horrible fantasies" of stabbing and shooting her parents, pouring gasoline around their house and burning them up. She didn't do it because she had schizophrenia. A grade-school teacher showed me a series of drawings done by two boys in her class which showed figures labeled Mom and Dad hanging by the neck, lying prone with knives sticking into them, kneeling under the axe of a guillotine and impaled on sharp black spikes. When the psychiatrist, Dr Dorothy Lewis, was in training, she had to spend time observing a nursery class, where a preschooler, bored with blowing soap bubbles, told the teacher that "he wanted to go to the costume corner, play soldiers and kill people" (*Guilty by Reason of Insanity*, 1998).

Virtually every child, no matter how meek and polite, has had killing fantasies, though they may be a mere firefly flash escaping from the dark of the taboo. Most of us commit our first murders in childhood, fantasy murders. The first real victim of serial killers is often a dog, but long before they bash the dog, they've killed a family member in a fantasy. Few children become killers, but throughout history, billions of children, in the safety of fantasy, have committed murders and got away with it.

Burying Mr Hyde

A child who chalked "I HATE MY FATHER" on a sidewalk near my house would soon forget the hatred in his or her heart, and would swear on a Bible—"Cross my heart and hope to die"—it never existed. The "I hate you, I hate you" that chants in children's heads when they're mistreated gets fainter and fainter. Most of their fantasies of family murder, like dead bodies weighted with concrete blocks, sink to the bottom of their unconscious. They usually stay there. If Lori Schiller hadn't got schizophrenia, she would have remained unaware of wanting to kill her father. Without the grace of Ecstasy, I wouldn't have become aware of the hatred that pervaded my life. I would have been like Oliver Sacks' patient who, until the frontal lobes of his brain were damaged, was completely unaware he'd committed a murder (*An Anthropologist on Mars*, 1995).

Why do children bury their killing fantasies? They have to. The Mr Hyde that develops in children is not a welcome guest in the family. Children whose angry passions rise soon learn to conceal them. In Biblical times, kings required slaves, when in their presence, to smile and look cheerful, literally on pain of death; kings wanted to pretend that their slaves liked their servitude. Similarly, Franklin Roosevelt's mother wanted everyone in her family, no matter how they felt, to look happy. She believed that the social rule that one should always look pleasant ought to be a household rule. No wonder that little Franklin was described as "always bright and happy." The mother of the cellist, Jacqueline Du Pré, taught her never to show her anger, which was why she smiled all the time. A lot of us display the Jimmy Carter, "I aim to please" smile, the grin of chimpanzees when they have to ingratiate themselves with superiors. When I was a child, a man who passed me in the street told me to "Smile. Nothing could be that bad." The happy-face cartoon was created and became popular because parents want to see a smiling face on their children who, eager to please their frightening parents, smile.

Children are anxious to keep their Mr Hyde hidden for another reason. They want their parents to believe they belong to the superior race, the good race. When the poet Robert Browning was a little boy, the first sermon he preached was, "Be good!" One of our deepest drives becomes to pass as one of the good people. At the beginning of Dickens' *Great Expectations*, the child Pip is wandering at twilight in a graveyard when up from behind a gravestone looms a massive, filthy, chained escaped convict, who growls, "Keep still, you little devil, or I'll cut your throat." Pip's shock and terror are what ours would be if the mass of hate we keep in chains suddenly broke free and we were revealed not to be a good, civilized citizen, but a monstrous outlaw, ready to cut someone's throat. We therefore deny that we hate, even to ourselves.

In July 1999 in an A&E report, "Teenagers Under the Gun," a group of fifteen high school students in Coral Shores, Florida, who called themselves Evilcon, admitted that they went on three day retreats to play blood and gore video games. They used the games, they said, to vent their aggression, but, they insisted, since they killed only fictional people in games, they were not violent. That reminded me of a headline I'd seen the previous February: "Defendant Called 'Full of Hate'." The defendant was a white man who was being tried for viciously killing a black man in Jasper, Texas, and he was full of hate, but the headline seemed to me smug, to imply that the killer, because he was full of hate, was unlike the rest of us. Whenever someone crosses the line from fantasy to reality and actually kills, we puff ourselves up as superiors, as members of the good race not the bad race that hates, or as I once put it in a poem:

> The child is taught to smooth its rage into a smile;
> It sets its mask and looks civilized.
> Hate, like a felon, is walled out of sight;
> Breakouts are promptly manacled by guilt.

Mr Hyde at Large

The other night in a TV drama a church functionary said that without moral rules and restraints we'd all be devils, a fundamentalist belief that was held by parents long before organized religion became our home away from home. Societies, copying families, have also believed that civilization depends on keeping our Mr Hyde in chains. Freud said that without strong parental coercion children would remain savages. (*The Future of an Illusion*, 1927).

The coercions of home, church and state are strong, but despite beatings, Commandments, laws and social pressure, Mr Hyde is always making his presence known. Just as locking criminals in jails doesn't reform them, neither does locking Mr Hyde in a dungeon in our unconscious reform us. For Mr Hyde can't be locked up. We think our hate is hidden, but it's hidden in plain sight. Children commit murders in their heads and when they grow up, they draw fantasy murders in comic books, write about them in mystery novels, movies and video games. Children imagine their parents blown up in airplanes and when they grow up, they love to watch disaster movies. The shootings, the fights, the cars bursting into flames on TV every night are our collective Mr Hyde exposed on film.

Unfortunately, Mr Hyde doesn't always remain chained in fantasy; the mad dog gets loose. Some children grow up who have an epileptic seizure of hate, which results in a flesh and blood murder, most often of a family member. A few children grow up and become the mass murderers who enter mosques, office buildings and other public places and shoot many people. Their guns and rifles are the material manifestations of the hate in their hearts, the hate that has blown up cars and buses in cities all over the world and has caused every war. The thousands of pounds of ammunition that were stored in the Branch Davidian compound in Waco, Texas was the amount of hate stored in the collective heart of that religious community, which in 1993 incinerated them, the same hate that in 1995 blew up the Federal Building in Oklahoma City, the same hate that on September 11, 2001, crashed into the twin towers of the World Trade Center, the same hate that built up to the critical mass that produced the hydrogen bomb. When Richard Rhodes was a child he had to endure the daily cruelty of a vicious stepmother. Years later when he was in psychotherapy, he dreamed that mushroom clouds were "boiling up" from the city where his persecution took place (*A Hole in the World*, 1990). The cruelties we endure in childhood can make us want to blow up the world:

> Let the nuclear wars begin,
> Kin of the killer within.

Yet even nuclear blasts are local and mild compared to the acts of hate destructing among us—the millions of unkind deeds and words humans commit against each other every day. Mr Hydes manifest everywhere, but unlike the Mr Hydes on the cover of paperbacks and in movies, they don't have evil faces. The Mr Hydes we encounter in daily life look like you and me.

I was at a conference on violence in children, listening or rather falling asleep to a dull talk on evolution when my nodding head snapped up. A human grenade had gone off; a furious voice was screaming, "This is supposed to be a conference on childhood and violence!" I looked around. The chairman of the conference was on his feet, his face red, his finger pointed at the culprit. The chairman was right: the talk had had nothing to do with childhood. But why should that trigger such rage?, which sent a shock wave throughout the room until the man who was giving the talk apologized, then babbled a few words about childhood violence. Two more times during the conference the chairman's Mr Hyde distorted his usual genial face, but since he was the head honcho, no one dared to rebuke him, just as when we're children we don't dare to rebuke an angry parent.

Because of his superior status, the chairman felt free to "blow" more than the rest of us, but almost everyone has a grenade within that can go off unexpectedly. Who hasn't during an argument felt a flash of rage flare up from who knows where?, rage that's far more than the occasion requires, rage that can turns us into fire-breathing dragons. Our blood boils, we see red, we go berserk, ballistic. On April 14, 1998, I heard on the radio that during a fraternity hazing at a Maryland university the pledges were spanked so hard with paddles that they had to be hospitalized. The Mr Hyde in their soon-to-be 'brothers' had got loose.

Dr Jekyll needed a powerful drug to get his Mr Hyde to come out of hiding, and many of us also take drugs to give our Mr Hyde free rein. We get drunk to make it easier to beat or rape, or simply to rage. An Israeli friend who grew up in a kibbutz had a father who, after an extra glass of wine, would smash dishes, sweep books off bookcases, knock down lamps, overturn tables and roar through the house like a whirlwind while his children cowered. Methamphetamines, a drug popular in California in the late 1990s, will, if taken long enough, change the chemis-

try of the brain and make some people paranoiac. One man encased himself in a M60 tank and crashed into cars and into the plate glass windows
of stores. That drug did damage the man's brain, but the hate it let loose
had been brewing since childhood.

Epidemic in modern society are what's called "road rage" (cutting in
front of cars on the highway, hurling curses into car windows), "airline
rage" (passengers assaulting flight attendants), and many other kinds of
"rages," like the woman in a grocery check out line who beat up another
woman who had more than twelve items in her cart. You'd think that
when your team wins a big game, Mr Hyde wouldn't be part of the celebration, but more and more often the winning team celebrates by going
on rampages and committing mayhem (torching cars, flipping them over,
fist fights, looting).

It's Mr Hyde who intimidates, browbeats and bulldozes. It's Mr
Hyde who spits out, "You idiot!" "Bitch!" "Pig!," and who strafes people
with the ethnic bullets of Kike, Nigger, Spic, Jap, Whitey, Polack, Chink,
Frog, Wop, Kraut, Mick. Backbiting is a Mr Hydean pleasure, the verbal
equivalent of stabbing someone in the back. Gossip can be verbal poison.
Wit often slashes. A catty remark is a cat scratching someone. We pound
down judgments on each other as if with a gavel. Candidates for office
run TV ads that crucify their opponents. We chew someone out. We cut
someone down to size. We cut him dead at a party. Tell her to drop dead.
We poke fun at people. We roast a friend. We give someone enough
rope to hang himself. Wishing that looks could kill, we look daggers at
our enemy or give her the evil eye, the ancient equivalent of the ray gun
in science fiction. It's Mr Hyde who boasts about his wealth and achieve-
ments so others will burn in the fire of envy.

It's Mr Hyde who tells truths that hurt. I proudly showed off the first
sweater I'd knitted to my cousin Selina, an accomplished knitter, who
could not choke out one kind word. "Let me show you how to sew a
seam right," she said, tapping her index finger hard into the errant seam
on my shoulder. It was Selina who said to a friend's child, "Your mother
told me you were getting fat, and you are," and then looked surprised
when the child cried. Selina should have read William Blake's, "A truth
that's told with bad intent/ Beats all the lies you can invent," except that
she'd insist on pain of death, that she'd meant well. She had no idea that,
just as Mr Hyde bludgeoned an old man to death, truth-telling was her
bludgeon. I know she didn't know her Mr Hyde had come out because I
once heard her proudly say that she was incapable of hate.

We deny we hate because we don't see it in ourselves. The millions
who get their daily dose of shoot-em-ups on TV don't think they're like
the killers in the programs but like the guys living with gusto in the beer
ads. The hate we may swear on a Bible we don't have is alive and kicking in others.

Chapter 14 **Original Sin**

Sinners, Beasts and Savages

If readers of Dr Jekyll and Mr Hyde had got the faintest whiff of my theory that Stevenson unconsciously knew that the hate in human beings is generated in children by family life, it wouldn't have become a best-seller. The book became and remained popular because Mr Hyde's hate was explained in ways people approved of, as the devil within us or as a throwback to our monkey ancestors, in either case, as an inborn force.

That inborn force for centuries was called original sin, a theory that was turned into a World War I cartoon that showed an infant emerging from a hatched egg brandishing a bayonet, delivering the message that evil is in the egg. That cartoon was a modern version of Genesis 3, in which the first humans God created disobeyed one of his orders, thus making not only themselves sinners but all their progeny. Or, as a seventeenth-century American schoolbook, *The New England Primer*, explained to its ultimately five million young readers: "In Adam's Fall, We sinned all." But how could Adam and Eve have been capable of sin since God (in Genesis 1) said he'd created them in his own image, and God was perfect?

Trying to solve that conundrum has plagued religious thinkers. In the fifth century, for example, Augustine thought he'd solved the problem when he said that man disobeyed God because the pleasures of the flesh had made his will imperfect. Paul had previously pointed out that the body isn't "for lust; it is for the Lord" (1 Corinthians 6:14), and Augustine explained that the pleasures of intercourse and orgasm drowned us in fleshly sensations, sucked us into human love, so that we utterly forgot the love of God. But Augustine may have said that the act of sex (not, for example, overeating) made our will defective because of his own difficulty in controlling his sexual drive. He's famous for asking God to give him "chastity … , but not yet."

Some scholars contend that Augustine did not blame sex for the fall, but after Augustine most Christian divines preached that sin was transmitted to each generation through the "loins" (the sex act), as if Adam's initial act of disobedience changed his "seed" permanently so that humans were forever after born with what Lamarck in the early nineteenth century would call an acquired trait, in this case a propensity to sin.

Not everyone believed in original sin. Earlier theologians, like Pelagius, a contemporary of Augustine, had said that babies were born innocent and became sinners only when they chose to act badly, and they had the choice because God had given mankind free will. But, if we were created in God's image, how could our will become defective? On the other hand, many people have argued that humans have no free will, that everything was predestined by God, though some people insisted that that didn't mean God predestined Adam and Eve to fall. You figure it out. I can't.

Round and round the religious merry-go-round spun, keeping theologians in a whirl of words, words, words for centuries, and ordinary Jews and Christians obediently accepting that, in some way or another, in Adam's fall, we sinned all. In 1677 when Leeuwenhoek put semen under the powerful microscope he'd developed and saw wriggling spermatozoa for the first time, he saw each sperm (he drew pictures of them) as an homunculus, a human-in-little, who, according to the theory of original sin, would already be a sinner. Theologians liked to explain that just as a newborn viper already has the nature of an adult viper, a human newborn already had the wicked nature of an adult human. It was therefore accurate to call children "limbs of Satan," "imps of hell," "the devil's spawn" since the devil was roiling within them. Fear that the devil might break loose was one reason newborns were tightly swaddled. When a baby cried, what parents heard was not a cry for help, but the baby's sinful nature making its loud presence known. A nineteenth-century Polish schoolteacher who beat his students mercilessly concealed his sadism behind his theory that the "Evil Spirit" was located in the buttocks.

When Darwin put forth his theory that humans hadn't originally been created in the image of God but of apes, many people no longer had to figure out how beings created in the image of God could have become evil. For if mankind had evolved from animals, there was no fall from unity with a perfect God. The German biologist Ernst Haeckel thought that embryology proved Darwin's theory because the embryo and fetus repeated the history of the race—from a single cell in salt water, to backbones like reptiles, to gills like fish, to a hairy body like the first mammals, and so on.

Thomas Huxley, the late nineteenth-century popularizer of Darwin, became an agnostic, a word he invented. His loss of religion required him to find another explanation for evil, and he used Haeckel's theory as the basis for his contention that at birth we've evolved only to the level of brutal, aggressive savages struggling to survive. Freud, influenced by his times, also thought that humans, having progressed in utero from fish to ape, were born little savages who knew "nothing of any restrictions on [their] instincts," who were aggressive, lustful, incestuous, killer cannibals (*The Future of an Illusion*, 1927). Melanie Klein, a disciple of Freud, described the baby as eager to bite the breast that fed it, a bite that merged cannibalism, incest, lust and the desire to kill in a pint-sized savage.

Back in the sixteenth century, when John Calvin said that the "whole nature" of children "is a seed of sin," he at least didn't mean that newborns were born lusting after mama or papa. Freud added a new vice to the sin of being born a baby.

Freud and the Freudians may not have believed in original sin, but they believed in original savagery. Every baby is born "a selfish, jealous, impulsive, aggressive, dirty, immodest, cruel, egocentric and conceited animal," to quote Ernest Jones in his biography of Freud. W H Auden made that Freudian gospel the subject of his poem, "Mundus et Infans" (1942), which begins, "Kicking his mother until she let go of his soul," and goes on to describe the baby as aggressive, self-centered, competitive, "resolved, cost what it may, to seize supreme power," a "cocky little ogre," a "beast."

Popular culture eagerly waved the 'savage' banner. In Richard Hughes' *A High Wind in Jamaica* (1929), a group of English children from Jamaica are held captive on a pirate ship and prove to be worse than the pirates. A ten-year-old girl kills the captain, demonstrating, said Hughes, "the depravity of human nature." The book quickly became a bestseller in England and America, as had Dr Jekyll and Mr Hyde before it, and as William March's *The Bad Seed* did in 1954. The bad seed was in this case Rhoda, an eight-year old serial killer, who forced her mother to learn the lesson that "violence" is in every heart, where it lies "like a bad seed," "ready to appear … in all its irrational dreadfulness." The same moral lesson was also preached by William Golding in *Lord of the Flies* (1954), another bestseller in England and America, in which school boys who were wrecked, naturally, on a tropical island, quickly reverted to man's ancestral savagery—to superstition, cruelty, warfare and murder. T S Eliot, a convert to Anglo-Catholicism, pronounced the novel theologically sound.

Innate savagery had already been pronounced scientifically sound. When Raymond Dart, a paleoanthropologist well-known in the 1950s, found piles of ancient animal bones in caves, he concluded they were stockpiles of weapons and that man had originally been a killer ape whose murderous instincts led him, for example, to use a leopard jaw with a tooth in it to gouge out eyes, a theory about original human nature that was treated as true in the movie, *The Planet of the Apes* (1968), and it's five sequels.

In the nineteenth century the public and most scientists had been horrified by Darwin's theory that man's ancestors had been apes. They protested that humans, as God clearly said in Genesis, were unlike animals, that they were a separate creation made in his own divine image. But by the end of the twentieth century the public reveled in being totally ape. Men, especially, liked to point out that they rape, fight and wage war because chimpanzees rape, fight and wage war. Ignorant humans for centuries had believed they were polluted by some ancient sin, but science had discovered the truth; humans were polluted by the ancient genes they'd inherited from their closest animal relatives, the chimpanzees.

But wasn't the new theory merely a scientific explanation for the old theory of original sin? To such questions as—Are we born with a seed of sin that inevitably flowers into evil? Are we born programmed to get drunk and commit mayhem? Is the urge to create guns latent in our genes? Were the "causeless hatreds" that Stevenson said were boiling in Mr Hyde's soul already simmering when Dr Jekyll was born?—to such questions, both religion and science have answered, "Yes."

In regard to original human nature, religion and science are not at odds. Scientists compared the genes of chimpanzees and humans and discovered that 98.6 percent of chimpanzee's genetic material are the same as humans'. But that small difference had obviously made an enormous difference physically and intellectually, though, just as obviously, not in regard to violence. Therefore, among the genes we inherit from chimpanzees must be the ones that make us violent. They haven't been located yet, but we have complete faith they will be, for we want to go on thinking that babies, like Pandora when she opened her box, bring evil with them into the world.

Why has mankind had such a bias against babies? I think it is a bias, a prejudice that existed long before religious or scientific theories about sinful or savage human nature, theories that supported an already existing prejudice. What's been overlooked in explaining our ancient bias against babies is a fundamental fact, one that's very real and that is innate in babies.

Original Shits

When Dr Frederick Leboyer was studying how babies were born, he observed that right after birth women were reluctant to touch their babies. He sensed they were feeling an "immense disgust" because babies emerge next to where we have bowel movements, are delivered by bearing down as if at stool, and are "warm and sticky" (*Birth Without Violence*, 1974).

In late May 2000, I heard on the radio that a woman had given birth to her baby while sitting on an airport toilet and, after covering it with toilet paper, left to catch a plane. Many women who want to get rid of their babies give birth on the toilet. It's a convenient receptacle for the blood and other detritus, and, expresses their wish to flush the baby away like feces. Feces, because they're dirty, were given a name that became a 'dirty' word, shit; babies, because they're associated with the dirty place where women shit have often been treated like disposable waste.

From ancient times unwanted babies were disposed of in dumps. Just outside of Jerusalem in a valley called Gehenna, parents used to burn their children alive as sacrifices to Gods. Gehenna was later turned into the city dump. The fires in which the children had been burned alive became the fires that perpetually smoldered in the dump, which stank from rotting garbage, among which was undoubtedly unwanted babies. In modern cities all over the world newborns are regularly thrown into dumpsters, disposal sites that are chosen because they're handy but also because the babies are, like garbage, unwanted and, live or dead, stink like dumps.

Shitting is sometimes called, "taking a dump," and babies take a dump where they are and their smelly shit has to be cleaned up. To put off the unpleasant job as long as possible was another reason (besides keeping the devil within them from breaking out) why babies used to be swaddled, their whole bodies (except for the face) tightly wrapped in bands of cloth, a process that could take two hours and so wasn't done often. Babies would stew in their pee and shit for days. Mothers or nurses used to hang swaddled babies up on a nail, not only so they were free to go about their business but to get away from the smell.

In September 1999, a little girl in southern California was found chained in a crib and covered with shit, which reminded me of my infant self, whose face used to be wiped with her shitty diaper. I didn't have to be chained to my crib. I hardly stirred because I'd learned who I was. By covering me with smelly shit, my mother had established my identity: I was shit.

You don't have to be covered with shit when you were a baby to think of yourself as shit. Edward, Prince of Wales, didn't confess, "I feel such a bloody little shit," because his nannies didn't change his royal nappies. Lori Schiller's mother kept her clean, but when Lori was in the hell of schizophrenia, her Voices would often yell, "You are shit." "You're nothing but a piece of shit," "a worthless piece of shit." Lori's Voices were merely saying more loudly one of the favorite put-downs of inner critics. Why? Perhaps because when our diapers were changed, our mothers turned up their noses or held their breath. Who can blame them? It's the rare parent who can manage not to. But unless the parent is genuinely not repelled, babies get the message that their shit is disgusting, which to them means that *they* are disgusting. Parents may beat bad children on their bare buttocks because that's where they once had the nasty job of cleaning up their children's smelly shit.

When we want to make people feel bad about themselves, we call them a shit, a piece of shit, a shithead, an asshole, which is a shit by *association*. "Ein Stück Scheisse" [German for "a piece of shit"] was the pet name the father of the therapist, Fritz Perls, smeared him with. Children smear school outcasts by flinging the word, "Shit!" at them, and at high school and college hazings both girls and boys fling the real stuff at kids they dislike. When we say to someone, "You're a shit!" we mean they're a bad person. The insult hits home because we're reminding them of the time when their shit disgusted others and made them feel they were bad. A sinner was originally a shitter.

Mater Ecclesia, the Holy Mother Church, was the name the early Christian church gave itself because it wanted to become the true "mother of us all," a far better mother than women were. The Church used to say that whereas women gave us mortal birth, only the Holy Mother Church could give us immortal birth. But to become immortal we had to reborn by the Church, a birth far superior to the foulness of physical birth. Birth was foul because it took place next to where women shit, so that newborns were often smeared with shit. Church officials, who'd all had to undergo the indignity of birth, may therefore have decreed that to be born of a woman was to be born in sin, and replaced baptism by shit with baptism by the Holy Mother Church, who washes away the stench of human birth by purifying us with Holy water.

My theory of the fundamental origin of baptism may be a stretch, but that Christians, like everyone else, equated sin with shit is not. Otherwise, Ignatius of Loyola (1491-1556) wouldn't have said that a sinner as great as he was should be exposed on a dunghill after he died.

Groups judged to be morally defective are often accused of being dirty and smelly like shit. Hitler said that Jews were sly, cowardly degenerates, and filthy and foul-smelling. Americans said that Indians were lawless heathens, and dirty and stinking. Whites said that blacks were more like animals than humans, and dirty and stinking. Because of their moral inferiority, untouchables in India were barred from doing any work except shit work (cleaning latrines, sweeping shit from streets, scavenging dumps), and of course they were dirty and stank. To stink became the sewer gas of the racially impure.

Montaigne reminded us that "the greatest prince in the world never sits but on his ass" because we don't like to think of our superiors with asses bared, shitting. I didn't. I never forgot the moment when I was a child and walked into the teachers' lounge to deliver a note and smelled shit coming from the adjoining bathroom. My horror wrestled with my incredulity. Morally dirty people like me shat, but august creatures like teachers? Can you imagine God shitting? Wouldn't it be blasphemy to imagine Christ, even when he was mortal Jesus, shitting? One of Michael Jackson's fans asked him: "Do you go to the bathroom?"

Shit, the real smelly stuff, has often been used to deliver the message that someone is a sinner. Greek peasants were so angry at Kazantzakis for depicting them in *Zorba the Greek* as greedy and coarse that when he died in 1957 they shat on his grave. When parents get angry at bad children, they sometimes plunge their heads into shit-befouled toilet bowls. When children get angry at parents, they may shit on the floor. They know what offends parents, and so do dogs. Friends of mine had a dachshund who used to shit on their bed whenever he was left alone too much. Burglars, to add insult to injury, sometimes leave their brown, smelly calling cards. In August 1997 a New York City policeman assaulted a Haitian immigrant by ramming a broom handle up his rectum, then shoving it into his mouth, which was his way of saying, "You're a dirty asshole. I equate you with shit." The policeman, when he went to jail, may have been told he was a shit in similar ways. Not only did he have to bend over and have a finger rammed up his rectum when he was strip-searched, he may have had his head shoved in a toilet bowl as an insult or as a prelude to the deeper insult of buggery.

Because water cleansed us of our first offense—foul-smelling shit— humans may have the misconception that water has the power to cleanse us of sin. Hindus are cleansed of sin when they submerge themselves in the holy Ganges; Christian are cleansed of sin when a holy man submerges them in water or sprinkles them with water. When children say 'dirty' words, we may wash out their mouths because we washed off their dirty behinds when they were babies.

Shit became the outward and visible sign of the sin within, which may be why humans developed the further misconception that washing out their insides cleansed them of sin. In the late 1940s in Nebraska a two-year-old was sent to stay with her grandmother while her mother had a second baby. Her grandmother, who was religious, seized the opportunity to cleanse her granddaughter of sin by giving her twice daily enemas to "wash out the bad in her," which is how she explained it to the child.

Babies and children may have been given so many enemas and adults may have taken so many because of the confusion of shit and sin. Not shitting regularly was a sign of sickness, and since sickness was thought to be caused by sin, if you were full of shit, you were full of sin. That being so, cleansing the body of shit could also cleanse it of sin. Madames at high class brothels report that their clients frequently request high colonics, perhaps to wash themselves clean of the sin of whoring. The members of Marshall Applewhite's Heaven's Gate cult had to take daily enemas to keep themselves clean inside, a way to insure that their resurrected bodies would be pure enough to be picked up by alien space craft and transported to heaven, which was their hope when they committed communal suicide in March, 1997. Many people fast, take laxatives, or colon cleansers because they think their intestines are dirty. The slogan of "Elimitox, 21 Days toward Detoxification" is, "How much cleaner you can feel inside and out!" People would probably not be addicted to purgatives if they hadn't been brought up to think of themselves as sinners.

People shouldn't have confused shit with sin. If they'd properly appreciated shit, it wouldn't be a dirty word. Shit is the remarkable feat that begins at the mouth, the end product of the food processing of the intestines, of assimilating what the body can digest and getting rid of the rest. If people in the past understood the complexities and efficiencies of digestion, they might have regarded shit as another example of God's divine ingenuity. When we call someone a shit, we're insulting shit, which is necessary for health, whereas what are the redeeming features of a shit? Benjamin Franklin said that farting would be socially acceptable if it didn't smell bad. Shit got a bad reputation because it smells bad, and so, at the beginning, may babies have acquired their bad reputation.

My theory that shit and sin merged in human minds may be full of shit, but I've discussed what's usually regarded as an unmentionable subject because I'm trying to understand the actual reason why babies were treated like shit, as offensive, bad, unworthy of respect, in short, as if they were the worst sinners.

Chapter 15 The Original Sinners

A Despised Race

At present, when pictures of happy boys and girls flood the media, when politicians kiss babies and promise to give every child an equal start in life, when parents try to do the best for their children and say how much they love them, it's hard to believe that for most of history children were labeled animals, imps of hell, little savages and bad seeds, that they were the objects of the most virulent and widespread race prejudice known to man. I say race prejudice because they were despised as an inferior race, like the Untouchables in India. The Hindu religion created four castes, from the Brahmins (the religious leaders) down to the Sudras (the craftsmen). The rest of the population, the Untouchables, were without a caste, a vast underclass who could be reviled, beaten, starved and killed without consequence, like children.

Hardly anyone registered that children were mistreated. Beating children, using them for sex and treating them with contempt were taken for granted, like eating and sleeping. In *Tom Jones* (1749), Henry Fielding didn't include any account of Tom's childhood. No need. As Fielding explained, "Nothing happened worthy of being recorded." Samuel Johnson dismissed childhood as a time when one cannot truly be said to be alive, rather like the Brahmins who, when they classified the four stages of life omitted infancy and early childhood, designating the first stage of life as the time when boys started school. Because people thought that what happened to children didn't matter, studying the history of childhood didn't become a separate branch of scholarship until the second-half of the twentieth century.

Even then, few scholars were interested and the public hardly at all. When the brutal way children were treated was brought to their attention, they were hostile. When in 1994, a collection of quotations about the treatment of children from 2000 BC onward was published, *The Penguin Book of Childhood*, a reviewer in the *Times Literary Supplement* (November 4, 1994) rebuked the editor, Michael Rosen, for presenting a "bleak" picture of childhood: "dismal" stories of children being beaten or sexually abused, of "cruelty, neglect and excessive punishment." He accused Rosen of excluding stories of "children's creativity and playfulness." The reviewer lamented the book's publication near Christmas, for the book, which he said would appeal only to a "sadistic pedophile," might by mistake be given to children or young parents.

If the anthology had been filled with accounts of happy childhoods, it's highly doubtful that the reviewer would have called the editor on the carpet for omitting accounts of the mistreatment of children. The reviewer, blinded by the modern delusion that childhood is the happiest time of life, didn't get the point, that the childhoods the editor document-ed were not unlucky exceptions to the rule of golden childhoods, that golden childhoods have been the exceptions. When he said that the book would appeal only to a "sadistic pedophile," he was inadvertently admit-ting that sadistic pedophiles had more often than not ruled the lives of children.

Trampled On and Left Screaming

The first act of violence that Mr Hyde commits is to trample on a child and leave it "screaming on the ground," an act that typifies the attitude of mankind to children who, for generation after generation, have been beaten, raped, despised and left "screaming on the ground." Virtually no one cared. If child abuse is to stop, people have to care. I therefore decided, though I've already said a fair amount about cruelty to children, that I should include a review of the most common kinds. I had to read the long, bloody history of God's crimes in the Old Testament before his brutality became real to me, before I knew Edward Gibbon was right when he said that God's violence "stain[s] almost every page of the Jewish annals." Violence stains every page of the annals of childhood, violence that must become real to us before it will stop.

Physical Violence

Physical violence often began at birth, when the baby was smacked on the butt after it left the birth canal. We used to think that smack start-ed babies breathing. But would nature have been so stupid as to depend on a human smack for so vital a function? Considering the history of childhood, smacking babies on the butt at birth was an initiation rite, a forecast of smacks to come, baptism into the violence of family life, where parental wrath, like God's, was always "flar[ing] up in a moment" and striking "down in mid course" (Psalms 2:11-12).

Parents didn't beat children because the Bible told them to; the Bible sanctified an ancient, cruel custom that continues to be passed on by each generation of powerful parents doing to their children what was done to them. I know of no one who has described parental wrath more forceful-ly and succinctly than Montaigne (1533-1592): "I have seen" young boys, he said, "attacked, beaten, and flayed by some father and mother insane with wrath! You see them sally forth, their eyes on fire and their throats aroar, often against a babe just come from the breast."

If a judge, "had condemned a criminal out of anger," Montaigne continued, he'd be sent to the gallows, but parents are not prosecuted because the courts take "no notice … as though these … victims were not members of our commonwealth." Adults could try to get justice from the courts; children couldn't. For most of history they were outside the law.

"A man's house is his castle" where even the king couldn't enter, said the law because parents used to be a law unto themselves in the private state called the home. Until late in history, parents could do what they wished to their children without the law intervening. The assumption was that children were under the rule of loving, wise and just governors, but children were generally the helpless victims of unjust and cruel parents, and there was no remedy. Whereas parents who beat, raped or killed someone outside the home were liable to prosecution, parents who beat, raped or killed their children were not. And beat, rape and kill them they did, especially beat them.

When Montaigne described fathers and mothers "insane with wrath" beating children in mid sixteenth-century France, he could have been describing the early twentieth-century father who, "his face black with fury," a face like a "madman" or "murderer" stood ready to "Teach his Boy a Lesson" he wouldn't soon forget. He did, as he'd done many times before. As soon as his son, Alfie, "unbuttoned his pants and let them down on the floor," he bent him "across the kitchen table" and beat him with his leather belt. After the tenth blow, Alfie screamed though he'd sworn not to give Papa the satisfaction. The eleventh blow cut the skin of his buttocks, but Papa lashed down a twelfth blow right into the blood (Shirley Abbott, *The Bookmaker's Daughter*, 1991).

Alfie was the victim of his father's exultant ferocity around 1913 when he was about ten, but I wanted to bring Alfie's beating back alive from the past because beating children continues to be the most common way of trampling on children, and not merely with a slap on the face or the behind. Many children continue to be beaten raw and bloody. In a survey made in the 1970s in West Germany eighty percent of parents admitted to beating their children, a full thirty-five percent with canes. In 1989 almost one thousand West German children died from beatings. In November 1999 in Sunnyvale, California a fifteen-year-old boy was found bound and gagged in his locked bedroom and beaten so badly the police described it as torture. His torture was not exceptional. Social workers frequently uncover similar atrocities and know that most of them remain undiscovered.

I used to wish that an Eyewitness News Camera could be in every home, connected to a central viewing site where the world could observe the daily violence against children. Late in the twentieth century, my wish partly came true. Investigative reporters for programs like *20/20*, *PrimeTime Live* and *Dateline* put hidden cameras in child-care centers and in day-care provided in homes. In addition, some parents, to oversee nannies, installed hidden cameras in their homes. The cameras revealed babies in the crib slapped hard on the face and on the back of the head; babies cowering in fear before a raised arm; a baby picked up and carried by one leg; a baby thrown across a room onto a sofa; a baby kicked as it lay on the floor; a baby held upside down and slapped on the butt to the screaming refrain of "You're bad!"

The nannies and the staff at child-care centers didn't know cameras were observing them. But parents who agreed to have cameras put in their homes also smacked their children across the face and whomped them on the behind. The cameras recorded a little girl thrown on a bed and hit and hit. Why? Because she'd used her mother's lipstick. A child is standing watching TV; her mother orders her to shut it off; the child continues to watch. Screaming, "Shut off the damn TV!" the mother wrenches the child away and gives her a resounding smack on the butt. A child reels from a slap on her face that's supposed to teach her not to pick her nose. A child hits his sister, and daddy hits the child harder to teach him not to hit his sister. Since these parents knew that cameras were recording their actions, they must have regarded such mauling as socially respectable. Alfie-like beatings are no longer socially respectable, so some parents must have restrained themselves until the cameras were shut off at night.

Sexual Violence

The cameras didn't show parents raping their children, which doesn't mean they didn't. Next to beatings, rape is the most common way children have been trampled on and left screaming. A 1994 movie, *Bandit Queen*, filmed the rape of an eleven-year-old Indian girl, whose father, for a cow and a rusty bicycle, forced her to marry a much older man, who said he needed a wife to do the work his aging mother could no longer do. The man wasn't telling the whole truth. He also wanted to rape a child. We see him shove her against a wall, then her huge terrified, trapped eyes, then her mother-in-law, smiling with pleasure and approval, walk out of the room as the screams begin.

Phoolan, the name of the eleven-year-old, was a real child who was raped in 1968, legally raped. Millions of little girls have been legally raped in virtually all countries. It was the custom for girls to be married off when they were very young. The second wife of Mohammed (570?-632), the prophet of the Islamic religion, was nine years old. Until 1924 in England men who liked to rape children could marry a twelve-year-old. But raping little girls outside of marriage was an ordinary fact of life that few people thought was wrong. A first century writer, Petronius, described women standing around a bed clapping while they watched a seven-year-old girl raped, a rape similar to the whorehouse rape of a child featured in the 1978 movie, *Pretty Baby*. Petronius also described men fondling the penises of boys, who were no more exempt from rape than girls. In ancient times many unwanted babies who'd been left in the countryside to die were rescued in order to be sold to brothels, boys as well as girls. Boy brothels flourished in every city.

Brothels featuring children continued to flourish. In the 1880s in London every brothel had at least one child virgin, and midwives could make a living by patching up children who'd been raped so they could be raped again. In the 1990s, child brothels existed in major cities all over the world, especially in third world countries. Forty percent of the two million prostitutes in Thailand were children, most of whom had been sold into sex slavery by their parents. Lust for children also produced the one and one-half billion dollar international child pornography business, which advertised its wares on the Internet. Videos with titles like "Slave Boys in Bondage" sold by the thousands, as did videos featuring alluring Lolitas being raped.

Sexually assaulting one's own children in the privacy of home has always been a fact of family life, a fact that wasn't discussed until the nineteenth century in France when, as Jeffrey Masson has documented, many articles and books were published on the subject. To give one example, Paul Bernard's *Sexual Assaults on Young Girls* (1886) recorded that between 1827 and 1870 in France there were 36,176 cases of children 15 years and under who were sexually assaulted (some as young as four), and that single men were not the sole rapists, that a large number of the cases were acts of incest. Influenced by their work, Sigmund Freud in 1896 was emboldened to give a paper in which he maintained that the cause of hysterical symptoms in adulthood was sexual abuse in childhood. (*The Assault on Truth: Freud's Suppression of the Seduction Theory*, 1984). Freud's paper met with hostility, and the belief continued to prevail that children who claimed to have been raped were lying or the victims of their own depraved fantasies.

Not until fairly late in the twentieth century, when hundreds of thousands of adults and children revealed what used to be closely guarded or 'forgotten' family secrets, did we begin to take in that throughout history millions of parents (mothers as well as fathers) have thought of their daughters and sons as fair sexual game. In the fifth century when Augustine said that the pleasures of sex sucked us into human love so that we utterly forgot the love of God, he was thinking of his own obsession for sex, which he didn't know is a common effect of sexual abuse, and that may also explain his excessive attachment to his mother. Christians will cry sacrilege, but why should Augustine have been spared when in 1984 Dr Henry Smith could say that even as he wrote, experts were reporting "that every two minutes a child in the United States is sexually abused," that "one in every five children will fall victim" ("Notes on the History of Childhood," *Harvard Magazine*, July-August, 1984).

Adults find it hard to stop molesting children. In May 1999, the TV program *Dateline* reported that incest is the most common form of sexual abuse in America. In August 2002, Tom Green, a polygamist, was convicted of child rape for conceiving a baby with a thirteen-year-old, whom he'd made his "spiritual" wife. He was one of an estimated 30,000 Mormons who still practice polygamy, in part because many Mormons like the old custom of having sex with children (April Daniels and Carol Scott, *Paper Dolls: A True Story of Childhood Sexual Abuse in Mormon Neighborhoods*, 1993).

Another sexual brutality of family life that has left children screaming is circumcision. Billions of male infants have had their penises grasped while the foreskin was sliced off. From ancient times onward, little girls in African and Middle Eastern countries had to undergo far worse mutilation. At the end of the twentieth century it was estimated that every year two million girls had their legs held apart (usually by their mothers) while a dirty razor cut off all or part of their clitoris. On a *Law & Order* episode, an Egyptian grandmother who lived in the United States was arranging to have her granddaughter's clitoris excised when the law intervened. "This is not abuse," she indignantly objected. "This is a family matter."

A similar "family matter' went on in China where for centuries little girls had to submit to a mutilation that was as bad as female circumcision. Because men were sexually aroused by women with small feet, the feet of female children were bound, which meant bending their toes under, then tightly binding them so the nails grew into the soles. The girls were in constant pain and their feet were often infected, which sometimes killed them. Those who lived were crippled for life. Add them to the pile of children trampled on and left screaming.

Killing Children

In twentieth-century China, after the government decreed that parents could have only one child, hundreds of thousands of infants (mostly female) were dumped in orphanages where, because of overcrowding and mistreatment, sixty to seventy percent died. According to a *PrimeTime Live* report, these orphanages had "dying rooms," dark rooms where babies lay unfed and unattended. One baby girl called Mai Ming (which means no name) took ten days to starve to death. Babies who were exposed in the countryside died more quickly, often eaten by animals.

The Chinese government did little or nothing about these murders because killing newborns used to be a universal custom. Unwanted Arab babies were buried alive in the sand; Eskimo babies froze to death in the snow; African babies lay in dry streambeds scorching in the sun till they died; female babies in Kaach, India were drowned in milk; female babies in China were strangled. Babies used to be murdered as casually as newborn puppies were drowned. In the thirteenth century, Roman fishermen complained that the dead babies thrown into the Tiber river were clogging their nets. In 1720 in England, Thomas Coram noted on his walks to London the large number of infants thrown on dunghills or on the sides of the road, "sometimes alive, sometimes dead, and sometimes dying." He was unusual. People were so accustomed to equating babies with disposable garbage that on their own walks to London they hardly noticed them. In 1879, 276 babies were reported found dead in London streets. Nowadays, killing babies is frowned upon, so they're hidden in dark plastic bags before being thrown into dumpsters. Every day, virtually everywhere in the world, newspapers report the discovery of dead babies in dumpsters, and, probably, the majority of such babies rot away as if they'd never lived.

Getting rid of unwanted babies became an organized business in Croatia, where midwives taught peasant mothers tried-and-true ways—like mixing gypsum in milk—to kill "fachooks," the Croatian name for illegitimate babies. Louis Adamic, a fachook born in Zagreb in 1889 who managed to survive, later exposed the custom (*Cradle of Life*, 1936), a custom he knew was practiced "nearly everywhere else in Christendom." Legitimate and illegitimate babies, rich and poor, were sent to "baby farms," which were notorious for neglecting babies to death. Babies were also disposed of at home. It was well-known that babies who slept next to their mothers were often 'accidentally' overlaid and smothered to death. Since opium was used to quiet infants as far back as ancient Egypt, overdoses were common. Called "Quietness" in fifteenth-century Italy and "Godfrey's Cordial" in nineteenth-century England, an overdose would quickly send a baby to its grave and many parents off to collect insurance money.

Mothers haven't stopped killing babies. Dr Ronald Reeves, a Chicago Medical Examiner, reported on a 1993 Oprah Winfrey show ("Mothers Who Kill Their Children") that he had autopsied "hundreds, thousands" of children whose diagnoses had been misclassified as natural or accidental when they had in fact been shaken to death, beaten to death or killed in other ways. A large percentage of crib deaths are actually infanticides, it being just as easy as it used to be to put a pillow over a baby's face and smother it. A study published in the August 1999 *Journal of the American Medical Association* revealed that the number of young children who were killed by parents or caregivers had been underestimated by sixty percent.

Killing children remains widespread because it used to be legal. According to the law of *patria potestas* (Latin for "father power"), fathers had total power over their children, including the right to kill them, and I'm not referring to the right to kill babies at birth. A father could kill a child for any reason no matter how old the child was, a right that fathers had for centuries. In the Massachusetts Bay Colony (1628-1684), for example, a father could have a disobedient adult child put to death. This extreme form of patria potestas continues to be practiced in some

Third-World countries. Men in Pakistan commit many "honor killings" of women in the family who commit adultery, seek a divorce, or in other ways defy male rules. Similar killings occur in developed countries. Among sects of American Mormons who remain polygamists, fathers from time to time 'discipline' a child to death, murders that, according to an A&E exposé are rarely reported, even in the twenty-first century. The Christian Science church and other religions keep demanding the right of parents to let a sick child die without calling in medical help.

Abandonment

Children could be got rid of in less direct ways. Hansel and Gretel were led to "the thickest part of the wood" and, their parents hoped, 'lost'. Children were often thrown out of their homes to fend for themselves. Dickens' novels describe the many "Artful Dodgers" who prowled the streets, begging, thieving, scavenging for food and sleeping under bridges. It was estimated that in 1876 there were 30,000 half-naked, half-starved homeless children in London alone. In the late twentieth century in Brazil millions of abandoned children roamed the streets, children who from time to time were shot at like rats to keep their numbers down.

Brazil is a poor country, but many parents in rich countries also abandon their children. An old New Yorker cartoon showed a couple walking down the steps of a hospital, a nurse chasing after them with a bundle in her arms. "You forgot the baby!" was the caption. The truth isn't funny. In the last decade of the twentieth century in America, every month 1000 babies were abandoned in the hospitals where they were born. Others were sold. In 1996 a Florida couple tried to sell their four-day-old twins for $25,000 each. But selling babies was far more common in poor countries like Russia, China and India, where babies were sold to rich Americans for as much money as the traffic would bear.

Child Labor

Throughout history, millions of children were sold to be slave laborers. They still are. In the late 1980s in Pakistan the parents of Iqbal Masih, aged four, in exchange for a small loan, sold him to the owner of a rug factory. For six years he worked at a rug loom to which he was chained for twelve hours a day, surrounded by other children sold to be work-slaves. Children have always worked, and at the earliest possible age. Five-year-old orphans in eighteenth-century England were set to winding silk or making hemp. In 1791 Alexander Hamilton pointed out that one of the advantages of opening cotton mills in America was that factories made children "more early useful" since children were employable after the age of six. The belief that it was good for children to work continued to be so acceptable that in 1915 Scott Nearing, then a professor of economics at the University of Pennsylvania, was fired when he spoke out against child labor.

Nearing wouldn't have been fired a few decades later, but children continued to labor. A 1996 report on worldwide child labor estimated that 250 million children under the age of fourteen worked for fourteen hours a day at ten cents an hour. In Brazil in the 1990s sixty percent of the working population in the country were children between the ages of three and seventeen, who for a pittance performed stoop labor and sprayed pesticides in sugar cane fields. In the twenty-first century many poor parents in West and Central Africa sold their children to entrepreneurs who resold the boys to work in cotton and cocoa plantations and the girls as domestic servants or prostitutes. America doesn't have a clean slate. Hundreds of thousands of the children of illegal immigrants were allowed to labor in the fields, and in the 1990s a Dallas contractor who made clothes for J C Penny and Sears was caught employing children under five.

The cruelties to children I've summed up are of the most brutal kind. I haven't mentioned the less obvious cruelties that have affected virtually every child who's ever lived, cruelties that got a name only in the late twentieth century—emotional abuse—but which has always been endemic in the family, even in seemingly good homes, where children are ignored, rejected, ridiculed, frightened, shamed, lied to, where one child is favored over another or forced to fulfill parental needs and ambitions.

"He was despised and rejected, rejected of men,/ A man of sorrows and acquainted with grief." That song from Handel's Messiah refers to Jesus, whose suffering on the cross is regarded as the ultimate in suffering. But compared to the suffering of children, Jesus' suffering was minor. He was, after all, an adult and knew why he was being crucified. Children don't.

The Greatest Holocaust

Both the English Bill of Rights (1689) and the American Bill of Rights (1791) barred "cruel and unusual punishments," but the bills applied only to adults. Children were not included because what we call child abuse wasn't regarded as abuse. It was accepted without an emotional flicker, much as we watch the daily violence on TV. "Custom will reconcile people to any atrocity," said George Bernard Shaw, and the atrocities people have been most reconciled to are the ones committed against children.

Since Homo sapiens evolved, most of the billions of children born have been treated cruelly. If they were piled up, the pile would reach higher than Mount Everest. All the telephone books in the world wouldn't be enough to list the children who've been mangled in body, mind and spirit. The Holocaust Museum in Washington DC, which memorialized the Jews exterminated by Hitler, only occupies a medium-sized office building. To memorialize the children who were abused in the past, the twenty-nine acres of the Pentagon wouldn't be large enough.

At the end of the twentieth century the population of the world reached six billion, which means that another Pentagon will have to be built as a memorial to the children who are certain to be abused in the twenty-first century. For although fewer children are now beaten and raped and though more children lead happier lives, all the crimes against children committed in the past continue to be committed. In every nation in the world, in cities and in the country, in tenements and mansions, in shacks and middle class homes, in basements and penthouses, children will have to live with drunks, rage-aholics, fanatics of every religion, racists, perfectionists, disciplinarians, and the huge midden heap of abused children will grow.

The Jews think that the Holocaust committed against them was the greatest holocaust in history. It was unique, as every holocaust is, but the greatest holocaust ever committed was not of the six million Jews under Hitler. Nor was the greatest holocaust that of the American Indians, whose population, estimated at 125 million in 1492, was by a series of slaughters reduced ninety percent by the end of the nineteenth century. Nor was the greatest Holocaust the murder of 85 to 100 million people by various Communist regimes from 1917 to 1989. Nor was the greatest Holocaust the uncountable millions who were slaughtered in the name of the God of Wrath, Christ or Mohammed in the planet's many 'holy' wars.

The greatest genocide committed by Homo sapiens has been of its children, and not only because so many millions were murdered, but because those who lived were emotionally shattered. "Almost from childhood she knew that a concentration camp was nothing exceptional or startling but something very basic, a given into which we are born." (Milan Kundera, *The Unbearable Lightness of Being*, 1984).

During the Spanish Civil War David Siqueiros painted a picture of a wailing baby in rags sitting on debris from bombed buildings. The painting is a virtual copy of a news photograph, except that behind the baby is a huge duplicate of its head, its mouth open enormously wide. Siqueiros called the painting *Echo of a Scream*, as if he wanted the baby's scream to echo out of the picture and stop wars. Children have suffered much in wars, but their fundamental suffering hasn't been caused by wars. Siqueiros's screaming baby shouldn't have been sitting on bombed-out rubble; it should have been inside a home, the site where billions of children have been beaten, raped, terrorized, rejected and demeaned day after day, year after year, century after century, and left trampled, "screaming on the ground."

"The history of childhood," said Lloyd deMause, "is a nightmare from which we have only recently begun to awaken" (*The History of*

Childhood, 1974). We haven't awakened much. Despite our atrocious treatment of children, we go on accounting for evil the way we used to, as original sin, original savagery, an aggressive gene inherited from animals, an extra Y-chromosome, or some other innate defect. In the Bible, Adam and Eve are blamed for bringing evil into world. That story has to be a myth because it blames evil, the fall of man, on adults, whereas in the real world adults have blamed children.

In the parable of the woman caught in adultery, Jesus told the mob eager to stone her to death that he who was without sin should cast the first stone. The mob dropped their stones. Jesus then told the woman to go and sin no more. The psychiatrist, Fritz Perls, changed the ending. After the mob dropped their stones, there was a short silence, then the thud of a stone hitting flesh. The woman, terrified, turned around, and her mouth dropped open. "Mother!" she shouted (*In and Out of the Garbage Pail*, 1969). We laugh at the story because, like the best humor, it tells the truth, in this case, that parents have traditionally set themselves up as without sin and cast stones at their children.

In December 1832 a native father in Tierra del Fuego "mercilessly dashed" his infant son "on the stones" for "dropping a basket of sea-eggs." We'd like to think that this murder, recorded by Charles Darwin in his *Journal ... During The Voyage of HMS Beagle*, was what could be expected from uncivilized savages. But what of the twentieth-century parents in civilized countries who smashed babies heads against walls?

"Depraved New World" was the headline of a 1993 review of *Genie*, a book about a thirteen-year-old who'd been tortured by her parents from the day she was born (*Times Literary Supplement*, August 6). The headline was inaccurate. We're not living in a depraved *new* world; the depraved old world is continuing into the present, depravity that has been worldwide. Throughout history, uncivilized savages called parents have tossed unwanted infants onto dunghills, beat them black and blue, locked them into closets, screamed "stupid" at them, forced their huge penises into tiny mouths, vaginas and anuses, cut off their foreskins and clitorises, sold them into slavery, and on and on and on. And yet, these brutes have accused helpless children of being the original sinners, and their blatant passing the buck has been accepted as true.

Parents were the original sinners, adults who set themselves up as Gods who could do no wrong and accused children of being "shaped in iniquity" and "by nature children of wrath." The theory of original sin was a religious rationalization for doing to children what had always been done. Parents didn't beat children because the Bible told them to; the Bible sanctified an ancient, cruel custom. No theologian had to put the idea of original sin into parents' heads. That idea had been put into their heads long before when they were children. Virtually every child who has grown up in a family has been trained to believe they were born bad; the unjust ways they were treated imprinted that lie into their every cell.

Chapter 16   Vigilante Justice

Montaigne said that child victims of parental wrath couldn't get justice because courts didn't regard children as "members of our commonwealth." That Montaigne thought children needed justice was remarkable. The conventional view was that children had no need of courts, that they were guilty without a trial and their parents took care of it.

A dumbfounding idiocy descends upon most adults when they become parents; they become incredibly stupid about children. Emotionally stupid. For when parents hit an adult, they know their victim will want revenge. But when parents discover that, after a beating, their children have fantasies of killing them, parents are shocked and convinced more than ever that they were right to beat them, that children are innately evil.

A friend told me that when he was a boy he spent many happy hours thinking up ways to kill his father, like beheading him with a guillotine. Was he a bad seed at the mercy of his killer genes? Who knows? But I do know that he was at the mercy of a father who frequently beat him for minor offenses, like being late for a meal, or forgetting a chore. If you think the imaginary death sentence the boy meted out didn't fit his father's crime, did the real, severe sentence his father imposed on his son fit his crimes? Would the boy have been merciless if his father hadn't bellowed at him to go outside and cut a switch, "And it better be thick enough!"?

Put yourself in the boy's place. Feel the degradation of having to cooperate in your own punishment. Feel the conflict between the instinct for self-protection and fear of a powerful parent. Feel the mortification at having to bare your behind and bend over to be thrashed. You can't run away, though every sensible cell in your body tells you to. You can't object because you know the beating will be worse. You have to listen to the whoosh of the switch as it comes whacking down, over and over until Simon Legree's arm gets tired. For days afterward when my friend sat down his physical pain and humiliation were resurrected, and his hopelessness, for it seemed to him, a young boy, that he'd be locked forever in his cruel prison. Can you blame him for getting back his self-respect the only way he could? His fantasies of killing his father was the only justice available to him.

In *Time Will Darken It* (1948), William Maxwell confessed to chasing his brother "round and round the summerhouse with a butcher knife." He didn't do it because he was a victim of his chimp genes, but of his brother who, said Maxwell, would get "people and animals to love him and then turn on them suddenly when they were least expecting it."

The family dog's feelings had been so hurt he'd bitten his brother, who wouldn't have turned on the dog or people if a parent, who'd made him feel loved, hadn't turned on him. Children become violent not because a gene that's programmed to go berserk goes berserk, but for a reason.

When I was little, I threw open scissors at my middle sister. I can still see the point of the scissors sticking into her flesh just below the knee and a red drop of blood beneath it. I don't remember why I threw it, but I had gallons of rage stored up, for whenever she was near me, she'd flick her finger against the side of my head, as if to flick a bug away. She was never corrected. My mother had set me apart as the family scapegoat, the one it was okay to hate. Throwing the scissors at my sister was a long overdue retaliation. Mousy me, for the first time in my life, had become the lion who roared.

Mousy me again became a lion when I was eleven. A hurricane had struck the city and as I stood at a window watching huge branches snap off trees and fly through the air, I wished that my older sister, who was out there somewhere in the storm, would be hit by a branch and killed. I felt guilty and puzzled by my murderous wish, for she was the sister I loved. Not until I was in my fifties and had started my inner journey did I remember that she used to sexually and physically assault me in various cellars in the neighborhood. My wish to kill her when I was a child was a stirring of self-worth rising from the coma of my degradation.

Children are vigilantes in fantasy because they can't get justice any other way. Children, no matter how old, who kill their parents are trying to remedy an injustice. Even Lizzie Borden. Whether or not she killed her father and stepmother continues to be debated, but if she did, she had a good reason. She was in an intolerable situation. She was thirty-two and a spinster, to use the demeaning word for older single women still current in the late nineteenth century. Convention still prevented middle class spinsters from venturing into the world and earning a decent living. They had to live at home and, like Lizzie and her older sister, Emma, confine themselves to church activities or other good works, and remain financially dependent on their fathers.

Their father could have given them an abundant life. He was the richest man in Fall River, Massachusetts (his fortune was estimated to be the equivalent of twelve million dollars in late twentieth-century money), but he was the classic miser. He forced his daughters and his second wife to live in the worst part of town in a small house that had no bathroom, only a toilet in the basement. Worse, Lizzie and Emma had to be subordinate to their stepmother, whom Emma hardly spoke to, and whom both of them actively hated when they discovered that their seventy-year-old father was secretly planning to will the bulk of his fortune to his wife and her family. It was about a week after that discovery that their stepmother and father were found axed. Soon after Lizzie was acquitted, she and Emma bought a luxurious house in the best part of town.

If Lizzie did axe them to death, or if, as Frank Spiering argued in *Lizzie*, (1984), she made sure the coast was clear so Emma could do the hatchet job, it's hard to blame them: they were about to be sentenced to a life of poverty. They shouldn't have done what they did, but neither should their father have done what he did. Patria potestas, the total power that Roman fathers used to have over their children from birth to death, was still strong at the end of the nineteenth century, so that Mr Borden felt it was his right to impose his miserly lifestyle on his daughters even after he was dead.

I feel for Lizzie's plight, especially since she paid dearly for her crime. Despite the great wealth she inherited from her father, she was ostracized by most people her age in Fall River. I suspect they couldn't forgive her for acting out their own secret rage at their controlling parents. Consciously though, I'm sure they felt justified because Lizzie had broken two of God's commandments: to honor thy father and mother and not to kill. But in their own way, they cut her dead. After her acquittal, Lizzie went to church, the church she'd gone to for years and where she'd taught Sunday school, the church that had been the center of her social life and whose pastor had defended her after she was arrested, but when she entered the family pew and sat down, everyone sitting near her got up and moved away.

The members of Lizzie Borden's church called themselves Christians, but they were not followers of Jesus. The mercy and forgiveness that Jesus advocated was sometimes preached in churches, but rarely in the secular world, and especially not in the family, which continued to function as if Jesus had never lived. When fathers and mothers dealt with their children, they didn't remember Jesus telling his followers to "never despise one of these little ones." Parents valued children for various reasons—as workers in the home and farm, as a future means of support, as bearers of the father's name into the next generation—but they didn't think of them as "of the kingdom of heaven." Whatever love parents had for their children didn't prevent them from beating them. Parents were the first vigilantes, often no better than lynch mobs, for without a trial, they pronounced their children guilty and punished them forthwith.

In an *Apology for the Christian Faith*, written about 160, Saint Aristides said that what differentiated the new religion, Christianity, from others was that Christians "avoid doing to others what they do not wish done to them" and "are kind." In their relationship with their children, parents remained pre-Christian. The new Christians may have tried to observe the golden rule with adults but I doubt that they tried with their children. Parents continued to do to their children what they wouldn't want anyone to do to them. Otherwise, the history of childhood wouldn't be a history of abuse. If parents had observed this golden rule, if parents had been "kind," their children would have repudiated the Old Testament. Their children and their children's children continued to cling to the Old Testament because it was the world they knew at home. An almighty God would suddenly descend from heaven and punish his children, and so would parents pounce on people less than half their size. If family life hadn't numbed our sensibilities and our reason, we would always have regarded parents who hit children as criminals.

For what respectable boxing match would be allowed between a six foot one-hundred-fifty pounder and a four foot fifty pounder? Yet such assaults are routine in most homes. A parent who hits a child is a bull attacking a puppy. Parents should be forced into a boxing ring with someone three or four times taller and heavier, so the gross wickedness of what they do would hit home. Perhaps, as the giant knocked them about, they'd realize that beating up a midget is the act of a coward. Perhaps, as the giant knocked them about, their fear would also teach them that they beat children not to establish an orderly government at home but a reign of terror.

Beating a child isn't an unfair fight; it isn't a fight, for children are not allowed to fight back. A cat lashes out when threatened, but children are forbidden to. In that regard, parents are worse than torturers. Amnesty International defined torture as an extreme physical and mental assault on a person who's been rendered defenseless. The victim of a torturer is rendered defenseless by restraints. Some children are tied up before they're beaten, but it's hardly necessary. Almost all children are rendered psychologically defenseless so that they cooperate in their own torture.

My friend who was ordered to cut a switch so his father could whip him, should have refused to cut it. With a roar of defiance, he should have kicked his father. He would have lost the fight, as virtually all children would, but children would go down fighting, and fathers and mothers, if they knew they'd encounter resistance, might think twice before beating children. But the great difference in size and strength between torturer and victim makes my wish another fairy tale, like "Jack, the Giant Killer." Except that in November 2001, I heard the Irish actor, Richard Harris, say on 60 Minutes that he was expelled from his Catholic school because when a nun hit him he hit her back! He was one in a million, a kid whose self-respect would not let him submit to violence (and I'm sure injustice), from a so-called holy nun.

Richard Harris was unlike most children, who are rendered psychologically defenseless in the presence of authorities. Parents brainwash them to believe that they can do no wrong, that "true and just are [their] judgments" (Revelation 16:7). Children, being new to the world, trust they're being told the truth, despite the force in them that doubts. A boy whose mother told him that she loved her sons equally at first knew she was lying and had fantasies of killing her. But he couldn't hold on to the truth, and soon believed that Mom mistreated him because he was unworthy of love, a lie that washed the truth (that he was worthy of love) out of his head. Children are forced to submit to injustice from their parents and, what's worse, come to believe that the injustice is just, and sentence themselves to a lifetime of feeling inferior.

"I will not submit to injustice from anyone," said Gandhi, who was forgetting that children have to submit to injustice, that in the home vigilante justice is the only law they know. In the last chapter, I told you about Alfie whose behind was beaten bloody by his father. His daughter was so affected by stories of her father's beatings that when she was an adult, Alfie appeared to her in a dream. Looking like the "aggrieved child" she'd seen in old photographs of him, he climbed into her arms and cried, "Injustice, injustice. Will you right my wrongs?"

When Gandhi was in Bengal, he visited the temple of the mother Goddess, Kali, saw the "rivers of blood" flowing from the many sheep being sacrificed, and was horrified. A friend told him that what with the noise and the drums beating, the sheep felt no pain. Gandhi knew that if the sheep could speak, "they would tell a different tale." "I hold," said Gandhi, "that the more helpless a creature, the more entitled it is to protection by man from the cruelty of man." Children in some ways are more helpless than animals, and for most of history they were not protected by man from the cruelty of man.

Gandhi tried to improve the lot of India's Untouchables by changing their name from one that was a label of "inferiority and shame," to Harijans, which means Children of God. The lot of Untouchables did improve theoretically. In 1931 the Indian Bill of Rights proclaimed that when India was freed from British rule, Indians, regardless of caste, would have equal rights. But when India became free, Harijans continued to be thought of as inferiors and to be demeaned and exploited. Children will also have to submit to injustice until their parents are able to treat them as "Children of God." That will take a while, as John Gray learned. In 1993, he'd published *Men Are from Mars, Women Are from Venus*, which became, as ads put it, a "phenomenal #1 bestseller" (it sold over ten million copies). In 1999, he followed it with *Children Are from Heaven*, a book that began, "All children are born innocent and good." It made the bestseller list once. Parents may piously say we're all God's children, but they treat their own as if they were bad, a judgment children soon agree with.

Chapter 17   **Good Children Know They're Bad**

When the first-century Greek philosopher Epictetus said, "If you would be good, first believe that you are bad," his was no original insight. He was unwittingly echoing the philosophy his parents had taught him, the philosophy parents for eons have dinned into children.

Good Beatings

In the TV documentary, *Influenza, 1918,* a woman, who was five years old during the epidemic, recalled overhearing the doctor tell her mother that "it wasn't necessary to beat me anymore because I wasn't going to live." The child survived the flu, so I assume the beatings resumed. Beatings were believed to be as necessary for children as milk or doses of castor oil. Good beatings made children good. A fundamental doctrine of family life has always been that without beatings, reprimands and other punishments children would remain the way they were born—bad.

The adults who wrote the Bible put no children in the Garden of Eden, only Adam and Eve, who, having been created by God in his own image, were without sin. Children don't appear in the Bible until after the fall when they could be born sinners. According to Christians, not until Christ was sired by God's Holy Spirit did the first sinless child appear on Earth, an event so momentous that wise men from the East traveled to Bethlehem with gifts to pay him homage. From this extraordinary event, recorded in their Holy Book, early Christians could have concluded that the birth of Jesus was ushering in a new era when all children would be born of God's Holy Spirit, especially since their new Messiah preached that children were heavenly beings.

"Of such is the kingdom of heaven," said Jesus when his disciples tried to prevent children from being blessed by him. The disciples had shooed them away because children, like the poor, insane, lepers, and women, were despised. Jesus didn't despise them because they have "guardian angels in heaven, who look continually on the face of my heavenly Father." Once when his disciples were disputing who among them would be "the greatest in the kingdom of Heaven," Jesus stopped the dispute by saying that a child would be the "greatest," and that "unless you turn around and become like children, you will never enter the kingdom of Heaven." "His arm around" a child, Jesus also said that whoever accepts a child, accepted him and his God.

Jesus was suggesting that children were one with God as he was, which he knew was blasphemy. For when he'd said, "My Father and I are one," his fellow Jews had "picked up stones to stone him" to death (John 10:30-31). They did because Jesus had defied Jewish law, which said that though God had created man in his own image, they were not one with God, but lowly sinners ruled by a perfect God up in heaven.

Jesus' idea that the nature of children was like the nature of God was unique for the times. According to some Christian scholars, like A E Harvey, Jesus was the only one in ancient literature who had a high opinion of real children (not children as symbols). It hardly mattered; for centuries, Jesus' words were not taken seriously, which was not surprising. For if people had changed their opinion of children, if they'd believed that children are "of the kingdom of heaven," it would have meant the collapse of a family structure that had been built on the assumption that parents were better than sinful children, whom it was their duty to discipline. In church parents had to acknowledge they were sinners, but at home with their children, they didn't.

The new Christians couldn't deal with Jesus' most radical idea. They continued to have the same view of children as their parents had had toward them. In the New Testament (Hebrews 12:5-14), early Christians discussed the question of disciplining children and concluded that their fathers had been right to beat them, that although the application of the "rod" was "never pleasant," and at times "painful," without beatings they wouldn't have led, "an honest life." The new Christians were not following Jesus but the religion of the Jews, whose Holy Book had many proverbs which told parents that "a good beating" was the best moral medicine for children: "it purges the mind," and humbles "the inmost being" (20:30); it drives out the "foolishness … bound in the heart of a child" (22:15); it imparts "wisdom" and keeps a boy from running "wild" (29:15).

Jesus's high opinion of children remained in the Christian holy book, but, like laws that aren't enforced, his words were dead letter; they weren't regarded as literally true until the nineteenth century. The early Christians decided that Jesus' words referred to them, "the new babes" in Christ. Christians had no foolish notions that a little child was going to lead them out of the wilderness of sin. They were the ones who must lead children out of their wildness by using discipline. Having had many "good beatings" at home, their flesh, which had so often smarted with pain, told them that children were bad.

Impressment

In the past young men were seized by thugs and forced to serve in the army or navy. Children undergo a worse form of impressment; they're forced into lifetime service by the family into which they're born. Men who were impressed were often flogged. The men bore it because they'd been flogged by parents who'd taught them they deserved to be flogged. In the late twentieth century, scientists became eager to clone humans, ignorant that parents had preceded them, that they'd been mass-producing psychological clones—children who, among other likenesses, have an almost identical sense of their badness.

Parents have been able to mass-produce children who feel bad about themselves because it's partly a physiological process, which can begin in the womb where embryos and fetuses have receptors that are able to receive their mothers' feelings. When a mother discovers she's pregnant and doesn't want the baby, she can't help hoping she'll have a miscarriage. If the pregnancy continues, mothers often displace their feelings about their pregnancy onto the baby. When my mother discovered that another baby would soon be pushing up her belly, another baby she'd have to take care of, she became a Nazi and I a Jew who should be exterminated. The excruciating pains of labor may also make mothers judge the baby bad, not the unfortunate fact that humans, unlike chimpanzees, have to give birth to babies with large heads.

No minister at the baptismal font has to tell newborns whose mothers blamed them for their pain or who didn't want them that "by nature" they're sinners. No human magic (sprinkling with holy water) can make them feel they've become "children of grace," for their badness had been impressed upon them by the Great Mother God Herself at a time when humans are most open to influence.

Before I was born, the Pope couldn't have been a more confirmed believer in my original sin than I was, which having to live with my mother ground into me. In grade school my belief about myself once popped out of my unconscious. I was being taught to spell by writing the same word over and over in a column. One day I received my corrected paper back with a huge X on it and was indignant until I saw that, whereas I should have copied 'baby' over and over, I'd copied 'bady'. My heart sank at my stupidity. I didn't know why I'd made the mistake.

Yet, even when mothers very much want the baby they're carrying, they soon make it feel it's a 'bady'. The first sermon that the child Robert Browning preached was "Be good!" He'd already learned he was bad and had to become good. The first duty of parents has traditionally been to teach children they're bad, a lesson children learn in the same physiological way fetuses do: because they have built-in sensors that receive their parents' low opinion of them. No sweet talk can hide from children that their parents don't like them, or hate them and wish them away. The younger the child the more sensitive its antennae. People who have near-death experiences report that in the "other reality" speech is unnecessary since they're able to read thoughts. Fetuses and young children have the same capacity. A couple, their eight-month-old baby in his father's arms, were telling me something funny he'd done, and we all burst out laughing, whereupon the baby burst out crying; he'd sensed we were laughing at him. No adult wants to be laughed at and neither did that baby, who felt he'd been unfavorably judged.

A raised voice can bowl a child over like a bowling pin. I know a mother who prides herself on never hitting her son. She thinks parents who hit children are an abomination, but from time to time she smashes her son to smithereens with her loud, angry voice. Usually though, loud angry voices are accompanied by physical assaults, and nothing more directly impresses 'bad' into children than hitting them. Slaps, spankings and beatings are so effective because they remain in the body. In 1948, Dr Robert Moody reported in *Lancet* that during a psychotherapy session a bruise appeared on a patient that looked like the carved death's head on the walking stick her father used to beat her with. (That and similar cases are described in Michael Murphy's *The Future of the Body*, 1992). In the early 1990s a woman in my incest survivor group showed up at a meeting with a black eye. No one had punched her. Her black eye was a body memory of a parent's punch surfacing from childhood.

When babies' are smacked at birth, the pain smacks 'bad' into their butts. Infants who are circumcised have 'bad' penises. So are the genitals of female children who are circumcised. "The bad thing down there has to be cut off," mothers tell little girls whose clitorises are about to be excised. These mothers know their child's clitoris is bad because their own mutilated clitoris told them so. In Dickens' *Great Expectations* (1861), the child Pip, an orphan, was brought up by his older sister, who never tired of saying that she'd brought him up "by hand," by which she meant that she'd hit him for all his offenses. Pip's body knew it was bad on the butt, the head, the face, wherever she lit into him.

Little children rarely understand why a hitting hand descends upon them. The psychiatrist, R D Laing (1927-1989), couldn't have comprehended when he was learning to walk why his mother gave him "a good spanking" every time he fell down (*Wisdom, Madness and Folly*, 1985). In one of his workshops, the Buddhist, Stephen Levine, recalled running across a room naked when he was a toddler and suddenly peeing, for which his mother whacked him. He had no idea what he'd done wrong, so he concluded *he* was wrong, bad, as do the children who are smacked or yelled at for sucking their thumbs, picking their noses, touching their genitals.

Children have been judged 'bad' for everything natural they do. In *Great Expectations*, Pip's sister catalogs all the "troubles" she'd had bringing him up: "all the illnesses I had been guilty of ... and all the high places I had tumbled from ... and all the injuries I had done myself ... and all the times she had wished me in my grave, and I had contumaciously refused to go there." Pip's sister's complaints were identical with my mother's, who always made me and my sisters feel we were bad when we fell down or got sick or caused her any trouble. I also felt, like Pip, that I was bad for being alive because I knew my mother wished I was dead. My sisters did too, for my mother would often say, with a heavy sigh, that having had children was the biggest mistake of her life. I later discovered that many mothers shoot that arrow into their children's hearts.

"You're stupid. You always have been and always will be. The day of your birth was the worst day of my life," said a father to his adolescent son in the TV series, *I'll Fly Away* (1991-93). Parents often hurl "stupid" at children like hockey players hitting a puck. In Paul Scott's *The Division of the Spoils* (1973), a Muslim father says to his adult son, "You're not as stupid as I thought." His son winces and his father apologizes. Parents rarely apologize: they're Gods who know the truth about their defective offspring and think it their duty to tell them. When Paolo Picasso was a toddler, his famous father pointed to him and said, "Isn't it terrible for a man like me to have a son like that?" Gloria Vanderbilt revealed that her husband, Wyatt Cooper, had a father who often told him, "You'll never do it. You're no damn good" (*A Mother's Story*, 1996). In his late seventies, when Charlie Chaplin was directing his son, Sidney, in a movie, he shouted at him, "Don't you have enough brains to place your hand on a doorknob? You know what a doorknob is, don't you?" Sidney told Marlon Brando, who was on the set, that his father had treated all his children (eight of them) with the same contempt. (Kenneth S Lynn, *Charlie Chaplin and His Times*, 1997).

I could go on and on, such put-downs are as common as dust mites. Ride on buses, shop in supermarkets, sit on a bench at playgrounds and you're sure to hear children 'dissed,' a term adolescents invented that means disrespected. Verbal assaults make as deep an impression as blows. When children are told, "You're stupid," "You're no damn good," the sound waves dissipate in the air, but nerve cells in children's brains get "Bad!" branded into them as surely as inmates in Nazi concentration camp had numbers tattooed on their arms. By one means or another children soon learn in their bodies and brains that they're bad through and through.

The Steady State of Badness

What's called "low self-esteem" is so difficult to transform because it becomes a physical part of us, not a wrong opinion that can be reasoned away. In the late 1980s and early 1990s, it was popular for people to repeat "affirmations," say good words about themselves to counter their inner critics' put-downs. When the affirmations were chanted in a group with a charismatic leader, they worked. But only for a while. It was like being infused with the energy of a powerful singer, or getting high on alcohol or other drugs; the high soon evaporates and we're back in our steady state of feeling bad. "I've got you under my skin. I've got you deep in the heart of me," says a romantic ballad, but romance rarely lasts. What lasts, what we've got under our skin and deep in the heart of us is an absolute, unquestioned faith in our badness.

In his autobiography, Benjamin Franklin commented on the Reverend George Whitefield, who came to Philadelphia in 1739 and was so dynamic a preacher that multitudes came to hear him, audiences comparable to the twentieth century crowds who packed stadiums to hear rock singers. Franklin was surprised that the public came in droves to hear Whitefield's "abuse of them": he told them they were naturally "half beasts and half devils." Franklin, who always had a healthy self-respect, couldn't comprehend the comfort of having one's faith in one's badness confirmed.

If I'd lived in 1739, I would have gone to hear Whitefield. I was magnetically attracted to gurus who told me I was bad. I used to listen to the radio talks of the California guru, Roy Masters, who was always telling his audience that they were full of pride, ambition, resentment and every other sin. I used to read and reread the talks of the guru, Krishnamurti, because he often told his readers that they led "shoddy little lives." If asked to list good things about myself, I couldn't think of one. The good words that my Kind Force sometimes whispered in my ear, I soon forgot. On the other hand, when I chanced on the "Jesus Prayer," for over a month I constantly repeated, "Lord Jesus Christ, have mercy on me a sinner."

The Jesus Prayer reinforced my fanatical belief in my badness; 'bad' stuck to me like crazy glue. It was the rock on which I stood and gave me a perverse pleasure. I was an emotional masochist. When I felt low and let my hand write, out would flow, "I'm bad, bad, bad. I'm the worst there can be, a blot on the earth. I deserved every failure and every bad thing that's happened to me. I should be exterminated like a rat covered with plague fleas. I should kill myself. I shouldn't be alive." My hand didn't write such words only at the beginning of my inner journey, I wrote the above words in 1999, thirteen years afterward. I was still repeating variations on the theme "You are evil" that my mother had whispered into my embryonic ear.

You may think I have an extreme case of the 'bads', and I may, but I'm in good company, the best, the company of the saints, some of whom seemed to have a worse case of the bads than I did. Ignatius of Loyola (1491-1556) was sure he was such a great sinner that he didn't deserve Christian burial. The nun, Teresa of Avila (1515-1582), felt "so wicked" that she had a vision of the tortures God had specially reserved for her in hell. The minister, Jonathan Edwards (1703-1758), was sure he was as bad as the saints, that his heart was "so corrupt," so "abominable in [God's] eyes" that God would send him to a particularly painful perdition.

They thought they were utterly wicked and consigned themselves to hell because children used to be beaten so severely they would now be called 'battered', like the six-year-old Elisa Izquierdo who was beaten to death by her mother in New York in 1995. The neighbors used to overhear her sobbing, "I'll be good," "I'll be good." Elisa's mother, in late twentieth-century America had created a daughter who had the same psychology as the saints and the sects of Christians who, starting in the twelfth century, used to whip themselves in public as a penance. They were doing to themselves what used to be done to them at home, for each lash was saying, like Elisa, I, who have been bad, now promise to be good!, good!, good!. In 1349 the Pope prohibited the practice, but sects of flagellants kept forming because children kept being beaten. In many monasteries and nunneries, as late as the twentieth century, monks and nuns were required to lash themselves on the back with scourges made of thorns, leather straps, clusters of chains. The Cabalists, a sect of Jewish mystics, not only flogged their flesh but subjected themselves to other bodily mortifications to try to get rid of their badness. When I was in Santa Fe, New Mexico in 1996, I visited the site where flagellants still celebrated the crucifixion of Christ by nailing themselves to crosses.

You didn't have to be religious to have a virulent case of the 'bads'. Lori Schiller, though she was brought up as an atheist, had as bad a case of the 'bads' as Christian saints. When Lori developed schizophrenia, her Voices constantly told her what the voices of saints had told them, that she was so bad she deserved to go to hell, a hideous hell she saw in visions. So did Teresa of Avila, but Teresa's visions were not an effect of schizophrenia, nor were Dante's, whose Inferno contains vision after detailed vision of the excruciating tortures the bad suffered in hell. When Dante and Teresa lived, and for centuries before and after, it was essential for good Christians to consciously know they were sinners and wallow in it. They would proudly declare they were the chief of sinners, a socially approved outlet for the faith in our badness we learn at home.

In the past couple of centuries, it has become less and less fashionable to boast we're sinners, which doesn't mean that our faith in our badness lessened; it went underground. Lori Schiller got in loud touch with her belief in her badness only after schizophrenia developed. If it hadn't, she would, like the rest of us, have been aware only of occasional jabs from her inner critic. But if you believe what your inner critic says to you (and you wouldn't have one if you didn't believe it), you too think you're "bad, bad, bad," which occasionally drives some of us to take pleasure in showing off our true colors. A fair number of children become like Lucifer in Milton's Paradise Lost (1667) who, when he could no longer surrender to God's ideas of goodness, defiantly proclaimed, "Evil, be thou my good." "DevilBoy," who in 1999 stenciled his name in red on sidewalks near my home, was a modern Lucifer, announcing to the world that he was no longer 'good' but had revolted back to his original 'bad' nature.

I did something similar when I was in my twenties and went to a Christmas party on tony Beacon hill in Boston. Standing in the living room filled with the de rigueur red and green decorations, including a huge fir tree dressed to the nines and "Come all ye Faithful" sweetly playing in the background, my DevilBoy took over. I sidled to the record player, looked through the records and, presto chango, Eartha Kitt's "I Want to Be Evil" was blasting through the room. I thought I was reacting to the hypocrisy of Christmas, when everyone pretends that love makes the world go round. I didn't then know that I was announcing to the world what my mother had announced to me when I was an embryo: "You are Evil." "I Want to Be Evil" wouldn't have become popular if it didn't appeal to the Devilboy in all of us.

At the end of my first Ecstasy trip, after I'd seen "You are Evil" chalked on a blackboard and after I'd lain in the dark for over two hours facing the harsh truth that I was filled with hate, I had another vision. I saw a black screen like the ones with "The End" on it in old movies. But on my black screen, what suddenly confronted me, and in much larger chalked letters than "You are Evil" was one word, the shocking — FORGIVENESS. I say "shocking" because for me it was. I was so shocked I couldn't take it in. A few days later when I told people about my drug trip, I didn't tell them about FORGIVENESS because it had dropped to the bottom of my mind. A few years later when I reread my journal, I was again startled by that final FORGIVENESS; I'd completely forgotten it, and I forgot it again. In 1993 when I again reread my journal, FORGIVENESS once more hit me like a chocolate pie in the face. The first truth about me that Ecstasy had revealed was what I continued to hold as self-evident — I was evil. I clutched it to my bosom like a radioactive teddy bear.

I continued to go through life with the sense of my badness emanating from my being. Millions have the same affliction. *I'm Okay, You're Okay* (1969) wouldn't have become a best-seller if we did feel okay about ourselves. Look in the eyes of people you pass on the street and you'll find in almost all of them the pain of feeling they're bad. Notice the many people who walk slightly stooped, head forward, as if begging the world's pardon for their existence. Remind yourself of the millions who've killed themselves, people who, even when they had a rational reason like a terminal illness, also wanted to be released from the lifelong sickness of feeling they were bad.

In a 1999 TV documentary about Christianity, Germaine Greer, talking about a mass she'd heard sung in a Russian church, couldn't help crying. Classical Christian music often opens us to the wound in our hearts. When Barbara Hendricks sings the "Benedictus" from Gounod's *St Cecilia's Mass*, its cry of anguish has nothing to do with Christian mysteries but is an expression of a universal human misery, the misery of feeling we're bad.

Get Me Out of Here

"I'm a despicable asshole," says a man in the 1990s' TV series, NYPD Blue. He's standing on a ledge outside the window of an office building. "I'm a train wreck," he rants on. "I don't deserve to live," and jumps to his death. Most of us don't stop feeling we're despicable assholes by committing suicide. We run.

On TV I see hundreds of people come up over a wide slope and run across a vast plain, like a herd of stampeding buffalo. According to this 1997 ad, they're running to buy mutual funds because there's "Safety in Numbers." For me that stampede was a symbol of the huge number of us who think our safety lies in running, not to a goal or a place, but away from knowing how bad we feel about ourselves.

"Black care," wrote Theodore Roosevelt, "rarely sits behind a rider whose pace is fast enough." Roosevelt was in the Bad Lands (the Dakota Territory) working hard on his ranch to get over a deep depression. He'd recently lost his mother, his beloved young wife and a political battle. He had good reasons to be depressed, as we usually do, but every depression gets its root power from the "black care" we acquired in childhood when we were judged and judged ourselves 'bad'.

Roosevelt actually did ride a fast horse to run from his inner Bad Lands. At the faintest whiff of noxious vapors rising from our Bad Lands, we too run, using the thousands of ways humans have devised to escape from emotional pain. Having learned that nicotine gives us an almost instant high, we light a cigarette. We drink a cup of coffee or a Coke to get a caffeine high. We dose ourselves with sweets and fatty food. We stone out on TV and rock music. We turn on the radio, or tune into the endless chat show in our heads. We take in a movie, run a few miles, pump iron, phone a friend and gossip, go shopping and buy ourselves presents. We work sixteen hours a day, fly off on a trip. We space out on science fiction, dream away with a romance, get lost in the maze of a murder mystery. We burrow into a crossword puzzle. We watch ball games and root for our team to win so we can feel like a winner, too.

In the last decades of the twentieth century, New Agers invented many new devices guaranteed to make them feel good. We learned different forms of touching, like Reiki, Reflexology, Rolfing, new breathing techniques, traditional yoga postures, kung fu, aroma therapy, color therapy, lucid dreaming, ancient tantric sexual techniques that blew our minds with super orgasms. We drummed ourselves into happiness, investigated our past lives, discovered the goddess or warrior we really were, contacted our angels, changed our voices, our handwriting, drew mandalas, woke up our psychic powers by laughing, chanting, singing, reexperiencing life in the womb and birth. I could go on and on. In the nineties in San Francisco the annual Whole Life Expo offered at least a hundred courses that promised quick fixes for happiness.

Long before mankind invented these New Age cures, humans put their faith in rituals, rituals we still use. Christians get immersed in water or sprinkled with water so they'll be washed of sin. For the same reason, Hindus immerse themselves in the Ganges. In their voodoo rites, Haitians rub themselves with the blood of a slaughtered animal, then wash themselves clean of sin in a river. South American shamans would put an unhappy person in a hut and suck the demons out of their heads and bodies.

Eastern gurus suck out the 'bad' demon by shaktipat, a touch that, like a benign lightning bolt, shocks us out of the misery of feeling bad into the ecstasy that some gurus say they always live in. Muktananda told his followers that to feel good, they merely had to let his divine energy "irradiate" them, which reminded me of God in the Sistine Chapel reaching out his hand and touching Adam into life. In the 1990s thousands traveled to Germany to receive darshan from Mother Meera, who would hold your face in her hands, look deep into your eyes, and fill you with her powerful love energy. As Andrew Harvey put it, the Divine Mother's "force seized me and … I felt as if … molten radiance was being poured directly into my mind and body" (*Hidden Journey*, 1991).

What some people get from darshan or shaktipat, Sufis get from twirling round and round until they twirl themselves out of their damning heads into ecstasy. To find the same ecstasy, an astonishing number of people, even in the twenty-first century, have been willing to sit in the lotus position for long periods of time, despite the severe pains in their knees or the torment of hemorrhoids. They repeat a mantra (a sacred word) over and over, chant for hours, do concentration exercises, observe silence for days, weeks, months, years, study thick volumes of holy scriptures, perform hundreds of prostrations to the Buddha or a God or guru, fast for weeks. The goal was to be rocketed into a world beyond suffering, into enlightenment, satori, samahdi, nirvana, Buddhahood.

The arduous work of classical eastern meditation is not for the many, who want an instant way out. Getting drunk has been the most common release from emotional pain. In Brian Moore's *The Lonely Passion of Judith Hearne* (1956), the lonely spinster called alcohol "holy water" because it lifted her spirits far better than going to church. Alcohol is legal, but we'll risk jail to take illegal emotional painkillers—marijuana, cocaine, crack cocaine, heroin, speed, LSD, Ecstasy. Adolescents invented Raves, parties where they take Ecstasy and dance until dawn in order to bliss out for a few hours, out and far away from their condemning heads.

They did what mankind has done for eons. The Aryans, a tribe that invaded Northern India in about two thousand BC, used an elixir called Soma to get intoxicated when they worshiped their Gods. Devotees who worshiped at the oracle of Apollo at Delphi also used a drug to get into an altered state. Hippies liked to think it was a natural form of LSD, but no one knows what it was. What's certain is why they used it—to feel good instead of bad.

In 1932 in *Brave New World*, Aldous Huxley predicted that someday everyone would achieve a state of perpetual bliss because they'd be on a happy-drug, which he named Soma after the Aryans. He was right. Millions of people began taking Valium and later Prozac and other drugs that suppressed their emotional pain. In the late 1990s, 23 million Americans were on some such FDA-approved drug, and there were serious discussions of putting children on Prozac.

In America, feeling good about yourself is thought to be achieved naturally by becoming a success. In a TV interview the ice-skater, Dorothy Hamill, admitted that what got her into ice-skating and impelled her to become a champion was not that she was particularly good at it but that she'd always felt, "I wasn't good enough. I was inadequate." She therefore determined to prove she was adequate, no, perfect, at skating. But it was obvious in the interview that, despite her Olympic gold medal and long career, Dorothy Hamill still didn't feel "good enough." "Nothing fails like success," said W H Auden because success doesn't dissolve the 'bad' identity that sits like a heavy stone in our chests.

When people get the blues, feel depressed, in the dumps, hopeless, suicidal, they sometimes talk about their "low self-esteem" and feel they're aliens in a world where everyone else feels good about themselves. Few of us know that most of us are carrying around the weight of feeling bad about themselves, misery they try to obliterate by using the temporary escapes I discussed above, and also by leading the "good life," the socially approved ways that are supposed to assure us we're A-Okay—making lots of money, buying expensive houses, cars, clothes and jewelry, sleeping with the most beautiful women or the most prominent men, marrying and living happily ever after, having a baby, finding God, becoming a football hero, getting a PhD, and so on for as long as we live.

What escape artists we have to become! Taught we're bad when we're children, we spend the rest of our lives trying to keep the 'bad' news from infiltrating our consciousness, thus guaranteeing that the 'bad' identity impressed into us at an early age remains our identity.

Chapter 18   Bad Children Know Their Parents Are Good

Going Home

I've never forgotten the longing in the voice of a young woman who said at a workshop, "I want to go home." Her voice had the passion of great baritones when they sing "Swing low sweet chariot, Comin' for to carry me home." Since it was a Buddhist workshop, I didn't think the woman was longing for an old man with a long white beard to welcome her into sky-heaven. I didn't know what she meant. Years later, when people who'd had near-death experiences were writing about meeting a Being of Light who made them feel totally understood, totally accepted, totally loved, I thought of her.

The Buddha said that the cause of suffering was desire. He should have added that everything we desire is a substitute for what we really want: to stop feeling bad about ourselves and rest in the 'home' of feeling loved. The Buddhist teacher, Deepa Ma, used to put her hand on the shoulders of meditators and say, "It's okay." She knew how much we need comforting. Dr Kathleen Grant, a San Francisco oncologist, told her patients that she wanted them "to get well" and that they had "a right to try to get well." Dr Grant felt she had to counter their conviction they were "unimportant" and that cancer was a punishment for their badness (*Focus Magazine*, March 1997). Experience had taught Dr Grant that changing one's view of oneself from bad to good can heal. The Unity Church came into being because in 1886 when Myrtle Fillmore was dying of tuberculosis, she went to a health lecture where she learned she had a radiant spiritual identity that was her real identity. She was able to look at herself in a different way and in a matter of months was healed.

I doubt that Myrtle Fillmore, Deepa Ma and Dr Grant made the connection between family life and our belief we're bad and therefore illness is a punishment for sin. Few of us realize how badly we feel about ourselves, and fewer locate the source of the trouble in the home. And yet everyone does know, but the part that knows is like a child playing hide-and-seek who hopes she won't be found.

Instead of finding the child in us who feels 'bad,' we spend our lives searching for love, a search that has pervaded our culture. Sleeping Beauty lies in a coma in a castle until a Prince wakes her into love. The ugly Beast is changed into a handsome Prince only when Beauty finally kisses him. In romance novels, which sell by the billions, women find a doctor, lawyer or Chief Executive Officer who sweeps them off their feet into happily-ever-after. In a Wagner opera, Tristan and Isolde drink a magic potion that makes them fall eternally in love. Our favorite

Wagnerian music surges with the deep yearning to be loved, and most of Puccini's arias say, no matter what the words, "Love me! Love me!" In that sense, they're like romantic ballads that croon, "I want you, I need you," "I can't live without you," "You must love me," "Always." When we "wish upon a star," we wish that someday he or she will come along, the one I love, who'll return my love, and take away the pain of feeling unloved.

Every new love is a hope that this time we'll feel loved forever, a hope we rarely give up no matter how many times love fails. Hope keeps us looking forward to another, better love, not back to the family we came from. Perhaps, we fear that, like Lot's wife who looked back when she was fleeing from Sodom and Gomorrah, we'll turn into a pillar of salt.

I say this although many of us have nostalgia for home, a sentiment expressed in Elizabeth Akers' popular nineteenth-century poem, "Backward, turn backward, O Time, in your flight, Make me a child again just for tonight" (*Rock Me to Sleep, Mother*, 1860). But nine times out of ten, the home we long for isn't our real home but an idealized one. Before the Buddhist, Gavin Harrison, began his inner journey, a psychologist at a job interview asked him what his family and parents were like. When he answered, "My family is perfect. My mother and father are perfect," the psychologist looked skeptical, which made Harrison furious. He was furious because the child in him knew the truth. After he began meditating, he slowly, reluctantly remembered that he'd been sexually abused when he was an infant. The Buddha then became the perfect home he hadn't had. He named the book he wrote about his spiritual journey *In the Lap of the Buddha* (1994), which has on the cover a picture of the lap of a gold Buddha, the lap that's our first chair, Mama's lap, the golden lap Christians also long for when they're sure "Jesus loves me," unaware that they have to feel Jesus loves them because mama and papa didn't.

We don't want to find that out. Sleeping Beauty was cursed by an old wicked fairy, Cinderella was mistreated by a stepmother, Hansel and Gretel first by the stepmother who wanted to 'lose' them in the woods and then by the wicked witch who planned to eat them. Even in fairy tales, we substitute wicked stepmothers and witches for the real mothers we don't want to see. In the last chapter, I listed a few of the many escapes we've developed to fend off the 'bad' news about ourselves. We have to fend it off; otherwise, we're in danger of finding out who made us feel we were bad. To avoid that grievous revelation, children develop the delusion that their parents are, if not "perfect," as Gavin Harrison wanted to believe, but essentially loving and good.

The Social Contract

A mother is beating her three-year-old son. "He'll be good," pleads his four-year-old sister in this 1697 version of the fairy tale, "The Sleeping

Beauty." Beauty is not presented as a bad mother but as a good one doing her duty to society by beating her children, just as her children are doing their duty by promising to be good.

When a parent hits a child and the child says, "I'll be good," both are acknowledging the social contract between parent and child, which designates the party of the first part, the parent, as good, and the party of the second part, the child, as bad. If the first duty of parents is to make children understand they're bad, the first duty of children is to understand that parents are good and know how to make bad children good.

"So you have brought wild animals into the world, eh old woman?" said the grandfather of the writer Maxim Gorky. He was pretending to his wife he didn't relish the duty of beating the wildness out of his children, a philosophy that this nineteenth-century peasant shared with the philosopher Immanuel Kant, who'd said in 1775 that "Man must be disciplined, for he is by nature raw and wild."

Considering the "raw and wild" babies delivered into their care, the Draconian methods used by parents to civilize them made sense. For how could law and order be maintained if babies were allowed to retain their wildness, their innate deviltry, their primitive savagery, their bad seediness, or whatever an era chose to call children's dreadful defect? Strong measures were needed if children were to become good. As Edgar Allen Poe joked in 1850, "Children are … like tough beefsteaks, the more you beat them the more tender they become."

Beating children and disciplining them harshly made parents good too: they were doing their duty to society, a duty they had to keep up. Drunks have to keep going to AA meetings to maintain their sobriety, and children have to keep on being corrected to maintain their goodness, just as Catholics need constant confession and absolution for their sins. That parents are good and children are bad is not called into question even when parental discipline doesn't make children good.

I once spoke to a group of African-American men released from prison into a halfway house, who admitted that they'd been severely whupped when they were children but who insisted that the whuppings had done them good. I suggested that if the whuppings had done them so much good, how come they'd landed in jail? After a few seconds of silence, one man said that maybe they hadn't been whupped enough. A few men laughed, uneasy laughter. They didn't want their faith shaken, their faith that their parents had been right and good when they'd whupped them.

The belief that parents are good keeps the social contract going, a contract we personally reaffirm whenever we witness a child being beaten or harshly corrected by a parent and stand by and do nothing. By not intervening, we act the way governments used to. Not until late in the nineteenth century, when organizations for the prevention of cruelty to children were established, did the law interfere between parent and child, no matter how badly a child was mistreated. It took so long because most people feared that abridging parental rights would mean that children wouldn't learn to be good and civilized society would collapse. But that wasn't their real fear. Their real fear went deeper.

In 1994 in my living room, I witnessed my second cousin Dana scream at her three-year-old daughter, Lily, merely because she'd gone out on the deck and hadn't come in when called. Dana, grasping Lily's arm, yanked her inside and, in a voice like trumpets blasting, ordered her to sit on the sofa and not move "one inch." Lily uttered a defiant, "No!" but she was already on the sofa, where she sat like a stone. Lily was more courageous than I was. To my shame, a shame I'll have till I die, I sat like a dummy. A part of me wanted to yell back at Dana, to give her a taste of her own strong medicine, but I didn't.

I couldn't. Her ferocious voice, her parental status, had triggered my frightened child, the child who'd learned that she'd be punished if she questioned parental authority. Governments took so long to intervene when parents mistreated children because the child who'd once submitted to mistreatment lives on in us. The frightened child in me was sure that if she talked back, raging Mom would scream, "This is my child. Mind your own damn business!" My consolation for not yelling back (or speaking calmly) was that if I had, Dana would later have taken her anger at me out on Lily. And yet, if I had talked back to Dana, Lily would have got the message that a mighty grown-up thought her Mama had treated her badly, for in some tiny corner of her being, Lily sensed the truth—that Mama was the one who'd been bad not her.

If that light had gone on in Lily's head, she would have turned it off instantly. Breaking the social contract not only outrages parents, it upsets children who learn that parents are good and children bad at so early an age it seems a law of nature, like night and day. It doesn't matter that the parent-child social contract violates what Confucius, Aristotle, Rabbi Hillel and Jesus, to name a few, said was the right way to treat others: the way you would want to be treated yourself. The golden rule is constantly violated by parents, who are nevertheless regarded as good. We don't accuse them of inheriting a be-cruel-to-your-children gene, whereas violent children are accused of having inherited wild animal genes.

College students put on a mortarboard when they graduate into the adult world. Men and women put on a halo of goodness when they graduate into parenthood. To become a parent is to become the perfect, omnipotent, omniscient ruler of the universe called home and of the "chosen people" parents create. The rite of becoming a parent is like the rite of becoming a priest; it changes flesh and blood people into magicians who have the ability to turn bad children into good adults.

If we didn't believe in that magic, we'd require prospective parents to pass tests in childcare, just as people do to get a driver's license. Since 1946, millions of parents voluntarily studied Dr Benjamin Spock's *Baby and Child Care*, which supplied them with information about the physical nurture of babies that nature apparently hadn't programmed into the maternal instinct of mothers. Nevertheless, Spock told mothers they should trust their instincts. What trustworthy instincts was he thinking of? The instinct that made parents hit their children? The instinct that made Dana yell at Lily? The instinct that made Dr Spock not hug and kiss his own children? Dana screamed at Lily because her own mother used to scream at her. Dr Spock didn't give his children physical affection because his own parents hadn't hugged and kissed him. Doctors used to advise parents not to hug and kiss their children because they were sure it was bad for them.

No matter how badly parents treat children, children accept them as good Gods. Children's unwillingness to see the truth about their parents constructed Mothers and Fathers we worship as if they were divinities. James Madison, the fourth president of the United States, called his father "Honored Sir" all his life. Children 'Sir'-ed and 'Ma'am'-ed their parents, and upper-class children curtsied to them. In October 1999 a newspaper published a photograph of a son of the Indonesian despot, Suharto, kneeling and kissing his father's hand. Children used to give parents the place of honor, open doors for them and not speak until they were spoken to, which is still the rule in the presence of royalty. Children in many ways act toward parents the way commoners still act toward royalty. Subjects were expected to be loyal and to submit to their king or queen for life, just as children were expected to be loyal and submit to their parents for life.

Parents wouldn't shout, "How dare you talk to your mother (father) like that!," if they didn't believe they deserved worshipful respect. Not to honor them used to be equivalent to treason. A child who struck or merely cursed his father and mother was "put to death" (Exodus 21:15, 17). Death was the proper punishment for children who disrespected parents. "Honor thy Father and thy Mother" was written by the 'bad' child in all of us who's trained to believe that their good parents made them good.

Chapter 19   Goodness Has Nothing To Do With It

In a Mae West movie, a woman looks with envy at West's sparkling diamonds, and exclaims, "My goodness!" to which West with a smile and a swing of her hips, replies, "Goodness had nothing to do with it!" The world might think that sleeping with rich men was bad, but West didn't, or, as she once quipped, "When I'm good I'm very, very good and when I'm bad I'm better." West hoped that her unashamed pleasure in sex would upset the sexual applecart, stop people from thinking of sex as bad, and she did help bring about the change. She did what Emerson advised: not be taken in by "the name of goodness, but ... explore if it be goodness." Society needs hundreds of Mae West's to knock down the false ideas about goodness that are the sacred pillars of family life.

The Prison of Good

A few months after my cousin Dana screamed like a fire siren at her daughter Lily, they visited again. I'd put cookies on the coffee table, little ones, healthy ones made without sugar, but even when I explained that to Dana, she told Lily she could eat only one, that she'd spoil her dinner (though dinner was four hours away). Lily ate the cookie, but kept eyeing the plate. When Dana went across the room to make a phone call and turned her back, Lily's hand moved toward the cookies. "Take one," I silently said. One eye on her mother, Lily's finger touched a cookie. "Do it," I silently urged. Dana, still talking, shifted her position. Lily's shoulders jerked; her trembling hand was off the cookie and behind her back in a flash. Lily had resisted temptation; she hadn't eaten the forbidden fruit. A few months earlier, Lily had managed a loud "No!" when her mother for no sensible reason had screamed at her to sit on the sofa and not move "one inch." Lily had now become a good girl.

In the past, to make children good, parents would take them to hangings and solemnly whip them to impress upon their young minds what their fate would be if they didn't become good. In strict Muslim countries where executions are public, children can still see criminals killed or their hands chopped off to teach them what will happen if they don't behave. Nowadays, more and more parents make children good by gentler means, and a slap on the face or the butt, time-out, reprimands, yelling, name-calling seem to do the job just as well. Children become good, but how good?

In the early 1960s I taught Emerson's essay, "Self-Reliance," to college freshmen. I thought they'd love it because it's a passionate plea for nonconformity. "Whoso would be a man, must be a nonconformist," had been an inspiration to me, but it wasn't to my students who, to my astonishment, were genuinely afraid that if they became nonconformists, they'd rob banks, rape and kill. I tried to explain what Emerson meant by the "self" we should rely on, the inner, divine "intelligence" we're born with, but they didn't get it. Emerson said that we're "ashamed of [the] divine idea which each of us represents," but I didn't think my students were ashamed. For them, the problem was simply one of conforming or rebelling, which they felt was occasionally necessary. They admitted they needed their drunken parties as a release. But, they insisted, conforming was best because society had become civilized by developing rules of right conduct, which parents pass on to children.

They assumed the rules were good, that just as chimpanzee babies learn from their mothers which foods are safe to eat, children can trust their parents to know what's good and what's bad, what's right and what's wrong. So why not do what they say? Not to would be as time wasting and foolish as requiring each generation to reinvent geometry, moral geometry.

Having arrived in a world in which everything is strange, why should babies question the rules? On the contrary, they're eager to learn them, to do what they're supposed to and not do what they're not supposed to, especially not do what makes Mom and Dad angry and yell, "Bad boy! Look what you've done," "You bad girl! You're going to get it," followed by a smack. On the other hand, when children follow the rules, they're safe and happy. Mom and Dad smile and say, "What a good boy you are!" "There's my good girl," says a smiling mother, her arms opening wide to welcome her little daughter. Parents may tell children they love them no matter what they do, but children learn that's not true, that they really love only good girls and boys.

Children want to be good even more than their parents want them to. They swallow daily mistreatment as if it were the Eucharist, the sacred food that will make them like their Gods. In their hearts, children are goody-goodies, like little Jack Horner who pulled a plum out of his Christmas pie and said, "What a good boy am I!" Jack was right; he had got his plum because he'd been a good boy and followed the rules. But sweeter than the sweet plum he got for being good was the plum of belonging, of being accepted as a good member of society. To become and remain a member in good standing, children have to agree that they're bad when they wet the bed, spill milk, disobey, talk back, fight, make noise, refuse to cooperate, sneak cookies, lie, steal a toy from a store, not do their homework, get low grades at school, stay out late, swear, dent the car, sleep around, behavior that children agree deserves the punishments parents mete out.

The price—alienation from the 'good' world—is so high that children rarely question if what they've done is really bad. Would Lily have been bad if she'd eaten another cookie? And what about Dana who, after she got off the phone, ate several cookies, oblivious of Lily watching each cookie disappear into her mouth? Why was it good for the goose and not for the gosling?

Children grow up accepting a double standard of goodness. Take lying. Children are never supposed to lie, not even fib. But parents are allowed whoppers. My favorite is the standard parental bullshit when they spank a child: "This hurts me more than it hurts you." What's worse is the common lie used to cover up a family injustice. A friend of mine, whose sister had been Mom's favorite, traveled some distance to help her mother move into a new house. "This will be Dorothy's room when she visits," said Mom when they were in the spare bedroom. My friend, stung, asked, "You mean, not my room too?" "You misunderstood, dear," Mom promptly answered. My friend let it pass although she'd always seen through her mother's blarney that she loved her children equally. She let it pass because the child in her still hoped that someday Mom would love her as much as her sister, that is, if she became good enough.

That my friend hinted to Mom that she played favorites took guts. For she'd been trained in the usual home where whatever parents said was The Truth, which children must never challenge. According to Gandhi, "Civil disobedience is the inherent right of a citizen," but the civil disobedience of challenging their authorities is not the inherent right of children. Gandhi advocated non-cooperation as a form of civil disobedience, but children are expected to cooperate when a parent says, as millions do daily, "Be a good girl, and do what your mother wants," or "Boy, just do what you're told."

Children are supposed to be like the Light Brigade that Tennyson celebrated when in 1854 without a murmur—"Theirs not to make reply, Theirs not to reason why, Theirs but to do and die"—they rode to their deaths in the Crimea. The Light Brigade died without a murmur because the blind obedience they'd learned as soldiers confirmed what they'd learned early in childhood, that being 'good' meant: "Do what you're told or you'll be punished." Children are obedient because they've been trained to believe that their own impulses and desires are bad and that only by doing what parents tell them will they be good. P M H Atwater was a most unusual parent when "from infancy" she taught her three children "to trust their own inner guidance, question all authority, and think independently" (Coming Back to Life, 1988). Average parents don't think their children have "inner guidance." They think that what children need to be good is to follow their parents' guidance, that without parents children wouldn't know right from wrong.

Average parents are like God in Genesis, who wanted his children to blindly follow his commandments, especially not to eat the fruit that would give them independent knowledge of good and evil. The students with whom I discussed "Self-Reliance" had been taught that what was innate in them was bad, that knowledge of what's good came from the outside, that goodness was a matter of following the agreed-upon rules of good behavior. At the end of the twentieth century, when a fair number of parents stopped spanking their children or spanked them less, many American parents clamored to have the Ten Commandments posted in classrooms and other public places so that children would be reminded of God's rules.

The result is that 'good' doesn't mean any more to children than it does to dogs. When dog owners order a dog to "Sit!" "Fetch!" "Stay!" and the dog does what it's told, the owners say in a pleased voice, "Good, dog!" When children "Sit!" "Fetch!" "Stay!," parents say in a pleased voice, "That's a good girl!" or "What a good boy!" Like dog owners, they count on children's desire to please to get them to act the way parents want them to.

In *Self-Reliance* Emerson said that "A foolish consistency is the hob-goblin of little minds, adored by … statesmen and philosophers and divines." He didn't mention everyone's first "divines," the hobgoblins who condition children to have "little minds," minds that stay locked into rules, minds that have been trained to comply "with the commands, orders or instructions of one in authority." That's the dictionary defi-nition of obedient, whose synonyms are tractable, docile, submissive, traits that parents regard as virtues, just as religions do. Parents and religions want minds whose brain matter has been rolled out like dough and shaped with stock cookie cutters. Schooling used to consist mostly of rote learning (children repeating what the teacher just said). Original thinking was subversive. "Great souls," said Emerson have "nothing to do with" consistency, whose core meaning is "to stand still." Great souls break through status-quo thinking into the unknown. That has never been the duty of parents; for children who questioned rules and conven-tions were dangerous moles who would heave up orderly societies.

To maintain the status quo, children have to learn to be convention-al, to believe in God and eat with forks, to go to church and wipe their mouths with napkins, to observe Thanksgiving and Christmas and have identical weddings, to obey the law and not fart in public. Conforming to convention locks us into a prison of 'good' behavior, a life sentence that's soon self-imposed because we stop being aware that we're in a prison. Being good comes to mean doing what we're supposed to do, what everyone else does. That becomes our happiness.

Power Trips

In *Parents and Children* (1914), George Bernard Shaw said that, instead of admitting that noisy children are behaving in "a perfectly healthy and natural infantile" way and telling them to shut up, parents call them "naughty" as if they were "offending God," not parents for whom 'good' means behaving "with a single eye" to their own "personal convenience." Parents do have a strong tendency to want things to go their way, to have only their wishes count, to define good as what's good for them. Having unrestricted power over subordinates tends to make parents me-first-ers. "Power tends to corrupt; absolute power corrupts absolutely." Lord Acton's truism is often quoted when we speak about corrupt dictators, but I haven't seen it applied (though it must have been) to our first dictators, parents.

I'm sure that many readers are sick of my denigrating parents, for children have to behave, don't they? Yes, if it's a matter of their own protection, of not harming others and respecting others' rights as equal to their own. Some parents try to teach their children that code, but if they've been brought up by the usual all-powerful parents, it's hard for them not to want total power, no matter how they disguise it. If Lily had sneaked more cookies, her mother would have judged her bad not because Lily might have ruined her dinner but had defied parental power, which parents want to be as absolute as the power their parents had over them. When we grow up in a tyranny, we look forward to being a tyrant in our turn.

Being a parent is the hardest job there is; it has endless duties, responsibilities, cares, concerns. The difficulties are compensated by many joys and pleasures—from a baby's first steps to seeing a child married. But among the pleasures, some are never talked about, the pleasures of power.

Fathers who have little or no power outside the home, can have total power over their children. Mothers, who for centuries had little power in the outer world and had to submit to their husbands' authority at home, had a free hand in the nursery, where they could strike and insult children who weren't allowed to strike and insult back, children who were taught that every parental punishment was deserved, every criticism valid, everything parents said gospel. The Pope wasn't decreed infallible until 1870, but parents have almost of necessity set themselves up as infallible to their children. One of the great pleasures people acquire when they become parents is the divine right of always being right, at least to their children.

When Jeffrey Masson was training to be an analyst and became uppity, his psychoanalyst announced to him as if banging a gavel, "This is my kingdom. I rule" (*Final Analysis*, 1990). Since his analyst had the power to have Masson kicked out of the training program, Masson had to comply. Masson fumed but learned to say nothing, allowing his analyst to ascend to the heaven that parents enjoy, the heaven of total power.

Another pleasure of parenthood is the pleasure of disciplining children, of using them as whipping boys, as dogs always on hand to kick around whenever parents feel the urge to let their rage climax. Parents often pretend they're doing their parental duty when they're actually getting their jollies. "I'm doing this for your own good," parents lie as they enjoy the pleasures of seeing children's eyes go wild with fear and of smacking their bare bottoms red. When Dana was screaming at Lily, the enjoyment of her power was as palpable as lust. But parents don't admit, even to themselves, that power turns them on. To allow such 'bad' feelings to surface would endanger the social contract that parents are good and children bad.

Parents conceal their sadism under a cloak of respectability, wear a crown on their swelled heads and sit on a high horse from which, in their role as parents, they never have to get off. To their dying breath, they feel they have the right to judge their children, a right they zealously hold onto because parenthood rescued them from the humiliation of being a victim and transformed them into a depersonalized force of nature, like the thunderbolts the God of Wrath wielded to get his vengeance. My turn to turn children into victims! To become a parent is to be promoted from the serfdom of childhood into the master race.

Nietzsche looked forward to the era of the master race, the time when Supermen would rule the world, an idea that didn't come from abstract thought but from having had a father, mother, aunts and a grandmother who viciously whipped him and who strove to control him totally. The battered, powerless child who lived on in Nietzsche created the idea that whatever increases our feelings of power is good (*The Antichrist*, 1888). He also set up power as a good because his role models had been the authority figures he needed to believe were good and loved him. He managed to go on believing they were good, though their absolute power destroyed him. In his mid-forties, he saw a horse being viciously beaten and ran over and dragged the cruel master away. He'd finally acted, let his justified hatred out, but it drove him insane because he couldn't stop loving those he should have hated. Future Nazis admired his superman philosophy because they too had been severely beaten in childhood, as German children usually were, including Hitler. The Nazis loved Hitler because he allowed them to become Supermen like their parents and blessed them for it. They became good members of the Third Reich as they beat, tortured and killed Jews, gypsies, homosexuals and other innate 'badies'.

Bad Is Good

"I am an uncompromising opponent of violent methods even to serve the noblest causes," said Gandhi, for even "when it appears to do good, the good is only temporary; the evil it does is permanent." To gain the temporary good of getting children to do what they're told, we've created many evils. The do-what-your-told mindset has deprived the world of a wealth of originality and has been positively harmful. Adults retain a simple-minded, black and white concept of goodness. Moreover, teaching children they must take their knocks without a protest (in the good cause of making them good) produces adults who think that the end justifies the means, and that freedom is rebellion. Having to surrender to mistreatment in childhood leads to helplessness in adulthood, to difficulty in acting to improve one's lot, and to an inability to fight against unjust authorities. Instead, we go limp with fear. Having to surrender to mistreatment in childhood makes us put up with mistreatment in relationships, or makes us demand that others surrender to us. Another evil created by do-what-you're-told training is moral blindness. Taught not to trust our own inner guidance, or rather, not to know we have any, we do what we were trained to do at home—think we're good when we go along with others, which often means overlooking the immoral actions of authority figures.

If children didn't have that training, millions of Bible readers wouldn't have called the God of Wrath good when his actions were so obviously bad, and I'm not thinking of his unashamed lust for vengeance. I'm thinking of the story of Cain and Abel (Genesis (4:2-16). In that story, Cain has traditionally been judged to be evil, the first murderer in the Bible, the man who killed his brother Abel out of jealousy. When I read the Bible, that interpretation seemed wrong, but I couldn't see why until I cleared my mind of parents-are-good-and-children-are-bad thinking.

In Old Testament times, to stay in God's good graces it was necessary to appease him with offerings. Since Cain was a farmer, he gave God some of his best produce. Since Abel was a shepherd, he killed a few of the first-born of his flock and gave God the fatty parts. God was no vegetarian; he demanded twice-a-day offerings of fat meat and blood, so he smiled on Abel's gift and scorned Cain's. Cain became "very angry and his face fell," whereupon God told him that his gift wasn't accepted because he hadn't done well. Cain refused to believe that lie, and he was right not to. For if God had been just, he would have accepted both gifts since both brothers had given him the best they had.

God warned Cain that unless he believed that his gift had been justly rejected, the devil would take him over. Cain couldn't swallow God's lie, and the devil did take him over. He killed Abel, but not because he was jealous. He killed him because God had unfairly favored Abel. If God had admitted that he'd been unjust, Cain wouldn't have killed Abel. He shouldn't have killed Abel; Abel was a scapegoat for the guilty party.

God knew that Cain would be unable to suppress his rage unless he believed the lie that he hadn't done well. God was like parents who, to maintain power, know that children have to be forced to repress the rage they feel when they're mistreated, which parents do by insisting that they're right and their children wrong. God's devious dealings with Cain reminded me of the mother I discussed above who, caught favoring her older daughter, told her younger daughter that she'd "misunderstood."

Few people are able to see the biblical God as a bad parent because that would put them in danger of seeing that their parents were not Gods of goodness. Society continues to believe that children are bad and parents are good because the child in us needs to believe it. It makes our world seem just, which lets us repress a chaos of unbearable feelings, feelings fundamentalist Christians in the twentieth century repressed further by championing a set of values they called family values: a man, woman and children sharing a home blessed by hard work, right thinking, discipline, wholesome food, loyalty, love, and, above all, God. Except that their "family values" were like a mirage floating on the heat waves of a desert. The family values that have misshaped the world were created by fear, hate, harsh discipline, shame and guilt, reinforced by religion.

Chapter 20   **Family Values: Fear**

The Beginning of Wisdom

The first family value, the one on which the others depend, is fear, the same fear that the Bible tells us "is the beginning of wisdom" (Psalms 111:10). Over and over we're advised that "The fear of the Lord is a training in wisdom" (Psalms 15:33); "The fear of the Lord, that is wisdom" (Job 28:28). After Moses received the Ten Commandments, thunder pealed, "lightning flashed ... and all the people trembled and stood at a distance." Moses told them not to worry, that God wasn't going to kill them, that he'd put on the scary spectacle "so that the fear of him may remain with you and keep you from sin" (Exodus 20:18-20). God drum-rolled his thunder and flashed his lightning for the same reason parents scare their children — to make them good. Parents with wicked sons were advised to have them stoned to death, so "all Israel will hear of it and be afraid" and therefore good (Deuteronomy 21:18-21).

The good, those who feared the Lord and obeyed him, would be rewarded in various ways. "Blessed is the man who fears the Lord and finds great joy in his commandments" because "in the end he will gloat over his enemies" (Psalms 112:1-2). Moreover: "fear the Lord and grow rich" (Proverbs 24:21); fear the Lord and be "untouched by evil" and your sons will be safe too (Proverbs 19:23; 14:26). Fear the Lord, and he'll prolong your life, just as the Lord will shorten the life of those who don't fear him (Proverbs 10:27).

The Bible teaches us what we've already learned in the family — that when you fear the great Father/Mother and do what you're told, you'll be judged good and treated well. But when you're bad, there'll be hell to pay, a hell you'll deserve. No wonder people want to believe that bad things happen to bad people, who deserve their misfortunes because they didn't fear the Lord. Little Lily learned that fear of her Lord was the beginning of wisdom when she resisted the temptation to eat another cookie, that is, when she developed the gut-fear that produces what families call goodness.

In the home, as in the Bible, fear was elevated to a virtue. Whereas the base definition of 'fear' is "a feeling of agitation and anxiety [in] the presence ... of danger," the third definition of fear (in *The American Heritage Dictionary*) is "extreme reverence or awe, as toward a supreme power." When the Prophet Jeremiah, speaking for God, said, "They shall fear me at all times" (32:39), and when the book of Revelation (11:13) said that people "in terror did homage to the God of heaven," no criticism of God was implied; it was a compliment. An ancient Egyptian inscription referred to "dread of his majesty's might" because the more a Pharaoh-

God filled his subjects with dread, the greater he was judged to be, which explains why David boasted that his God was "more to be feared than all gods" (1 Chronicles 16:25-27). Terror, fear, dread, awe (which used to mean the power to inspire dread) were positive emotions, the proper ones to have toward Parents, God, Kings, and Authorities. Fear of those above us was good because it not only made us good, it ensured our safety.

Boogeymen and Boogeymoms

That God wanted his people to fear him at all times would be considered irrational, strange and sick if family life hadn't accustomed us to being afraid of our parents. The future George VI of England was so terrified of his cold and severe father that once when he was five minutes late for breakfast "he fell down on the floor in a dead faint," although he was "a huge teenage boy" (Caroline Blackwood, *The Last of the Duchesses*, 1995). A friend, whose father would suddenly pounce on his children and beat them up, remained so frightened of him that even in her mid-fifties, when she returned to her apartment after work, she checked the closets to make sure he wasn't hiding there, ready to pounce, and she did this though her father had been dead for twenty years.

Most children soon repress their raw fear of their parents. Only years after I began my inner journey, did I realize that fear was the blood that flowed through my veins. I learned that in 1999 when I read the words of a student who'd had a gun pointed at him during a massacre at a Colorado high school. "I was so afraid," he said, "I wanted to die to stop being afraid," which brought a scary dream I'd had in childhood back to consciousness. In the dream I was being chased down a dark road. Feet thudded behind me, closer, closer until my fear became so intense, I couldn't bear it. Being caught, hurt, killed seemed better than that fear. The student stopped being afraid when the gun didn't go off. In my dream, I stopped the unbearable fear by turning to face my pursuer, only to wake in a sweat without seeing who was after me. My fear also surfaced after my mother took five-year-old me to a movie in which anyone who sat on a particular chair disappeared into it. That night and for months after, I looked under my bed before I went to sleep, sure a monster was there who'd 'disappear' me.

Every culture has created scary monsters—boogeymen, goblins, ghosts, spooks, zombies, demons, vampires, werewolves, ghouls and other phantoms. Jewish parents used to warn their children that if they were bad, Lilith (a female demon) would eat them raw, and Christian parents would tell their children that ghosts or the Black Man stole away naughty children, cut them up and sucked their blood, and that God himself would hold them over the pit of hell or put them in a red-hot oven. In the 1697 version of Sleeping Beauty, the castle where Beauty lies asleep is in a wood that's rumored to be the home of an ogre, a giant with long teeth and claws, who "runs away with naughty little boys and girls and eats them up."

Parents who warned children that Lilith or an ogre would get them if they were bad were scaring their children the way their own parents had scared them, and so on back in history. Parents, however, didn't invent monsters; the minds of frightened children do.

Alfred Hitchcock said that he made scary movies because fear dominated his childhood. Every night he had to stand at the foot of his mother's bed and make his "evening confession." To pay for his sins, his father once gave the four or five-year old Fred a note to take to the police station, where a bobby locked him into a cell saying, "This is what we do to naughty boys," and kept him there for five endless minutes. At his Catholic school, a rubber strap was lashed so hard onto the palms of bad boys that if they were sentenced to twelve, three strokes were given on each hand on one day and the other six on the next day because three strokes made your hand numb and God wouldn't like it if you didn't feel the pain with full force. What fear the boys must have suffered anticipating the next day's torture! Fear of authority figures and of being helpless in a scary world dominated Hitchcock's movies (Donald Spoto, *The Dark Side of Genius, The Life of Alfred Hitchcock*, 1983).

"The Green Monster will get you," a modern father says as he shoos his children, squealing and screeching, off to bed, and when children grow up, they eagerly put on special glasses at 3D horror movies the better to screech with fear. People lined up around the block to be scared at *Psycho* (1960), *Scream* (1967), *Scream 2* (1969), *Night of the Living Dead* (1969), *Jaws* (1975). A movie critic reported that one of the young men who crowded in to see *The Blair Witch Project* in 1999 got so scared he threw up. Video stores have a special section for the hundreds of horror and suspense movies that keep on being made because they make tons of money. The Scream movies each made 100 million dollars, and the low-budget *The Blair Witch Project* also cleaned up.

A nightmare means a goblin who comes out in the night, and there we sit in dark movie theaters, having paid to have film-goblins scare us to death, which we regard as entertainment, "A Fun House of Shrieks and Screams," to quote the copy for promoting *The Haunting* (1999). Cultural madness, except that we need these shrieks and screams to keep us sane. For the fear generated in children to make them good doesn't vanish like an exorcised ghost. It stays in our system and continues to haunt us but not with its original full intensity or in its original form. We create monsters and scary movies because we need to vent our fear without being exposed to our original fear. We do what parents do, who deflect their children's fear away from them, the scary Mom and Dad they really fear, onto witches and ogres parents pretend are out there.

Psycho was an unusual scary movie because Hitchcock crudely revealed his childhood demon. "A boy's best friend is his mother," says the boyish-looking, candy-eating Norman Bates, who kills the domineering mother who'd originally frightened little Fred Hitchcock. As a rule, scary movies don't even hint at the original fear, and Hitchcock, in this case obeying the rules, located *Psycho* (1960) in a spooky house in the country off the highway, whereas he should have located it in a house or apartment in the city or the suburbs. But that would have been too close to home for comfort. We can screech when the bandages of an Egyptian mummy slowly unwind, though we were struck dumb with fear at our real mummy coming with a hairbrush to spank us or to force an enema up us. We can scream at a huge shadow on the wall, though fear constricted our throats when Daddy loomed over our bed, ready to put his hand into our pajamas. It's less scary to be afraid of a ghost in a haunted house than of Mom/Dad suddenly materializing. Better to endure scary movies than go crazy with the knowledge that a Boogeyman or Boogeymom did haunt our childhood. I had no idea that the monster who'd chased after me in a dream was my scary mother and that I looked under my bed every night because I unconsciously knew my mother wanted to 'disappear' me.

To keep the real monsters from our consciousness, we almost always make fictional monsters look scary. In Hollywood movies it's usually as easy to tell the bad guys from the good guys as it is to identify the demons in Tibetan dances by their ghastly masks. Scary movies sometimes try to break the mold, but they rarely succeed. *Copycat* (1995) begins with a criminal psychologist giving a lecture on serial killers who, she says, look like ordinary people, but then the camera focuses on a man in the audience whose face has such a scary expression that we're sure if he smiled he'd reveal fangs, the man who, of course, turns out to be the copycat killer. In *The Silence of the Lambs* (1991), Anthony Hopkins, who played Dr Hannibal "the Cannibal" Lecter, stared out of the cage he was kept in with the intensity of a lion stalking its next meal. Movie monsters are required to look frightening, not like the Mom and Dad who looked like everyone else and were often good-looking and often smiled.

Making monsters scary-looking is emotionally accurate. They reflect children's fear, fear so powerful that millions of adults need scary movies so their fear can get a controlled release, fear so powerful we often get irrational fears. We can't leave our houses (agoraphobia); we're afraid of enclosed spaces (claustrophobia). We're so terrified that the plane we're on will crash that we can't fly. We screech when we see mice or spiders. We're sure an earthquake will demolish our house, that a business venture will fail, that indigestion is stomach cancer. When I was a child, I was so terrified of dogs I'd cross the street when I saw one. I thought my fear was rational: dogs bark, they go mad and attack you. I didn't know dogs were stand-ins for the mother who did bark at me, who did attack me. I projected my real fear on to one I could manage. I could cross the street when I saw a dog. I could do nothing when my mother attacked me.

Many of us release some of our original fear by courting physical fear. We go on steeper and steeper roller coaster rides. We take up sky-diving, bungee-jumping, base-jumping (jumping off tall buildings or high cliffs); we learn to fly through the air on a trapeze. A woman I knew is lying frozen in a crevasse in the Himalayas because she overcame her physical fear by mountain climbing instead of confronting the husband who'd treated her as an inferior. Dealing with physical fear is infinitely easier than dealing with psychological fear.

Not long after *Jurassic Park* (1993) was a hit, a theme park based on the movie was opened, and one of the ads said, "Face your fears." By screeching when a phony dinosaur lunges at you? Encountering witches or slasher killers in movies or in Stephen King novels, even fear of flying are on the level of spook-rides through dark tunnels in amusement parks, kids' stuff compared to our original raw fear.

Fool's Gold

To make sure our raw fear doesn't surface, humans have developed a strategy far more powerful than creating monsters. Ancient alchemists thought they could turn base metal into gold. Children manage to turn the base metal of fear into love.

In *The Blair Witch Project* (1999) three young people try to discover if a witch that's rumored to haunt a wood really exists. After two spooky days hiking in the woods, they get lost, then one of them disappears and outside their tent, they find a bundle with a bloody heart. The remaining two are terrified. Sure that the witch will get them too, one longs for his mother's mashed potatoes, and even the bossy leader moans out, "I love you Mom and Dad. I'm so sorry." These babes lost in the woods got so afraid they retreated to childhood, to the time when we first learn to love Mom/Dads who frighten us. A witch still haunted the woods in this movie because she/he still exists in homes. Witches will continue to wander in the wood of our unconscious as long as we're afraid to iden-tify the real witch.

When Machiavelli said that to maintain power it's better "to be feared than to be loved," he was naive. He didn't understand what par-ents intuitively do, that they maintain power over their children because the fear they instill in them turns into love. We call it love; we think it's love, but it's the kind that the God of Wrath inspired. Children become like the Israelites who, no matter how harshly their "fearful and terrible" God punished them, worshiped him with all their "heart and soul and strength." Fear makes the party of the second part, children, sign the social contract, and 'love' keeps them from breaking it. Until I remembered my horrendous childhood, I used to believe with all my "heart and soul and strength" that my older sister, who tortured me for years in various cellars in my neighborhood, was the most noble, loving saint who ever lived. Fear make us bedfellows with the enemy.

In 1973 in Stockholm a woman who was held hostage by bank robbers fell in love with one of them, after which the phrase, the Stockholm Syndrome, came into the language, as if the phenomenon was a newly discovered psychological disorder. The disorder is ancient and should be called the Family Syndrome, for it's when we were held captive in the family that we find ourselves loving those who make us afraid, a phenomenon that social workers who deal with abused children frequently observe. Here is a true story that's common. A mother is finally in court for beating her son so severely he'd been repeatedly hospitalized. The judge sentences her to jail and, as she's led out of the courtroom, her son, held in a social worker's arms, cries out, "Mummy! Mummy!" as if he were losing the love of his life.

Making a frightening Mummy the love of one's life is common. Young Isabel, the main character in a Kathryn Harrison novel, had a mother who raped her with hairbrush handles, wooden spoons and letter-knives so that she became unable to conceive. Nevertheless, she "desperately" loved her mother: "There is no one I love so much as you" (*Thicker than Water*, 1991). A scientist in his sixties would listen to Puccini arias sung by females and cry to be reunited with the love of his life, the mother who'd masturbated him, had him suck her clitoris, and rented him out to pedophiles.

To love a frightening parent is preferable to feeling the fear, which I didn't know was true of me until I woke up one morning with, "Bring back, bring back, bring back my Mummy to me" singing in my head. More than a minute went by before I realized I'd changed "Bring back my Bonnie to me," to "Bring back my Mummy to me." I was shocked. I'd deluded myself into thinking that only mutual hate had existed between my mother and me, but that message from my unconscious forced me to take in that the brutally savaged baby I'd once been was no different from the brutally beaten boy who'd cried out, "Mummy! Mummy!" when his vicious mother was being taken to jail.

Despite years of working on myself, I hadn't discovered that I'd once loved my "Mummy," and so desperately that baby-me was singing for her to come back. I'd arrogantly thought I'd escaped that shameful love. But I too, like all the other ducks, had bonded with whoever had been around—my monstrous mother! I'd bonded with her because if my fear hadn't turned into love, I might have gone mad with terror. The morning I woke up with "Bring back my Mummy to me" singing in my head I'd reached a stage in my inner journey when my fear of my mother was thudding closer and felt as if it was about to catch me, so I invoked the Mummy-love I'd originally created to rescue me from fear.

These are extreme cases, but a slap across the face, spanking or yelling, produce fear that so frightens children they have to turn it into love. Parents desperately need them to turn their fear into 'love'. Since the foundation of the family is supposed to be love, parents don't want to consciously know that their children are afraid of them, and for a good reason. Parents have to protect their image of themselves as loving, and also protect the image they had of their own parents. For parents were once children who had parents who beat, smacked and yelled at them but who, they were sure, loved them. Parents want to maintain their own illusions as much as children want to create them. Both parent and child collude in the pretense. Parents either deny they're violent, or assure themselves that their violence is love, "tough love," as the religious right began to call parental violence in the second half of the twentieth century.

In 1993 children who'd been in a cult were studied for two months by a team of psychiatrists. The head of the team, Dr Bruce Perry, reported that the leader of the cult had forced many girls (some as young as eleven) to become his 'wives', had beaten all the children with a wooden paddle he called "the helper" for offenses as small as spilling milk, and so severely that several girls "had circular lesions on their buttocks that probably came from being paddled with 'the helper'." Another punishment was to deprive them of food, sometimes for a day. Dr Perry said that the children were still so afraid of the head of the cult that, though they were separated from him, they were sure he'd punish them if they told family secrets. They were so afraid that for three weeks after their release from the cult their heart rates were extremely high (140 compared to the normal 70-90). And yet they "drew pictures of hearts, under which they wrote, 'I Love David.' " Perry concluded that they had "learned to substitute the word 'love' for fear" (*The New York Times*, May 4, 1993). They'd done far more than that; they'd transmuted fear into 'love'.

The cult leader was the notorious David Koresh of the Branch Davidians, but his mistreatment of the children under his care used to be the normal way children were treated and is still the norm for multitudes of children, who also draw pictures of hearts under which they write, "I Love you Dad," "I Love you Mom."

"The lion has roared; who is not terrified?" said the Prophet Amos (3:8). He was speaking of his wrathful God but probably remembering how terrified he'd felt when his parents roared at him. Lily's body trembled when her mother roared at her. I'm sure that children are more frightened when parents assault them than animals are when lions assault them. Attacked animals can fight back or run away. Children can't. Moreover, the lion who attacks an animal isn't the one who fed and protected it. A parent's sudden transformation into a monster terrifies children because it delivers the scariest message of all, that the Mummy or Daddy who are supposed to protect and love them will attack and hurt them, fearful knowledge too awful to take in. Children have to believe that Mummy and Daddy do love them.

Loving those who make us afraid is the sick tie that binds most children to parents. I call it 'sick' because I can't help feeling that "There is no fear in love; but perfect love casts out fear." I thought Jesus said that, but a man named John did in a letter he wrote to early Christians (1 John 4:18). I also thought it meant that love is free from fear, but John was merely saying that only those Christians who love perfectly—who don't hate their brothers or commit sin—can cast out the fear of going to hell on Judgment Day, which John said was about to take place. "This is the last hour!" he warned. Though John insisted that "God is love," his God is the same old frightening God who taught his chosen people they'd better be good, or else. John could think of such a fearsome God as loving because God was like the parents who'd made him afraid to make him good. Many people call the Bible the Book of Love because they were brought up with Biblical love, a kind of love that should be called fear-love.

In 1965 three Unitarian ministers went to Selma, Alabama to help register blacks to vote. They were beaten up, one so severely he died. Thirty-five years later, a survivor, Clark Olsen, told a CNN reporter that "the terror is still in me." The fear we feel in childhood stays in us for the rest of our lives too; the beatings may not have been severe; but a child's tender skin and emotions feel the pain more than adults do; besides, unlike Clark Olsen, they usually don't understand what they did that was so bad, and children are beaten up not by a known enemy but by those who say they love them. They're emotions become twisted, as they were meant to; parents have to initiate them into the ways of the world. They have to teach children to love what they fear, and also to love those they should hate.

Chapter 21   Family Values: Hate

The physicist Stephen Hawking in an interview on *Larry King Live*, (December 25, 1999), was asked to name the most important problem the world would have to deal with in the twenty-first century. His answer was aggression. Early man, he explained, needed it to survive, but the world was now in danger of being destroyed by it. Since evolution takes too long, Hawking suggested that the twenty-first century should use genetic engineering to modify aggression.

In the last two decades of the twentieth century, it grew more and more fashionable to believe that all the ills of humans and the society they created lay somewhere in the genes and that genetic engineering not Jesus would be man's salvation. That aggression is in the genes, an inheritance from our animal ancestors, is believed by most scientists and layman with the same faith that Catholics believe in original sin.

The Cradle of Violence

"I got plenty of trouble trying to get that boy right. I got to beat him all the time, but it didn't seem to do no good," said a grandmother about the grandson she'd brought up. In a photograph taken in 1943 when he was two years old, his eyes were a mixture of "hurt and anger," but his grandmother didn't connect the beatings with his hurt and anger or with the robberies and murders that Willie James ("Butch") Bosket later committed. She thought that Satan had taken him over. (Fox Butterfield, *All God's Children: The Bosket Family and the American Tradition of Violence*, 1995).

She didn't know that she'd been Satan. Like parents in the past who thought they were beating the devil out of children, she didn't know she was beating the devil into her grandson. She thought her beatings were love, just as the Bible said they were: "Whom the Lord loves he corrects [beats]," just as a father does (Proverbs 3:11-12). But no beatings, no slaps on the face, no smacks on the butt come from love. They come from the hate that had been festering in the grandmother since she'd been beaten in childhood, the hate she passed on to her grandson.

Nowadays the causes of violence are discussed endlessly, but the finger is rarely pointed at family life. Animals don't beat their children; only humans do, and yet when children become violent we talk about inheriting aggressive genes from animals. We refuse to see what seems to me screamingly obvious, that home is the cradle of violence, that treating children violently makes them violent. And the violence is not merely physical. More subtle but equally powerful ways of creating hate in children guarantee they'll grow up fighting mad.

Creating Hate—No Fight, No Flight

A preborn, as an amniocentesis needle was inserted into her mother's womb, batted the needle away. The needle was removed, then reinserted, and she batted it away again. The physician who observed it was taken aback; he told me he feared that her action was proof of mankind's innate violence. Was it?

The fetus was able to bat away the needle because she'd been developing her muscles. From a mere six weeks after conception, the embryo begins to arch its back and neck and, for a moment, lifts itself off the bottom of the amniotic sac. By two months the fetus is deliberately moving its arms and legs, which further strengthens its muscles. Not only do fetuses exercise, they suck their fingers and toes and drink amniotic fluid. At thirteen weeks when their taste buds reach adult form, they stop drinking when a bitter taste is added to the fluid but drink double when it's sweetened. Fetuses know what they like. When their hearing develops, which is early, they like to vocalize and imitate their mothers' speech patterns. They communicate: when they feel their mother's belly prodded, they may poke back. They try to get their needs met. Motion calms them, so when their mothers are still, they sometimes gently kick and punch. Nor are fetuses wholly dependent on their mothers to be born. Their own brains transmit many of the signals that begin labor. Fetal life is not months of passivity. The new humans are not just acted upon; they act.

From the beginning of human history, fetuses have been physically active until they get so large they can't move much, restriction they may sense will end when they're pushing and being pushed out of the womb. But until the recent past, coming out of the womb, didn't mean they could again move freely. Newborns used to be wrapped from head to foot with bands of cloth so they could hardly move. Swaddling was said to be beneficial because it kept the devil within from getting loose, assured that babies' bodies grew straight and kept them from the disgrace of moving on all fours like animals. Turning infants into a package also had practical advantages; they'd stay where they were put and could be hung on a hook. At the same time, swaddling taught infants the most important lesson they had to learn, that they were not free.

In 1874 Robert Louis Stevenson wrote *The House of Eld,* a fable whose hero, Jack, lives in a country where as soon as children begin to speak, an iron shackle is riveted onto their right ankle, which makes it difficult to walk and rubs against the skin producing sores. When Jack is ten and sees people who don't wear shackles, he asks his uncle why he has to wear one. His uncle, who teaches catechism, gives the religious answer, that without the shackle he wouldn't be "good," "respectable," or "happy." Besides, if he takes it off, Jupiter will smite him with a thunderbolt. The unfettered, his uncle assures him, are "brutes, not truly human." Jack's uncle was wrong. Fettered children become "not truly human" when their healthy emotional growth is stunted by being forced to suppress the fight or flight instinct.

When a snake feels threatened, fear and action are instant and simultaneous: it bites. A hand that touches a hot stove instinctively jerks away. Threat and pain set off an alarm in the nervous system of animals and humans, a signal to take action. Batting away the amniocentesis needle — fear in action — was a fetus's instant reaction to danger. The doctor who told me the story was shocked by her evasive action because he was used to babies who submit to whatever is done to them. When babies are born, they have no choice but to submit. Unlike fetuses, babies, even when they're not swaddled, aren't strong enough without the support of amniotic fluid to push against gravity, and by the time babies are old enough to have acquired more muscle power, they've become psychologically swaddled. They've been trained not to take evasive action, trained to suppress what I call the "Hey! Get away from me" instinct.

Having to submit to whatever is done to them makes babies afraid unless they're in a loving atmosphere, one in which they are safe. Far too often babies learn they're not safe, that their Gods scoop them up like sacks of dough and do whatever they want to them, that their Gods yell and hit. What's worse, babies learn that they must not retaliate. In the Bible David was grateful for having been saved from "the guilt of giving way to my anger" (1 Samuel 25:34), and yet he worshiped a God who gave way to his anger whenever the spirit moved him, which was often. God declared his wrath holy, but the wrath of his chosen people was anathema, just as it is in families, where anger is the sole right of parents. All babies can do is cry, but parents often yell when they do.

When parents yell and hit, children react as if a fanged monster had suddenly said "Boo!" in their face. I've seen a child's whole body jerk when a parent merely raised his voice at him. Healthy "Hey! Get away from me" anger leaps up, but can a child roar back at a roaring father? Can it hit back at a hitting mother? Little children can't compete in yelling and hitting. Parents are huge and children are small. The law of physical survival precludes children from doing to their gigantic parents what their parents do to tiny them. For who else will feed, clothe and protect them in the dangerous world in which they find themselves?

Nevertheless, some children do run when they know they're going to be hit, but they're easily caught and, even if they manage to run away, they're safe only for a while. They have to go home; they get hungry and cold. Moreover, and this is confusing, the same parents who scream and hit may also smile, kiss and hug, and children have to feel that someone cares for them. Running away is a short reprieve from mistreatment but isn't a reprieve from resentment and anger.

No fight, no flight, means that children's healthy anger, having no outlet, seethes within. Unable to act in a scary situation, fear, like a car accelerating, revs into hate, another getaway (besides love) from fear. Hate is a defense against fear, and children need a defense. Frightened cats hiss, dogs snarl, rats trapped in a corner leap up and bite. Helpless, frightened children protect themselves by hating, but soon learn they can't show it. Hate has to go underground. It becomes an imaginary fortress where we're on our feet, upright, no longer a downtrodden, passive victim. It's virtual action. As long as we're buoyed by the energy of hate, we can pretend we're big and powerful; Nietzsche's Supermen originated in childhood fantasies, his defense against beatings. The first violent video games were played inside children's heads. Hate is a karate stance, a posture that says my rights have been violated. Hate is inner flight and fight when we can't flee or fight. Hate is an antidote to the paralysis of fear.

Creating Hate—I Own Your Body

In August 1996, I saw a billboard for a Health Maintenance Organization that read: "You've been with your body since day one. You should be the boss." What a lie, I thought. When you join an HMO, they become the boss of your body, though not as much as when you were a member of that first Maintenance Organization, the family, where children's bodies are treated as if they belonged to their parents.

Millions of children have had their penises and vaginas manhandled and womanhandled, and I'm not talking about children who are raped. Parents often play with their children's genitals as if they were toys created for grownups. The mother of the poet Anne Sexton used to lie her down on the bathroom floor and intently examine her vagina, a form of sexual abuse almost as harmful as rape. Even when parents merely put a child's bare behind over their knees and smack it till it's red, or whack a child across the face, they're delivering the message: "I'm the boss of your body. I can hurt it whenever I please."

When babies tiny ankles are grasped and their legs jerked straight up to wipe their bottoms, when their arms and legs are bent like pipes and thrust into clothes, when children's faces are firmly held and a washcloth reddens their tender skin, when their ears and noses are swabbed out, when food is shoved into their mouths to get feeding over as quickly as possible, when they're forced to eat food they don't like, or to eat everything on their plate, they learn who's the boss of their bodies. Franklin Roosevelt wasn't allowed to take a bath by himself until he was eight and a half, and then only because his mother was away. These may seem like minor matters to adults, but to children they're not; their bodies become objects that don't belong to them. Adults who feel detached from their bodies, and many do, are trying to forget the time when their bodies were taken over and mishandled. Children so easily submit to pedophiles because they've learned from day one that their bodies belong to adults and that their private parts aren't private.

In jails when prisoners are strip searched and a guard makes them bend over to stick a finger up their rectums, many go berserk and assault the guard. They go berserk because children are outraged and humiliated when their bodies are invaded by enemas. In the past it was routine to give children daily enemas. Little Louis XIII of France (1601-43), besides being beaten daily, was given enemas four times a day before he was fed. The custom of giving children daily or weekly enemas still continues in many homes and tells children that even their bowel movements are not their own but belong to their parents.

At my incest survivor meetings, a few courageous men and women talked about the degradation of having enemas forced on them, almost always by their mothers, enemas they described as a power play as coercive as rape. In August 1993, thirteen-year-old Eric Smith of Savona, New York killed a four-year-old neighbor, then turned him over and pushed a stick up his anus, degrading him as he must have been degraded. Shoving pencils and pens up a victim's anus is a favorite sport of participants in high school and college hazings. During a college hazing in Connecticut in March 2000, two members of a wrestling team were sodomized with plastic knives.

When attackers force objects up a victim's rectum, they may also be passing on the pain and shame of childhood anal rape. In May 1999 Justin Volpe, a New York City policeman, confessed in court that in August 1997 he'd sodomized a prisoner with a broken broom handle, then rammed it into his mouth, then swung the shit and bloodstained broom handle around as if he were triumphantly flourishing a sword. He said he'd done it in a fit of uncontrollable rage (*The New York Times*, May 25, 1999). But why did his rage take that form? I'm certain his ancient animal aggression hadn't got loose, that his rage came from his past, rage at the man who'd sodomized him when he was a child, then forced his shit-befouled penis into his mouth, a common atrocity of pedophiles. The tall, powerfully built Volpe chose a slight Haitian, a despised minority, to use as the helpless victim he'd once been. He thus got revenge against the man who'd raped him, who must also have told the child Volpe what Volpe told his victim, "You'd better not tell or I'll kill you!"

Creating Hate — I Own Your Life

Parental control of children doesn't stop with their bodies. "You are clay in my hands," Jeremiah said (18:6-8), pretending he was God who, like parents, wanted children to be putty in his hands. In May 2000, one of the mothers who attended the Washington DC Million Mom March against guns gave a speech in which she said she was going to deliver the same message to Congress she delivered to her children: "Do what you're told, and just because I say so." Her confident, self-righteous voice made me shudder. I was thankful that when her children got older, they could leave home and do what they wanted.

Children in the past did not gain freedom when they grew up. Parents, like God, felt, "I alone know my purpose for you" (Jeremiah 29:11). Upper and middle class fathers used to order one son to enter the clergy, another the law, a third the army. As late as the 1940s in parts of Serbia, fathers decided what their sons would do in life. Ivan Stambolic, who later became president of Serbia, was told by his father to be an industrial worker, just as he'd ordered another son to get a higher education and third to be a farmer.

The right of a parent to determine their children's careers has deprived the world of great gifts. The father of the composer, Handel, intended him to study civil law, and no pleas from his son could move him until a Duke, his father's new employer, by chance heard Handel play the organ and convinced his father that being a musician was an honorable profession. In lower class families, sons were expected to follow the same trade as their fathers. A farmer's son became a farmer. An upholsterer's son upholstered furniture for the rest of his life. At the age of thirteen, Thomas Paine became an apprentice staymaker in his father's shop, a trade that, luckily for the world, he became financially able to abandon.

Mozart's father earned his living by exploiting his son's and daughter's musical gifts. When Mozart grew up and proved to be a far greater musician and composer than his father, his father nevertheless felt he had the right to tell his son what direction his music should take, and, of course, what direction his life should take. When Mozart married without getting his father's permission, his father was outraged; he'd been denied a sacred parental right. Children's marriages used to be arranged so that parents could gain money and power. When that was no longer the custom, a father's permission continued to be a prerequisite to marriage. In 1758 the historian, Edward Gibbon, then twenty-one, broke off his engagement when his father forbade it: "I sighed as a lover; I obeyed as a son."

The belief that children were not supposed to shape their own destiny has in its grosser forms faded away. In its subtler forms it's alive and well. In *The Prophet* (1923), Kahlil Gibran told parents that "Your children are not your children," they have their own thoughts, their own souls and, since children represent the future, parents should not try to make their children become copies of themselves. Rare are the parents who encourage their children to be different and go their own way, and rare are the children (in their eagerness to please their parents and fit into society) who don't conspire in the loss of themselves.

Many adolescents become aware of their loss, and rage against it. In the early 1980s, adolescents listened to songs like the Commodores' "Easy," which was about everyone wanting you to be what they wanted you to be, and hating that you had to fake it. That theme still resonates with teenagers, as do songs about loneliness, depression and suicide. When we were little, we may have thought we'd be free when we grew up, but in adolescence we discover that society is like home. We have to follow rules, aim to please, try to be perfect and, above all, fit in, enter the rat race and succeed, which means having to think and act like everyone else and, no matter how we feel, pretend we're happy. Otherwise, no one will like us. Our drive to be like everyone else pulls against our need to be who we are. But who are we? Having been brought up to believe we're bad, we're afraid to find out, and yet we sense that if we don't find out who we are, our life will be wasted.

"Man's greatest pain ... is the sense of personal insignificance, of being helpless and of no real value as a person, an individual." Wilbert Rideau, a convict at Angola prison, was referring to the plight of prisoners, who often convert their need for a "sense of individual worth" into an assertion of power that's violent. (*Life Sentences: Rage and Survival Behind Bars*, 1992). Many children become violent for the same reason. In the 1990s children began going to schools with guns and killing, violence that made the headlines. Much more common, though it never makes the headlines, is the violence students direct against themselves in increasing numbers. A report issued by Surgeon General David Satcher in March 2001 said that "roughly 1 out of 13" high school students in the United States attempted suicide in 1999, and that among people between the ages of "10 and 24" suicide was the third leading cause of death. Why not get out of a world that makes us feel we have "no real value as ... an individual."

Evolution depends upon animals and humans having small differences. How can the world evolve when parents, governments and religions do their best to destroy differences? As long as the attitude of parents toward children is, "You are not your own person. I own you, body, mind and soul," as long as children are brought up in a society that trains them to be like everyone else, children, whether conscious of it or not, will rage at the waste of themselves, existential rage that eventually makes us feel that life has no meaning, that the world has no meaning, so why not destroy it. Conformity keeps society stable but sows the seeds of violent rebellion.

Re-Creating Hate — Mind Transplants

When the God of Wrath said that he visited the sins of the fathers upon succeeding generations, he was, as usual, taking credit for what he didn't do. Parents are the Gods who transmit their sins to their progeny, and not by means of their genes.

Paul Mones, a children's rights advocate, represented an eight-year-old boy who'd been beaten by his mother for three hours until he was senseless. After he got out of the hospital and was in a church shelter for battered children, he slammed a GI Joe doll against a table and screamed over and over at the top of his lungs, "I want my mommy!" (*When A Child Kills*, 1991). The boy hadn't merely learned to confuse cruelty with love. His fear, physical pain and anguish had been so great that he'd stopped being a helpless child and had become his powerful mother. For when he slammed and slammed the male doll against a table, he was not a little boy; he was his mother slamming him senseless. His mother had slammed him as if he were a doll who couldn't feel, and he slammed a doll who couldn't feel and who was much smaller than he was. If the doll were a tiny child, it would also be screaming, "I want my mommy!" while it slammed a doll smaller than itself. The boy needed the doll because as his mother, he needed a child to 'love', that is, beat up. When physical flight is impossible, some children flee from unbearable emotions by becoming one with a hate-filled parent.

In his *Personal Narrative* Jonathan Edwards liked to speak of being "swallowed up" by God. He was unaware that the God who'd swallowed him up was his God-of-Wrath mother, that the person who delivered his hell and damnation sermons was the mother with whom Edwards had fused when he was a helpless infant being beaten. The hate and vindictiveness that filled his mother had become his hate and vindictiveness. Her drive to make her children feel the power of her wrath had become Edwards' drive to make the members of his congregation feel as convinced as he'd once been that they were eternally damned.

Where was the original Jonathan? His individual essence was there; that can never be swallowed up, but it was deeply buried, covered over by the cruel mindset of his mother, whose essence had also been covered over by the insane religious community she too had been born in. Children do imitate those around them, but what happens in fusion goes far beyond imitation; it's a form of incarnation.

In Hitchcock's *Psycho*, Norman Bates killed the mother who'd tried to control every aspect of his life. He'd hoped thus to be free of her. It didn't work so he killed mother substitutes. But he could never kill her off, for she was still living in him, a fact symbolized by her dead body sitting in a rocking chair in his house. At the end of the movie when he goes totally insane, he's wearing his mother's clothes.

Norman Bates is an extreme case. In real life, not Hollywood, fusion is subtler and never total. For example, in my incest survivor group many newcomers spoke with anguish of the guilt they felt because of their abusive sex fantasies, which they thought they'd been born with, proof of their badness and the reason they'd deserved the punishment of rape. How relieved they were when others told them that their sex fantasies were not their own; that they'd absorbed the feelings of those raping them — the rapists' pleasure in having power over helpless children, in frightening and hurting them, and in corrupting innocence.

Infants and children who are raped pay a heavy price when they use fusion as an escape from fear: they acquire the perverse feelings of their abusers. It's as if they'd undergone psychic surgery, as if a part of their abuser's mind had been transplanted into their mind, and without their consent. A crime has been committed against their person, and they don't know it's happened.

At one point in my inner journey I felt that an evil presence was in me, so much so that I read the case histories of possession in Malachi Martin's *Hostage to the Devil* (1976) and Thomas Allen's account of an exorcism in *Possessed* (1993). Those cases of possession were too extreme to compare to mine. I was forced to accept that the evil presence I felt in me was not the devil but the sister whom I thought was my best friend but who also tortured me, abuse I wiped out of my consciousness so I could go on loving her. But I carried her abuse within me, or rather, the child who'd partly fused with her did, the child who from time to time would bite my lip as my sister did, trip me as she did, make me feel as if my head had been hit by a board, my hip feel as if it had been kicked. My sister also became part of my inner critic, smearing me with put-downs the way my mother'd smeared me with shit.

Our inner critic may not simply be attacking us with variations on the theme of old family criticisms; it may be a mind transplant. When a son who had a controlling father exerts total control over his own son, he may not be following in his father's footsteps but walking in his father's shoes. Bossy children who order other children around may not be *like* their bossy mama; when they're bossy they may *be* mama. When Dana screamed at Lily, she'd become the mother who used to scream at her. When the policeman, Justin Volpe, went into a rage and sodomized a prisoner with a broom handle, he *was* the man who'd raped him in childhood.

In Orthodox Jewish homes, adults light a candle on the anniversary of a parent's death. Little do they know that the dead parent they're commemorating may not be six-feet under but alive in them, that the sins their fathers and mothers committed against them are alive in them. The vehicle of transmission is not parental genes but parental mistreatment. A child can be frightened out of its own mind into the mind of the person who's frightening it, fusion that exists because it's a psychological lifesaver. Fused with their abuser, children feel powerful not helpless, somebodies not nobodies, in control, not controlled. In the process, they're infused with a dose of their parents' hate. Children thus, in addition to the hate they develop as a reaction to abuse, acquire some of their parents' hate, hate their parents acquired by fusion with their parents, and so on back in time. We may be heirs to thousands of years of accumulated hate, a bit of it going back to the first families. If that seems far-fetched, it hardly matters. Treating children brutally produces hate and violence, and children have been brutally treated in every era.

Gods of Wrath

In 1993 floods devastated northern California. When the water receded and the children were back at school, I heard on the radio that psychologists had been hired to help the children — get rid of their fear — that's what I expected to hear, but the newscaster didn't say that. He said that psychologists had been hired to convince the children that they hadn't caused the floods.

Caused the floods?! I shook my head in disbelief, then thought of the mad astronomer in Samuel Johnson's *Rasselas* (1759), who thought he controlled the weather. I hadn't read the Bible back in 1993, but if I had, I would have been reminded of the mad God of Wrath who claimed he caused every natural catastrophe. But why would young children think they'd caused floods? Psychologists say that children have such delusions because they're totally self-centered, which is why they blame themselves for human catastrophes like divorce. But egocentricity was not why the children thought they'd caused the floods.

They thought they'd caused the floods for the same reason God said he caused catastrophes. "The Assyrian! He is the rod that I wield in my anger," said God (Isaiah 10-5), by which he meant that the Assyrians' bloody conquest of the Israelites was really God punishing the Israelites for their sins. Similarly, the upbringing of the California children had filled them with so much rage that the sight of the raging floods became their own dammed up rage got loose, 'the rod' they would have liked to wield in their anger at parents and society for the sins committed against them.

Stevenson said that "fear and hatred" "raged like a tempest" within the evil Mr Hyde, but seemingly ordinary people who have the courage to look into themselves are appalled by the firestorm of their rage, which makes them feel, as they sometimes say, that they want to blow up the world. The Pathwork lectures (channeled lectures referred to in Chapter 4) say that "fear and anger take up most of the room" in everyone's psyche, which the lectures treat as givens of human nature. The educator, A S Neill, knew that wasn't true. In 1920, he founded Summerhill school to prove that when children are given freedom they lose the fear and hatred engendered in them by family life. As Neill put it, "Children are good when the necessity to hate and fear is abolished," but "under adult discipline, the child becomes a hater."

"Rigid authority ... breeds hate" and so do "storming and beating," said Neill, who tells the story of a mother who smacked a child for dirtying his clothes when he was playing in the garden. She took the weeping child indoors, changed his clothes and sent him out again, where he got dirty again and got smacked again. Neill wanted to tell her "that her son would hate her for life, and worse, hate life itself," but he knew it would do no good. When he lectured to mothers and told them that every time they spanked a child, the child hated them and they hated the child, the mothers shouted at him "savagely." They thought hitting children was love because if "children have nothing to fear," they'd never become good. Neill knew that fear makes children bad, that "only hate can flourish in an atmosphere of fear" (*Summerhill*, 1960).

Parents have deluded themselves into believing that punishing children is the key that winds them up like toys into good behavior. It's true that most of us do behave ourselves in the sense that by and large we obey the laws and conventions of society, but our goodness can only be skin deep because, like Mr Hyde, fear and hate are raging within us "like a tempest," filling us with a craving for revenge as obsessive as the God of Wrath's. "The result of fear," said Gandhi, is "violence." So much hate and violence is in the world because so much fear is created in children.

People who have multiple personalities often have a violent one, an alternate personality that embodies the rage created by their severe childhood abuse. Multiples are not the only ones afflicted. All of us have a violent 'alter'. That sane, civilized gentleman, Dr Jekyll, discovered the rage existing in his alter when he took a powerful drug. But drugs don't create rage, though they sometimes release it. The story of Dr Jekyll and Mr Hyde has universal appeal because as we grow up most of us acquire a Mr Hyde; the hidden rage within us has always been the heart of darkness in mankind.

Chapter 22   Family Values: Kissing The Rod

In the early 1990s a popular bumper sticker said that "Hatred is not a family value," which proves the truth of a remark made by that renowned philosopher, Archie Bunker: "Lies is what holds families together." Those who wrote the bumper sticker didn't know they were lying, didn't know that when they were children, their need to be loved was so powerful they accepted whatever they got as love, that their need was so powerful they covered up the truth their feelings at first told them—that yelling, beating, judging and reviling aren't love.

Having had the fight and flight instinct trained out of them, children run toward those they should run from. They become like dogs who, conditioned in experiments to feel they're helpless, don't leave a bad situation even when there's a way out. The way out for children is to see the harsh truth about their parents and face the emotional consequences. Instead, they sell their many birthrights for a mess of lies, and the healthy love they were born with degenerates into a form of family masochism that used to be called "kissing the rod."

"I Love You Too"

"Thou shalt break them with a rod of iron," says Psalm 2, celebrating God's dreaded instrument of power. God's rod of iron became "the rod of empire," the scepter symbolizing a monarch's might. The origin of these rods was the rod parents wielded to maintain their power, which was first a parents' arm with its attached weapon, the hand. When the writer Anton Chekhov (born 1860) was under five, his father started beating him on his bare behind almost every day, after which Chekhov was required to kiss his hand. In some Eastern countries adult children still greet their father by bowing and kissing the same hand that used to beat them. That kiss is a way of saying "I love you" to the very person who physically and emotionally hurt them. When, despite the many punishments he inflicted on his people, God demanded that they love him with all their "heart and soul and strength," he was imitating parents, and so were kings when they required their subjects to kneel and kiss their hand as a pledge of lifetime loyalty.

"A testy babe," said Shakespeare, "will scratch the nurse" and, after being beaten, "all humbled kiss the rod" (*The Two Gentlemen of Verona*). Children no longer kiss the rod, but most of them at an early age humble themselves by sealing the social contract (Children are bad and Parents are good) with the hot wax of a kiss. I witnessed three-year-old Lily pledge her loyalty to her mother with a kiss on the day that Dana screamed at her for not obeying instantly, which sent Lily into a deep depression.

Although we'd planned to go to the zoo, Lily's favorite entertainment, she had to be cajoled off the sofa where she'd been ordered to sit. At the zoo, her spirits didn't lift; she hardly looked at the animals. We therefore went to the zoo playground, but Dana had to coax, then order Lily to use the slide. Lily obediently slid to the bottom, where she stayed, oblivious, until Dana yelled at her to get off, that other children were waiting. Back in the car going to my house for dinner, Lily sat in her car seat cuddling a small rag doll, holding it to her chest as if the doll were breast-feeding and murmuring to it in a soft, gentle voice. Dana, glancing at her, shrugged and said, "Lily's been doing that a lot lately." I don't think she realized that Lily was remembering the good old days when Mummy had cooed at her while she was sucking at her breast. Having been kicked out of paradise for disobedience, Lily wanted to go back. She did. Within the hour, her arms were hugging Mummy's legs, who picked her up. They exchanged kisses. "I love you," said Dana. "I love you too," lisped Lily.

But what does "I love you" mean when a baby says it? At three years old, love has nothing to do with words. Lily was saying what Dana had taught her to say, saying the magic words that, after one of Dana's outbursts, assured them both that the social contract was intact, that Baby was bad and Mummy was good and they lived in a world of love. Parents often take out a you-must-love-me-no-matter-what-I-do insurance policy by teaching their children the "I love you" game. Children are grateful. They appease their Gods and assure themselves that the world they live in, despite their mistreatment, is loving, which keeps them from feeling their raw fear. The parents who create the fear, teach children how to deal with it. Rarely does the original fear resurface, but if it does, children know how to make it go away.

When I was in my forties, every month or two, I used to have lunch with Ruth, a former next-door neighbor. At one lunch, she looked so exhausted that I asked what was wrong. Ruth said that she'd been having dreams that were so frightening she slept with the light on, or rather tried to sleep, for when she felt herself drifting off, terror would wake her. When I asked what the nightmares were about, Ruth said she couldn't remember, but her face turned dead white, then red, then white again. I'd never seen anyone look so afraid. I told her to feel free to phone me when she couldn't sleep and suggested that, instead of seeing the conventional therapist she'd been going to, she should try hypnosis, that I'd heard it got to the heart of a problem quicker.

When I didn't hear from Ruth for over a month, I phoned and asked her how she was doing, if she was still having nightmares. "Oh, those," she said, "they were really nothing. I'm fine. I even dropped therapy." We arranged to meet for lunch, where when I asked if she'd found out what the nightmares were about, she shook her head, but her face turned white and she changed the subject. We did what we always did at lunch:

exchanged news about our lives. The chief item of Ruth's news was that she'd treated her mother to an expensive dinner. My eyebrows rose. Ruth didn't get along with her. During the years when we'd been neighbors, Ruth (and her sister and brother) had complained at length about Mom, who wouldn't let them live their own lives, who so dominated the household with her rages and tears that everyone, including Dad, walked on eggs. And yet Ruth said she'd taken Mom to dinner to apologize, to tell her how sorry she was for all the trouble she'd caused her, especially when she'd been a rebellious teenager and would sneak out on dates and, in defiance of Mom's edict not to have sex until she was engaged, had slept with every Tom, Dick and Harry. "Mom was really a trooper," said Ruth, "putting up with all my shit." Ruth looked down. "I know now," she said, her eyes filling with tears and her voice breaking, "that Mom unconditionally loved me."

"You're kidding! What about all *her* shit?" I blurted out. Ruth, looking as stern as her mother sometimes did, glanced at her watch. Saying it was late, she stood up. I sensed she was dropping me, that she didn't want to remain friends with someone who didn't accept her elevation of Mom to sainthood. Over the years, when I thought about Ruth, I became sure that something far beyond the antics of a domineering Mom had happened between them, something so frightening it had produced nightmares, which had to have been about Mom; otherwise Ruth wouldn't have taken her out to dinner to re-sign the social contract, reestablish that she was bad and her mother good, and comfort herself with the lie that her mother's domination had been unconditional love.

Ruth reminded me of Winston Smith, who at the end of George Orwell's *1984* looks up at a poster of Big Brother's enormous face and tears trickle from his eyes. Winston was realizing that at long last he'd come home, that he'd been a "stubborn, self-willed exile from the loving breast!" but now "everything was all right, the struggle was finished. He had won the victory over himself. He loved Big Brother."

Winston Smith's fear and hatred of Big Brother had been hammered down and reshaped in a building called the Ministry of Love, where dissidents in the totalitarian state he lived in were tortured into conformity, a fact superficially concealed by the state's official language, Newspeak, in which words often signified their opposites. Many of the totalitarian states we call home also pretend to be Ministries of Love when they're Ministries of Hate, where dissident children are trained to love their oppressors. In March 1995 a woman on *Family Living*, a religious radio program, complained that her children got angry after a spanking. As God's agent, she felt it was her duty to train them not to get angry but to submit "cheerfully." She didn't say how she was going to manage that. Did she plan to make them kiss the brush she spanked them with, or kneel and kiss her spanking hand, or teach them the "I love you" game?

Linda Gray Sexton (the daughter of the poet Anne Sexton), besides being beaten by her mother and father, was beaten by an uncle who, after lashing her bare bottom fiercely with a strap, would hug her, and Linda would enjoy the "sweet pleasure of being forgiven" (*Searching for Mercy Street*, 1994). Forgiven for what? Her uncle was the one who needed to be forgiven. A father in a 1994 TV movie at least knew that. He regularly punched out his two sons who, after a punching session, were required to hug him and say, "I forgive you, Dad," whereupon Dad would say, "I love you" and the sons would say, "I love you too." The movie was fittingly called *The Ultimate Brutality* because to force children to forgive and love the parents who beat them is to pervert love into masochism. When Linda Sexton had children of her own, she one day passed on that "sweet pleasure." Unable to control herself, she smacked her five-year-old son's bare bottom "until we were both exhausted," whereupon she hugged him and he hugged her. "Love follows the purge that violence provides," she said, forgetting that when she was beating her son, he was probably doing what she remembered doing when her mother beat her — silently repeat, "I hate you!" "I hate you!"

"I hate you! I hate you!" had to have been repeating in Lily's head as she sat obediently on the sofa after her mother screamed at her. Her hate was justified for being screamed at, deprived of free will, disrespected, publicly shamed, turned into a slave by her mother's need to show off her power. That's why Lily got depressed and couldn't enjoy the zoo or the playground, a depression that lifted only after she humbled herself by hugging her mother's knees and playing the "I love you" game.

The "I love you" game was invented to keep childhood fear and hate at bay by teaching children to love their Gods of Wrath. Just as children play ancient games like "London Bridge is falling down," they play the "I love you" game handed down from parent to child, a game so successful that most of us forget we once feared and hated our parents and don't tell family secrets because we don't think there's anything bad to tell, and send "I Love You" cards and call home on Mother's and Father's Day, calls that end with an exchange of "I love you's." The lethal undercurrent in that family custom was exposed in an Elaine May-Mike Nichols comedy skit in which a mother, talking to her adult son on the phone, complains endlessly that he doesn't call her enough and whines and whines about her health until her son whimpers in a baby voice, "I love you, Mommy."

Taking the Fifth

When Dana and Lily were exchanging "I love you's" and Lily lisped, "I love you too," tears came to Dana's eyes, which touched my heart for it revealed how much Dana was aching for love; otherwise a three-year-old's parroted "I love you" wouldn't move her to tears. Dana had married a man she didn't love in order to have a baby. Like many women, she wanted to create someone to love her, unconsciously hoping that a baby's love would heal the pain of not having being loved by her mother. I was a witness at Dana's childhood and saw the daily acts of rejection little Dana endured from her mother, who'd made her first child, her son, the king of her universe. For over two years the love between Dana and Lily seemed to heal Dana's wound. I once saw them running toward each other, arms open wide, eyes smiling, so eager were they, after a short absence, to be together again. They could have been lovers meeting. They were lovers meeting.

But as Lily grew older, she reached out to her father as much as to her mother and seized her own independent life. She stopped doing what she'd been born to do—love her mother with a hot, exclusive love—and Dana's wound opened as if it had never healed. Although Dana didn't consciously know what her wound was or where it came from, she rejected Lily as she'd been rejected, raging at Lily the way her mother had raged at her, using the boom-box voice her mother had blasted her with, although Dana couldn't stand loud noises. Lily had had to be much quieter than children normally are to cater to her mother's aversion to loud noises, an aversion she didn't realize was a manifestation of her hatred of her mother, to whom she was devoted. Dana, having buried her hatred, taught Lily to do the same, to drink the home brew that passes for love in most families, the home brew that stupefies children's original honest feelings, the homemade moonshine that elevated "Honor Thy Father and Thy Mother" to fifth place in the top ten Hits called the Commandments.

The fifth Commandment made the cut because it expresses the fear-based love that's the foundation of the family. The fear is obvious in the complete commandment: "Honor thy father and thy mother, that you may live long in the land which the Lord your God is giving you" (Exodus 20:12). God's usual threat: Be good, or you won't live long. An early nineteenth-century children's poem by Ann and Jane Taylor (famous for *Twinkle, twinkle, little star*) expresses the fear in the fifth commandment: "For God, who lives above the skies Would look with vengeance in His eye, If I should ever dare despise My mother."

To keep up the pretense that the Biblical God of Wrath is a loving God, when the Ten Commandments are posted in public places, the threat that follows "Honor thy father and thy mother" is omitted, as is God's threat in the second commandment that he'll "punish the children for the sins of the fathers to the third and fourth generations of them that hate me." By "hate me" God meant those who didn't love him with all their heart and obey him no matter how he treated them, that is, unless they kissed the rod.

The sign above the entrance to Buchenwald read: "My Fatherland, Right or Wrong." The sign wouldn't have been there if the motto of homes hadn't been: "My Father and Mother, Right or Wrong." The fifth commandment means the same thing, for it doesn't say honor your parents if they treat you honorably, and dishonor them if they treat you dishonorably. "Honor thy father and thy mother" is a blanket statement. It's the security blanket babies cling to, written by the child in us who conceals its fear and hatred of Mom and Dad by hugging them to its bosom. You "kiss the hand you cannot bite," was an underground joke during the reign (1965-1989) of Ceausescu, the vicious dictator of Romania.

"A son honors his father, and a slave goes in fear of his master" says the Bible (Malachi 1:6-7). "Honor" here has the stench of fear, as it often does. The fifth commandment says honor your parents for the same reason we call judges and mayors "Your Honor" and defer to them: they're higher on the scale of being. Childhood teaches us to be afraid of those above us, our "betters," our powerful parents.

The "I hate you" that first rages in children's minds when they're mistreated soon becomes taboo. When they notice a flash of rage, they pound the 'Bad!' gavel on their own naughty heads, and soon their hate stops emerging. Before I spent a few hours under the drug Ecstasy, observing the hate that pervaded my life, I was as unaware of it as everyone else, and so was my mother. I was a model child. I did what my mother wanted even before she knew she wanted me to do it. I was a good girl. I "took the fifth" and honored my mother as all good little boys and girls should.

What got me to study the Bible was my assumption that "Thou shalt not hate" must be one of the Ten Commandments, probably the first. It took me a while to learn that "Thou shalt not hate" didn't have to be engraved on stone tablets; during our early years it gets etched into our brain cells and tattooed on the valves of our hearts. In that sense, "Thou shalt not hate" *is* the first commandment we learn and the one we obey most because we have so much hate to keep down under. If family life didn't fill children with hate, a commandment to honor mothers and fathers wouldn't have been in the Bible, nor would the commandment that follows it.

I've sometimes felt that putting "Thou shalt not kill" right after the commandment to honor parents was a 700 BC Freudian slip, that those who wrote the Bible unconsciously revealed what they'd learned from their own childhood, that having to honor the parents who mistreated them made them want to kill.

Not that children at first know what 'kill' really means. They think that a dead animal or person is asleep and will wake up. Children may regard the killings they see every day on television as a temporary wish fulfillment. So they run around with a pointed finger or a toy gun, yelling, "Kill! Kill! Bang! Bang!" and thus regain the power they lost when fear cut them off at the knees. "Bang! Bang!," and children can pretend they're rid of the parents who are always in their face, judging, hitting, yelling, hurting their feelings, too often forcing them to do what they don't want to do. "Kill! Kill! Bang! Bang!" is the child's version of adults' "Drop dead!"

In childhood our rage at having to surrender to the powerful parents who mistreat us is often acted out, but rarely against parents. Before her mother began screaming at her, Lily used to run into nursery school, arms open wide, and hug her little friends. Afterward, she began hitting the smaller children, bopping them on the head hard. Lily wouldn't have dared bop her mother, who towered above her. Besides, she feared she'd lose her mother's love.

Killing parents doesn't happen often because the child in us rarely gives up hope that some day over the rainbow Mom and Dad will truly love us. That hope keeps parents safe from their children's wrath, which is almost always directed against someone else—a school wimp, a step-parent, or one of the ethnic groups the culture sets aside for hating. Scapegoats were invented by children so they could go on loving Mom and Dad. As a result, the culture rarely has to deal with what's regarded as the most shocking crime there is—killing parents. But to honor parents no matter what they do covers up what's far more shocking—that parents, those who should protect and love children, often treat them so badly that a few children, having lost all hope of being loved, kill them. Considering how badly parents have traditionally treated children, it's amazing that so few children do kill them.

When I was a child, I crossed the street to get away from those four-legged demons who barked, snarled, bit and gave people rabies. My fear of dogs, originally fear of my raging mother, was also fear of the mad dog within me, the bad child who hated and wanted to kill. I needn't have worried. The mad dog in children rarely gets loose; they learn to love those who mistreat them, and should hate threaten to escape, guilt pulls at them like the choke collar that makes dogs obey.

Chapter 23 Family Values: Guilt

The Shackle of Guilt

Robert Louis Stevenson's fable, *The House of Eld,* takes place in a country where an iron shackle is riveted onto the right ankle of children, a shackle that their religion says makes people "good," "respectable" and "happy." But when the hero, Jack, is fifteen, he wanders in the woods and sees a boy without a shackle dancing freely, joyously. He tells Jack that the religion they were taught isn't true. Other atheists tell him that their God, Jupiter, doesn't exist, that he was an invention of a sorcerer. Jack then knows his mission in life is to free children of their shackles. He sets out to find the sorcerer, who has to be killed three times, and meets apparitions of his uncle who teaches catechism, and his father and mother. He kills them, sure he's killed the sorcerer because the iron shackle drops from his right ankle, and when he gets back to his village, the shackle is gone from everyone's right ankle. But to his horror, he finds his uncle, mother and father dead.

Stevenson fantasized killing his father and mother because shortly before he wrote "The House of Eld," they'd discovered he'd become an atheist. His mother got hysterical and his father was in such a fury he argued with Stevenson for months, threatened to disown him and wished him dead to his face. Stevenson's father was like Martin Luther when he said, "I would rather have a dead son than a disobedient one." A Jewish friend told me that at the funeral of a cousin who'd died in an automobile accident, his grandmother said she was glad God killed him because he was about to marry a woman who wasn't a Jew. The mother of the cellist Jacqueline Du Pré told her that she got multiple sclerosis because in order to marry a Jew, she'd converted to Judaism. That mother and grandmother, and Luther and Stevenson's father felt justified when they wished their children ill or dead. Jack, in Stevenson's story, is inconsolable as he weeps beside the dead bodies of his parents; he didn't want them to be really dead. As a punishment, he (and everyone else) must wear a shackle on their left ankle, the shackle of guilt.

After Lady Macbeth commits murder, she pretend-washes her bloody hands, saying, "Out, damned spot! out" Children think their guilt should never wash off for their fantasy killings.

It's My Fault

One morning I was on my regular walk, which is down the steep hill where I live. It was a Sunday, very early, no cars, no people, when a metallic noise broke the silence. I looked back. A bicyclist, his brakes shrieking, was tearing down the hill. I was admiring his daring and his bright clothes, when, as he whizzed by, "Asshole!" shot out of his mouth. I stood, stunned. "Why was he angry at me? I wasn't in his way!" My intellect then reminded me that "Asshole" hadn't been a judgment of me, that the bicyclist was using a stranger to vent his wrath. But my feelings had at first reigned. They'd instantly taken "Asshole" personally, told me I'd done something wrong and was guilty as charged. I might as well have been embryo-me back in the womb, the poison dart of my mother's judgment — "You are evil" — entering my heart.

Back in the womb, I didn't understand that my mother's "You are evil" was not directed at me but at an unknown embryo. I took it personally and continued to, especially when she'd tell visitors about the various ways she'd tried to get rid of me before I was born. Abortion was illegal then, and her attempts to unwomb me — scalding baths, castor oil, enemas, jumping up and down — didn't work. Every time my mother told the story, I hung my head in shame for causing her so much trouble, for not passing out of her like the piece of shit I was, for defying her will by surviving, by being when I wasn't supposed to be. I'm not alone. Millions of unwanted fetuses have felt guilty for being alive, guilt that doesn't go away.

A woman was convinced all her life that she didn't belong in the world until, under hypnosis, she remembered her birth, which took place in the family car. Her father was driving her mother to the hospital and yelling at her that she'd better not "have the baby in his car" and mess it up. But out the baby came, feeling "overwhelming guilt" because she'd "done something which brought disapproval from my parents and it was all my fault" (Barbara Leahy Shlemon, *Healing the Hidden Self*, 1982).

Her father might have controlled his anger if he'd known that the new baby could feel the thrust of what he was saying. But until late in the twentieth century, virtually everyone thought that preborns, newborns and babies were *non compos mentis*. People didn't know that a baby could comprehend parents' feelings about them, and that they took them to heart, made them a part of their being, as babies at that stage in their development are meant to do. Babies are being socialized. Just as they absorb the language and customs of the country in which they happen to be born, they absorb the ancient parental custom of blaming children. The woman born in the car and embryo-me felt "overwhelming guilt" because her father was blaming a baby for messing up his car and my mother was blaming an embryo for messing up her life. They weren't blaming us personally, they didn't know us; but we took it personally and felt guilty.

A woman in my incest survivor group remembered that her mother used to watch when her father raped her. When she confronted her mother, her mother yelled that it hadn't happened, that that filthy stuff was coming from her filthy mind, not from a mother's pure mind. When

Jeffrey Masson was undergoing training analysis, he was told by one of his analysts that if, during a session with a client, he felt "bored, or restless, or disgusted, or angry," the feelings weren't his; he was picking them up from the client (*Final Analysis*, 1990). Clients, like children, were the ones with bad feelings, not beyond-reproach analysts.

The social contract exists because 'good' parents blame 'bad' children, who are physiologically designed, like sponges, to soak up their parents' judgments of them. The bicyclist who shouted "Asshole!" at me turned himself into a condemning parent, which for a while turned me into a child who thought she was an asshole, or to use parental parlance, "bad." When the nature writer, Sally Carrighar, was a child, she thought that she "was somehow monstrous," not the mother who tried to kill her (*Home to the Wilderness*, 1973). When children are raped, they almost invariably believe that it's a punishment for doing something wrong, that "it was all their fault."

"You are bad. Punishment. God hates you," wrote one of the estimated two million people in the United States who slash their arms, legs, faces, genitals with razors, knifes, scissors, pins, anything handy. They press the burning end of cigarettes into their flesh, hold lighted matches to the soles of their feet, bang their heads against walls. These men and women were raped and beaten in childhood and/or severely neglected or rejected, and yet they insist that they were to blame, even when they were raped at age two or three. A dance therapist who worked with mutilators said they "don't want to believe Mom or Dad could do anything wrong. They think they must be at fault" (Merilee Strong, "A Bright Red Scream," *San Francisco Focus*, November, 1993).

Mutilators are no new phenomenon; they're latter-day saints, like the medieval saints who beat their bare flesh with hooked chains, the saints who drank pus and ate vomit, the saints who developed stigmata. They invented their own cruel punishments while on earth and condemned themselves to everlasting suffering in hell. They punished themselves for the same reason present-day mutilators do, because "it was all my fault."

In ancient Greek drama, a chorus would stand on stage and comment on the action. On the stage of the world, a chorus of children silently comment on the action at home. No matter what's going on — divorce, drunkenness, death — "It's all my fault." Children don't know that their mouth strings are pulled by parents who conditioned them to feel so bad about themselves they take on blame for everything bad that happens. But conditioning is not the only reason why children pour ashes on their guilty heads. Deep inside they have a secret that fills them with shame.

Our Guilty Secret

Most of us never become conscious of our guilty secret. In late middle age, I thought I'd become aware of mine when Ecstasy forced me to face that "I'm all hate." I'm quoting what I screamed out loud when, soon after I'd taken the drug and was meditating with my husband, and the hate snarling in my head wouldn't stop. "Of course, you're not all hate," soothed my husband, but I knew better. I was in an agony of guilt.

At that time, though, I didn't know why I felt guilty. I didn't begin to understand until the day my sister phoned and announced, "Mama died." I took the news calmly. That's an understatement. I felt nothing, no tears, no grief, which puzzled me. Three years before, I'd cried when my sister phoned to announce that Mama's health was failing. (She'd felt faint during a walk and had to sit down on a curb.) But now when she was dead, I wasn't crying. What's worse, about twenty minutes after I got the news of her death, "Free, free at last!" was singing in my head. I felt jubilant!, and the song didn't go away for two days when it was replaced by chorus after chorus of "We shall overcome someday." I found out why after lunch, when I felt so tired I had to nap. When I woke up, I consciously knew what I hadn't known before, that though I'd dutifully turned my fear of my mother into love, I'd hated her, that a war had existed between us; she was out to kill me and I was out to survive. As I lay there absorbing that, "Live, live, live" began pulsing in my head. *I* had won the war. *I* had overcome. I was free, free at last of my scary mother.

I'd cried three years before when I got the news her health was failing because I'd recently flown east to see her and had committed the sin of family sins. When Mama was complaining as usual about how much she'd suffered her whole life, I'd dared to tell her that everyone suffers, and that, strange as it might seem, many people suffered far more than she had. Her eyes turned to steel and I sensed she'd pay me back for desecrating her "Poor Mama" image, which her children had had to worship all their lives. By (almost) fainting in the street, she'd resurrected Poor Mama, hoping I'd feel guilty, and dutiful daughter that I was, I did, and cried too for what I'd done.

I didn't cry when she died because I'd started my inner journey a year before and was remembering her crimes against my person. The truth had set me free, had released my honest feelings. The child whose mother had tried many times to kill her was jubilant because Mama was dead and she wasn't, and that Mama hadn't killed her; she'd killed Mama. The child-in-me was certain that she, not old age, had killed her, that telling Poor Mama she was not the chief of sufferers had been the blow, the stone in the slingshot that had at long last slain Goliath.

I used to say that I had to jackhammer through ten feet of concrete to remember what I'd suffered when I was a child. In the process, I had to jackhammer through ten feet of conventional opinion, what Samuel Johnson meant when he said, "Clear you mind of cant." The world is full of it, false beliefs we hold sacred, one being that we should grieve when close relatives die. A group of ministers and rabbis once told the psychiatrist, R D Laing, that over fifty percent of their parishioners didn't mourn at all when a "loved one" died; they were relieved, glad to be rid of them. The oppressed child in me, set free when she'd heard Mama was dead, had her personal French Revolution and shouted huzzahs—"I offed my mother! I finally killed her!"

If you're shocked, you shouldn't be. Why shouldn't I have been glad to be rid of the mother who, again and again, had tried to kill me? Why shouldn't I have been glad to be rid of the mother who'd turned me into a hater? Because she started it. I didn't. Hate isn't a gene-in-the-box that pops up for the hell of it. Hate begins in children as retaliatory hate. I wouldn't have hated my mother if she hadn't hated me first. There I was, a soft transparent grub you could flush down the toilet, and there she was trying to flush me down the toilet, and oh how she'd wished that would be my end!

My mother wanted to destroy me because she wanted an easier life, one without another baby. I don't blame her now, but then I was fighting for my life. Besides, hating her was beyond my control. My life force took over. Since mothers are supposed to protect children and mine wanted to destroy me, my life force, which drives us onward to "live, live, live," was up in arms. Warriors used to slash at each other with swords. In my battle with my mother, her sword was the various ways she tried to kill me, and my sword was hate, which cleared my mind of the infant's expectation of love and correctly identified my mother as the enemy. I needed to know the truth to help me withstand her powerful wish for my death.

Without my powerful life force, I would have died. I almost did many times, but hate—"I'm going to defy her; I'm going to live despite her"—kept me alive. I needed the strength of hate to counter the good little girl who wanted to die to please Mama. When I was a baby, I slept lightly, my hearing alert for the slip slop of my mother's slippers as she came down the hall, which instantly woke me. I knew she was coming to hurt me, but I'd lie there, eyes closed, not breathing, wanting to give her, if only for a few seconds, the pleasure of thinking I was dead.

Freud postulated that we're born with a death instinct (in addition to a life instinct). He was wrong. At conception the life instinct is wholly a creative force, a force that can be partly perverted into a death instinct when, among other things, a mother wishes the fetus within her dead. I suspect that anti-abortionists are willing to kill to prevent women from having abortions because their own mothers wanted to kill them before they were born. But most unwanted babies turn their mother's hatred of them against themselves: they frequently have accidents; they're careless with knives; they stumble; they drive recklessly, sometimes they commit suicide, heeding their mother's siren call for their non-existence, and thus finally freeing themselves of their guilt for being alive.

Unwanted babies wouldn't want to die if they were evil at conception. If children were created evil, the child born in the car wouldn't have grieved that it was "all my fault"; she would have danced a little demon dance for messing up her father's car. Embryo-me would have stuck my incipient thumbs under my incipient armpits when my mother judged me evil, overjoyed that I'd managed to be conceived despite her wish for my non-existence. In a 1996 novel, a mother used to force her daughter, Trixie, to stand in front of a mirror for hours "until you recognize the badness in you" (Lesley Glaister, *The Private Parts of Women*). If Trixie had been born bad, recognizing her badness in the mirror would have made her smile and want to raise a toast to the devil. Instead, Trixie split—into multiple personalities.

If children were born bad, they wouldn't feel guilty for hating the parents who mistreat them. In her autobiography, Teresa of Avila was sorry that when she was a child, she'd "been so wicked" she hadn't profited from having "such virtuous and pious parents," virtuous and pious because they must have given her many Bible-ordained beatings to free her from sin, beatings that had to have filled little Teresa with outrage, resentment, dark hatred, and then guilt. If she hadn't felt guilty for hating her parents, she wouldn't have whipped herself with scourges (doing to herself what her parents did) or had a vision of the torture that God had reserved in hell specially for his wicked child, Teresa.

Saints accuse themselves of every deadly sin, unaware of what makes them feel guiltiest—hating the parents they were supposed to honor. If Ignatius of Loyola hadn't had that secret guilt, he wouldn't have said that his dead body should be thrown on a dung heap and eaten by birds and dogs. The Italian poet, Petrarch, wouldn't have said, "God indeed is the best and I am the worst," if he hadn't felt he was "the worst" for hating his first Gods. Jonathan Edwards, though he dutifully honored his mother, had within him the rage of the baby she'd beaten, rage that made him sure that, like Teresa, he was going to hell. Teresa, Petrarch, Loyola and Edwards belonged to the same Guilt Club.

Almost all of us belong to the same Guilt Club, the largest in the world, in which every member has the same guilty secret. "Everyone has a secret they don't know they're keeping," said the twentieth-century drama critic, Kenneth Tynan. It's been my experience that we have more than one. But our guiltiest secret, bar none, is that, whatever other feelings we have for our parents, we also hate them and want to kill them. Children, having been conditioned to believe they're bad, guiltily cry out, "I'll be good" when they're beaten. But having been made to feel guilty also breeds the desire to kill. It skulks in the shadows inside our skull, a Mr Hyde whose presence we hide from parents, from the world, and mostly from ourselves.

That unconscious hate is the source of the guilt of all guilts, for how evil we must be to hate the Gods who conceived us, fed us, clothed us, watched over and cared for us. We ought to owe the authors of our being eternal gratitude, not hate them, not want to kill them! That unconscious guilt keeps us silently repeating "mea culpa, mea culpa, mea culpa," guilt we cling to as if it were a life raft on a stormy ocean. Guilt *is* a life raft because it has a hidden payoff.

The Balm Of Guilt

For two decades my husband and I had a bad marriage, so bad that (as I explained in Chapter 1) we were persuaded to take the 'love' drug, Ecstasy, which started us on our inner journeys, but didn't make the marriage better. It became worse. My husband flew off on even more business trips to Venice, Madrid, Athens and other romantic places and insisted that he couldn't take me with him (though other men in his firm took their wives). Perhaps to ease his guilt, he'd phone me nightly, calls I dreaded, for he'd always tell me about some interesting place he'd gone to on an afternoon off or about some splendid meal he'd eaten with his colleagues. He would rattle on like a little boy reporting his day to Mummy, not to the wife he'd excluded from the good times, the wife he must have wanted to feel rejected.

One night I turned off the phone. Let him think *I* was out having a good time. I lay on the sofa reading and fell asleep until I was jerked awake by my husband's voice describing a boat trip along the Seine. Cursing myself for forgetting to turn the sound off the answering machine, I was about to get up and turn off his damn voice, when a pain clutched my chest, a pain so intense I could hardly breathe. Was it a heart attack? I feared it was because the pain got so bad I wished I'd die, so bad I no longer heard my husband talking on the phone. I stared in front of me in shock, my hand on my breastbone, the pain expanding till it filled my whole chest. The agony became so intense, my mouth opened. I panted.

I had to get away from that pain. I struggled up, then downstairs to my study, where I sat in the dark, my eyes closed, trying to meditate. Instead, I found myself thinking of the many times I'd dreamed of meeting a man who'd carry me off to a happier life. Oh, how I'd longed for that dream to come true, to be rid of my husband who, I was sure, wouldn't miss me. Nor would I miss him, not for one moment. Had my husband sensed that? He must have. No wonder he took trips without me. He was right to get away from someone who didn't love him, who, in fact, hated him.

I looked down at my chest. The pain had totally vanished! Why? I went upstairs, erased my husband's words from the answering machine and put on water for tea. In the kitchen, I was standing by the stove waiting for the water to boil, when I saw myself as a baby, alone in my crib, forced to listen to my mother and sisters in the kitchen while I was condemned to solitary confinement and starvation. My husband's exclusion of me from the good times had caused me intense anguish, but it was nothing compared to the anguish I'd felt when I was a rejected baby. It was that infantile agony that had escaped from the place where we store unbearable feelings. It escaped because my guard was down. I thought I was safe: I didn't expect to hear my husband's voice and had dozed off, which put to sleep the watchdog that kept my old agonies from becoming conscious.

Then a sun rose in my head; I understood why my agony had suddenly vanished. It left as soon as I decided that my husband had been right to reject me. In infancy I'd also decided that my mother had been right to reject me, and for the same reason: I was the one who'd been bad, not my mother. I was to blame; I was the guilty one. In the present as in the past, blaming myself took away my emotional pain; no shot of morphine could have taken it away faster than the soothing balm of guilt.

Guilt was more bearable than feeling the agony of my mother's rejection. Millions of children have felt the same way. "Had I been good enough, wouldn't my mother have loved me?" asked Carol Buckley (*At the Still Point: A Memoir*, 1996). My former friend Ruth, when her childhood fear of her mother came back to haunt her, couldn't face that her mother had been a boogeymom. Instead, she shouldered all the guilt and totally absolved her God-of-Wrath mother. The baby born in the car felt overwhelming guilt, not because her father was yelling that she was messing up his car; her guilt was protecting her from the agony that love wasn't welcoming her into the world. When I was a baby isolated in my crib, I suffered a psychic heart attack that I reexperienced the night I heard my husband's voice on the phone. When children aren't loved, their hearts do break. Better to take on blame than feel the heartbreak of being unloved.

Once when I was cooking, I saw myself put my hand on the red-hot coils of an electric burner and letting it fry there until my blackened skin curled off. I didn't realize it at the time, but I'd had that fantasy because anguish at not having been loved must have been surfacing, and I chose to fantasize an excruciating physical pain rather than feel emotional pain.

I did to myself in fantasy what mutilators do in reality, who would rather inflict the bloody marks of Cain on various parts of their body than face that their Gods, instead of loving them, frightened them, beat them, treated them like lepers, used them as sex toys, as scapegoats on whom they could freely take out their displeasure, irritation, hate. Mutilators would rather mutilate themselves than think anything bad about the parents who emotionally and physically mutilated them. Only with great difficulty can even a few of them feel anger at their parents.

Mutilators in that respect are like the rest of us; we find it extremely difficult to be angry at our parents. We prefer to keep the faith we were taught: that we were born bad and parents made us good. For if we did get seriously angry at our parents, we might discover we had good reasons to be angry, and then we'd be in danger of releasing the greatest emotional pain children can feel, the pain of having been judged inferior goods, rejects, defectives, pieces of shit, which all mean unworthy of love. Guilt, like an ancient breastplate, guards our hearts from that supreme anguish.

Chapter 24   Family Values: Religion

On This Rock

In the New Testament, Christ says to Peter, "On this rock, I will build my Church" (Matthew 16:17), a passage that most scholars agree wasn't said by Christ since he was sure the world would end soon. They think "on this rock" was added to the Gospels after the Church was established to give it divine authority. That passage is false for a more profound reason. The rock on which the Church was built was not the teachings of Jesus but the teachings of the family. Once, when wandering in a cemetery, I chanced on a Christian tombstone that was a granite, life-size double bed with two granite pillows plumped at the head on which were engraved "Mother" and "Father." I laughed, thinking it would make a hilarious Mother-Father's Day card. Years later, when I read in the New Testament, "On this rock, I will build my church," I remembered that tombstone, designed by children to "Honor Thy Father and Thy Mother," and it became, for me, a symbol that the Family, not Jesus, was the bedrock of the Church.

In September 1999, the Supreme Judicial Court of Massachusetts agreed to decide whether or not a father, who beat his son once or twice a month with a leather belt, was abusing or disciplining him. The case came before the court because the son told his teacher about the beatings, who reported them to the Department of Social Services, which filed charges of abuse. Social Services was willing to drop the charges if the father would agree to stop the beatings. The father, a minister, refused, arguing that the state was interfering in the practice of his religion. The minister may have thought he had the Court by the proverbials because to prove he was practicing his religion he cited many Biblical passages from Proverbs that advise parents to beat their sons to make them good. The minister didn't understand that the court wasn't interfering with his religion but with an old parental custom. Parents beat their children long before the Bible sanctified beating. The Family came first, then religion.

Although God claimed to be an invisible heavenly being from outer space, he was, as I've pointed out many times, modeled mainly on parents. To sum up: God wouldn't have been regarded as all-powerful if parents didn't seem all-powerful to children. Nor would God have been called omniscient if children didn't think parents knew everything and that every word they said was true, a childish misconception that became the religious misconception that every word in the Bible is true. God's invisibility may also be a delusion of children, who are sure parents can see them wherever they are and can even read their minds.

The God of Wrath continues to be worshiped as the supreme judge of the world because in the world of our childhood Mother and Father were the Honors whose gavels banged down judgments from which no appeal was possible. "The terrible judgment of God upon sinners" was originally the terrible judgment of parents upon children. Parents, not God, created the first laws, the first punishments. The wrathful God of the Old Testament was originally the wrathful Gods who punished children. In the Bible, God's chosen people tremble with fear when his wrath gets loose because children used to tremble with fear when Mom or Dad's thunder violated their eardrums and their lightning bolt was readied to strike.

What most enrages the God of Wrath is disobedience, the sin that most enrages children's household Gods, whose motto, "Disobey at your peril," became God's, for whom blind obedience is a virtue because parents prefer children who instantly do what they're told, and when they don't, accept that however severe their punishment, it's deserved.

"I repent for offending you. Do with me what thou will," Catholic children pray to God, a prayer children first pray to parents, who teach children that if they don't want to offend them, they must totally surrender to parental will. If surrender hadn't been a virtue in the family, surrendering to God wouldn't have become a highly regarded Biblical virtue, especially at times of dire need. The Swiss minister, Zwingli, when he had the plague in 1519 and feared he'd die, prayed to God: "Do with me as you will … I am your vessel to be restored or destroyed," the prayer of helpless children who have to surrender to their all-powerful Gods and who can only pray that the worst won't happen. God wouldn't regard his chosen people as his "special possession" to do with as he wills if children weren't the "special possession" of parents to do with as they will.

"Almighty God, Father of all mercies, we, thine unworthy servants, do give thee most humble and hearty thanks for all thy goodness and loving-kindness to us," says The Book of Common Prayer because children, no matter how harshly they were treated, were trained to feel unworthy, humble and thankful for the loving-kindness of parents.

The tyrannical God of the Old Testament continues to be honored because children cling to their household tyrants. To quote a popular hymn, we speak of God as "our help in ages past, our hope for years to come, our shelter from the stormy blast, and our eternal home" because "in ages past" we were vulnerable children who needed the physical protection of parents, no matter how frightening and unjust they were.

The harsher parents were, the more children craved for their approval, like the son of the writer, John Middleton Murry. When "the Olympian figure who had control over my destiny," once "sang my praises. I doubt whether I had ever been happier," said Colin Middleton Murry (*I at the*

Keyhole, 1975). He experienced the glow Christians expect to feel if they're good and go to heaven, where God, they hope, will say, "well done, my true and faithful servant." I heard a famous radio minister quote that Biblical passage with a sob in his voice that revealed his father had rarely if ever given him the praise he'd longed for.

The dysfunctional world of the Bible is the world of home. The playwright, Moss Hart, said that a family is "a dictatorship ruled over by its sickest member" (*Act One*, 1959). The sickest member in the dictatorship described in the Old Testament is God, the Father.

The dysfunctional world of the Family that's mirrored in the Bible became the dictatorship known as the Church. Since the first Church officials grew up in families, the Church couldn't help imitating the family structure. Priests ranked themselves into a hierarchy, each rank wanting to be treated by those beneath them with the same awe that they'd treated their all-knowing and all-powerful fathers, who were collectively transfigured into our Father who art in Heaven and, a little below him, his earthly agent and mouthpiece, the great Papa, the Pope.

The Church, since its role model was parents, naturally set itself up as an authority who could do no wrong, a supreme judge who had life and death power over its 'children', on whom it could inflict punishments from which there was no appeal, who ruled by fear and violence and demanded total surrender of their subjects' minds, hearts, souls and bodies. In the *Brave New World* Huxley predicted in 1932, people's minds, hearts, souls and bodies would be controlled by the state, who at last could have the total control over children that parents, God and the Church had aspired to in the Old World, a world that was finally made possible by science — by cloning babies and by designer drugs.

Not having genetic engineering and modern chemistry, the Church had to establish its authority in another way. Christ may have told Peter to build his Church on a rock, but the Church was built on something far less substantial, on a set of beliefs that the Church Fathers demanded must be regarded as facts as indisputable as that the world was flat. Among them was the belief that death wasn't natural but a punishment imposed by God on humans for their sins, a punishment that Christians need not incur if they agreed that Christ died so their sins could be forgiven. Only if they accepted these doctrines as literally true, would Christians be saved from death and become immortal: their actual bodies would be resurrected. Not to believe these and other Church dogmas was called "heresy," which was decreed to be so great a sin that about 1260 Berthold of Regensburg, preached that he would rather his brother had killed 100 men and his sister slept with 100 men than that they be "in a single heresy."

Heresy, because it was the gravest of sins, incurred the severest punishments — torture, burning at the stake, being kicked out of the Church and, after death, kicked straight into hell. And quite rightly, said Thomas Aquinas, who argued that it was more important to excommunicate and kill heretics than "forgers and other malefactors." Heresy was so great a sin because the Church is a house of words; it depends for its existence on the acceptance of a set of beliefs, which, if not believed, would reveal that the "rock of ages" was a hill of sand, but if believed by everyone would become as real as the Emperor's new clothes.

Magical Thinking

The Christian plan for man's redemption continues to be believed not because it's true but because the need for man's redemption is so great. Unkindness, injustice, cruelty, war have always ravished the world. The desire to create a world in which people are kind, honest and peaceful is one of the highest goals of humankind, a world that the Prophets imagined God could create. They didn't know he couldn't because he was a heavenly stand-in for threatening and punishing parents. The Prophets themselves, since their bodies had been beaten like carpets to flog the bad out of them, also knew no other way to make people good except by threatening them with more and more punishments. Church officials, having been brought up in the same way and identifying with parents, punishment for sins became essential to religion and will continue to be as long as parents are in the punishment-for-sins business they founded. The Church and the Family were like the founder of Dotheboys Hall, Wackford Squeers, who knew no other way to educate boys but by whacking them (Charles Dickens, *Nicholas Nickleby*, 1838-9).

If the Family plan for producing good children — threats, beatings and other punishments — had worked, the Church as we know it wouldn't have come into existence. The Church knew no better than parents, but set itself up as a power higher than they were, a divine power whose job was to keep children good, be their Father always. But long before the Judeo-Christian Church made its power-play, kings and priests in pagan religions had declared that, by smearing special oils on their skin, *they* had become endowed with *kharisma*, the Greek word for divine power.

"Priests and conjurors are of the same trade" said Tom Paine, but priests claimed they could perform a greater miracle than pulling rabbits out of hats; they could pull sin out of people, a feat the Church boasted it accomplished soon after birth. "Being by nature born in sin, and the children of wrath, we are hereby made the children of grace." I'm quoting from the baptismal ritual in *The Book of Common Prayer*, in which "hereby" is the key word. For by that simple ritual (sprinkling with holy water), newborns, having been purified from sin and become "children of grace," could henceforth, so the words seemed to promise, go on their sinless way.

If that baptismal promise had been effective, all that would have been required to free humans of sin was a band of Church officials, like notaries public, who would show up wherever babies were born, perform the ceremony and issue a document certifying that "grace" had taken place. The notaries of the Church, of course, would have had to be anointed with holy oil in order to acquire *kharisma*, the divine power that enabled them to make infants kosher, ritually clean.

The Church didn't remain a simple baptizing institution because the ritual didn't do what it claimed to. The baptismal ritual turned out to be merely a certificate of membership in the Christian club, a guarantee that newborns could get into its exclusive heaven. A substantial benefit, except it applied only if they died in infancy. An inevitable restriction, for no matter how much kharisma a priest acquired, baptism didn't ward off the effects on infants of growing up in families that mistreated them. The first Christians, who were baptized as adults, must have thought they'd go and sin no more, unaware that the long-term effects of parental mistreatment can't be abracadabra-ed away. The baptismal ceremony necessarily became an initiation into a lifetime of rituals since Christians had to keep being absolved of their sins.

In Alcoholics Anonymous, which is worldwide and has many meeting places, drunks are told that they must "keep coming back" if they want to remain sober. In the Church, which is worldwide and has many meeting places, we're also told that we have to "keep coming back" because we remain sinners who need to be saved. AA has its twelve steps, and the Church has many more, for example, Sunday school, Bible study, religious instruction, communion, mass, confession, rosary beads and, before we die and sin no more, last rites. To keep back the constant tide of our sins, Christians fast during the forty days of Lent, Jews on the Day of Atonement, Muslims during the month of Ramadan; the religious make pilgrimages to Mecca, walk on their knees to holy shrines, scourge themselves with whips. Christians unceasingly repeat the Jesus Prayer ("Lord Jesus Christ, have mercy on me a sinner") because they're perpetual sinners whom Christ unceasingly has to forgive. The Church's very existence depends on people continuing to be sinners. If they were not, the Church would be out of business.

Cathy Ladman, in a 1991 comedy skit, defined religion as "guilt with different holidays." The audience let out a howl because religions never let us forget that we're sinners, far worse sinners than our parents taught us we were. Parents merely teach us we're bad. The Christian Church bludgeons us with the horrendous crime that resulted from our badness—causing the death of the greatest man who ever lived. Christ, the only begotten son of God, the one perfect being ever born, had to be born into this world of suffering, be nailed to a cross and die in excruciating pain so that the sins of wretches like us could be forgiven and we could escape the damnation we deserve and go to a heaven we don't deserve. Oh, *mea culpa, mea maxima culpa!* My far from perfect mother used to tell my sisters and me that she'd sacrificed her life for rotten us, which ravaged us with guilt. So imagine the guilt of having a good person's blood on your hands, Christ's innocent, sinless blood! How can such guilt ever be washed away?, especially from the child in us who was taught to believe its very essence was bad. What a miracle that Christ was willing to die to save offal us.

Despite the hundreds of rituals and services that churches kindly provide to ease our guilt, the blood on our hands isn't washed away. It can't be. It's the wrong blood. The blood on our hands isn't Christ's. It's the blood of the parents we killed in our hearts when we were slapped, beaten, rejected, slandered, raped. Jesus said that lust in the heart is as bad as lust in the act. I don't think it is, but murder in the heart does produce 'as if' guilt in children, who at first confuse the thought with the dead — I meant to type deed — but 'dead' parents was what we wished for, a deed we thought we'd buried six feet under in our unconscious, but which lets off a stench of guilt that the Church doesn't deal with. It can't, for though Church officials were anointed and made holier than thee and me, they'd also grown up in families and have the sin of fantasy murder buried in their unconscious. The Church turned Christ into a scapegoat who died for our general sins so we wouldn't have to disinter the specific heinous sin that we're guilty of — parricide.

What a wonderful religion that absolves us of sin and lets us get away with murder! We gladly perform the Church's rituals, obey its rules, and believe that Christ is our Savior and whatever else the Church tells us to believe, because doing what we're told allows us to keep our secret hidden. Unfortunately, it doesn't work. Multitudes of Christians who've obeyed the rules and dutifully believed what they were supposed to and led decent lives have nevertheless doubted that God would choose them as one of his elect. On their deathbeds, they fear they'll soon be in hell. They can't help being terrified because a part of them knows their guilty secret.

The Church's rituals turn out to be mumbo jumbo, to have no real power. Real absolution isn't a matter of priestly forgiveness or acts of contrition, but of understanding, in this case, what parents do that turns children into fantasy killers, knowledge, alas, that puts us in danger of feeling the agony of not having been loved. Since church officials were once children who preferred to bear a heavy burden of guilt than feel that agony, the Church hasn't been able to help us.

"So much straw"

In the thirteenth century, Thomas Aquinas devoted much of his life to writing *Summa theologiae* to prove that Christianity, as expressed in the Bible and Church doctrine, was the true view of the world. In one place in the *Summa* Aquinas says that in order "That the saints may enjoy their beatitude and the grace of God more abundantly, they are permitted to see the punishment of the damned in Hell," in other words, that in heaven God increases the enjoyment of the saints by letting them watch the suffering of the damned, "the fierce laments of tortured souls" as they boiled in blood or hot tar, floated in excrement, were eaten by wild dogs, or their stomachs ripped open until their guts spilled out, to name a few of the tortures Dante described in his *Inferno*. Aquinas didn't question that a God who made enjoying seeing the suffering of others a heavenly pleasure might not be God. Nor did Dante question the reality of a God who would subject his people to more and more vicious punishments in the twenty-four concentration camps known as the circles of Hell.

The philosopher David Hume (1711-1776), in a conversation he had on his death bed with James Boswell, said that the morality of every religion was bad. Religion is supposed to supply people with a moral code that makes them good, but a religion can't be moral that takes a man like Aquinas, who was said to be gentle and kind, and teaches him not to recoil with horror at a God who thinks that watching people tortured is a saintly pleasure. By defending the indefensible, Aquinas damaged his morality. So did Dante, and so do the people who read his literary Belsen and are not appalled by his and God's sadism.

It's not sufficiently known that Aquinas repudiated the God he'd been taught was the true God. On December 6, 1273, he was at Mass when a flood of light entered his mind, an ecstasy that lasted so long that the friar sitting beside him, not knowing what was going on, pulled at his cloak to see if he was all right. Aquinas came back to himself, but from that day on, he stopped writing his defense of Catholicism. When asked why, he once answered: "Because all that I have written seems to me like so much straw compared to what I have seen and what has been revealed to me." If, in his ecstasy, like those who have near-death experiences, he was immersed in the total love of a Being of Light, no wonder he thought that all he'd written about the Church was "so much straw" and hoped he'd die soon. And the shock to his belief system was so great that three months later, though he was not yet fifty and was in vigorous health, he did die. He could thus say "No!" to the Christian God without having to commit heresy (Father Angelus Walz, *Saint Thomas Aquinas, A Biographical Study*, translated from Italian, 1951).

The Catholic Church still clings to its punishing God. Starting in the 1970s many books were published about near-death experiences, which the Church maintained couldn't be true because God doesn't allow the dead to be in his presence until they've suffered in purgatory. The Church clings to its cruel God because family life conditions most of us to regard parental punishments, even when severe, as a means to goodness, not as the sadism it is.

Nevertheless, something deep within humans has been gravitating toward a kinder God, like birds migrating south in winter.

"The Possibility That God Could Love Us"

Father Merrin, one of the priests performing the exorcism in William Blatty's *The Exorcist* (1971), said that the demon in a possessed person tries to make the priests and everyone present see themselves "as ultimately bestial; as ultimately vile ... ; without dignity; ugly; unworthy." For Merrin and the demon, "unworthiness" is mankind's core problem. But, according to Merrin, what demons don't understand is that belief in God is "not a matter of reason at all." Considering our unworthiness, it's a matter "of accepting the possibility that God could love *us*."

"Accepting the possibility that God could love *us*"! Pope Gregory the Great (540-604) would have empathized with Merrin. Living at a time when few people questioned that God was the God of Wrath, Gregory lamented that he found it difficult to feel close to a God he knew nothing about, whom he couldn't talk to, a God who made him feel guilty, exhausted, only able to cry. Unwittingly, Gregory was describing how he'd felt toward his parents who, he'd wished, hadn't been remote, hadn't made him feel guilty, hadn't made him cry. Gregory was weary of feeling he was a sinner in the hands of an angry God and yearned for a more loving God, whose presence, since he was a mystic, he could sometimes feel.

Few of us are mystics. Besides, to believe in a loving God used to mean that you didn't believe in God. When he died in 1809, Thomas Paine was labeled an atheist and refused burial in consecrated ground because he insisted that the God in the Bible wasn't God, that the real God was benevolent. In the popular mind, belief in the God of Wrath persisted for centuries because most children grew up in households that made them feel bad and guilty, sure they ought to be punished and didn't deserve to be loved. And yet "the possibility that God could love *us*!" or, as the hymn, "Amazing Grace," puts it, the possibility that God could love "a wretch like me," has remained a hope.

In the twentieth century, that hope became a demand among some Catholics. The internationally-known priest, Henri Nouwen (1932-1996), said that people "can no longer relate to the powerful God of the Middle Ages but are searching for a tender, compassionate God, who can heal their wounded hearts." For Nouwen, that was the fundamental reason for religion. He frankly admitted that his wounded heart needed to be healed, a need that was so great he imagined Jesus saying to him, "I am your God ... You are my child ... . Come, let me wipe your tears, and let my mouth come close to your ears and say to you, 'I love you. I love you,

I love you' " (*The Road to Daybreak*, 1988). Nouwen's passionate need for God's love pervaded his life. In his last book, to comfort his readers, he told them that God constantly says to us what he said to Christ: "You are my beloved child, on you my favor rests" (*Life of the Beloved*, 1992).

Nouwen's search for "a tender and compassionate God," and Merrin's belief in "the possibility that God could love us," would have interested the anthropologist, Raymond Firth. Their search would have been more proof of his theory that "a marked feature" of all religions is the human need to have a "personal relation" to a higher being who makes us feel we're worthwhile and that our lives matter (*Religion, A Humanist Interpretation*, 1996).

When I first read about Firth's theory, I was dismayed. I didn't want to accept that God was a figment of my need, for in 1996 I was trying to believe in the Christian God and was sampling churches and reading religious books. I desperately wanted to have faith that God or Christ was really out there and loved me, and (as I described in Chapter 4), repeating "God is always loving me" did make me feel loved. If I'd continued to feel loved, I might have lived my life comforted, like the old man I saw on Bill Moyers' TV documentary, *On Our Own Terms* (September 2000). As he lay dying in a hospital, he sang in a soft voice, "Jesus loves me — this I know, For the Bible tells me so." That touched me, made me glad that religion lets people who are afraid and alone believe God loves them, thus satisfying a need for love that wasn't satisfied in the Family.

For would we sing, "Jesus loves me"?, would we stretch our hands up high to a God in heaven, if the love we'd received in our earthly homes hadn't been tainted with fear and hate? Would we long to believe in the possibility that God could love us, if parents' beatings and rejections hadn't made us feel unworthy of being loved?

Some of us feel so deprived that we long to be utterly possessed by God. "I want you to touch the deepest places of my heart so that I won't belong to anyone but you," Nouwen said to God, like the nineteenth-century Indian swami, Ramakrishna, who would say to Kali, the Goddess he worshiped, "I long only for my divine Mother." "I cannot live without You." "Please merge me constantly into Your Reality." Another devotee of another Divine Mother, the Virgin Mary, was Pope John Paul II, whose motto, directed to her, was *Totus tuus*, "I am all yours." John Paul was certain that Mary also felt that he was "all hers," that it was she who saved his life when he was shot in 1981. The need to feel loved is so powerful that even the Pope's emotional well-being depended on thinking that he and Mary were each other's "special possession."

The need to feel loved is so powerful that it grew breasts on God the Father. Clement, one of the early Christian theologians, compared seeking Christ to suckling: "for to those babes that suck the Word, the Father's breasts of love supply the milk." "My own breast I prepared for them, that they might drink my holy milk and live thereby," says God in an anonymous second-century Christian ode. The early church called itself *Mater Ecclesia*, and the mother aspect of the church didn't die. Despite the triumph of a warrior God who thought going on crusades and killing as many infidels as possible were Christian virtues, in the twelfth century a cult of the Virgin Mary arose. At first a mediator between man and God and painted in the stiff Byzantine style, Mary in the Renaissance plumped into a human mother suckling a child, the holy Madonna that the Church has since been unable to do without, just as people in the Paleolithic era couldn't do without their full-breasted mother figurines. I "will hold you against my breast," Nouwen imagined Jesus saying to him, as if Mary were his mother, which he was sure she was because Mary was the mother of everyone who believed in Jesus.

Nouwen was emotionally no different from the young child who, separated from his alcoholic mother, said that when he went home he was going to pretend to faint "so that Mama would carry me again like I was her baby, like she used to" (Jennifer Toth, *Orphans of the Living*, 1997). He too wanted to pretend he was still his mother's "beloved child," on whom her "favor" rested. Though God became male, in the heart of the baby who lives on in us, God remains female.

Being fed and held by a mother, that infantile concept of love, remains an underground spring in religion because most children experience it for too short a time and because it often ends violently. The child who wanted his Mama to carry him "like I was her baby" was looking back to the paradise before she slapped and beat him, threw dishes at him, and branded him with lighted cigarettes. In the past, Japanese little girls must also have longed to go back to paradise, to the time before Mama put red pepper on her nipples to stop them breast-feeding. I've sometimes wondered if Christians insisted that "in my flesh shall I see God," because heaven still meant having their flesh held against their first God. We look back with longing to infantile love because, as Wordsworth said, "shades of the prison house" soon darken our lives—the yells, smacks, beatings and the devastating knowledge that being loved depends on obeying our jailers.

Infantile love is paradise for a deeper reason than our need to be fed and held. That time in our lives is an Eden because our Gods usually haven't yet made it wholly clear that we're bad, imperfect, inferior goods. Augustine (354-430), who believed that human hearts were congenitally evil, is the theologian who's credited with inventing the idea of original sin. He didn't invent it; it was implanted in his head the same way it's implanted in every child's head. In *The Exorcist* when Father Merrin said that the demon in a possessed person tries to convince us that we're "bestial ... vile ... ; without dignity; ugly; unworthy," he was unaware that we're all possessed by a demon, an inner critic who constantly tells us we're vile, ugly, without dignity, unworthy of love, a demon who doesn't rise up from hell but is the child in us dutifully repeating parental indoctrination. The Church tells us we're born evil because it too is repeating parental indoctrination.

The underlying assumption of the Family and the Church is that children are born bad. The Family performs the initial indoctrination, which the Church confirms. The Family tries to transform bad children into good ones by threats and punishments, and so does the Church. The Family makes it clear to children that in order to be loved, they have to become good. The Church offers the same conditional love we get at home: only if we believe what we're told to believe and obey Church rules will the Church love us and ultimately God love us, though that's iffy because only a few people are good enough to make it into God's inner sanctum.

The Family and the Church as we know them wouldn't exist if they didn't believe that something is innately wrong with babies that need fixing, and that the first step in redemption is making children understand that they're bad. We named our species, Homo Sapiens, wise man, but no one who was wise, who had a bit of common sense, could have reasoned that teaching children they're bad would produce loving adults. They would have known it would produce haters, as it has, a species remarkable for its personal and global violence, a species who, because of its conditioning, thinks that a sprinkle of holy water can change a baby's nature, or its genetic engineering.

What if that basic premise of the Family and the Church is wrong? What if the truth is that babies are born loving and that immersion in a hell of mistreatment shocks them into hate? The children who were sure they'd caused the floods in California identified with the raging rivers not merely because they were in a rage at being slapped, spanked, rejected, humiliated, overly controlled. They were also in a rage because they'd been maligned, slandered, libeled.

When children's original capacity to love and be loved is not reciprocated, when children are rejected and despised, the rage that's ignited is Biblical. In the Old Testament, when God's need to be loved by the Israelites was thwarted, the fire kindled by his anger would pour from his mouth and could set fire to "the very roots of the mountains" (Deuteronomy 32:22). If God had lived at the end of the twentieth century, he might have been sent to Hillcrest, an institution in Massachusetts that specialized in treating children who act out their rage by setting fires. In the Bible, God's wrath is tremendous because he was a child who'd received severe mistreatment instead of love. The God of Wrath may insist, despite his insane jealousy and lust for vengeance, that he's a loving God because, originally, he was a loving child. God's destructive wrath is an expression of children's cosmic rage at not being loved. What most of us want from God is the love we didn't get when we were babies. "Heaven has no rage, like love to hatred turned," said William Congreve (*The Mourning Bride*, 1697) because hate is a reaction to not being loved. At the heart of hate is always the child's bewildered, angry cry, "I loved you. Why didn't you love me? Godamn you for not loving me."

And yet beneath the rage, our original capacity for love remains, which knows there's a better love than the love mixed with fear, hate and guilt that families provide. The idea of a loving God was created by the original loving nature of children.

Chapter 25   **Original Love**

The Sun That Lies Within

"The sun that lies within" means 'soul' in a tribe in Uruguay. When I read that in Wade Davis's *One River* (1996), my face lit up, and when I read the dictionary definition of 'sun', I understood why. The sun is the star that's "the basis of the solar system and sustains life on Earth, being the source of heat and light," and the sun lying within is our personal 'soular' system, the source of the 'heat' (our capacity for love) and 'light' (our quest for truth) that sustains each of us on Earth. Then it struck me that if we were brought up differently, our sun within could give off much more heat and light, and I imagined an Earth without the thick smog of hate and lies that pollute it, and, for a moment, I breathed the intoxicating air of freedom.

I had a similar feeling on the morning of October 5, 2000 when I turned on TV and saw the crowds in Belgrade, shouting, waving, carried away with joy, sure they were going to overthrow Milosevic, the dictator who'd brutalized their country for over a decade. I was so excited, I kept on watching, though I should have been working. Even when the reports began repeating, I didn't return to my computer. I drove to my favorite café and celebrated the revolution by eating a brownie and drinking coffee (forbidden foods in my health regime).

I bought a newspaper, though it had only yesterday's news: "Mass Protest Planned by Yugoslavian Opposition," the protest I'd just seen on TV. It had been forecast by an incident the day before, when striking miners, ordered to get to work by the police, refused and had been joined by 20,000 people who crowded into the mine to defend them and, to everyone's amazement, the police backed off. We're "more democratic" than people think, said one policeman, who was also "fed up" with Milosevic and sure that this was "the end of him."

I wanted to stop time or, better, put my excitement in a time capsule so that whenever I needed to, I could open it and inhale the high of victory over tyrants, the intoxicant of the child in us who longed to triumph over our household tyrants. Revolutions are realizations of that childhood dream. In the French Revolution, the guillotine that cut off head after head was a child cutting its oppressors down to size.

The heart that leaps up when we behold a dictator overthrown is part of the sun that lies within, the part that's revolted by injustice and leaps with joy when justice triumphs. Wordsworth's heart leapt up when he saw a rainbow in the sky because the part of the mind that's able to recognize beauty saw it. The part of my mind that can recognize truth leapt up when I read the Uruguayan definition of soul because a 'sun' does lie within us. Such leaps are mini-second unions of like to like. When Hindus, palms together at the chest, head bowed, greet each other, their divine essence is acknowledging the divine essence in the other, the Uruguayans' sun that lies within, the soul that Socrates said contains the "jewels" of justice, courage, nobility and truth.

But how can violently triumphing over a dictator be a jewel of human nature? Because the impulse to overcome injustice is sublime, though the means may not be. Children wouldn't dream of revolution if they weren't born with a strong sense of justice. When mistreated, their soul cries out for justice, but since children can rarely get it except in fantasy and since their parents are violent, they have violent fantasies. And yet we can't help feeling that if children were born truly good, they wouldn't be violent even in fantasy. We have that feeling because in early childhood we're trained to think that goodness means submitting to authorities.

True goodness has nothing to do with submission. Goodness (if it gets out from under the rules of conduct imposed by parents and society) doesn't come from "Thou shalts" and "Thou shalt nots" but from our "Buddha nature," from the Atman, the Hindu name for the life energy they say permeates everything in the universe. In the fourth century BC Socrates called that energy the "seed of divinity," the "spark of the true light" in humans. In the twentieth century, Jane Goodall called it "the flame of pure spirit" which is our essential nature (*Reason for Hope*, 1999).

A common name for that energy is love, "bakti," the divine love that the swami Muktananda (1908-1982) said creates and sustains everything in the universe, which reminded me of Dante's "Love that moves the sun and the other stars." Muktananda said that the love energy that creates and sustains the universe is also the core of us, our "Inner Self," our "I AM," "the greater consciousness dwelling within every human soul." The channeled Pathwork lectures (mentioned in Chapter 4) described love as our "innermost core" as "free, spontaneous, creative, loving, giving, all-knowing, and capable of uninterrupted joy and bliss," as "the most powerful, creative and intelligent force" we have, an "inexhaustible fountain of strength and inspiration."

As I was summarizing the Pathwork's discourses on love, one of Archie Bunker's jeering "Whoop-di-do!"s from *All in the Family* echoed in my head. For to hear love, which most of us associate with romantic love, described in grand, cosmic terms seems wildly inflated. Even the dictionary mainly defines love as a tender or intense desire and attraction to another, the love that's celebrated in popular songs. We celebrate romantic love because it's usually our most powerful positive emotion, and when we remember how it feels to fall in love, Muktananda's description of divine love energy, or the Pathwork's tributes to love don't seem so wild.

Since Freud, love has been downgraded to the sublimation of the sex drive. At our core, according to Freud, men are still chimpanzees for whom love is lining up behind a female in heat and waiting their turn for what Jane Goodall timed as a ten to fifteen-second fuck. But in humans sex can occur because the nature of "the spiritual being as originally created" is love (to quote the Pathwork again), and our capacity to love and be loved has been resurrected. We return to the time when ovum and sperm united into a new being, who is fearless, vulnerable, trusting, positive, vibrantly alive, eager to grow and change in a growing and changing universe.

The resurgence of this positive love energy is a tour de force because mistreatment in early childhood stifles our dynamic growth, makes us wary of humans, afraid to trust, numb, tough, cynical. What blasts us through our negative conditioning and lets us risk being vulnerable again is the same energy that created the universe, which is concentrated in the part of the body that creates life. Sexual arousal is feeling the creative energy that's radiating throughout the universe radiating in us. When we fall in love, we're back in our original, expansive state of consciousness, a cosmic safety net that allows us to let go of our separateness and fall free, like an acrobat who lets go of a swing in a high wire act and joins another.

Bakti, love energy, the "powerful, creative and intelligent force" we bring into the world does more than generate personal love; it's also the force that drives us toward truth. Socrates said that the "divine agency" that led him to the truth was in everyone, which meant that humans, since they can know truth, have the highest destiny. About 400 years later Jesus tapped into the same "divine agency," a "Spirit of truth" that made him feel he'd come "into the world" to "bear witness to the truth," the truth that sets us free (John 18:37; 8:32). According to John, Jesus promised that after he died, his Spirit of truth would be transmitted as a gift to future Christians (14:16-17). If Jesus actually said the "Spirit of truth" was unique to him, he was wrong, as Socrates' life proves, and that "the still small voice" mentioned in the Old Testament (1 Kings 19:11-12) also refers to. Millennia before Jesus was born, humans were able to tune into something within that recognizes truth, and after Jesus' death, they continued to, whether Christians or not.

We tend to describe truths that suddenly strike us as "divine" because we think they come from a mysterious source outside us. Thomas Paine said that "almost all [his] knowledge" had "bolted" into his mind of its "own accord," and many others have spoken with awe of the leap in consciousness that, coming from who knows where, produces new ideas, truths, facts, and profound life changes. Francis of Assisi (1182?-1226) was on his way to join a Crusade when a voice in his head told him to return home, where he stopped being a well-to-do young man about town, gave away his possessions and founded a new religious order based on personal poverty, helping the poor and loving animals and nature.

Centuries later George Fox (1624-1691) also founded a religion because, he said, "a still small voice" in his head told him that since Christ's Holy Spirit was in everyone, it followed that men and women were equal, that people should not tip their hats or bow to their "betters," and, most shocking of all, that Churches and priests were unnecessary. No wonder Fox was imprisoned eight times and that Quakers were persecuted. But his truths helped undermine the social and religious order and spark the revolution that created modern democracy.

Inner Self-Helpers

The truths of George Fox and Francis of Assisi were communicated to them by a voice they heard in their head. Socrates' truths also came to him by means of "a kind of voice," an inner voice he "was first conscious of as a child," a voice he heard all his life and that also served as a moral guide. In the last quarter of the twentieth century, many psychiatrists who used hypnosis began reporting that a voice was speaking through their clients that acted as a similar guide. Ralph Allison (in the 1974 *American Journal of Clinical Hypnosis*) called it an inner self-helper because it acted as a personal therapist, one who knew a client's history and how to solve his or her problems, was "free from emotion," had "good judgment," a strong "awareness of God" and a "sense of right and wrong" that could be highly unconventional. Because his clients had multiple personalities, Allison assumed that their inner self-helper was an alternate personality (*Minds in Many Pieces*, 1980).

Other therapists and psychiatrists who worked with "multiples" also encountered inner self-helpers they assumed were "alters." But a voice that spoke through a client of Dr Robert Mayer told him that it wasn't an "alter" but a "trinity of angels" sent here to help his client. When Mayer asked where they came from and who they were, they told him they came from "beyond" and were guardian angels. Mayer was highly skeptical, whereupon the trinity told him that his "spiritual awareness [was] that of a flea," and treated him with "patronizing disdain" (*Through Divided Minds*, 1989).

A hypnotherapist who encountered inner self-helpers in clients who were not multiples wasn't skeptical about their origin. Perhaps because she'd had a near-death experience, P M H Atwater thought she'd discovered the soul when she heard a voice coming from her clients that gave wise, personal advice, a voice that was "a detached and loving source of limitless knowledge and endless compassion," a voice that sounded the same or similar no matter who the client was. When she later read about inner self-helpers in psychiatric journals, she wrote the authors suggesting they may have established that the soul is real (*Coming Back to Life*, 1988).

The psychiatrists were not prepared to come out publicly and say so, and yet more and more therapists validated the reality of inner self-helpers. Robert Mayer, despite his skepticism, acknowledged that we all have one, and the best contemporary therapists use it as an ally. David Calof, a Seattle hypnotherapist, taught his clients self-hypnosis so they could more easily contact their inner self-helper since it knew far better than he did how to solve their problems (*The Couple Who Became Each Other*, 1996).

When 'something' began writing through my hand and speaking in my mind, I'd never heard of inner self-helpers. I feared I was going crazy, for schizophrenics heard voices. But I heard only one voice and I knew it was inside my head, nor did it scream put-downs at me or demand that I kill myself or someone else. The voice I heard was kind, which was why I called it my Kind Force. Like the inner self-helpers Ralph Allison described, it was a reservoir of wisdom and had a "sense of right and wrong" that was highly unconventional. It not only knew the history of my abuse, it made sure that the memories came up at a pace I could handle and encouraged me to believe them. Once when an unusually violent memory was about to surface, my Kind Force said as if with a megaphone: "DO NOT DOUBT!" It did because when memories of child abuse surface, the most common response is not to believe them. Or, one day when I was sweeping the patio and was about to trip on a hose, my Kind Force made me aware of the danger by whispering, "Be careful. You are precious."

I stood, holding the broom handle, incredulous. "I, precious? How ridiculous!" I was awed though, but only for a short while. Instead of taking the reality of my Kind Force to heart, I tried to reason it away. I decided it was merely an extension of instinct, a more sophisticated form of the programming of animals, that, just as the body knows how to heal a cut, the human mind knows how to heal emotional wounds. I didn't want to take in that my Kind Force was not following a program. When the body heals a cut, it does follow a program, but my Kind Force knew about my particular wounds and dealt with my particular problems. It was not a mechanism. It was alive, aware, adaptable. It *was* a "most powerful, creative and intelligent force."

I doubted the reality of my Kind Force not only because it defied reason but because it frightened me. It threatened to destroy my 'bad' identity, the self-hate most children acquire in the family, where parents condition children to think they're bad by steady doses of that most addictive home-brew — love laced with fear and hate. I'd never before been exposed to pure love in action, love whose goal was to uncondition me, to help me regain my original love so I could experience to the fullest "the greater consciousness dwelling within every human soul."

The appearance of my Kind Force wasn't a sign I was going crazy; it was a sign I was becoming sane, getting back the bright blue sky that had appeared at the very beginning of my first Ecstasy trip. That blue sky, a symbol of the original love we all have at conception, lasted only a second because my mother's hatred began contaminating me as soon as she knew she was pregnant. To heal, so my Kind Force told me, I had to go back to who I was before my mother knew she was pregnant. For years I didn't know what that meant, and if anyone had told me that my Kind Force came from my original self-love, I would have been equally uncomprehending.

When I was trying to become a Christian, I thought the voice that had said, "You are precious" was Christ's. After I discovered "Christ" was a myth manufactured from a man, I could no longer believe that. Nor could I believe what a religious friend told me, that it was God speaking within me. I refuse to call my Kind Force "God," which evokes images and concepts that repel me. When I was a child, "God" meant the old man with a white beard who presided in heaven. After I read through the Bible, God was the madman who hurled plagues and storms down from heaven. That millions have worshiped that vengeful demon will always astonish me. So will the twentieth-century feminists who resurrected the big-bellied, heavy-breasted female Gods of prehistory and boasted that all women were Goddesses who embodied the wise, kind, nurturing archetype of ideal motherhood.

A pox on all such Gods. He-Gods and She-Gods are glorifications of the matriarchs and patriarchs who so frightened us when we were children that we bowed down and worshiped them to retain our sanity. The results have been catastrophic. Training children to believe that varieties of mistreatment are acts of love has greatly diminished our capacity to see truth, and to love. Family life almost eclipses the sun that lies within; rarely, if ever, can we open to the "free, spontaneous, creative, loving, giving, all-knowing" energy that is our innermost core at conception.

Original Play

In the early thirteenth century, Francis of Assisi, having received a message from his inner voice, left the respectable calling of killing infidels in Crusades, and founded a religious sect that broke with the violence, luxury and lack of compassion of the Catholic Church. In the mid-1970s, O Fred Donaldson, convinced that "the gods" were calling him to his true vocation, left the respectable profession of teaching at a university and got a job playing with preschool children (*Playing by Heart*, 1993).

Francis of Assisi, like John Wycliffe in the fourteenth century, Martin Luther in the sixteenth century and many others tried to reform a Church that was essentially corrupt. When Donaldson began playing with children, his goal, far more difficult, was to reform a culture whose attitude toward children was essentially corrupt.

How corrupt it was, he didn't fully comprehend until he learned that play wasn't what philosophers in the past and modern psychologists said it was: a way to use up surplus energy, act out hidden desires, release aggression, master anxiety, strengthen the ego, and learn physical and social skills (like teamwork, fair fighting and competition). Others who'd studied play observed children playing, or supervised or coached them. Donaldson played with children as if he were another child and discovered what he called "original play," the way children instinctively play until they're about three or four.

Down on his hands and knees and following children's lead, Donaldson learned that play is initiated by a meeting of eyes that say, "You're lovable and there's nothing to be afraid of." Children also taught Donaldson that when he wanted to play with them, he should first touch their feet, then nudge their legs. A sense of safety having been established, children let what happens happen, exploration and adventures, like chasing, hugging, rolling on the ground, lying together and gazing at clouds, watching insects in the grass, looking for elves and finding them, patting each others' faces, giggling, being a horse, a chicken, a leaf, staring into a pond, smacking hands in mud puddles. Whatever happens is always different.

What's the same is that young children don't normally push each other around, hit or use weapons. Original play remains "roly-poly"; it doesn't turn into a fight. The children who are "most appeasing, conciliatory, friendly" become the leaders. Aggression is unnecessary because in original play no one wins. The "curiosity, trust, resilience, awareness" of healthy children generate mutual love and respect, and more: the joy of being alive in an exciting world, and the feeling of belonging. A "we" is born. As a five-year-old put it, "Play is when we don't know we are different from each other."

From the initial eye contact that says, "You're lovable and there's nothing to be afraid of," to the exhilarating peace of feeling one with another, all young children play the same way. Whether girl or boy, rich or poor, Asian, Caucasian, African, whether from Italy or China or Timbuktu, whether autistic, mentally retarded, or physically disabled, the original play of children all over the world is an expression of our original love and kindness, a fact Donaldson proved by the effect playing with children had on him. It slowly resurrected the playful attitude toward life and the loving kindness that had lain dormant in him since he was a child.

The French obstetrician, Frederick Leboyer, observed that when a baby is placed in warm water a few minutes after birth, it plays. Its eyes "open wide" and it looks around, exploring its new world with "utter concentration … astonishment [and] curiosity." It turns its head to the right and left as far as it can. One hand opens, closes, emerges from the water, then the arm does, whereupon the palm feels the air. That arm descends and the other hand and arm similarly emerge. Soon the hands play with each other. A little later "a foot shoots out," or a leg hits the edge of the tub and "propels the whole body" backward and the child, enjoying the feeling, does it again. Its mouth opens, closes, lips part, the "tongue flicks out, retreats," the hand finds the face and "slides over it," the thumb finds the mouth. Thus, uttering "soft little cries of … surprise and joy," the baby experiences the delights of being alive in a new, exciting world. (Birth Without Violence, 1974).

Early in the nineteenth century, Wordsworth, remembering his childhood when everything seemed bathed in a "celestial light," fancied that "trailing clouds of glory do we come from God who is our home." Wordsworth's poem, Ode, Intimations of Immortality, was a forecast of the new faith in original goodness that was about to occur, a shift in thinking that became widespread for several decades and was accepted by many of the best minds of the period. But by the end of the century, in part because of the influence of Darwin, the belief was fading away. Thomas Huxley, a popularizer of Darwin, argued that the "liberal popular illusion that babies are all born good" couldn't be true, for our inheritance from ancestors who were engaged in the brutal, aggressive, competitive struggle for survival meant that we were not born good or innocent but with an "innate tendency to unlimited self-assertion" (Evolution and Ethics and Other Essays, 1916).

Freud similarly argued that mankind's noble qualities—conscience, cooperation, civilization, love—were not innate but developed by suppressing or sublimating man's original savagery and were therefore much weaker than our brutal qualities. Freud and Huxley had been influenced by the evolutionary biologist Ernst Haeckel, who thought he'd proved that the findings of Darwin had a basis in embryology by his "biogenetic law"—ontogeny recapitulates phylogeny—that the embryo, as it develops, repeats the history of the race, that having progressed in utero from fish to ape, humans were born savages. The vast majority of late nineteenth-century intellectuals assumed that the recapitulation theory was a scientific truth and therefore irrefutable.

During the first half of the twentieth century embryologists proved that Haeckel's theory was wrong. Although embryos and fetuses do develop characteristics of some of our animal ancestors, their growth doesn't repeat the history of the race. Evolution occurs, not when we inherit characteristics of adult ancestors but when we inherit juvenile ones. A fetal ape doesn't have low brow ridges like adult apes; its brow is like a human brow. Nor are the milk teeth of an infant ape like its parents' teeth; they're like human teeth. According to Gavin de Beer in *Embryos and Ancestors* (1958), evolutionary progress is made by "paedomorphosis," the retention by a species of the fetal or infantile traits of past ancestors. Adult forms rarely give rise to new species. Evolutionary change is most likely to occur when ancestral youthful characters become those of the adult descendant. "It is the young form that shows the way of future evolution."

According to the biologist J B S Haldane, if "human evolution is to continue along the same lines as the past," people in the future will never acquire many of the present adult characters but will remain more like children. Haldane predicted that in the future human beings would not mature until thirty, that they would put more value on pleasure than work, that they would not take religion or philosophy seriously, that they would retain the curiosity and uninhibited sexuality of children and be too sensitive and uncompetitive to fight wars ("Possibilities of Human Evolution," *The Inequality of Man and Other Essays*, 1932).

In original play children are acting like future human beings; they're "sensitive," "uncompetitive," don't fight, are sexually curious and "put more value on pleasure than work." They're "free," "spontaneous," "creative," filled with "joy and bliss," fearless, trusting, eager for the adventure of life. They're coming from their innermost core, living proof, as the Pathwork says, that the nature of "the spiritual being as originally created" is love.

Our culture doesn't define love as freedom, spontaneity, joy, creativity, fearlessness, the excitement of being alive that little children experience when they play. We think love is the intense attachment of romance, or a settled attachment, concern for another, serving others. Most of us wouldn't define children's play as love, but it hardly matters. By the age of three or four, it usually vanishes. As Donaldson sadly noted, the initial play-look of, "You're lovable and there's nothing to fear," is no longer exchanged. Eyes that were once "clear and free of fear" become "aggressive," or are cast "downward in submission." The kind of play that one of Donaldson's playmates defined as a sense of oneness and belonging, is replaced by the "thrill of victory" and the "agony of defeat." Original play becomes competition. Children "fight and call it play," and when we play to win, said Donaldson, "every victory is a funeral," and not only for the child who loses. Children play to win because they've already attended their own funeral, because the innermost core they had at conception, their "inexhaustible fountain of strength and inspiration" has been reduced to a trickle.

Chapter 26   The Fall Of Man

When Fred Donaldson in *Playing by Heart* said that children's initial play-look—"You're lovable and there's nothing to fear"—is replaced by eyes that have become "aggressive" or are cast "downward in submission," he was lamenting what's been called the fall of man.

Many cultures have myths about man's fall. We're most familiar with the Genesis story of Adam and Eve. Created by God in his own image, they lived innocently and happily in the garden of Eden until Satan flew up from hell, disguised himself as a serpent, and tempted Eve to disobey God by eating fruit from a forbidden tree. Incensed, God drove them out of Eden and condemned not only them to death but all their children and their children's children forever and ever. Christians later decided that God's punishment was just because "In Adam's Fall, We sinned All." "Out of a man's heart," declared the New Testament, "come evil thoughts, acts of fornication, of theft, murder, adultery, ruthless greed, and malice; fraud, indecency, envy, slander, arrogance, and folly; these evil things all come from the inside, and they defile the man" (Mark 7:21-23).

A Mexican Myth

The ancient Mexican sorcerers also believed that long ago man became defiled. Don Juan, Carlos Castaneda's teacher, told him that, according to the ancient sorcerers, man was originally a "complete being" with full psychic powers which made him capable of "stupendous insights, [and] feats of awareness that are nowadays regarded as mythological legends." But the "magical being" man was "destined to be" lost his power ("Mud Shadows," *The Active Side of Infinity*, 1998). In the Christian myth, Satan flies up from hell to make man evil. In the Mexican myth, "predators" fly up "from the depths of the cosmos" to destroy man's potential. They do that by displacing what don Juan called our "true mind" by the "mind we use every day." We think it's our own mind, but it's a "foreign installation" acquired from the predators.

The ancient sorcerers developed that theory because they'd developed the ability to see the energy flowing in the universe and saw humans as "luminous cocoons of energy" and infants as "balls of energy" covered from top to bottom with a "glowing coat of awareness" unique to the human species. Infants lose that awareness, said the sorcerers, because predators, craving an awareness superior to their own "heavy awareness," eat infants' "glowing coat of awareness." Just as we rear chickens in chicken coops to be our food, "predators rear infants in human coops" to be their food and, by the time they become adults, their glowing awareness is gone, except for "a narrow fringe" "from the ground to the top of the toes." Predators leave that "point of awareness" because it makes us capable of self-reflection, which gives off energetic "flares of awareness" that predators continue to eat.

Predators, said don Juan, thus take "over the rule of our lives," become "our lord and master," and make us "docile and helpless." "If we want to protest," they "suppress our protest. If we want to act independently," they demand "we don't do so." They displace our glowing awareness with their own "systems of beliefs," "ideas of good and evil," "social mores," "hopes and expectations and dreams of success or failure." They make us greedy, cowardly, chained to routines, "complacent," "obedient," "meek," and yet "egomaniacal." Humans, who were once destined to be "magical beings," become "sedated man," "trite, conventional, imbecilic."

The Mexican sorcerers' explanation for the fall of man was more accurate than the Christians because they saw the "glowing coat of awareness," emanating from babies and knew it was the great, creative energy humans are born with. But their explanation of how babies lose their original awareness — that predators eat it up — is fantastic. I was surprised that the highly intelligent don Juan thought predators were real. But he told Carlos he believed in predators because nothing else could explain the "contradiction between the intelligence of man the engineer and the stupidity of his systems of beliefs … and contradictory behavior." He railed at his own plight. "Nobody ever asked me," he protested, "if I would consent to be eaten by beings of a different kind of awareness." My "parents just brought me into this world to be food," "meat" for the predators.

When don Juan told Carlos about the predators, Carlos said they were "preposterous, incredible." And yet, he felt "a profound sense of unease and discontent," and his body shook "from head to toe." Later, when he glimpsed the predators' shadows and heard them buzzing in his ears, he screamed "his head off." Eventually, the mere thought of predators made him pant, nausea rise from "the bottom of [his] being," and his body convulse. When the predators appeared as fifteen-foot black shadows leaping fifty feet high and landing beside him with "a silent thud," Carlos let out a scream and kept on screaming until he passed out. When he came to, he was lying in bed, towels soaked in ice-cold water on his head to bring down his high fever. Fear, not reason, made Carlos finally accept that malevolent entities flew up from the depths of the cosmos and "crushed us ages ago," leaving us "weak, vulnerable, and docile." He "wept" for his "fellow men" who'd continue to be eaten by predators.

To prove they exist, don Juan told Carlos that "in the depths of every human being" is "an ancestral, visceral knowledge" of predators, knowledge Carlos felt and that the ancient sorcerers must also have felt, a gut knowledge that long ago and far away something happened that undermined and almost destroyed the best in them. When the sorcerers described that 'something' as being eaten by scary predators, they did what many cultures have done.

Eating Children

In legends and fairy tales, scary monsters who eat children are common. The Roman God Saturn, among other Gods, ate his own children. The monster Grendel in Beowulf ground up babies into sausages. A wicked witch wants to shove Hansel and Gretel into the oven so she can eat them roasted. The big bad wolf wants to eat little Red Riding Hood raw. The ogre who lives in a wood near the castle where the comatose Sleeping Beauty lies is a giant with long teeth and claws, who "runs away with naughty little boys and girls and eats them up." The mother of the Prince who later marries Beauty is an ogre. She's no giant with long teeth and claws; she looks like an ordinary woman, but she plots to make a meal of each of her grandchildren.

Children have literally been eaten. A chimpanzee mother will sometimes eat a newborn, and so will mothers in native tribes. In 1927 Daisy Bates, an amateur anthropologist, published in an Australian newspaper, "Aboriginal Cannibals: Mothers Who Eat Their Babies" because she'd often observed the custom, as others had. (Elizabeth Salter Daisy Bates, 1971) In eleventh-century China, human-meat restaurants were common, where children's flesh was regarded as the tastiest (Hans Askenasy, *Cannibalism from Sacrifice to Survival*, 1994).

When Jonathan Edwards spoke of being "swallowed up" by God, he'd actually been swallowed up by the God-of-Wrath mother who beat him without mercy. Children who are sexually used often feel "swallowed up" by their abusers. A friend, whose mother started to suck on his penis when he was two months old, was so overwhelmed by feelings he couldn't comprehend that he felt himself dissolving into her.

Mexican sorcerers thought predators compensated for their "heavy awareness" by partaking of babies' "glowing awareness," and Catholics drink the blood (wine) and eat the flesh (wafer) of Christ to partake of his virtues. Catholics may find it easy to believe they consume "the real presence" of Christ in Communion because they have visceral memories of having been somehow mysteriously consumed by their parents. Mothers often hug and kiss their babies as if they were hungry to get back something they once had.

Most of us have seen mothers who kiss babies all over, saying, "I'm going to eat you up!" The anthropologist, Sarah Blaffer Hrdy, was one of them. She found her babies "luscious." When her three children were young, she'd say to them, "You're so adorable I could eat you up," and called them "sweet potato," and "muffin." Being a Darwinian, she asked herself if, because of her animal heritage, she was drawn to eat tender "delectable" new flesh because it was "so healthy, not to mention parasite free"? She didn't ask if, like animals, she was drawn to eat the young because they're so easy to kill, for she was "positive that I never had any inclination whatsoever to [really] eat my children." She theorized that babies' are born plump so mothers will find them attractive and want to take care of them, that babies need "to seduce at birth," that "the erotic appeal and sheer deliciousness of a baby's soft, plump flesh" helped insure its survival (*Mother Nature*, 1999).

Hrdy used the theory of evolution to partially conceal her real motive, for when she said she had no "inclination whatsoever to eat" her children, she acknowledged "desiring ... control over them, body and soul," "more control ... than their own strong wills were ever inclined to grant." Hrdy thought that her children's opposition made it a fair fight, and I hope they had wills strong enough to resist her, but most children don't. They succumb to their parents' desire to control them "body and soul."

Gods, in some ancient statues, have a huge open maw, as if they were waiting to be fed, and millions of real children did become meat for Gods. But virtually all children have been sacrificed to the Mother and Father Gods who demand total control over them, who by various means—from fear to possessive love—hook their children and eat them up like the mythic predators. It's as if parents also wanted to exchange their heavy awareness for children's fresh, expansive awareness, but in the process they make their children as much as possible like themselves.

The Family Theocracy

In the sixteenth century John Calvin established a theocracy in Geneva in which a governing body judged and punished his followers and tried to control the most minute aspects of their lives. What food they should eat, what time they should get up in the morning and go to bed at night, even regulations about coughing could be found in the statutes of Geneva. Calvin modeled his theocracy on the Old Testament God's 613 commandments, which also controlled trifles. Calvin demanded absolute control because God had absolute control over his chosen people. But Calvin, like the Israelite God, was imitating his first Gods. Families, whether Christian, Muslim, Jewish, Buddhist, Atheist, or Communist, rich, poor or middle class, educated or uneducated, cruel or kind, creates a theocracy with many rules children must obey, and they are anxious to obey. They learn fast that their safety and sense of well-being depend on it.

Thoreau said that "Every child begins the world again" and James Agee that in every child "the potentiality of the human race is born again." That's true. The trouble is that children quickly absorb their culture as if by osmosis. Every family is a cult where children are en-cultured by learning to worship the great God of conformity, to want, above all, to belong, to be like everyone else (except better).

To become like everyone else, children first have to undergo spiritual circumcision. Parents perform that initiation rite when they pervert the original love children are born with into the belief they were born bad. Like boys who have their foreskins cut, and girls who have their clitorises excised, children are scarred for life. They feel so bad about themselves, they're sure they can only seem good, that they must do and think what everyone else does, and thus pass as good.

To be stripped of our conformity would feel like being naked in public. That common dream may express the common fear of being caught with our naked self showing. Or we may have to dream of revealing our naked self because in daily life we're confined in a full-body straitjacket. The trouble is we don't feel confined; we're unaware that virtually everything we think, feel, even see is a cultural implant and, that beneath our programming is the hidden treasure we had at conception, the capacity to be spontaneous, original, joyous, in tune with the vast possibilities that exist beyond convention.

During Dannion Brinkley's second near-death experience, he was told to build various therapy rooms to help people understand that they're "powerful spiritual beings" (*At Peace in the Light*, 1995). We need that therapy because families don't grow children up; they stunt them. It's as if we had lobotomies, which merge us into the mass of confused beings who wander about at the mercy of parents, teachers, ministers, gurus, fashions, public opinion, tethered to the multiple leading strings of our particular culture.

The Real Predators

Mexican sorcerers developed the ability to see that humans are born with a "glowing coat of awareness," but they were unable to see what seems far less difficult, that those who try to take "over the rule of our lives" are not predators who fly up from deep in the cosmos.

The gigantic black shadows of the predators filled Carlos with a "sense of foreboding," as if "something imminently dangerous" was about to attack him. They reminded him of "an infantile fear" he associated with his Catholic "religious background," with "dark results and punishment … like the wrath of God, descending on me." However, he realized that his fear also came from the "wrath and impotence" raging within him. He didn't connect his rage and sense of helplessness with the scary parents he and all children are cooped up with. The gigantic predators the Mexican sorcerers conjured up reminded me of the scary movies conjured up in our culture, which people flock to see so they can release some of the fear we accumulate in childhood, without being aware of its real, human source.

The sorcerers of Mexico were courageous warriors, but in one area they remained scared children, unable to see that the frightening, bossy predators who rule children's lives are not a "foreign installation" but a domestic one. Don Juan said he believed in the reality of predators because "every human being on this earth seems to have exactly the same reactions, the same thoughts, the same feelings." They do because the "human coops" we're raised in are families, where parents, who've already been shaped by the culture, do everything they can to mold their children into the same shape.

Children say, "I'll be good, I'll do whatever you want, think what you tell me to think" because they're afraid of scary parents, not scary predators. We don't need aliens called predators to make us, "docile, helpless," "trite, conventional, imbecilic," when parents are right at home doing the job.

It's strange that Don Juan went along with the ancient belief in predators because he knew that parents and teachers create the internal dialogue that keeps us stuck in the same reactions, thoughts and feelings all our lives. He also knew that children suffer: "Life is hard, and for a child it is sometimes horror itself." He further knew that the helplessness of infants has serious negative effects, and that childhood humiliations make people mean. He usually listened sympathetically when Carlos talked about the "fear and loneliness" of his childhood, but when Carlos discovered the truth about his relationship with his mother, don Juan refused to listen.

Carlos had been sitting with men who'd taken peyote and, though he himself hadn't taken any, he slipped out of his regular mind and heard his mother's voice calling him, her slippers "shuffling" and "her laughter." It was so real "he turned around" expecting to see her. She wasn't there and he was trying to get her out of his mind when he again heard her calling his name, and was submerged in the "anguish and melancholy" of his infancy. "I whined involuntarily. I felt cold and lonely and I began to weep" because "I needed someone to care for me." He closed his eyes and had "a clear vision" of his mother standing beside him, which made him tremble and want "to escape," but "a very peculiar feeling," like "an outside force," compelled him to think about her critically, and he suddenly felt weighed down by "the horrendous burden of my mother's love," and knew that he'd "never liked her." This "shocking revelation" turned into a series of "emotional certainties, indisputable evidence about the nature of my relationship with my mother" before she abandoned him when he was six.

Carlos wanted to talk about his mother, but don Juan forbade it. He told him that whatever he'd "experienced was nonsense in comparison with the omen," the pink glow that don Juan had seen hovering over him. Carlos said he didn't care about the omen, but don Juan, in a "very forceful" tone, told him that being engulfed by the light of Mescalito, the spirit within peyote, was all that was important (*A Separate Reality*, 1971).

For don Juan and the sorcerers, a shocking relationship with a mother was insignificant compared to a sign that the spirit within a drug would help one achieve what should be our primary goal—changing our view of the world. "If the doors of perception were cleansed," said William Blake, "everything would appear to man as it is, infinite." The sorcerers tried to cleanse the doors of their perception so they could see the infinite, mysterious world that's beyond ordinary reality. Don Juan fought against having been consumed by his culture by using various disciplines, the most helpful being learning to turn off his internal dialogue, the endless chat in our head that maintains our identity and the beliefs we acquire in childhood. Silencing that chat is immensely difficult, but don Juan didn't know the primary reason—that the eternal chat is a Hoover Dam keeping back a flood of devastating feelings, those that threatened to overwhelm us in childhood.

Don Juan didn't talk about parents who beat children up, 'play' with their penises and vaginas, sodomize and rape them, scream "You're stupid" at them, abandon or totally control them, the routine horrors that took place in ancient Mexican homes as surely as they took place in homes in every country and in every century and are taking place now. The mistreatment of our childhood frightened us into becoming good little boys and girls, who repeat the approved cultural mantras that keep fear at bay, but which also shut the doors of their perception.

Don Juan wouldn't have downplayed Carlos's revelation about his mother if he'd understood that revelations from childhood can shock us out of our routine ways of seeing, that our conventional world was partly created because frightened children refused to see the truth about their parents.

When don Juan told Carlos that "in the depths of every human being there's an ancestral, visceral knowledge" of predators, Carlos' viscera registered that he was hearing the truth, but a truth so frightening he didn't want it to surface in "a million years." Mescalito dredged up for Carlos a home truth about his mother's predatory love that most of us wouldn't want to surface in a million years. Unpleasant truths about parents have been slow in surfacing because we find them so frightening we lock them up, like madmen in insane asylums.

The Mexican sorcerers thought that "the topic of topics," the most important one in the world, was solving the problem of the fall of man. They were right, but their answer that predators fly up from an alien world and eat babies' glowing coats of awareness was almost as wrong as the Christian myth that Satan flew up from hell and made Eve, Adam and their progeny sinners forever. I say 'almost' because at least the sorcerers knew that man's fall wasn't what we now call genetic, that predators have to "eat up" each generation of children.

By discovering that every child has its glowing awareness taken from it, the sorcerers made a great advance in knowledge. They broke from the ancient, static view of children. Buddhists, from ancient times on, said that every child is born with its own identity, that parents therefore have no responsibility for what the child becomes. That idea prevailed in medieval Germany when children were thought to have immutable natures that revealed themselves as they grew up, that the then common traumas of medieval life — death of parents, abandonment by parents, or being sold into slavery — did not affect their character. (James Schultz *(The Knowledge of Childhood in the German Middle Ages, 1100-1350, 1996)*.

Only recently have we been able to comprehend that what happens to us in childhood has profound effects. As late as the 1940's and 50's most psychologists, influenced by Freud, held that children's innate aggressive and libidinal drives were the source of their problems. They refused to admit that a child's relationship with its parents could be the source. In the 1960s and 70s, Mary Ainsworth and John Bowlby actually had to compile statistics from years of scientific experiments to prove that a mother's treatment of her children influenced their behavior! (Robert Karen, "Becoming Attached," *The Atlantic*, February 1990).

Not until the mid 1980s did the connection between family life and crime begin to be studied. Only then did we learn, for example, that ninety percent of the death-row inmates in California's Folsom prison had been severely abused when they were children. Before those studies and the work of the heroic child advocate, Paul Mones, lawyers defending children who killed their parents were not allowed to mention the cruelty parents had inflicted on them. The law, like psychiatrists and the public, maintained that having been beaten daily, raped and reviled, had no connection with a child's later conduct, an attitude that continues into the twenty-first century, when the public assumes that children who kill were born bad, and juries and judges rarely let the facts of a horrendous childhood lighten the harshness of a sentence.

And yet, in the nineteenth century some people did point a finger at the guilty parties. Among them was Sigmund Freud. Soon, though, he reverted to the traditional view that forces innate in children were to blame. Investigating why Freud changed his mind helps us understand why mankind has taken so long to face the real cause of man's fall.

Chapter 27   Freud's Fall

As part of their observance of the 2000 millennium, the A&E television network compiled a list of the 100 most influential people in the past one thousand years. Sigmund Freud (1856-1939) was among the top ten. For decades he was honored as if he were a God whose psychological wisdom sprang full-grown, like the Goddess of Wisdom from Jupiter's head. But what shaped most of his thinking were the traumas he experienced in childhood, traumas the adult Freud for a while tried to confront. He finally couldn't and developed theories that enabled him to deny what had happened to him and enabled others to do the same, theories that shaped the world's thinking.

Freud didn't begin his psychiatric career by creating theories that were a cover-up. He began by writing an exposé, the answer to what the Mexican sorcerers said was the "topic of topics," the reason for man's fall. Psychiatrists in the late nineteenth-century had dealt with the topic by trying to find out the reason for hysteria, why some people developed symptoms, like blindness or paralysis, that had no physical cause. Jean Charcot, a well-known French neurologist with whom Freud studied, believed, as everyone else did, that a defective heredity was the cause. Freud decided Charcot was wrong; he was sure he'd found the one cause of neuroses: childhood sexual abuse. Though sexual abuse was and is common, it's not *the* cause of neuroses. Freud, however, had pointed mankind in the right direction—to mistreatment in childhood.

I   Freud, The Revolutionary

In April 1896 Freud read a paper to his fellow psychiatrists that was a watershed in human history, and Freud knew it was revolutionary. He dared to announce that the real cause of hysterical symptoms was not, as had been believed, heredity, the constitution a child was born with, but sexual abuse at home. Nowadays, when many of us are aware of the prevalence of child sexual abuse, that's not news, but Freud's colleagues were so outraged they gave his paper, as Freud said in a letter (April 26, 1896) to his friend Wilhelm Fliess, an "icy reception."

In 2001 when I read "The Aetiology of Hysteria," it didn't get an icy reception from me. I kept exclaiming, "Yes, that's true, that's what happens, that's how I felt," and the people in my former incest survivor group would have had the same reaction. For example, if one woman had read Freud's observation that "painful sensations in the genitals" can be the first hysterical symptom of early sexual abuse, she would have said, "My God, that's what happened to me!" Her first symptom had been pain in her vagina, plus bleeding unconnected with menstruation. Doctor after doctor had found nothing wrong, but the pain and bleeding continued, until she remembered that her father had raped her when she was a baby.

Some of his patients suffered from "choking," or "vomiting," "indigestion," or "disgust at food," symptoms, said Freud, that "the bucal cavity" had been "misused for sexual purposes," or as the most angry sufferers in my group would have put it, that Dad had fucked them in the mouth.

Freud compared his patients' discovery of their sexual abuse to finding the "one piece" that fills "the empty gap" in a "child's picture-puzzle." That "one piece" completed the picture, made the reason for their symptoms "self-evident." Virtually everyone in my group (except those who'd always remembered their abuse) said that only when they realized they'd been abused could they understand why their lives had been so messed up. A few people even used the "picture-puzzle" analogy.

Freud also understood that sexually abused children may as adults repeat their sexual past. A gay man in my group told us that he usually sodomized his partners, but that at other times he wanted to be sodomized. He'd never forgotten his father's assaults and eventually realized that in sex he'd either be the powerful father who'd forced his penis into his rectum or the child who'd learned to get pleasure from the pain. In his own way, he was constantly revisiting what Freud called the "scene" of the assault.

Some people stay in the "scene" of the assault. Freud said that "a regular love relationship" that "often lasted for years" could develop between a child and the adult who "initiates sexual intercourse." One woman in my group, in her mid-twenties, had only recently managed to stop sleeping with the father who'd molested her from early childhood, a father she confessed she still loved. "How could she?" I wondered because at that time, I hadn't yet realized I still loved the sister who'd sexually tortured me.

Freud uncovered much that was sexually bizarre. "In one of my cases," he said, a man who'd been trained in childhood "to stimulate the genitals of a grown-up woman with his foot" later developed hysterical paralysis of his legs. When I read that, I rushed to my husband, exclaiming, "Can you believe it?, one of Freud's cases was a foot case!" He knew what I meant because he'd had a mother who'd stimulate her genitals with his tiny foot, which she would also insert into her vagina and move around. Another man in our group had had a mother, and a third a grandmother who'd done similar things. We later met a man not in the group whose mother had used his foot as a sex toy. When he was telling us about it, one leg seized up so he couldn't walk for about ten minutes. When he was able to walk again, I told him that he should become a member of a recovery group that needed to be founded, Mother Fuckers Anonymous. He managed a laugh, but we both knew it wasn't funny because if, in my small world, I'd chanced on four cases, there had to be many more, including women, the daughters of mothers who'd used their babies' feet as dildos.

Most people still don't want to believe that a woman would train a child "to stimulate her genitals … with his foot," but Freud believed his patient, and the others (twelve female, six male) whom he'd recently analyzed. By believing them, Freud knew he was breaking with psychiatric tradition; the doctors his patients had previously consulted had accused them of lying. Freud was sure they were telling the truth because, strange as it may seem, they didn't want to remember. The fact of their sexual abuse was dragged out of them "with great distress and reluctance," for they were trying "to conceal" what they regarded as their own shame. Even when, "piece by piece," their abuse was dredged up and they relived their fear, anger, disgust and sense of betrayal, and even though Freud accepted "the reality" of their "infantile sexual scenes," his patients "emphatically" assured him "of their unbelief."

I knew how they felt. When my first memory managed to escape from my unconscious, "I don't believe it. I'm making it all up" rang in my head. After I joined an incest survivor group, I learned my reaction was common and was often expressed in the same words I'd used. My ego, my almighty 'I' didn't want to face that it had been shamefully degraded. More important, a part of me knew that believing the truth would rip the scab off the excruciating feelings I'd repressed. Those feelings, plus his patients' reluctance to remember or to believe what they'd remembered, convinced Freud that their memories were true. I too learned that when a memory surfaced and I said, "I don't believe it, I'm making it all up," that the memory was true.

Believing his patients had serious consequences for Freud. Not only did he have to discard heredity as the cause of hysterical symptoms, he had to discard the traditional belief that masturbation was the cause of physical, emotional and moral dysfunctions, and that it could even drive people mad. For example, Freud's best friend at that time, Wilhelm Fliess, had no doubt that painful menstruation was caused by this "abnormal sexual satisfaction." Valentin Magnan, a French psychiatrist, thought that a paper he'd published in 1893 proved that masturbation could cause insanity. A five-year-old girl, after having been sexually abused by a young man, obsessively masturbated. Her obsession became so out of control that she tried to masturbate her mother, even ran her tongue over her genitals. Such depravity, Magnan attributed to the deadly combination of heredity and masturbation, which made putting the girl in an insane asylum the proper course of action.

I learned about Magnan's paper in Jeffrey Masson's *The Assault on Truth* (1984), in part of which he discussed what made Freud decide that sexual abuse in childhood was the cause of hysteria. Masson thought it probable that Freud read Magnan's case history. If Freud did, he didn't think of the child as depraved, but as a victim of abuse, who masturbated and tried to lick her mother's genitals because she was repeating what had been done to her. Such cases made Freud change his mind about masturbation, to believe, as he said, that "active masturbation ... is a much more frequent consequence of abuse ... than is supposed."

Freud made that revolutionary statement in a paper published in a French journal a month before his colleagues heard his theory of *The Aetiology of Hysteria,* which contained an even more revolutionary statement. After discussing the case of a young boy who'd molested a girl by doing to her "exactly" what his female molester had done to him, a case he knew was true because he'd been able to get outside proof, Freud was inclined, he said, to conclude "that children cannot find their way to acts of sexual aggression unless they have been seduced previously," that "the foundation for a neurosis would accordingly always be laid in childhood by adults."

Freud ended *The Aetiology of Hysteria* with confidence: "I cannot believe that psychiatry will long hold back from making use of this new pathway to knowledge." He was sure that his discovery of the cause of hysteria was the "solution to a more than thousand-year-old problem," like finding the "source of the Nile," and hoped, as one who'd "disturbed the sleep of the world," that he'd become famous and rich.

He soon found that those who disturb the sleep of the world meet strong opposition. His lecture not only received an "icy reception," Freud sensed, as he said to Fliess, but also that "word has been given out to abandon me" (May 4, 1896). He was right. A journal that summarized papers read at such meetings listed the title of Freud's without a summary. The editor didn't want Freud's unspeakable theory to appear in print, for it couldn't be true that parents, especially well-to-do, respectable parents, molested their children. Reviewers of Freud's 1895 *Studies on Hysteria* (a book he'd written with Joseph Breuer) were convinced that Freud (and Breuer) had been fooled by the "fantasies and invented tales" of hysterics, that they'd taken seriously what was "nothing but paranoid drivel with a sexual content."

Freud was aware that his discovery of the cause of hysteria might "meet with contradiction and disbelief." He therefore had assured his colleagues that his conclusions were not the result of "idle speculation" but were "based on laborious individual examination of patients which has in most cases taken up a hundred or more hours of work." He also told them that his belief in "the great frequency of childhood sexual abuse" had been confirmed by pediatricians, who in their publications stigmatized nursery maids for sexually tampering with children. Freud also said he'd read an 1895 paper by Dr Stekel on "Coitus in Childhood," but that he hadn't "had time to collect other published evidence."

Having read Jeffrey Masson's *The Assault on Truth*, I knew that Freud's conclusions had also been based on the thousands of hours of work that had been done for over forty years by French pioneers in the field of childhood abuse, work Freud knew about. Masson told Anna Freud that he'd found the records for the day in 1895 when Freud saw Paul Brouardel at the Paris morgue perform an autopsy on a child who'd been raped, then killed by her father. During his lectures at such autopsies, Brouardel would tell his audiences that sexual abuse of children was common and that the rapists were often "excellent family men." "Sexual assaults," he said, "are crimes of the home."

Paul Brouardel was the successor to the chair of legal medicine at the University of Paris, previously held by Ambroise Tardieu, who in 1860 had published *A Medico-legal Study of Cruelty and Brutal Treatment Inflicted on Children*, an emotional article he was compelled to write because he'd been horrified by the beaten bodies of the many children he'd autopsied. In that article he mentioned only one case of sexual abuse, but in his earlier, *A Medico-legal Study of Assaults on Decency* (1857) and in its six later editions he reported and continued to report, for example, that of the 616 cases he'd "personally examined, 339 were of rape or attempted rape of children under the age of eleven (1867 edition) and that some girls who'd been anally and vaginally raped were only four or five (1879 edition). Tardieu knew that the number of child rapes was much greater than those reported, and that fathers often raped their daughters, that "the ties of blood, far from constituting a barrier … serve only too frequently to favor them."

Tardieu's work had been preceded by that of Adolphe Toulmouche, a professor of medicine at Rennes, who in 1853 had written an article that Masson thought might be the "first ever recorded of a sadistic assault on a young child." The child was a four-year-old who'd been whipped to death by her godfather. Because twenty-eight years of experience had taught Toulmouche that beating children often occurred before or after a rape, he regretted that her genitals hadn't been examined during the autopsy.

Freud may not have known about Toulmouche's article, but Masson discovered that he owned the 1878 edition of Tardieu's *A Medico-legal Study of Assaults on Decency*, a collection of Brouardel's lectures, and Paul Bernard's *Sexual Assaults on Young Girls* (1886). Paul Bernard had been a student of Alexandre Lacassagne of the University of Lyon, who, deeply affected by Tardieu's work, encouraged his students to investigate sexual abuse of children. Bernard did and his book revealed how widespread it was, that between 1827 and 1870 in France there were 36,176 reported cases of "rape and assault on the morality" of children fifteen years and under, some having been raped as young as four. Bernard was appalled to discover that not just single men raped children, that "children living at home constitute rather a stimulus to evil acts," in other words, that he'd been "struck by the large number of cases of incest."

From these French investigators, Freud learned that the rape of children was an ordinary fact of life. Tardieu didn't doubt it because in the vast majority of his cases, the physical evidence proved that the children had been raped. Toulmouche, Tardieu and Bernard were also certain that when children managed to overcome their fear and tell someone in authority they'd been raped, that they were telling the truth.

Their work had to have helped Freud break with tradition and believe that his patients' memories of rape were true. Freud may not have known it, but if he hadn't believed his patients, they wouldn't have trusted him enough to let their memories surface, with the accompanying fear, shame and sense of betrayal. In other words, if Freud hadn't believed his patients, he wouldn't have made his discovery. Nor, if the French investigators hadn't established that child sexual abuse was widespread, would Freud have focused on it as *the* cause of hysteria, for analyzing eighteen patients wasn't sufficient proof.

In the *The Aetiology of Hysteria* Freud didn't mention the extensive work of the French investigators. He should have, for the irony is that if Freud had summed up the mass of evidence proving the prevalence of sexual abuse, his colleagues would have found it much harder to give his paper an "icy reception" or to accuse him of having been fooled by the "fantasies and invented tales" of hysterics.

Freud should also have cited his sources for another reason: he needed all the support he could muster. For to say that "children cannot find their way to acts of sexual aggression unless they have been seduced previously," and that "the foundation for a neurosis" was "always ... laid in childhood by adults" did more than rock the family boat; it sank it. Freud should have known that a society whose Bible commanded people to honor their father and mother was not likely to accept a theory that accused parents of raping children and of laying the foundation for their future neuroses. Such beliefs jettisoned the fundamental tenet of societies, that the family was the sacred institution in which honorable parents transformed bad children into good citizens.

To point to parents as the ones who harmed children, Freud had had to break a taboo, see what we're trained not to see. Freud managed to take off his cultural blinders, and what he saw filled him with so much compassion for the suffering of children that he told Fliess (December 22, 1897) that the motto of psychoanalysis should be Goethe's words: "What have they done to you, poor child?" He was like Ambroise Tardieu who, having autopsied the bruised bodies of so many children beaten to death by parents, felt that the fact they were executed by "the very people who gave them life" was "one of the most terrifying problems that can trouble the heart of man."

Tardieu was right, but until recently man's heart has not been troubled, even when presented with the facts. When in 1860 Tardieu published "Cruelty and Brutal Treatment Inflicted on Children," he expected others would feel the indignation he felt, but in 1879, the year he died, though he continued to publicize the high incidence of fatal assaults on children, he lamented that "writers in the field of legal medicine have subsequently remained completely silent" on the subject (*A Forensic Study of Wounds*, 1879). For a while he had some followers, but his discovery had to be virtually rediscovered 102 years later when C Henry Kempe (and others) published an article on what is now known as "The Battered Child Syndrome" (*Journal of the American Medical Association*, 1962).

Tardieu, until he died, continued to publish facts the public and his colleagues ignored, and it's most likely that Freud, if he'd pursued what he called the "seduction theory" (that parents molested their children) would have had few followers. A public that couldn't face that many parents viciously beat, even killed, their children, wouldn't have faced that parents raped them. We'll never know. Freud fairly soon decided that his seduction theory was wrong.

II   Freud, The Reactionary

To have accused parents of raping their children and causing future neuroses was almost as dangerous as committing heresy during the Inquisition. And Freud's colleagues did sentence him to professional death, or to use his own words, he was "despised and universally shunned." For well over a year Freud was defiant, but the lost sheep eventually found his way back to the fold. The Freud who'd agreed with Paul Brouardel when he said that "excellent family men" often raped their children, now reasoned that the very fact that fathers were so frequently "accused of being perverse" was proof the accusations were false because "such widespread perversions against children are not very probable." I'm quoting from a letter Freud wrote to his friend, Wilhelm Fliess, on September 21, 1897 in which he explained why "I no longer believe in my neurotica" (his theory that child sexual abuse was the cause of neurosis).

Back to The Past

Recanting required Freud to do what we all must do to be accepted by society: believe what our culture tells us is true. To do that, Freud had to reaffirm the theories that allowed the culture not to face that some parents sexually abuse their children. In 1896, Freud said that a boy's excessive libido had been "prematurely awakened" by his female molester. After he recanted, Freud would have said that the boy, compelled by an inherited strong, sexual drive, forced himself upon the woman. Freud had resurrected that old scapegoat, heredity, as the cause of neuroses, but with a difference: he said that heredity drove the boy to have sex with the woman, but only in fantasy.

In fantasy! Why did Freud accuse his patients of committing lewd fantasies? If he believed, as he now said he did, that the "scenes of seduction" his patients described "had never taken place," why didn't he call his patients plain liars? Because a part of him knew the truth, that children were often sexually abused, that therefore patients would continue to accuse parents of sexually molesting them. To give psychiatrists a way to 'prove' that the abuse hadn't really happened, he created a special kind of lie he called a fantasy, by which he meant sexual fantasies, ones he said had been stimulated by childhood masturbation. For in order to prove that sexual abuse was a fantasy, Freud had to resurrect not only that old source of sin, heredity, but that old bugaboo, masturbation.

In "An Autobiographical Study" (1925), Freud explained how heredity and masturbation conspire to produce fantasies of sexual abuse. Everyone knew, he said, that "childhood masturbation" was of "general occurrence." Although children forget they masturbated, the truth was revealed by fantasy encountered in most female patients," that "the father seduced her in childhood." When I read that, I frowned. How could Freud leap from masturbating in childhood to the fantasy of being seduced by a father? Freud said they were connected because the fantasy had a "grain of truth" in it. Not, of course, that fathers had sex with their daughters, but that fathers' "innocent caresses" sexually aroused infants, which caused them to masturbate. Since masturbation was harmful, "these same affectionate fathers" had to force their daughters to stop. Inchoate memories of this father-daughter scenario reappeared at puberty when intense sexual feelings arose. Afraid of those feelings, and not wanting to face their infantile guilt at masturbating and their anger at their fathers for stopping them, women got "revenge" by claiming that their fathers sexually abused them. Thus, according to Freud, arose the fantasy that their fathers seduced them. (In a parenthesis, Freud said that mothers' "innocent caresses" similarly aroused their sons' sexuality.)

Poor affectionate Papa, he innocently caressed his infant daughter and she got turned on sexually, which, according to Freud, happened to the vast majority of little girls, for he said that the fantasy of having been seduced by their fathers "dominated" the "entire life" of most women. But if, as Freud had earlier argued, "such widespread perversions" by fathers were "not very probable," why was such widespread perversity by children virtually universal?

Sexy Babies

Freud could say that babies were sexually aroused by innocent caresses because he claimed they were born sexy. Parents (as I discussed in Chapter 10) have traditionally regarded children as a different and inferior species, and Freud took pride in having discovered further evidence of children's inferiority—that they were not, as the world thought, born innocent of sexuality but sexual beings, and perverse ones. Freud was sure his belief was grounded in science. Like most intellectuals of his time, he accepted the theory of the Darwinian biologist Ernst Haeckel, who argued that in utero the embryo and fetus repeated the history of man's evolution, which was interpreted to mean that at birth babies had evolved to the level of savages, who were popularly characterized as innately aggressive, lustful and incestuous. The work of the evolutionary neurologist, John Hughlings-Jackson, had also supplied Freud with information that could support his equation of babies with moral savages, for Jackson had discovered that the brain was a hierarchical structure, the brutish, primitive levels at the bottom and the higher, civilized levels at the top. Since babies' 'higher' brains were thought to be virtually non-existent, it would have seemed scientifically accurate to describe them as primitive savages, like early man.

In 1905 in his paper on "Infantile Sexuality," Freud quickly (in the second paragraph) established the scientific basis of his theory by saying, à la Haeckel, that just as the life of the individual repeats the history of the race, a primitive period exists in humans—infancy and early childhood, thus predisposing his readers to accept what he was about to say, that the sexual instinct of infants was strong.

A species who reproduces sexually has to be born with the "germs of sexual impulses already present," but do these germs first flower in infancy when no possibility of reproduction exists? Freud said they did, and that thumb sucking was one of the "manifestations" of infantile sexuality, one that could be so intense it produced "a motor reaction in the nature of an orgasm." Moreover, since thumb sucking was sometimes combined with rubbing a "sensitive part of the body such as the breast and external genitalia," it could be a "path" to masturbation. Every one, said Freud, did not "indulge energetically in sucking during childhood," but those who did had been born with "a constitutional intensification of the labial" erogenous zone, which in adulthood could produce "constriction of the throat and vomiting," hysterical symptoms he'd observed in "many of my women patients." In 1896 in "The Aetiology of Hysteria," Freud had said that such symptoms meant that the child's "bucal cavity" had been "misused for sexual purposes." In "Infantile Sexuality" it meant that the "bucal cavity" was inherently so sexual that sucking the breast could climax in a virtual orgasm: "No one who has seen a baby sinking back satisfied from the breast and falling asleep with flushed cheeks and a blissful smile can escape the reflection that this picture persists as a prototype of the expression of sexual satisfaction later in life."

Not only was sucking the breast and the thumb oral masturbation, defecation produced anal sensations that went far beyond the satisfaction of relieving oneself, for babies turned defecation into an intense sexual pleasure by deliberately holding "back their stool." Since they then had a larger mass to void, the anus was stimulated more, and since compacted feces were hard to pass, babies enjoyed a masochistic thrill. Freud maintained that when "a baby obstinately refused to empty his bowels when he was put on the pot," he was choosing to hold back in order to enjoy that "subsidiary pleasure." Educators were therefore right to "describe children who keep the process back as 'naughty'." Freud had said that the bliss of breast feeding was a prototype of the later bliss of orgasm. He similarly said that the shape of the fecal matter in the rectum was the "forerunner of another organ, which is destined to come into action," by which he meant the penis.

Freud said that infants had a third erogenous zone, the urethra, for they urinated from (or near) their sexual organs so that the discharge gave "an early start to sexual excitation," as did washing and rubbing the genitals to keep them clean, which led to "early infantile masturbation which scarcely a single individual escapes." Freud further noted that in the second part of childhood (from about four to puberty) bladder infections were "sexual disturbances" and that peeing in bed at night corresponded "to a nocturnal emission" and was a sign of early masturbation. Freud thought that the sexual stimulation of urination was also nature's way of assuring "the future primacy" of genital sexual activity.

Urination, defecation and thumb sucking were the sources of what Freud described as the "polymorphous perversity" of infants, whom Freud compared to prostitutes because prostitutes retain into adulthood the "infantile disposition" to be sexually perverse, sexual perversity that also compelled infants to want to commit incest.

Incestuous Hans

Freud explained how infantile sexuality led to incest in his *Analysis of a Phobia in a Five-year-old Boy* (1909). Freud got his data from Max Graf, whom he'd asked to take notes on the sexual development of his son, notes that, he was pleased to discover, confirmed his theory of infantile sexuality. For little Hans was fascinated by his penis, animal penises, toilets, feces, behinds and the way his mother and baby sister peed. He got pleasure from defecating and often, naughty boy!, held back his feces to get even more "voluptuous sensations." He was observed with his hand on his penis, and once boldly asked his mother to touch it, and "regularly indulged" in "masturbatory gratification." Hans also had a "disposition to polygamy," for he loved everyone—his mother, the daughters of a family friend, even a boy cousin. When that five-year-old cousin visited, Hans would constantly hug him and once said, "I am so fond of you," which, for Freud, was "the first trace of homosexuality" and proved that little Hans, like all children, was "a positive paragon of all the vices."

But homosexuality was not the path Hans was to take. "Our young libertine," said Freud, proceeded to "an energetic masculinity" "in the most concrete and uncompromising manner," and confirmed what Freud had previously said "with regard to the sexual relations of a child to its parents," that every male child wanted to sleep with his mother and every female child with her father. Hans, too, longed to be alone with "his handsome mother and sleep with her," and to do that he wanted his father "out of the way." "Hans," Freud was pleased to announce, "was really a little Oedipus."

Whereas Freud had once blamed parents for imposing their sexual will on children, Freud's theory of infantile sexuality maintained that children were the guilty ones, that "the sexual constitution" of children was "precisely calculated to provoke sexual experiences of a particular kind—namely traumas," that is, that children came on to parents, tried to "provoke" sex (*On the History of the Psychoanalytic Movement*, 1914). Parents, of course, were beyond temptation. But naughty little girls, forbidden the real thing, perverted a father's innocent caresses into the fantasy that he'd actually molested them. Therefore, whenever girls accused their fathers of having had sex with them, "there can be no doubt ... of the imaginary nature of the accusation" (*Introductory Lectures on Psycho-Analysis*, 1916). Although from time to time a case would force Freud to acknowledge that a particular parent *had* sexually abused a child, the Freud who'd once regarded children as innocent victims of lustful parents, now accused them of being the sexual predators.

Early in the nineteenth century, Wordsworth expressed his faith that we come from heaven "trailing clouds of glory" that surround us "in our infancy." Throughout the century, most people praised children for being better than adults, for being, as Thomas Campbell put it, "freshest from the hand of God." Early in the twentieth century, Freud wrote "Infantile Sexuality" and his case study of little Hans in order to express his faith that children were born polymorphous perverse and had an innate incestuous drive that climaxed in the Oedipus complex.

At first Freud's characterization of children as sexually perverse was rejected as outrageous, but by the mid twentieth century the majority of people accepted as a fact that infants got intense sexual pleasure from their erogenous zones. When I was in college, my friends and I talked glibly about people being "oral" or "anal" and believed that sex was man's dominant drive and that everyone developed an Oedipus complex, that boys had castration anxiety and girls penis envy. We also believed that everyone made Freudian slips, which proved the power of the unconscious, and that the mind was divided into the ego, the superego and the id. Few of us had read Freud's work; his ideas were in the air, ideas which, since they'd been created by the greatest genius of the mind, were regarded as Gospel. Freud, though, didn't think his theories needed to be accepted on faith. He was certain they'd been discovered by a dispassionate seeker of psychological truths, a scientist of the first rank, a Darwin of the mind.

III   Freud, The Scientist

Anna Freud told Jeffrey Masson that if her father had continued to believe in the seduction theory (that parents molested children), he wouldn't have discovered the Oedipus complex and the importance of the fantasy life of children, and psychoanalysis wouldn't have become "a science and a therapy." She called it science because she was sure he'd discovered the truth, as sure as Freud was, who'd said that truth was "the absolute aim of science" and his own.

Freud had to have known that the kind of psychology he was interested in was not scientifically true in the same way physics is. But some psychological observations, like some scientific findings, are and remain universal truths. When in 2001 I read Freud's 1896 paper, "The Aetiology of Hysteria," my own experience and what I'd learned from many incest survivors, again and again confirmed Freud's findings about the effects of sexual abuse, symptoms he easily traced back to the abuse his patients had endured in childhood. But when I read what Freud wrote after he decided that parents didn't molest children, that simple cause and effect clarity was gone, and I kept doubting what he said.

Not Observing Babies

I'll never forget my reaction when I read that fathers' "innocent caresses" sexually aroused their children ("An Autobiographical Study," 1925). I thought Freud had lost his mind. For anyone who's had anything to do with children knows that a parent's innocent caresses make them feel safe and happy, not sexy.

Only later did I understand why I'd reacted that way. I'd read *An Autobiographical Study* out of order, before Freud's much earlier essay on infantile sexuality and his case history of little Hans. If I'd read those first, I would have been informed that innocent caresses turn children on because they're born with a sexual drive that makes them autoerotics, who need only a touch to be aroused.

But it wasn't ignorance of Freud's theory of infantile sexuality, it was knowledge of the period that made me balk at Freud's implication that it was normal paternal behavior for fathers to caress their infant daughters. In Freud's time, few fathers hugged and kissed infants, and Freud was no exception. I was also astonished by Freud saying that fathers were the ones who taught their infant daughters to stop masturbating. In the Victorian era, for fathers to perform that duty would have been grossly improper.

In these two instances, Freud was saying what wasn't true, so why, I asked myself, would the rest of that passage in *An Autobiographical*

Study be true? I reread the scenario: fathers' "innocent caresses" sexually arouse infant daughters, whose nature compels them to masturbate while imagining Daddy having sex with them, which forces Daddy to make them stop, which makes daughters want "revenge," which they get at puberty when they remember their sex fantasies as real and accuse innocent Daddy.

In Freud's scenario one event triggers the next like a domino effect. Since the chain reaction climaxed in the Oedipus complex, I dared to suspect that Freud had let his imagination roll, especially since he had no doubt that the premise from which the rest followed was true—the existence of a strong sexual drive in infants. Freud took special pride in having discovered the scientific truth on which he based the jewel in his crown—the Oedipus complex.

Freud was sure his theory of infantile sexuality was on solid ground because it was compatible with Ernst Haeckel's theory that the fetus repeats the history of man's evolution. But, as I said in Chapter 25, Haeckel's theory was later disproved; embryologists learned that evolutionary progress is made, not by a species repeating the characteristics of adult ancestors but by retaining fetal or infantile traits. Freud couldn't have known that scientific fact. However, if he'd spent time observing children, he might have registered that they were not miniatures of adult savages, nor would he have compared infants' sexuality with the adult perversities he read about in books like Kraft-Ebbing's *Psychopathia Sexualis*.

Freud had to draw analogies between children and adult savages and perverts because his personal knowledge of children was virtually nil. In "The Aetiology of Hysteria," Freud assured his colleagues that his theory that hysteria was caused by sexual abuse was not the result of "idle speculation" but had been based on "laborious individual examination of his patients," with most of whom he'd spent "a hundred or more hours." That Freud spent that much time with his patients has been questioned, but he did spend a lot of time with them. By his own admission, though, he spent little time observing infants. He wrote to Wilhelm Fliess (February 8, 1897) that at home he didn't visit the nursery because he didn't have the time and his wife and the nurses didn't want him there.

If Freud had had the mindset of a scientist, he would have regarded visiting the nursery as essential research, for he lived at a time when the psychological study of infants hardly existed. Max Graf did supply Freud with information about little Hans, but only *after* Freud wrote "Infantile Sexuality." Moreover, Freud said he "learnt nothing" from the Hans case that he hadn't already learned from his patients, who had "the same infantile complexes" Hans had.

Freud's theory that children were born sexually perverse didn't come from the mind of a scientist, not a modern one. Freud was like the seventeenth-century natural philosophers at the time of Newton who, unlike Newton, continued to create theories from a priori reasoning, theories unsupported by facts, experiments and observations. The infantile complexes that Freud said he learned about from analyzing patients may have been legitimate observations. But since, according to Freud, no one remembers their infantile complexes until they're psychoanalyzed, and Freud did the analyzing, we have to accept what he said on trust. Other analysts have confirmed his findings, but only those who were Freudians; Jungians, for example, don't. It's true that the kind of proof required in science and psychology are different. However, Freud expected to be believed on his word alone, which no one in the nineteenth-century who claimed to be a scientist would have dared to presume.

Nor would any scientist of his time have used the "everyone knows it's true" proof. But Freud, having reasoned that if infants were highly sexual, they'd masturbate a lot, asserted as a truth that masturbation was of "general occurrence." But if everyone accepted that as true, they did because, like Freud, they hadn't observed babies. In Freud's time, most infants were still swaddled, which made it impossible for them to touch their genitals. Moreover, if babies were sex bombs programmed to go off, as soon as they were unswaddled and had developed enough muscular control, their hands would glom onto their genitals like magnets. That's not what happens. Discovering genitals is a chance encounter. Liking the sensations, infants may touch their genitals again, but soon they're distracted by other things, even when their penis spontaneously erects. Infants do get stronger sensations from their genitals than other parts of their body, but the sensations don't have an urgent goal: babies don't have sex hormones arousing them and can't have orgasms. Infants much prefer sucking their thumbs to touching their genitals.

But for Freud, thumb sucking was oral masturbation, a substitute for that other form of masturbation, breast-feeding. "No one," said Freud, "who has seen a baby sinking back satisfied from the breast and falling asleep with flushed cheeks and a blissful smile can escape the reflection that this picture persists as a prototype of the expression of sexual satisfaction later in life." It turns out, though, that babies are blissing out on two hormones produced by breast-feeding, one that's like morphine and another called oxytocin, which create feelings of euphoria and contentment in both mother and child. Nature is making sure that mothers nurse their babies, not giving babies previews of future orgasms, or the proto-orgasms Freud thought babies were trying to reexperience when they sucked their thumbs. Freud didn't consider that babies might love thumb sucking, not to get a sexual high, but to try and repeat the drug high of breast-feeding, to trance out of a world in which they often feel helpless and frightened.

It wasn't nature's plan to make babies sex-pots; it was Freud's. He fantasized not only that the bliss of breast-feeding was a "prototype" of orgasm, but (as I said in the last chapter) that the shape of feces in the rectum was the "forerunner" of the penis "destined to come into action," and that the frequent stimulation of urination assured "the future primacy" of genital sexual activity. For Freud such 'erotic' stimulation was the necessary foreplay for later sexual arousal, as if without infantile sexuality, sex hormones wouldn't be activated at puberty.

Freud didn't understand that infants' sensitivity to touch has an important function that has nothing to do with sex. We're born sensate beings, alive in every pore, a capacity for pleasure that allows us to receive the world, and connect with others, become part of a community. Like animals when they're groomed, being touched gives babies and children a sense of well-being, makes them feel safe and not alone in a mysterious, scary world. So vital is touch to babies, they can die when they're not touched.

Hans as "Little Oedipus"

Freud insisted that babies' sensitivity to touch was sexual because he had an agenda. Hans could hardly touch himself or any one else without Freud happily labeling it sexual. I say "happily" because when Freud, as I said in the last chapter, called Hans "a positive paragon of all the vices," he thought he was paying him a compliment. Freud, however, was really congratulating himself. He beamed on Hans because Hans was proving his theory that infants were "young libertines."

For Freud, Hans was also living proof of his theory that the instinct for knowledge was not "elementary" in children but was "first aroused" when a child became curious about sex. "There can be no doubt," he said, that "Hans's sexual curiosity" "roused the spirit of inquiry in him." Freud had six children, but managed not to observe that infants are born curious, that they constantly look around and will even stop feeding to look at something.

Freud didn't observe infants but had no trouble seeing their unconscious. In the case history of Hans, Hans's father kept telling his son that he wanted to kill Daddy so he could have Mummy all to himself. Fearing that readers would think Hans was being brainwashed, Freud explained that Graf was merely making Hans conscious of what was already in his unconscious. Graf agreed. Freud chose him to take notes on Hans because he attended the meetings of Freud's Wednesday Psychological Society, and his wife had been analyzed by Freud. Consequently, Graf had, as Freud put it, the "special knowledge ... to interpret the remarks made by" his son, that is, he knew what he was supposed to find, especially about the cause of Hans's phobia.

Hans's phobia was a fear of horses, and his father, having acquired
Freud's "special knowledge," told him about the "connections between
the horses he was afraid of and the affectionate feelings towards his
mother." Hans steadfastly refused "enlightenment," so his father took
him to see Professor Freud who, after Hans revealed that he "was particularly bothered" by horses' blinders and the black around their mouths
(halters), explained to him that since his father wore blinders (eyeglass-
es) and had black around his mouth (a moustache), it was his father he
"was afraid of and "precisely because he was so fond of his mother."
"It must be, I told him, that he thought his father was angry at him on
that account." Little Hans dared to disagree. He said that his father
was "fond of him" even though he was fond of his mother, and "that he
could tell him everything "without any fear." But what did little Hans
know? Freud informed him that "long before he was in the world, ...
I had known that a little Hans would come who would be so fond of
his mother that he would be bound to be afraid of his father because of
it." No wonder that on the way home, Hans asked his father, "Does the
Professor talk to God, as he can tell all that beforehand?"

Freud didn't have to talk to God; he was God talking, and Graf was
God's mouthpiece when he told his son that his fear of horses was really
fear of his father's anger at him for wanting to sleep with Mummy. To
encourage Hans to express his hate, his father once asked him if he'd "like
to beat the horses as Mummy beats Hanna." Hanna was his baby sister,
whose screams Hans couldn't bear to hear "when Mummy whacks her
on her bottom." Hans's reply, that he wanted to beat Mummy with the
carpet-beater because she often threatened to beat him with it, Graf did
not believe. Nor did he believe Hans when he explained that his fear of
horses began when he was out with his mother and saw a horse who was
pulling a bus collapse on the street, and kick and kick with his feet. "It
gave me such a fright, really!" he insisted. His father would have none of
it. Why should seeing a big horse fall down and kick his feet make him
so afraid? Once more Graf told Hans that he was afraid "when he saw
the horse fall down" because he wished Daddy would "fall down like
that and be dead," so Mummy would be all his. Hans didn't disagree
with him this time, and later when playing with his father, he bit him, a
bite that proved to Graf and Freud that Hans did want to kill his father.
It's possible, though, that Hans, having learned he mustn't disagree with
his father on that subject, bit him, not because he wished Daddy dead,
but because he was angry at being told what he thought.

Freud told his patients what to think, and the world. In the Hans
case, he pronounced as a universal truth that little children knew without
being told that when Mummy got fat she was having a baby. He said that
Hans expressed a desire to climb on carts filled with big boxes because the
boxes were for him "symbolic representations of pregnancy," so when a

"heavily loaded horse fell down, he can have seen in it only one thing—a childbirth, a delivery." Freud, having just said that the horse was "only one thing—a childbirth," remembered he'd first said it was "his dying father," so he now said the horse was both. Moreover, that Hans hadn't seen his mother give birth or that the horse that fell down had been pulling a bus, not a load of boxes, didn't matter. No fact could stand between Freud and a theory.

Nor did Freud object when Hans's parents told Hans a conventional lie about where babies come from, that "children grow inside their Mummy" and were "pressed out" "like a lumf" (Hans's word for feces) after "a great deal of pain." Freud said "he would have told [Hans] of the existence of the vagina and of copulation" because the information was vital for "his comprehension of sexual matters." But though Freud often told Graf what to tell Hans, he hadn't told him to give Hans accurate information about reproduction, nor did he order him to correct the lie he'd told Hans about anal birth.

Freud ordered Graf to tell Hans something else. Having decided that Hans's "libido" was now focused on seeing his "mother's widdler," Freud told Graf to inform Hans that women "had no widdler." "Widdler" is an English translation of "wiwimacher," what Hans called where he made "wee-wee." But Hans, knowing that girls peed, decided that girls did have wiwimachers, but they were very small. He was right. For Hans, wiwimachers were for peeing. He was more naive than Freud supposed, who thought boys instinctively knew that their wee-wees also had a sexual function because of their instinctive drive to have sex with Mummy.

Freud wanted Hans to learn that women "had no widdler" so he'd realize that his unconscious fear was true, that Daddy would cut off his penis because he wanted to have sex with Mummy. For Freud believed that when boys saw that girls didn't have penises, they assumed that girls once had them but they'd been cut off. Freud didn't want Hans to get the correct information about vaginas and copulation, he wanted him to get castration anxiety.

Freud didn't think that castration anxiety was bad. At least, when Hans's mother "found him with his hand to his penis," and told him she was going to "send for Dr A to cut" it off, Freud didn't react with horror and order her to apologize to Hans for telling him that cruel lie. Freud didn't object because castration anxiety was a sign that little Hans wanted to have sex with Mummy and feared Daddy would punish him by cutting off his penis, that is, that he had an Oedipus complex. For Freud, castration anxiety and the Oedipus complex were Siamese twins conjoined at the penis.

Freud later decided that castration anxiety didn't depend on "a chance threat," or on learning that girls didn't have penises; he was sure that little boys on their own would "construct this danger" because they all had Oedipus complexes. To assure that the Oedipus complex would be regarded as a universal law of life, Freud gave it the permanence of heredity. Since the French naturalist, Lamarck, had said that physical characteristics acquired from adapting to the environment could be passed on to offspring, and since Darwin thought the idea had some validity, Freud felt he could say that the Oedipus complex had become an acquired memory of man, part of our "phylogenetic inheritance" (an idea similar to Jung's collective unconscious).

The Oedipus complex was itself dependent on another "inheritance," the sexual perversity of babies, which caused the "state of intensified sexual excitement" Hans felt when in bed with "his handsome mother." His mother took Hans into bed for a while in the mornings. Hans called those times "coaxing," fondling, which he loved. It may be that coaxing with Mummy was merely the snuggling all children love, but Freud thought that the "young lover" (as he called Hans) used the occasion to seduce his mother and that he tried to seduce her at other times. Once Hans showed his mother his penis and asked her to touch it. Another time, when his mother was powdering him after a bath and was careful not to touch his penis, Hans asked her why she didn't put her finger there. She answered, "Because it's not proper," to which Hans replied, "But it's great fun."

That can be interpreted as seduction, but would Hans have dared to expose his penis and ask his mother to touch it if she hadn't already touched it? Would he have told Mummy that touching his penis was "great fun," if they hadn't already had great fun? Hans may have been shamelessly confessing to masturbation, but Hans's mother may have had a hand in the "great fun." At least, Freud said in a footnote that "it was one of the commonest things" for "fond relations" to caress little boys' penises, "including even parents themselves."

Hans's father had suspicions. When Hans got afraid of horses, that is, when he wanted to kill Daddy so he could sleep with Mummy, his father wrote to Freud that "no doubt the ground was prepared by sexual excitation due to his mother's tenderness." My eyebrows rose when I read that. Was Graf actually saying that Hans's "mother's tenderness" had produced his "sexual excitation"? Did Graf, who informed Hans that big boys slept in their own beds, jealously suspect that his wife's tenderness included touching Hans's penis? Since that was a Freudian heresy, Graf added, "but I'm not able to specify the actual exciting cause," and Freud didn't explore Graf's suspicions. For he might have learned that Mummy, by playing with Hans's penis, had created his desire to have sex with her, and Freud wouldn't have been able to present little Hans to the world as a "little Oedipus." However, it may be that Mummy didn't play with Hans's penis. I may be guilty of "doing a Freud," of doing what Freud often did with his patients, use them as dummies on which to drape his theories.

Abducting A Dream

To prove his theories, Freud ran roughshod over his patients, dismissing what they told him had happened and telling them what had 'really' happened, making them feel, as Hans put it, that the Professor must talk to God. A flagrant example occurred in the case history of a young Russian ("From the History of an Infantile Neurosis"). Serge Pankejeff has come to be known as the "Wolf Man" because of a dream he told Freud he had when "I was three, four, or at most five." In the dream he was lying in bed in "winter" at "night-time" when a window opened "of its own accord" and there, sitting motionless on "the big walnut tree," were six or seven white wolves with "big tails like foxes" staring in at him. Terrified, sure the wolves were going to eat him, he woke up screaming.

Freud instantly dismissed the scary wolves as the cause of Serge's childhood terror. He told him they were created by his unconscious to conceal something scarier, something that had actually happened, and not at the time he'd had the dream, but when he was eighteen-months old. According to Freud, the infant Serge was lying in his cot with a fever "at about five o'clock" on the day before Christmas, when he witnessed his parents having "coitus a tergo" [his mother kneeling, his father entering from behind], an act that was "three times repeated," during which eighteen-month-old Serge saw "his mother's genitals as well as his father's member." But, said Freud, because he'd dreamed about the wolves when he was older and by then had had "sexual excitations" and made "sexual inquiries," he "understood" what he hadn't when he was eighteen-months old, that his parents were having sex, which was why "as a sign of his sexual excitement," and of "his congenital [anal] sexual constitution," Serge passed "a stool," which gave him "an excuse for screaming," and thus "interrupt[ing] his parents' intercourse."

Serge hadn't told Freud he'd defecated at the end of the wolf dream, but Freud had an elaborate explanation for why Serge did and why Serge was eighteen-months old when he witnessed his parents having sex. Freud also explained why he knew that Serge had had a fever, and that the time was "about five o'clock" on the day before Christmas, and that his parents had had sex a tergo three times. Unfortunately, Freud didn't explain how the infant Serge had been able to see his mother's genitals when she was kneeling, crouched forward.

The long case history of Serge consisted mostly of discourses explaining why Freud's interpretations were correct. Freud said he was aware that many people thought that an analyst forced a fantasy on a patient "on account of some complexes of his own," but he was so sure his analysis of Serge was correct that he ventured to say it either was "a piece of nonsense from start to finish, or everything took place just as I have described it above."

Anything But That

I decided it was "a piece of nonsense from start to finish," that Freud did "force a fantasy" on Serge "on account of some complexes of his own." For when I was reading the case history, I was struck again and again by what was to me overwhelming evidence that Serge had been sexually abused by his father, a conviction that was clinched when I later read what Serge said to Freud at their very first session. As Freud wrote to a colleague, Serge said that "he would like to use me from behind and shit on my head."

As soon as I read that, I had no doubt that Serge's father had sodomized his son, and that Serge was saying he wanted to do to father-figure Freud what his own father had done to him, and that he was still so angry at his father he wanted to shit on his head. Virtually everyone in my incest survivor group would have had the same insight, and so, in 1896, would have Freud. At the time he wrote "The Aetiology of Hysteria," it would also have been obvious to Freud why Serge, when he had sex with women, had to enter them "from behind," why he had to be given daily enemas by a male attendant, why, when he was a child screaming with rage and "his father came toward him," his screams redoubled, why Serge got masochistic pleasure when his father beat him, why he became anally erotic at an early age, and why he thought that "the part of the female body that received the male organ was the anus."

When Serge was taught religion, his first question was "whether Christ had had a behind too" and had "to shit." When he was told Christ did, he got so upset he decided that the behind was a continuation of the legs and that since Christ had changed water into wine, he changed food into nothing so he wouldn't have to defecate. That Serge didn't want Christ to have a behind and anus so he'd be spared the agony of sodomy, Freud was unable to comprehend. He went as far as saying that the *a tergo* primal scene he claimed Serge witnessed had made Serge wonder if he "could be used by his father like a woman," yet Freud couldn't register that Serge's father *had* used his anus as a vagina.

That Serge had been anally raped was screaming at Freud, but he tossed up other explanations like juggling balls. He said that Serge could have sex only when he entered a women "from behind" because (1) it was a trait of "the anal-erotic" constitution; because (2) he was imitating animals; because (3) he'd reverted to the "phylogenetically older" position; because (4) he'd "inherited this constitutional predilection" from his father. Anything but face what turned out to be the truth. In the 1920s, after Serge had a paranoid episode, Freud sent him to Ruth Mack

Brunswick to be re-analyzed. To her astonishment, she learned that he'd been anally "seduced," to use the Freudian euphemism for rape.

The source of Serge's symptoms was so clearly anal rape, it seems incredible that Freud didn't see it. It would be easy to say that he concealed the truth so his theory that parents didn't sexually abuse children wouldn't be undermined. Jeffrey Masson, who discovered Brunswick's notes of Serge's analysis, reported that she felt Freud didn't know that Serge had been sodomized. I don't think he did. At the end of his life Freud thought his analysis of Serge had been a success.

Freud wasn't a conscious fraud. Most analysts unconsciously steer patients away from areas of emotional pain they themselves haven't dealt with. For the same reason, Freud steered Serge away from the cause of his symptoms by endless, convoluted, far-fetched explanations. When I read them I thought of Dr Johnson's witticism: "A man might write such stuff forever if he would abandon his mind to it." But Freud didn't know he'd abandoned his mind, that his words, words, words were no more scientific than a child whistling in the dark to keep his fear away.

During their first sessions, Freud noticed that Serge, lying on a sofa facing away from him, would often turn his head around and give him "a very friendly," propitiating look, then stare at the large grandfather clock across the room, as if, thought Freud, he was eager for the session to be over. Much later in the analysis, Serge remembered a childhood fairy tale in which a wolf eats six little goats and the seventh saves himself by hiding in a grandfather clock. Serge then understood why, after giving Freud a propitiating look, he'd look at the clock. It meant, he told Freud, "Be kind to me! Must I be frightened of you? Are you going to eat me up? Shall I hide myself from you in the clock-case like the youngest little goat?"

When he started analysis, the child in Serge was entreating the father figure behind him to be kind and not turn into a big bad wolf, like the father who'd come up from behind and raped him. Serge must also have unconsciously feared that the famous Dr Freud would have the power to coax the child hiding in the clock-case to come out and remember he'd been anally raped. Serge, like all patients, despite his desire to get well, was terrified of facing his old agony. He didn't know he had nothing to worry about, that, if patients remembered being sexually abused, Freud would convince them that their memories were fantasies, their symptoms caused by something else.

Early in the case history, Freud said that Serge was "undoubtedly [afraid of] his father," but, since Freud now believed that parents rarely molested children, Serge had to be afraid of his father for another reason, a reason Freud already knew. Just as Freud had known beforehand that Hans would have an Oedipus complex, Freud knew that Serge's father would be "the terrifying figure that threatened him with castration." "Fear of castration" had to be the reason for Serge's "intense unconscious hostility" toward his father because all male children wanted to have sex with Mummy and therefore feared Daddy would cut off their penis.

Knowing beforehand the cause of Serge's neurosis enabled Freud to be unaware of Serge's childhood rape. Serge could keep his secret hidden in his unconscious because Sigi (Freud's childhood nickname) was another little goat hiding from a scary wolf.

On December 22, 1897, years before he analyzed Serge, Freud suggested to Fliess that Goethe's words about a suffering child—"What did they do to you, poor child?"—should be the motto of psychoanalysis. He made that suggestion after he'd spent over a year and a half struggling to find out what had been done to poor Sigi.

Opening Eyes

Freud began to sense that something had been amiss between himself and his father at the same time as many people who've been sexually abused feel safe enough to remember, when the parent is dying or dead.

In mid 1896, when his father became mortally ill, Freud found himself behaving, not like the loving son he thought he was, but as if he hated his father. He did dutifully cancel his planned meeting with his dear friend, Wilhelm Fliess, so he wouldn't be far from his father, and yet he ended up being away from home for altogether two months, the longest holiday, according to his biographer, Ernest Jones, that he'd ever taken. When his father died, Freud's hidden hostility surfaced again; he managed to be late for the funeral, which, to the disapproval of his relatives, he'd made as simple as possible. That night in a dream he saw a notice in a shop that said: "You are requested to close the eyes." He told Fliess (November 2, 1896) the dream revealed the "self-reproach" survivors of the dead usually feel. Freud's self-reproach was more likely guilt for having wished him dead, for in a few months he'd remember that his father had been a sexual pervert. "You are requested to close the eyes" sounds like the common warning from parents to children they molest: "Don't tell, close your eyes to what I did to you." But with his father dead, Freud's eyes began to open, not at first to his father's abuse, but to fathers as sexual abusers.

Daddy Did It

Many have pointed out that although Freud accused nursemaids, servants, governesses, grown women and siblings of molesting children, he didn't label fathers as sexual abusers until after his father's death. His father died on October 23, 1896, and six weeks later in a December 6 letter to Fliess he said, among other theoretical statements, that "heredity is seduction by the father" (which I think means that heredity doesn't cause neuroses; abuse by a father does). In that letter, he told Fliess about a "highly perverse father" who got sexually excited from licking "the feet of a wet nurse," and in many subsequent letters he told Fliess about the perverse fathers who'd molested his patients. On January 3, 1897, he reported that a daughter, who'd been raped by her father when she was eight, had suffered from a white discharge from her vagina and, when an adult, from "eczema around her mouth," and lesions at the corners that "do not heal," symptoms that reminded Freud of an earlier case, whose cause had been "traced back ... to sucking on the penis." On January 12 he told Fliess about a "loathsome" father who'd done something to his daughter that gave her convulsions before the age of one, but whose two younger sisters were "healthy," as though the father had "convinced himself of the damaging effects of his caresses."

Freud next (January 17 and 24) wrote to Fliess, not about contemporary evil fathers, but about sexual perversity in medieval times, tales of devils who "invariable abuse" their victims "sexually and in a loathsome manner," and he wondered if perversions were remnants of "primeval sexual" cults, for his paranoid patients complained they were "maltreated at night in the most shameful way sexually" [anal intercourse]. It was as if Freud first had to distance himself, go back to medieval times and prehistory, before he could face his own early history, for in his next letter to Fliess (February 8 and 11) he did. He said that "hysterical cold shivers" go back to "being taken out of a warm bed," and that "hysterical headache," was caused by perverts who hold their victims' heads "still for the purpose of actions in the mouth," then added "unfortunately, my own father was one of those perverts and is responsible for the hysteria of my brother ... and those of several younger sisters."

In 1951, when Ernest Jones was writing a biography of Freud, he remarked that it was strange that Freud accused his father of orally sodomizing "only his brother and some younger sisters" when Freud himself suffered from hysteria, that it was strange Freud didn't include himself. It wasn't strange. At incest survivor meetings, newcomers often said that Daddy had molested their siblings but not them, only to discover that they'd come to meetings, not out of sympathy for their siblings, but because they hadn't been spared. Freud, however, without realizing it, *had* included himself. Whereas in "The Aetiology of Hysteria," he'd said that "vomiting," "indigestion," or "disgust at food" were the symptoms that "the bucal cavity" had been "misused for sexual purposes," in the letter in which he accused his father, he changed the hysterical symptom to headaches "with sensations of pressure on the top of the head [and] temples," like his own, chronic severe migraines.

Psychoneurotic

Ernest Jones characterized the "hysteria" Freud suffered from as the "very considerable psychoneurosis," which began soon after he wrote the February letter accusing his father of orally sodomizing his siblings. On April 12 he complained to Fliess that "for several weeks" he'd been so drained of energy that in his free time all he could do was distract himself: "cut open books, play solitaire ... and the like." Freud attributed his lethargy to prolonged "overwork and tension," not, he emphasized, to any desire to "contradict my own etiological theory," by which he then meant "paternal etiology," identifying fathers as sexual abusers. He told Fliess on April 28 that he still had doubts "about matters concerning fathers," but that, luckily, that very morning, he got a new patient whose "noble and respectable father regularly took her to bed when she was from eight to twelve years old and misused her without penetration ('made her wet')," and that he'd also violated her older sister.

Freud became obsessed with discovering "the pederastic element" that he said men repressed, so obsessed that on May 31 he told Fliess that he was so eager to "pin down a father as the originator of a neurosis" he'd had a dream in which he had "over affectionate feelings" for his nine-year-old daughter. In that letter he also mentioned wishing parents dead and spoke of "the horror of incest," noting that "members of a family" used to have a "communal sex life (even in childhood)." These intellectual interests were the prelude to the "neurotic experience" that soon overwhelmed him, which he described to Fliess on June 22 as "curious states incomprehensible to consciousness, twilight thoughts, veiled doubts," which subjected him to a "period of intellectual paralysis" he'd "never before even imagined" existed.

"I believe I am in a cocoon," he ended that letter, "and God knows what sort of beast will crawl out." His "neurotic experience" continued, but the beast didn't crawl out. On July 7 he told Fliess that "something from the deepest depths of my own neurosis has set itself against" understanding what's going on "and you have somehow been involved in it," for he'd developed a "writing paralysis ... designed to inhibit our communication." He didn't find out why something within him wouldn't let him write to Fliess. He experienced an "obscurity" in his mind, which he thought might be a "defense against memories." He was right. When someone who has been sexually abused gets close to remembering, he or she will often get so frightened their minds shut down. Perhaps to make sure that memories of his father would stay buried, in mid July he had a stone laid on his grave.

But, as if to unbury memories, Freud courageously began self-analysis, which he told Fliess on August 14 "must be done" because, though he was on vacation, "the agitation in [his] head and feelings" hadn't diminished. "Things are fermenting in me," he confessed, so that "I have finished nothing." His "psychic strength" was so paralyzed he couldn't even write up his findings, and he was still "tormented by grave doubts about my theory of the neuroses," which continued to be to pin down fathers as abusers. But he'd pinned down many fathers as the source of his patients' symptoms and his doubts persisted, perhaps, he may have begun to realize, because he hadn't pinned down the right father.

Flight

Freud fled to Italy where, he told Fliess on September 6, he was "seeking a punch made of Lethe." Lethe in Greek mythology was the river of forgetfulness the dead drank from when they entered the underworld. Freud drank it. On September 21, back from vacation, he wrote what was to become his famous letter repudiating his theory that the cause of neuroses was sexual abuse. One reason was "the surprise that in all cases, the *father*, not excluding my own, had to be accused of being perverse" and "surely such widespread perversions against children are not very probable."

On October 3, less than two weeks after he'd reasoned it was "not probable" that "all" fathers were perverse, Freud announced to Fliess that a dream had revealed that his "prime originator" hadn't been, as he'd feared, "the old man," who "plays no active part in my case." His old, ugly nursemaid had been his "teacher in sexual matters." Freud thought that he'd projected onto his father what his nurse had done. How she abused him is unclear, but she couldn't have forced a penis into his mouth, the perversity he'd accused his father of committing.

Now that his father had escaped indictment, Freud should have rested his case against fathers. He didn't. On December 12, Freud told Fliess that his "confidence in paternal etiology has risen greatly," and he again wrote him about cases in which fathers were sexual abusers. On December 22, he recorded an especially brutal case: a two-year-old who, among other horrors, had been "brutally deflowered" by her father, who'd "infected her with his gonorrhea." She was the child who touched Freud's heart and made him suggest that the motto of psychoanalysis should be Goethe's:" What have they done to you, poor child?"

Freud's compassion for abused children didn't last. That heartfelt cry was like a sputtering candle flame that spurts up before it goes out. From then on, Freud mostly gave up trying to find out what had been done to sexually abused children. He was too afraid to find out what had been done to poor Sigi. "What have they done to you, poor child?" became a question Freud would never answer about himself, a question he would have denied needed to be asked. Nevertheless, the poor child he'd abandoned kept trying to tell him the truth.

Collateral Damage

When Serge was a child, he pretended he'd saved himself from the big bad wolf by hiding in a fairy-tale grandfather clock. When Freud was an adult, he pretended he'd saved himself from the "old man" by remembering that his old nurse was the one who'd molested him. Until he was re-analyzed in the 1920s, Serge wasn't conscious that his father had raped him, nor of the many illnesses, habits and feelings that revealed his abuse. For the rest of his life Freud remained unconscious of the symptoms that bore witness to his abuse.

Freud linked his siblings' headaches with his father's oral sodomy, but not to his own migraines, nor did he see a connection between oral sodomy and the cigar he usually had in his "bucal cavity." He smoked up to twenty a day, an addiction he couldn't give up even when he thought it was the cause of his heart trouble (chest pains and heart arrhythmias). He often quit but always started again; he said he felt better when he smoked. He told Fliess (April 19, 1894) that he hadn't had "anything warm between my lips" for three weeks, but that his "cardiac misery" was "greater than I ever had while smoking," so great he'd had visions of death and dying. His "cardiac misery," turned out to be what we now call panic attacks, which nicotine eased for a while.

When Freud had his "cardiac misery," he wondered if it was really an "anxiety neurosis," but he didn't go into it, and he told Fliess (December 22, 1897) that all addictions, including "tobacco," were substitutes for the "primal addiction," masturbation. By 1905 the author of "Infantile Sexuality" would have been able to say that he smoked cigars excessively because he'd been one of those babies born with "a constitutional intensification of the labial" erogenous zone. When Freud listed the many symbols of the penis in the 1910 edition of *The Interpretation of Dreams*, he didn't list the cigar.

The Phantom of the Rectum

Freud may have needed a penis symbol constantly in his mouth to divert his attention from the penis hidden in another erogenous zone, a penis he inadvertently made visible in "Infantile Sexuality." "The contents of the bowels," he wrote, "behave like forerunners of another organ, which is destined to come into action." When I first read that, I couldn't take in what Freud meant. I had to read it again, slowly, before I registered that Freud was actually comparing feces in the rectum to a penis. Though a mass of feces compressed in the rectum is shaped somewhat like a penis, how could feces be "the forerunners of *another* organ" since they're not an organ. And yet when I read "forerunners of another organ," I'd seen the organ that Freud said was "destined" "to come into action" in action, but not in a vagina. I saw it in a rectum! A surreal effect that made me suspect that Freud had been anally raped.

My suspicion was increased when I later read the case history of Serge and found Freud again saying that the "column of feces" "plays the part of an active organ," an organ that stimulated "the erotogenic mucous membrane of the intestine" "just as the penis" stimulated "the vaginal mucous membrane," as if they were comparable sex organs and the mucous membrane of the intestine and vagina were alike.

To refresh my memory of "the contents of the bowels" passage in "Infantile Sexuality," I reread it and this time noticed in a footnote that it hadn't been in the original text (published in 1905) but had been added in 1915. My suspicion that Freud had been sodomized became stronger. For in the winter of 1914-1915 Freud was writing up the case history of Serge. Freud's conscious mind may not have acknowledged Serge's rape, but analyzing Serge must have triggered memories of his own rape, for only a child who didn't yet know vaginas existed and for whom a penis in the rectum was his original model of intercourse would say that a "column of feces" and a penis were comparable sex organs. Freud summoned up the apparition of a penis in a rectum because the memory of a penis was still alive in the mucous membrane of his own rectum.

That Freud's body held the memory of his anal rape would not be unusual. Bodies often retain memories of traumatic assaults, memories that sometimes, like Rip Van Winkle, wake up after a long sleep, a fact Freud knew. In "The Aetiology of Hysteria" he'd said that "painful sensations in the genitals" can be the first symptom of early sexual abuse.

How Sigi distanced himself from the pain of anal rape was probably described in "Infantile Sexuality." Freud there said that infants held "back their stool" (stored up a mass of compacted feces that hurt to pass) because they enjoyed the "painful but also highly pleasurable sensations," as if all babies got constipated to get masochistic thrills. They don't. Children who've been sodomized get constipated to avoid the pain of defecating from a torn anus. When they must defecate, they deal with the pain by turning it into pleasure, one of the ways bodies transcend great pain, as those who've been tortured testify. Anal sodomy in childhood sexualizes defecation. When Freud said that Hans and all children got "voluptuous sensations from their evacuations," he wasn't describing all children; he was describing how little Sigi sexualized his anus to handle the pain of rape.

Freud's body had many pains that could have been memories of oral and anal sodomy:—his severe migraines, his addiction to cigars, the cancer of the jaw that killed him; the constipation and constant intestinal difficulties that climaxed in a fear of rectal cancer so great that in May 1914 he had an internal examination. But Freud's analytic mind had disconnected from his body; he'd forgotten what he'd once known, that painful sensations in the body can be symptoms of early sexual abuse.

Rape By Proxy

The part of Freud that remembered his abuse was driven to reveal it, but he could do it only by using a patient as a shield to hide behind.

Freud peremptorily commandeered Serge's childhood dream of wolves sitting on a tree outside a window and replaced it with an elaborate dream in which the child was not between three and five but eighteen-months old and witnessed, not scary wolves on a tree, but, said Freud, Serge's parents having sex. The dream, though, had nothing to do with Serge. In wealthy Russian families like his, babies didn't sleep in their parents' bedrooms, whereas Freud's first home was a one-room apartment where he most likely did see his parents having sex.

In the dream that Freud, not Serge, created, the parents have sex in the *a tergo* position (the woman kneeling, the man entering from behind). Freud was certain they did because, he said, "all" his patients who saw their parents having sex reported they were in that position. That all parents had sex *a tergo* is incredible, so I wondered if Freud's parents always had sex that way. Whether or not they did, Freud would have fantasized them in the *a tergo* position because Serge had told Freud he couldn't have sex unless he took the woman from behind, that is, unless he forced the woman to assume the position he'd been in when he'd been raped, a position that Freud's body had also been forced to assume when his father used his rectum as a vagina, the *a tergo* position favored by pederasts.

Jeffrey Masson pointed out that Freud used "primal scene" and "scene" interchangeably to refer to childhood sexual traumas until he wrote the case history of Serge, that only then did "primal scene" mean witnessing parents having sex. But Serge didn't witness his parents having sex *a tergo*. Freud said he did because he was compelled to write about his "primal scene," his sexual trauma.

Because Freud was using Serge to relive his own rape, he told him that he woke up from the dream screaming and "passed a stool," thus interrupting "his parents' intercourse." Freud explained that just as a "grown-up man" would have an "erection" when he saw sex, an infant's sexual excitement would make him "pass a stool." More likely, fear was the cause. Freud insisted that Serge screamed and passed a stool because in poor Sigi's primal scene he'd screamed with pain, interrupting his father, who withdrew his penis, whereupon the terrified Sigi "passed a stool." Serge denied defecating after the wolf dream, but Freud insisted that "everything took place just as I have described it" because unconscious memories of his own rape had written the script.

Ghosts

Ghosts of Sigi's rape haunted Freud. In 1906 in the dining room of a hotel in Munich, Freud fainted, and was to faint there two more times. Freud later guessed he fainted because he associated that room with Wilhelm Fliess, for whom he had homosexual feelings, feelings that even his conventional biographer, Ernest Jones, called "passionate." "How nice it would be, if this close harmony between us were a total one," Freud wrote to Fliess (March 10, 1898), sounding like a woman wanting to be totally absorbed into her lover. Long after their break up in 1901, Freud's feelings for Fliess remained so intense he transferred them to Alfred Adler and other colleagues. Freud was very much aware of what he called his "unruly homosexual feelings." He wasn't aware of their source and he didn't want to know. When he was tracking down fathers as abusers and was in the grip of his psychoneurosis, his hand became paralyzed so he couldn't write to Fliess, the man who'd resurrected the unruly homosexual feelings first aroused by his father's rape.

In 1909, this time at a lunch with his colleagues, Jung (a Fliess surrogate whom Freud called his "dear son") was talking about the well-preserved corpses recently dug up from peat-bogs, when Freud fainted.

Freud said he did because he was sure that his "dear son" was talking about dead bodies because he unconsciously wanted to kill him. But why should a son wanting to kill a father even raise the eyebrows of the author of the Oedipus complex, never mind make him faint? It may be that Jung's news item, coming unexpectedly, revealed, like a bolt of lightning, the well-preserved corpse in the bog in Freud's mind, revealed the father whose "dear son" had often killed him in fantasy. To use Freud's own insight, the sudden "return of the repressed" frightened him into a dead faint.

Love's "Erotic Pitch"

Soon after that fainting fit, Freud devised a few theories about the origins of homosexuality, none of which had anything to do with what he'd called "paternal etiology" (fathers as sexual abusers). In 1910, a year after he fainted, Freud published a study of Leonardo da Vinci in which he blamed Leonardo's homosexuality on his mother's excessive love. The next year in "A Case of Paranoia," Freud suggested several other reasons for the homosexuality of Dr Daniel Schreber, a man whose madness had long fascinated Freud.

According to Schreber's *Memoirs of a Neurotic*, his mental breakdown began the morning he woke up feeling that "it really must be very nice to be a woman submitting to the act of copulation." Schreber later feared that his physician would actually change him into a woman so he could handle his body "in all kinds of revolting ways." Freud knew that Schreber's physician was a stand-in for his father, which in 1896 would have made him suspect that Schreber was afraid of his physician because his father *had* handled his body "in all kinds of revolting ways." But having developed the theory that parents rarely commit such abominations, Freud was compelled to prove that Schreber's homosexuality had nothing to do with paternal sodomy.

Schreber's longing to be a woman, said Freud, "had its root in a longing" he'd had in childhood, first for his brother and then for "some one of greater importance," his father, a prominent man and eminent physician, "by no means unsuitable for transfiguration into a God." Schreber's "outburst of homosexual feeling" was therefore love of his father "intensified to an erotic pitch," which wasn't perverse because "every human being oscillates all his life between heterosexual and homosexual feelings." Poor Schreber, not knowing that his feelings were natural, struggled against his homosexual "libidinous impulse," a struggle that was "the exciting cause of his illness."

At a time when homosexuals were regarded as moral monsters, for Freud to define homosexuality as love "intensified to an erotic pitch," and to say that its frustration caused mental illness was extraordinary, as was Freud's argument that we're all born with "a bisexual predisposition."

However, in the study of Schreber, Freud also developed his theory that the root cause of homosexuality was Narcissism, regression to the "primitive stage" of sexuality called autoeroticism, when an infant can love only someone with genitals like its own. In other words, that we're all born homosexual, not bisexual. Freud ignored the contradiction.

In my incest survivor group in San Francisco there were many homosexuals who'd been orally and/or anally raped by a father or other adult male and whose sex life consisted of acting out the role of abuser or victim, or both. Since most men who are sodomized as children don't become homosexuals, it's not *the* cause of homosexuality. There are many causes, some of which may be genetic, but among the causes, sodomy is one, a compulsion to repeat in adulthood the sex life learned in childhood.

In the Closet

People who become hysterically blind can't see for psychological reasons. Freud became hysterically blind to his own homosexual abuse, which made him unable to pick up that Schreber and Serge had been sodomized. His fear of what was hidden in his unconscious forced him to lay down as an iron rule of psychoanalysis that patients' stories about sexual abuse must be treated as fantasies. But despite Freud's decree, real sexual abuse of children remained common, more common than people suppose; it has always been one of the best kept family secrets. Ironically, among those children (as Jeffrey Masson reported in *The Assault on Truth*) was the son of Freud's beloved Wilhelm. Robert Fliess in a 1956 book confessed that he'd been beaten "almost within an inch of his life" by his father and that he'd been sexually molested "in the most bizarre ways" by his father and mother, who'd both handed him "to others" to be sexually used.

Robert, who became a psychoanalyst, told Freud about his father and said that Freud believed him. Freud must have been appalled that, at the same time he was writing to Fliess about wanting to pin down fathers as sexual abusers, Fliess had been abusing his own son. Did Freud then realize why Fliess hadn't been enthusiastic about the seduction theory? Did Freud sense he'd been attracted to Fliess because Fliess was a pederast like his own father? I doubt it. That would have meant he'd become aware of the reason for his "unruly homosexual feelings," and he never did. He kept trying to understand those feelings; he once said he'd dealt with them by withdrawing a "piece of [his] homosexual investment" and using it to "enlarge [his] ego." Whatever that means, it was an escape into the intellect, a sign that his feelings in that area had turned to stone.

Freud rightly said that the goal of psychoanalysis was to make the unconscious conscious. It's ironic and tragic for Freud and the world that he couldn't practice what he preached. His inability to make his father's abuse conscious barred him from fully understanding himself, male homosexuality, and, of course, sexual abuse. For a similar reason, he couldn't explore another area of human psychology: women's sexuality. Though most of his patients were women, and though he told Hans's father that his notes on Hans were superfluous since he'd learned all he needed to know from analyzing patients, Freud, instead of writing paper after paper about women's sexuality, claimed it was a "dark continent."

V   **What Did She Do To You, Poor Sigi?**

The Seduction Theory

Freud called his belief that hysterical symptoms were caused by childhood sexual abuse the "seduction theory." I avoided using that phrase because having sex with a child is never seduction. To seduce means to persuade another to have sex, but even when a child is cajoled into letting its body be used, even when a child seems to like it, it's not seduction; it's coercion. Adults, especially parents, are not negotiating with an equal but imposing their will on a person much smaller and weaker who is dependent on them for survival. The child can't fight or run away and rarely dares to object. Trapped, afraid, the child is not seduced; it's raped, and the early Freud knew it. It may be that, living in the Victorian era, Freud thought that "seduction" was a genteel way to cover up an unpleasantness. But that he used the euphemism "seduction" may have had deeper roots.

By 1909, when Freud published "Analysis of a Phobia in a Five-year-old Boy," he no longer accused Mummy or Daddy of 'seducing' children. Five-year-old Hans was the "young lover," who in a "state of intensified sexual excitement" spent time in the morning in bed with "his handsome mother," where he was the sexual aggressor, not his mother. For Hans, like all children, was a "little Oedipus." And yet a mere year later, in his study of Leonardo da Vinci, Freud described a Mummy seducing a child in which he used words found in romance novels. Freud imagined Leonardo saying: "My mother pressed innumerable passionate kisses on my mouth."

Had Freud abandoned the Oedipus complex? Or, since life forced him to admit that occasionally a child was sexually abused, had Freud done original research that compelled him to present Leonardo's mother as a seducer? If he did, he never mentioned it. Very little was known about Leonardo's childhood, and nothing about his infantile relationship with his mother, except that he was an illegitimate child. Many mothers reject such children, but Freud was absolutely certain that Leonardo's mother smothered him with "excessive tenderness" and "passionate kisses." Freud also waxed poetic about the famous Mona Lisa smile, claiming it was the "smile of bliss and rapture" that "had once played on" Leonardo's "mother's lips as she fondled him."

Since Freud said that the Mona Lisa smile expressed the greatest "human happiness" mothers ever attain, and that the "love-relation" of a mother with her son was "completely satisfying," he may have thought he was uttering a general truth about mothers, not just Leonardo's. Isak Dinesen also observed the same "love-relation." "To watch our Southern mothers playing with and fondling their infants is to see the hearts aflame, and that an infant son, while still in swaddling clothes, may well be his mama's lover." The narrator in Dinesen's story was remembering his mother. Fifteen when she was married to a man three times her age, she poured her love into a son she thought of as "a divine power" in "human form," which made breast-feeding "like kisses—reciprocal givings and takings of vigor and bliss" ("The Cardinal's First Tale," *Last Tales*, 1957).

Dinesen was describing the intense love between mother and infant son that was common when marriages were arranged, when women were often much younger than their husbands and couples weren't in love, when men didn't think they had to satisfy women sexually and women were despised as inferior beings. Under such circumstances, it was understandable that a woman would pour her love onto the member of the superior sex she'd miraculously created and turn him into "mama's lover."

Freud's mother was barely twenty when in 1855 she married a man twice her age, an arranged marriage to a man she didn't love, a man who was a secret pederast and who may have had sex with her *a tergo* because that's how he had sex with children. It may, therefore, have been Freud's mother who, "in place of her husband" took as a lover her first-born son, a son she may not have regarded as "a divine being," but whom she called her "golden Sigi" all her life. Freud may have been positive that Leonardo's mother smothered him with "passionate kisses," and that the Mona Lisa smile was his mother's "smile of bliss and rapture" because Sigi was indulging in remembrances of times past with Mummy.

In the case history of Serge, Freud unwittingly revealed much more about himself than about Serge. He may have done the same with Leonardo and, since little was known about him, Freud may have felt free to write what he admitted was a "half-fictional production." Some of the fiction, though, was true to Freud's life. He made Leonardo the same kind of homosexual he was, one who "restricted" himself "to what is called ideal (sublimated) homosexuality," like his own "ideal," nonsexual attachment to Fliess. Freud summed up what he regarded as his own scientific genius when he said that Leonardo was a "modern natural scientist," whose intellectual "boldness," and "courage" were rewarded by "an abundance of discoveries and suggestive ideas." Leonardo da Vinci was one of the great geniuses of the world, and Freud, though he modestly said he couldn't be compared to Leonardo, secretly felt he'd been cut out of the same golden cloth, especially since they'd become geniuses in the same sexual way. In the case history of Hans, Freud had said that the instinct for knowledge was not "elementary" in children, that "the spirit of inquiry was first aroused" only when a child became curious about sex. Leonardo and Freud's sexual curiosity having been aroused when they were babies by a mother's "excessive tenderness" and "passionate kisses," their great geniuses got the same head start.

Having slipped into Leonardo's famous skin, Freud felt sufficiently anonymous to tell the world what he elsewhere claimed not to know. In *Three Essays on Sexuality* (1905), he'd said that women's erotic life was "veiled in an impenetrable obscurity," and in 1928 he told Ernest Jones that "the sexual life of the adult woman" was a mystery to him, "a dark continent." But when Freud asked his friend, Marie Bonaparte, "What do women want?," a part of Freud did know. Sigi had explored that dark continent and, as far as he was concerned, "the sexual life of the adult woman" was centered on the son with whom Mummy had enjoyed a "completely satisfying," loving relationship

A Secret Happiness

Mummy was not the only one who'd been completely satisfied. Freud noted that the Mona Lisa "smile of bliss and rapture" was mirrored on the faces of the beautiful young men Leonardo painted, who also, said Freud, "gaze in mysterious triumph, as if they knew of a great achievement of happiness." I couldn't help thinking of that great happiness when Freud philosophized (presumably about Leonardo): "How slowly anyone tears himself from his childhood, if in his childhood days he had enjoyed the highest erotic bliss, which is never again attained." I linked the great happiness with enjoying the "highest erotic bliss" because Freud said that the "smile of bliss and rapture" mirrored on the face of the beautiful young men was a happiness "about which silence must be kept," the silence that child abusers demand of their victims. Moreover, Freud tells us that Leonardo received more sexually than "excessive tenderness" and "passionate kisses" from his mother.

Freud does when he discussed a childhood memory that Leonardo recorded in his notebooks: "While I was in my cradle, a vulture came down to me, and opened my mouth with its tail, and struck me many times with its tail against my lips." Leonardo attributed that incident to his interest in the flight of birds. Since a tiny black bird perched on my head when I was a baby, I accepted Leonardo's memory as real, but Freud was certain it wasn't. Just as Freud said that Serge's wolf dream was a disguise for the sex *a tergo* Serge witnessed when he was an infant, Freud was sure that the "vulture opening the child's mouth and beating about inside it vigorously with its tail" was a memory of "*fellatio*, a sexual act in which the penis is put into the mouth of the person involved." Perhaps, but I doubt that Freud would have made that leap into sex if he hadn't had memories of his father opening his mouth with his penis.

Freud, of course, would have disagreed. For him, Leonardo's memory of the vulture fellating his mouth was a fantasy that went back to the origin of fellatio, to breast-feeding, when we put our mother's "nipple into our mouth and sucked at it." Freud, however, didn't leave it simply at that. He went on to say that the mother's breast "has been turned into a vulture that puts its tail into the child's mouth," a tail that "cannot possibly signify anything other than a male genital, a penis." To turn a mother's breast into a vulture, a vulture whose tail is really a penis confused me. I puzzled over what Freud meant and decided that it would make sense only to Sigi, a child who'd had his father's penis in his mouth as well his mother's nipple. That Sigi merged his mother's and father's abuse is also suggested by Freud saying that in fellatio "the penis is put into the mouth of the person involved," which could refer both to his father putting his penis into Sigi's mouth and to his mother putting Sigi's penis into her mouth. If she did fellate Sigi, she did what many female abusers do, an act that men, who've experienced it when they were babies, have told me can be so pleasurable they feel their very being dissolve, an act that may well be the "highest erotic bliss" about which "silence must be kept."

The study of Leonardo I read had the title, *Leonardo da Vinci and a Memory of his Childhood*, but Freud called it *A Childhood Memory of Leonardo da Vinci*. I think Freud emphasized Leonardo's childhood memory in the title because it evoked unconscious childhood memories that Freud could interpret in a sexual way.

A True to Life Romance

"The intensity of the erotic relation between mother and child," said Freud, was the effect Leonardo wanted to create in his paintings. I've looked and looked, but I don't see maternal eroticism on Mary's or Anne's face in "Madonna and Child with St Anne" (a painting Freud discussed), and how Freud could have described Mona Lisa's cool, mysterious smile as a mother's "smile of bliss and rapture" is beyond me, especially since no child is in the picture. Freud saw Leonardo's paintings with the eyes of the child who'd had blissful sex with Mummy. He confidently asserted that Leonardo remained as tied to his mother "by erotically colored feelings as he had been in childhood," because the child in Freud continued to have "erotically colored feelings" for the mother who'd seduced him, feelings Sigi thought were love, not the consequences of abuse, feelings so powerful he glamorized sexual abuse with the name of "seduction."

And yet, though Sigi glamorized his affair with Mummy, he knew their romance had been tainted, for when Freud wrote about Leonardo's mother, he told the whole truth; he admitted that, despite her "devoted tenderness," her "sensuality" could be "ruthlessly demanding" and her "caresses" violent.

Freud also spoke of "his mother's (the vulture's) activity," and described her breast as turning into a vulture. In 1923 it was pointed out that the translation of Leonardo's notebooks that Freud used mistranslated "vulture" for "kite," another bird of prey. Freud never made the correction. Perhaps because "vulture" had many mother associations that Freud cherished: it could mean a rapacious person; it was the Egyptian hieroglyph for "mother," and in some myths vultures were always female.

Freud accused the vulture-woman of psychologically devouring Leonardo. "In the manner of all unsatisfied mothers," she used him "in place of her husband." Being her "only solace," she smothered him with an "excessive tenderness" so that, "infatuated with his mother," he experienced "a union of the male and female natures" that "was fateful for him." It "robbed him of a piece of his masculinity," and thus "set the stage for his later homosexuality." "It was through this erotic relation with my mother that I became a homosexual," Freud has Leonardo confess, but the "I" startles the reader, who at first thinks Freud is writing about himself. Since Freud also said that Leonardo, like him, didn't act out his homosexuality, he may have been unconsciously revealing what he thought was the source of his own "unruly homosexual feelings"— maternal seduction.

Peter Gay, in his biography of Freud, was among those who noted that Freud "exiled mothers to the margins of his case histories." Why he did has puzzled Freudians. Freud's personal physician, Max Schur, in a 1955 letter to Ernest Jones, felt there was much evidence that Freud had a "complicated pre-genital relationship with his mother which perhaps he never fully analysed." But in his study of Leonardo, Freud did analyze their relationship at some length, and realistically: he complained about the violence of her caresses, blamed her for making him a homosexual. Gay said Freud wholly sentimentalized a "mother's love for her son." He didn't in his study of Leonardo.

That Freud, even in the guise of Leonardo, described a mother's sexual love for her son is surprising since it came from a Freud who no longer believed in the seduction theory. For over a decade, Freud's rock of ages had been his theory that the perverse sexual constitution of infants made them lust after parents, that it was little Hans, not his Mummy, who brought "erotic feelings" into their bed, that the "scenes of seduction" patients described "had never taken place." But in his study of Leonardo, Freud described "scenes of seduction" that had taken place, scenes of a mother's "passionate caresses," oral and genital. Before he repudiated the seduction theory, Freud said that a boy's libido had been "prematurely awakened" by his female molester, and in the Leonardo study he again said of a child that he'd been seduced "into precocious sexual maturity" by his mother.

Narcissus to the Rescue

Freud may have feared that his followers would think he was res-
urrecting the "seduction theory." Only a great need could have made
Freud take that risk. In the last chapter, I suggested that Freud fainted
because the ghost of his father's sodomy suddenly materialized. What
better way to lay that ghost, than to blame homosexual feelings on an
"erotic relation" with a mother? However, having contradicted his theory
that parents didn't seduce children, Freud had to repair the damage.

He did by devising a new theory, Narcissism, which Freud first pro-
posed in his study of Leonardo. Just as Narcissus was infatuated with his
own beauty, babies are infatuated with their genitals and only love others
with genitals like their own. Homosexuality is therefore regression to
the autoeroticism of infancy. That his new theory contradicted his statement that it was through Leonardo's erotic relation with his mother that
he became a homosexual, didn't disturb Freud's followers, who would,
anyway, have dismissed Leonardo's talk about his mother's passionate
caresses as Oedipal fantasies.

I'm sure they didn't realize that Freud's theory of Narcissism made
no sense. Babies (especially girls) can't see their genitals and for a long
time both sexes don't know their genitals belong to their own body any
more than they know their hands do. Besides, from the very beginning babies do love someone else, their mothers. Narcissism seems to
be another theory Freud created, not from observing babies, but in this
case, to smooth over an inconsistency. What rings true in his study of
Leonardo is not his theory of Narcissism, but the intimate details of a
mother's erotic relationship with a son.

The influence of that erotic relationship remained with Freud all
his life. Though angry at his mother for robbing him of "a piece of his
masculinity," in his book on dreams (1900) Freud called her his "beloved
mother," and "mother" stayed on a pedestal. The "most perfect of
human relationships," he said, was a mother's with her infant son (*New
Introductory Lectures on Psychoanalysis*, 1932). "Every tender and passionate relation among humans" has some hostility in it, "perhaps with
the single exception of a mother with a male child" (*Civilization and its
Discontents*, 1930). To describe a mother's relationship with a son as
"passionate" didn't seem wrong to Freud, attached as he still was to the
mother with whom he'd attained the "highest erotic bliss."

When Freud was writing about Leonardo, he was aware he was in
the grip of an "obsession," but his "Leonardo" remained his favorite
work, "the only beautiful thing I have ever written." His biographer,
Peter Gay, suggested that "the secret energy animating this obsession"
came from memories of his homosexual feelings for Wilhelm Fliess. That
Freud was writing about the pleasure of being seduced by Mummy,

would have appalled Gay, who had dismissed "the seduction theory" as an "absurdity."

Mothers As Abusers

Sigi's other "teacher in sexual matters," his nurse, wasn't put on a pedestal. Freud didn't describe the sex he had with her, except to tell Fliess (October 3, 1897) that she "complained because I was clumsy and unable to do anything." Freud would later remark that Leonardo's mother's "sensuality" was "ruthlessly demanding." Mothers (and mother surrogates) who use children for sex often are. When my husband was an infant, his mother forced him to suck on her clitoris and to vigorously move his tiny foot in her vagina, angrily complaining when he didn't make her come. When Freud told Fliess about his nurse, he said that "neurotic impotence always comes about this way," and he attributed his present feeling that he was impotent as a therapist to not being able to sexually satisfy his nurse. That he may also have not been able to satisfy his mother is a possibility.

The idea that mothers have sex with their children is, even in the twenty-first century, taboo. That father's often rape their daughters was, by the end of the twentieth century, more or less accepted as a fact. But in regard to mothers, we've hardly advanced beyond Alfred Fournier, a French academic (mentioned by Masson) who in an 1880 lecture described a mother's vicious sexual assault on her eight-year-old daughter, but then insisted that when a mother did it, it couldn't be sexual abuse.

Statistics compiled by the United State Department of Justice have forced us to face that when it comes to killing children under the age of five, mothers are almost equal with fathers. I'm therefore sure we'll someday have to face that mothers are equals in regard to sexual abuse. Perhaps more equal, for nature seems to foster it. As I said earlier, nature creates a drugged intimacy between mother and child by producing hormones during breast-feeding that make mothers and babies euphoric. Mothers are also exposed to the intense love that babies focus on them, which makes many new mothers feel loved for the first time in their lives. No wonder mothers often enclose babies in a hot, possessive love, which may become sexual. Breast-feeding is sexually arousing, and many mothers, especially when their husbands don't sexually satisfy them, do turn a child into "mama's lover."

"How slowly anyone tears himself from his childhood, if in his childhood days he had enjoyed the highest erotic bliss, which is never again attained," was written by a man who, like most boys who are seduced by a passionate mother, find it almost impossible to tear themselves from their early bliss. Freud may not have explored what he called the "dark continent" of women's sexuality because it remained sacred ground, a secret altar in his heart where he kept the light of his mother's love eternally burning, a love "about which silence must be kept," as Mummy had told him.

Real Skeletons in the Oedipus Complex

In his study of Leonardo, Freud turned a vulture's tail into a breast, which he then turned into a penis, a transformation that confuses the reader but would have made sense to Sigi, who, as I said, sucked on his mother's nipple and had his father's penis forced into his mouth. It also wasn't the adult Freud who insisted that Leonardo couldn't have gone to live with his father until he was at least three years old, or until "perhaps, his fifth year" because Leonardo needed a long time "alone with his mother" receiving her "tender seductions" in order to become a homosexual. Freud's readers may have assumed that an eminent psychiatrist would know how long it took to make a child a homosexual, but no knowledge on the subject existed then. Moreover, Freud had read a French study that said Leonardo's father took his son to live with him when he got married, which was a mere year after he was born. Freud didn't mention that study. It contradicted Sigi's wish that his traveling-salesman father would be away for a long, long time, that God would be good and kill Daddy so he'd never come home and Sigi would be alone with his beloved Mummy forever.

I said that Sigi wished God would be good and kill Daddy because Freud once told Fliess (June 22, 1897) about a young woman who had *not* been molested by her father only because the "Almighty" had been "kind enough to let the father die before the child was 11 months old." Sigi must often have wished that the Almighty had been kind and killed his father before he'd sodomized him. Why shouldn't Sigi have wished his sexually sadistic father dead, dead, dead?

When Sigi grew up, his hatred of his father surfaced in Freud's belief that patricidal wishes lurk in sons' hearts forever. But when Jung in 1912 told Freud a story about an Egyptian king who hated his father so much that after his death he had his name removed from the monuments his father had built in his own honor, Freud fainted. Why? He couldn't have been shocked by a son hating his father, and, as usual when he fainted, nothing was physically wrong with him. It made me wonder if a son obliterating the very name of his father ignited Freud's smoldering hatred of his own father and threatened to bring up memories so frightening he had to faint them away. At any rate, as if to keep him dead, Freud killed his father again in another fantasy; he soon resumed work on *Totem and Taboo*, his book about sons who murder their powerful father.

One reason the Oedipus myth appealed to Freud was that in the complete version he most likely read, King Laius, Oedipus's father, was a notorious pedophile (he'd abducted the beautiful son of a king), a pedophile whom Oedipus, using his superhuman strength, bludgeoned to death. By identifying with Superman Oedipus, Sigi got revenge.

Freud was also fatally attracted to the Oedipus myth because after eliminating Daddy, Oedipus got to marry Mummy. Some have wondered why, since most of Freud's patients were female, the Oedipus complex wasn't about little girls who want to sleep with Daddy. For Freud that was never a consideration. Oedipus had to be male because Freud was Oedipus. In the theater in his head, Sigi had many times played the part of a son who kills his pedophile Daddy and marries his Mummy.

In the Oedipus complex, Freud expurgated those fantasies. Since Freud never acknowledged his father's incest, the Oedipus complex doesn't acknowledge homosexual incestuous fantasies, but says that boys want Daddy dead, not because he molested them, but because they want Mummy all to themselves. The real sex Sigi had with Mummy was also expurgated; it was downgraded to a fantasy and Superman Oedipus was shrunk into an infant. But "little Oedipus" was no ordinary baby; he was a Superinfant, whose mouth, anus and genitals already pulsed with sexuality, who got sadomasochistic thrills from retaining his feces, craved titillation from every orifice and got virtual orgasms from breast-feeding and thumb sucking, the sexy baby Freud presented to the world as a prototype of all babies.

Freud managed to get the world to believe that babies conform to that prototype, that humans are born with an incestuous drive that makes them capable of generating sexual fantasies on their own, without Mummy or Daddy showing them the ropes. But human children are no different from monkeys who, when isolated at birth and unable to observe copulation, don't know how to copulate when they become sexually mature. Children have sexual fantasies about Mummy or Daddy only after Mummy or Daddy gives them an early sex education.

Freud told Hans that "long before" he was born, he knew a little Hans would want to sleep with Mummy, and long before Freud wrote about Leonardo, he knew a little Leonardo would have an erotic relationship with his mother. But it wasn't the adult Freud who'd psyched out Hans or Leonardo. "Long before" went back to Sigi, whose mind and body remembered what Freud had repressed. The baby in "Infantile Sexuality" is poor Sigi, whose mouth, anus and genitals had been stimulated "into precocious sexual maturity" by his father, mother and nurse.

When Oedipus discovered he'd committed incest, he stabbed his eyeballs. When Freud began to discover his incest, he became like his early critics, who'd also been frightened by the reality of sexual abuse. He too decided that children's stories about sexual abuse were "invented tales," fantasies. But the sex Sigi's mother and father forced on him had been all too real. Sigi's desire to kill Daddy stayed with Freud all his life, as did the taboo that prevented him from writing about women's sexuality.

Jeffrey Masson called his book on Freud's suppression of the seduction theory *The Assault on Truth* because "assault" was the word the French investigators of child abuse often used for rape. Masson's title was a polite way of saying that Freud raped the truth when he denied that children were sexually abused, for which Masson accused him of "a failure of courage." Freud did rape the truth, but not because he didn't have the courage to defy conventional society. He raped the truth because being raped drained him of the emotional courage to confront his own sexual abuse. He had to deny it. He was like his patients in "The Aetiology of Hysteria" who, though they slowly dredged up their abuse and relived the feelings, "emphatically" assured Freud "of their unbelief." His patients' reluctance to remember or believe what they'd remembered convinced Freud that their memories were true. "I don't believe it. I'm making it all up," is the most common first reaction to memories of sexual abuse and virtually a guarantee, as Freud once realized, of the truth of the memory.

But Freud couldn't do for himself what he'd done for his patients; perhaps because he didn't have the compassionate Freud of 1896 to help him remember and believe the truth. Trying to do it himself (self-analysis) almost drove him crazy. By claiming that the sexy baby he described in "Infantile Sexuality" was normal, a prototype of all babies, Freud denied he'd been sexually abused. But that oversexed baby wasn't normal; he'd been created by sexual abuse. Such babies often masturbate a lot because when the emotional and physical pain of being raped begins to surface, as it often does, feeling sexual pleasure is an escape, especially since the masturbation fantasies often romanticize the assaults. The Oedipus complex was Freud's masturbation fantasy, the fantasy of an abused child who, as if in a Hollywood movie, is transformed into a hero, an Oedipus Rex, who kills a corrupt, powerful Daddy and innocently marries Mummy.

The Oedipus complex was a defense Freud invented so he wouldn't have to deal with real mothers (like his) who seduced sons and real fathers (like his) who sodomized sons, or real victims of abuse (like him). The Oedipus complex had a function similar to those a defense lawyer might devise to prove a guilty client didn't do it. By attributing a patient's symptoms to other causes besides sexual abuse—to an inherited sex drive, an overly developed erogenous zone, castration anxiety— Freud could prove that parents didn't do it.

What's fascinating is that in the same case histories, Freud would supply readers with more than enough evidence to conclude, for example, that Serge and Schreber *had* been anally raped by their fathers. At first, I thought Freud liked the thrill of balancing on a high wire. But I was forgetting that Freud didn't consciously remember his abuse. Yet, there was the evidence in plain sight. Freud had a strong need to reveal his abuse and deny it, and the Oedipus defense allowed him to do both.

"Little-Suck-a-Thumb"

In his first case history (*Fragment of an Analysis of a Case of Hysteria*), we see Freud using the Oedipus defense to point out the cause of his patient's hysteria, but at the same time he supplied readers with information that undermined his diagnosis.

In October 1900, Freud began to have sessions with an eighteen-year-old he called Dora. She hadn't come willingly. Her father had forced her to see Freud because she'd accused his best friend, Herr K, of propositioning her, which her father insisted was a lie. It didn't take long, though, before Freud believed Dora, which made her feel safe enough to tell him what she hadn't told anyone, that Herr K had first made a pass at her when she was thirteen, that having connived to get her alone, he'd pulled her to him and kissed her passionately on the mouth. Disgusted, she'd pushed him away and fled.

Dora undoubtedly expected Freud to denounce Herr K and praise her for resisting his lewd advances. She must have been astonished when he said not a word against Herr K, but blamed her, and for a fault she'd never heard of. He accused her of having something wrong in "the sphere of sexuality." He said that a normal girl of thirteen wouldn't have had "a violent feeling of disgust, and torn herself" from Herr K, that a normal girl's lips would have been sexually excited by his kiss and her genitals by his erect penis, which, though Dora hadn't mentioned it, Freud said she'd felt when Herr K pressed her against him. Dora's failure to be aroused and her disgust proved to Freud that at thirteen she was "already entirely and completely hysterical."

Nowadays, Herr K would be guilty of a crime, and in 1900 too. In the case history, Freud raised Dora's age to fourteen, the age of consent in Vienna. But Freud didn't think it was a crime, and had no sympathy for a thirteen-year-old who'd been assaulted by a man old enough to be her father. On the contrary, he told her that her revulsion was abnormal. Freud thought he was spreading his sexual gospel, teaching Dora that a healthy thirteen-year-old, having been born sexy, would, at puberty, be greatly aroused orally and genitally when Herr K kissed her.

I was shocked, almost as much as Dora must have been, when Freud told her that during Herr K's kiss, she'd felt his erect penis pressing against her clitoris, and most readers of the case history have been disturbed by Freud's barely-disguised prurience. Why was Freud, who lived in a strait-laced culture, being so graphic with an eighteen-year-old virgin? I wondered if Freud had been aroused by Dora. I did because she was about as young as his mother was when she'd had sex with a man old enough to be her father, which was close to Freud's age, so that the erection he said Dora felt pressing against her was a projection of his own. Whether or not that's true, Sigi had surfaced. The child who'd been freely used for sex by adults had to have been shocked when Dora dared to push away a father-figure. Sigi's experience had taught him that you weren't supposed to object, that it was okay for adults to have sex with children. Besides, children liked it too. Freud was teaching Dora the sexual values he'd learned when he was a child.

When Dora abruptly stopped analysis, which she did after eleven weeks, Freud told her he regretted not being able to cure her hysteria. But for a thirteen-year-old not to have been turned on by a middle-aged man who suddenly assaulted her was not a symptom of hysteria. Dora did have genuine hysterical symptoms, which Freud knew had plagued her since she was eight. He listed them as: choking, tickling in the throat, hoarseness and nervous coughing, often accompanied by a loss of voice that could last for weeks. If Dora had been his patient in 1896, Freud would have known the cause. In "The Aetiology of Hysteria," he'd said that "choking" and "constriction of the throat" were often the "hysterical symptoms" of those whose "bucal cavity" had been "misused for sexual purposes," symptoms that Freud knew had recently recurred when Dora found out that her father was having an affair with Herr K's wife.

Dora's father had forced her to see Freud not only because she insisted that Herr K had propositioned her, but because she claimed that her father was sleeping with Frau K. Her father had sworn to Freud he wasn't. "With my state of health, I need scarcely assure you that there is nothing wrong" in the relationship. Dora's father had previously consulted Freud about certain paralyzing effects of syphilis, one of which was impotence. Nevertheless, Freud was sure her father was having an affair with Frau K, but, as if to counter Dora's accusation, he told Dora that her father was impotent. It turned out, though, that Dora knew. Why then, Freud asked her, did she think he was having an affair? Was she aware there were other ways of "obtaining sexual gratification"? When Dora said she was aware, Freud told her that "she must be thinking of … those parts of the body which in her case were in a state of irritation — the throat and the oral cavity." Dora, who didn't remember her abuse, denied she was thinking of "the oral cavity," and Freud didn't question her further.

He told her that her throat symptoms reappeared because she wanted to touch her father's heart so he'd stop sleeping with Frau K, as if Freud didn't understand that her throat symptoms were reminding her father that Dora's "oral cavity," not Frau K's, had once sexually gratified him. For Dora's physical symptoms were a kind of sign language. Her cough was coughing up the penis in her mouth and the semen she'd choked on. Her hoarseness was semaphoring how irritated her throat had been, and her loss of voice that she'd been unable to speak when it was happening and wasn't supposed to tell anyway. Dora's throat symptoms were crying out what had happened to her, and Freud signaled that a part of him did know. Otherwise, after he informed Dora that the mouth could be used for sexual intercourse, he wouldn't have said that her unconscious had visualized "a scene of gratification *per os* between" her father and Frau K.

But quickly sensing that he was getting too close to the real source of Dora's throat symptoms, Freud added that it wouldn't have been "very extraordinary" if, without learning about fellatio, her history of thumb sucking alone had produced a fantasy of that perverse sexual act.

Freud's belief in the dire effects of thumb sucking reminded me of a famous nineteenth-century "awful warning" poem for children in which naughty "Little-Suck-a-Thumb" had his thumbs cut off—"Snip! Snap! Snip!"—by the scissor-man. Heinrich Hoffman, the author of *Struwwelpeter* (1847) would have blamed Dora's excessive thumb sucking on the same thing Freud did, bad heredity. Dora was one of "those children whose constitution marks them down for a neurosis," a "predisposition" she'd inherited from her father's side of the family: her father's sister and brother were neurotics. Besides, her father had syphilis, which can give a child a neurotic constitution. It was this unfortunate heredity that had made Dora a "suck-a-thumb," so addicted that at four or five she was still sucking her thumb, a perverse habit that eventually produced her throat symptoms. (Why her bad heredity affected only her mouth, Freud didn't explain.)

Freud made Dora's thumb sucking the cause of all the manifestations of what he regarded as her hysteria, like her genitals not getting aroused when Herr K kissed her. Freud explained the connection when Dora told him she sometimes still felt Herr K pressing against her chest. Freud then informed her that she'd experienced "displacement": she'd felt the pressure in her chest instead of feeling Herr K's "erect member" against her "clitoris." That Dora, at thirteen, may have been sufficiently shorter than Herr K so his penis and her clitoris didn't meet, Freud overlooked. It would have nullified his theory that her fixation on "the erotogenic oral zone," made her get sexual excitement from the upper part of her body; hence she felt Herr K pressing only against her chest. Why Miss Suck-a-Thumb's mouth hadn't been sexually aroused by Herr K's kiss, Freud explained away by saying that her mouth *had* been stimulated, that her disgust was a reaction against the intense oral erotic feelings she did have but had repressed. Thus did Freud use "displacement" and "repression," the genuine defense mechanisms he'd discovered, to displace and repress the cause of Dora's throat symptoms.

Freud was determined not to acknowledge the real cause of Dora's throat symptoms. Otherwise, he would have understood why Dora knew the real reason her father refused to believe that Herr K had propositioned her: so Herr K could sleep with her in exchange for Frau K continuing to sleep with him. Her father had sexually used her when she was a child, so why wouldn't he use her again to get his sexual desires gratified?

Dora couldn't stop hating her father for being willing to hand her over to Herr K as if she were a prostitute. That annoyed Freud, but why shouldn't Dora have hated him for that? Perhaps, Freud was annoyed because he sensed that the reason Dora couldn't forgive her father was that he was the one she wanted to expose as a pervert. Freud was also irritated by Dora's constant lament that her father "had sacrificed her to this woman." Here again, Freud may have wished she'd shut up because it was so obvious that her father had replaced her with Frau K, that her jealousy was the sexual jealousy of a former lover.

Instead of comprehending the real reason for Dora's jealousy, he accused her of being in love with Frau K and therefore jealous because Frau K now loved her father, not her, that is, Freud accused her of being a homosexual. His proof was that she and Frau K had spent much time together, and that when visiting the K's, Dora shared Frau K's bedroom. Dora had also told Freud how much she admired Frau K's "adorable white body." But for a teenager to have a crush on an older woman is common and doesn't mean she's homosexual, even if she admires her body, admiration that contains the hope that her own body will someday be adorable. Dora had a mother whose sole interest was house-cleaning; Frau K was the intelligent, compatible mother she'd longed for. Dora might have had male friends if at that time young women were allowed to freely associate with young men. Moreover, Freud wasn't a good judge of homosexuality. Later, when little Hans hugged his five-year-old cousin and told him "I am so fond of you," Freud would say it was "the first trace of homosexuality." The truth may be that Freud, angry at Dora for breaking off analysis, did what some men still do when a woman rejects them: they accuse her of being a lesbian.

Dora had sexual feelings not for Frau K but for her father, which originated not from innate lust, or from inheriting an overactive oral erogenous zone, but from having had an affair with him, from being forced to suck on his penis, which she interpreted as love because it was the only love she got in her loveless household.

Dora's crisis with her father and Herr and Frau K might have made it easy for Freud to help her cough up what had happened to her as a child. But Freud couldn't help her as long as he thought her throat symptoms were caused by thumb sucking, an absurd diagnosis that Freud used because in the area of child sexual abuse he'd undergone a lobotomy. It was as if a doctor, no longer able to detect a particular common disease, tried to convince his patients they had another disorder. Freud said again and again that Dora's coughing symptoms were caused by thumb sucking because he had to keep telling himself that his father had *not* forced him to suck on his penis. And yet, it was Freud who told Dora that she'd unconsciously visualized "a scene of gratification *per os* between" her father and Frau K, a fantasy of fellatio he was sure she'd had because he was 'visualizing' his own abuse.

When Freud accused Dora of homosexuality, he was anticipating what would become his standard put-down for those who disagreed with his theories, and Dora had constantly disagreed with him and spurned him by leaving analysis. The disloyal colleagues whom Freud labeled homosexuals were not, and neither was Dora. But Freud's diagnosis of Dora was accepted, and not only in his own time. Philip Reiff in his introduction to a 1963 edition of the case history spoke of Dora's "unconscious Lesbian tendencies" and Louis Breger in *Freud* (2000) referred to Dora as "the young homosexual."

Freud once compared his discovery that sexual abuse was the cause of hysterical symptoms to finding the "source of the Nile." Recognizing the effects of abuse on children is far more important than finding the source of the Nile. Unfortunately, Freud's own abuse forced him into denial (excuse the pun). He developed the Oedipus complex as a defense against recognizing the effects of abuse, a defense Freud used for the rest of his life.

VII   Defending The Faith

With the zeal of a Christian missionary, Freud devoted his life to spreading his gospel. In 1907 we see him teaching it to Jung. Jung, who'd recently become Freud's disciple, wrote him about a six-year-old patient who was masturbating excessively and claimed that her foster father had 'seduced' her. Since she had no memory of the actual incident and expressed no emotions, Jung thought her story was false. But, he asked Freud, "where does the child get all those sexual stories from?" Freud assured Jung that he too had been taken in by such stories until he realized they'd originated in the unconscious fantasies created by the sexually perverse minds of infants.

Louis Breger, who quoted from this exchange of letters in his *Freud*, (2000), commented that the girl's excessive masturbation and lack of emotion were typical of "the effects of sexual abuse in a girl of this age" but that it was "not fair to expect that Freud and Jung could have known in 1907 what is now known." However, the Freud of 1896 did know that such six-year-olds had been molested, a fact that Breger should have known he knew, and that Freud would have continued to know if he hadn't consigned his own abuse to a private hell in his unconscious.

When Freud was a neurologist, the sexually abused child lurking in his unconscious didn't interfere with his work; he became a respectable scientist who made important discoveries. But when he became a 'scientist' of the mind, fear of that child made him incapable of recognizing the symptoms of sexual abuse, a common childhood trauma. In the Dora case, he used the genuine defense mechanism of displacement to prove his false theory that Dora's coughing symptoms had been caused by thumb sucking. He explained away Serge's terror of his father by invoking castration anxiety. Freud was considered a fearless researcher, but fear of uncovering his own sexual abuse made him a liar, not that he knew it.

Cover-Ups

To prove he was telling the truth, Freud became adept at the convoluted free association that passed for reasoning in much of his writing. He was like Stanley Fish, the godfather of the deconstructionists, who could twist a literary text into whatever meaning suited his thesis, or like theologians who, since organized religion was invented, have used scriptural texts as putty for their own ideas. Freud, though, used this ancient defect of the human ego not fundamentally to prove a questionable theory but to keep himself safe from the horrors of his childhood.

To remain safe, Freud also had to deny that sexual abuse was common. But since sexual abuse has always been widespread and since the unconscious never totally forgets traumas, the price of Freud's denial was eternal vigilance. He had to guard his unconscious as ferociously as the three-headed dog that guarded the entrance to the underworld. To keep the truth about the prevalence of child sexual abuse suppressed, he also had to be a strict warden of his theories. Darwin said that whenever he came across an idea that challenged his theory, he wrote it down so he wouldn't forget it. Freud tried to obliterate such ideas. Having abandoned the open mind of the scientist, he demanded total control over the minds of his followers; he even formed his own Inquisition to deal with heretics.

In 1912 a secret committee of six loyal Freudians was established as defenders of the faith. Their job was to quash ideas contrary to Freud's. The committee was thought necessary because in 1911 Alfred Adler had asserted, among other heresies, that mankind's ruling drive was for power, not sex. Freud, using his superior power, drove Adler out of the Freudian flock. In 1913, Wilhelm Stekel was also ousted, he for maintaining that masturbation, far from harming people, often did them good. That Stekel might be right couldn't be discussed, for the Oedipus complex depended on Freud's doctrine that the perverse sexuality of infants made them compulsive masturbators. The renegades, therefore, couldn't merely be expelled; Freud and his followers tried to banish their heretical ideas. Otto Rank, for example, found that after his excommunication he couldn't get his papers published in psychoanalytical journals. A rumor was also bruited about that he was a manic-depressive. All defectors were discovered to have become mentally disturbed, especially with paranoia.

When the secret committee was formed, Ernest Jones said its purpose was to keep Freud's "pure theory unadulterated by personal complexes," which implied that Freud's theories were 'pure,' that they hadn't come from his "personal complexes." In other words, colleagues who developed ideas different from Freud's were not having an intellectual disagreement with him; their ideas, unlike Freud's, had come from their "complexes." Freud accused them of being sick in the head because a part of him knew he was. His attitude came across as arrogance, but his arrogance was a shield against the fear of going crazy that overwhelmed him when memories of his father's sodomy were trying to surface. That Freud linked insanity with believing parents molested children is revealed by his saying of one colleague who defected that he was living in an imaginary world in which he actually thought that children were victims of cruel parents, that the poor deluded man had been taken in by "the fantasies of patients about their childhood."

Rediscovering the Truth

That colleague was Sándor Ferenczi, an unlikely defector. A member of the secret committee, he'd been Freud's special friend and devoted follower who'd taught his patients the true faith: if they said they'd been sexually abused, Ferenczi would convince them they'd conjured up incestuous fantasies. And yet after over twenty years of playing Follow The Great Leader, Ferenczi took off his Freudian glasses. In the sixteenth century, Martin Luther had taken off his religious glasses and not only saw the corruptions of the Church, but risked excommunication and death by speaking out. Ferenczi's version of Luther's nailing 95 theses to the church door was giving a paper in September 1932 at the International Psycho-Analytic Congress, where he shocked the psychoanalytic world by announcing that his clinical work had proved again and again that his patients' accounts of sexual abuse were not fantasies, that they were, tragically, memories of actual rapes.

Ferenczi's evidence was impressive. Not only had "a multitude" of his patients confessed "to assaults on children," he'd also learned that "children of respected, high-minded puritanical families fall victim to real rape much more frequently than one had dared to suspect," that "rape of girls barely beyond infancy, similar sexual acts of grown women with boys, even sexual acts of a homosexual character by force are commonplace."

For Freud, it was as if time had gone backward to 1896 and it was "The Aetiology of Hysteria" all over again. Worse, when Ferenczi spoke of sexual acts of women with boys and forced homosexual abuse, Freud's unconscious must have set off alarm bells. No wonder he was furious. Freud urged Ferenczi to correct himself as, over thirty years before, he'd done, and complained to his daughter Anna that Ferenczi had dredged up his old theory and "said it in virtually the same words I used then." I wonder if it flashed through Freud's mind that Ferenczi said the same thing in the same words because he'd rediscovered the same truth. But Ferenczi said far more than that sexual abuse was common.

The Discovery of Tenderness

Ferenczi agreed with Freud that children were sexual, but he thought their sexuality was totally different from that of adults, a difference he summed up in an alternative title he gave his paper: "The Language of Tenderness and the Language of (Sexual) Passion." Whereas adults speak the language of sexual passion, which is a mix of "love *and* hate," of "love … saturated with hate," children speak the language of tenderness, which is without the love-hate "split." Children are innocent beings who crave only touching, hugging, kissing, playing, and whose instant reaction to sexual acts is "hatred, disgust, … 'No, no, I don't want this … that hurts me. Leave me be.' "

When Ferenczi said that children didn't want sex, he threatened Freud's life work. For if what Ferenczi said was true, gone was Hans, the "young libertine," the "little Oedipus" eager to have sex with Mummy, gone was the sexy baby of "Infantile Sexuality," whom Freud had clutched to his bosom like a life preserver to keep from drowning in the fear, hate, grief and sexual feelings he hadn't been able to handle when he was a baby. Freud had to keep that sexy baby alive and well if psychoanalysis was to survive.

Freud and his inner circle went into action. They strongly advised Ferenczi not to give his paper. Ferenczi refused and couldn't be stopped because of his high position in the organization, status that obliged them to publish his paper in their German periodical. They also felt they had to translate his paper into English and publish it in the *International Journal of Psycho-Analysis*, where it would be read by the increasing English-speaking audience, as Ferenczi wished. But Ferenczi died before publication, and the type for his paper was broken up and thrown away, a symbol of the Freudians' desire to pretend his paper hadn't existed, just as they pretended that widespread sexual abuse didn't exist.

They almost succeeded in quashing Ferenczi's truth. It sank into oblivion for many years, and Freud's 1907 advice to Jung, that patients who remembered being sexually abused were the victims, not of their parents, but of their own sexual fantasies, remained the law of Freudian land.

Freudian Fundamentalism

The duty of Freudian analysts whose patients claimed they'd been sexually abused was to convince them they hadn't been, a duty they fulfilled with the assurance of priests expiating sinners after confession. For one of the purposes of psychoanalysis was to expiate such patients from the sin of dishonoring parents.

In Jeffrey Masson's *Final Analysis* (1990), he recorded a story told by Heinz Hartmann, a mid twentieth-century Freudian, about a patient who revealed at her first session that as a child she'd been sexually abused by her father. Hartmann informed her that "such memories were nothing more than wish-fulfilling fantasies," that the abuse had never taken place, "only the desire for it," to which the woman, at their next session, responded by informing him that she was stopping analysis. I hope Hartmann didn't tell her what he told a colleague, that the truth was "too much for her to bear," that to learn that "her most important memory was a fantasy" was "too great a narcissistic wound." Hartmann assumed that the woman created her incest fantasy out of childish conceit, to feel that Daddy specially loved her, which revealed how little he knew about the devastating effects of incest. As a good Freudian, though, he wasn't supposed to know; he'd been trained to follow the faith, not observe for himself.

That Hartmann's patient refused even to consider that her memories were fantasies was extraordinary. Virtually all patients try to believe what their analyst tells them because, surely, he knows more than they do. That was the misfortune of the poet and playwright, Anne Sexton (1928-1974). She began analysis because she'd had a mental breakdown and attempted suicide. During analysis, in a self-induced trance, she remembered that her father had had sex with her. She asked her analyst, Martin Orne, to let her take sodium pentothal, a drug that makes accessing the truth easier. Orne refused. He was convinced that her memories were false and that to be cured she had to face that, although her memories were emotionally true, she'd lied about the facts. Orne reasoned that since Anne sexualized everything, she'd sexualized her relationship with her father. Why she sexualized everything, Orne didn't ask. He must have thought, as a good Freudian should, that she'd been born that way.

Orne also didn't ask himself why Sexton kept writing about incest. For example, her play, *Tell Me Your Answer True*, is about revealing a family secret that turns out to be incest: a drunken father tells his daughter that he'll give her a back rub, but soon his hands are between her legs. As if repeating the incest with her father, Sexton slept with her second analyst, whom she called "doctor-daddy." She was also compelled to present herself to the public, not as a serious poet, but as a sexy woman, and in her first session with Orne, she told him that the only thing she could do well was "be a good prostitute and ... help men feel sexually powerful." Orne apparently didn't know that most prostitutes have been sexually abused; if he had he would have immediately suspected that Sexton had been. Prostitutes also think their bodies are evil: Sexton wanted to pour gasoline on hers and light it. She thought only death would expiate her guilt, made several attempts to kill herself, and finally succeeded. She might not have wanted to die if she'd been able to put the guilt where it belonged. Not being believed made her feel she was an actress who invented stories, that there was "no true part of me." Only the truth would have cleansed her of the sense of sin and guilt that her father (and mother and aunt who also molested her) should have felt. But Sexton was doomed by her analyst, who'd been blinded by the chief article of Freud's faith, that children's memories of incest were fantasies. (Diane Wood Middlebrook's *Anne Sexton: A Biography* (1991) went along with Orne's analysis.)

I hold Freud ultimately responsible for Anne Sexton's suicide and that of other patients who preferred death to being torn apart by their inner knowledge of the truth and their analysts' insistence that nothing had happened. I also hold Freud ultimately responsible for the misery of the hundreds of thousands of patients who were brainwashed to believe they'd made up lies about Mummy or Daddy. However, I may be wrong about that. Freud's denial of his abuse had given him a kind of peace, and he may have unconsciously tried to help his patients in the same way he'd helped himself. Since remembering abuse brings up harrowing emotions, most patients prefer, like Freud, the Valium of denial.

It's therefore generally and rightly agreed that psychoanalysis wouldn't have become popular if Freud hadn't repudiated the "seduction theory." The problem is that, as Freud knew in 1896 and Ferenczi in 1932, parents and other adults often molest children. But analysts, like most of the public, didn't want to know the facts and honored Freud for admitting he'd been wrong when he said that parents molest children, for it enabled Freud to make what Freudians claimed were his great discoveries: infantile sexuality, the perverse fantasy life of children, and the crowning glory of psychoanalysis, the Oedipus complex.

True Believers

Many twentieth-century dictators 'disappeared' those who opposed their regimes. Freud tried to disappear the abused child who endangered his regime by deep-sixing Sigi. Nevertheless, bits and pieces of Sigi's sexual abuse kept surfacing in Freud's case histories, as did evidence that his patients had been abused. But Freudians, being true believers, didn't notice the evidence. That Serge had been anally raped by his father was howling at them like wolves, but they didn't hear it. Freudians even managed to read his study of Leonardo and think that Freud was writing about Leonardo's real mother. They must have assumed that Freud's analytic genius could fill the almost total gap in historical knowledge about Leonardo's childhood. But how they managed to read Freud's nostalgic lament that it's hard to tear oneself from a childhood in which one has "enjoyed the highest erotic bliss" with a mother, and not suspect that Freud was speaking from unconscious personal experience, seems to me a sign of gross psychological retardation.

Freud's confession that his own father had orally sodomized his brother and sisters was also passed over lightly. Ernest Jones in a 1951 letter did wonder why Freud excluded himself, especially since he was then suffering from a severe psychoneurosis, but Jones didn't go into it. Nor did Freud's frantic search to pin down fathers as sexual abusers make Freudians suspect that Freud's father sexually abused him. Like Freud, paternal homosexual abuse may have been a horror they didn't want to talk about. Freudians seem to have felt the same relief Freud did when a dream enabled him to drop the "old man" and name a socially acceptable abuser, his "old nurse," as "his teacher in sexual matters." Freud said she'd scolded him for being sexually inept, but Paul Ferris (in his *Dr. Freud*, 1997) dismissed that evidence as probably amounting to "no more than soothing a bawling boy by playing with his penis."

Louis Breger, in his book on Freud, omitted the evidence of his nurse's sexual abuse, which allowed him to maintain that she was a wholly beneficent force in Freud's life. Breger argued that the loss of this nursemaid (who was fired for stealing) and the loss of his mother, whose many pregnancies were a form of abandonment, made early loss of love, "not seductions," Freud's core trauma. To prove his point, Breger also passed over Freud's account of the infant Leonardo's passionate sex life with his mother. Indeed, he doesn't mention the Leonardo study in his long book on Freud, nor, what's worse, Freud's boldest paper on the reality of sexual abuse: "The Aetiology of Hysteria." I can understand why Freudians wouldn't want to recognize that Freud had been sexually abused: it would destroy classical psychoanalysis. But Breger's aim was to show that Freud, because of his abandonment by his nurse and mother, became a flawed thinker, therapist and human being. Yet Breger, too, observed the quarantine and stayed away from the Black Death of sexual abuse.

Everychild

I've asked myself if I saw Freud as a sexually abused child because I was sexually abused. I worried that I'd been like the many people who recreated Jesus in their own image. In Germany in 1899, the anti-Semite, Houston S Chamberlain in *The Foundations of the Nineteenth-Century* argued that Jesus was a pure Aryan without a drop of Jewish blood in his veins; in 1991, the Buddhist, Stephen Mitchell, published a book proving that Jesus was essentially a Buddhist; *Corpus Christi*, a 1998 play, presented us with a gay Jesus, like its author, Terrance McNally. Freud often recreated his patients in his own image, and perhaps I too am guilty, although Freud's abuse was totally different from mine. I like to think that my knowledge of myself and the knowledge I acquired at incest survivor meetings enabled me to see the symptoms and effects of abuse that others don't want to see, and to accept what few of us do, that one of the awful facts in all periods of human history has been the prevalence of child sexual abuse. The 2002 statistics are that one-third of girls and one-quarter of boys in all countries are victims of incest. Since most abuse remains a family secret, the real number is far higher. Millions of children have run the gamut of abuse by a nurse, mother or father. Freud was not unusual; he was more like Everychild.

In the late 1980s and early 1990s, I and other incest survivors used to assure each other that we were getting better because we'd remembered the truth, that we wouldn't be getting better if we'd remembered lies. We clung to our conviction because at that time the culture still didn't want to acknowledge sexual abuse, and many therapists, not necessarily Freudians, were reluctant to accept that their patients had been molested.

Such therapists were like the Freudians who withdrew Ferenczi's paper from wide circulation because "the dissemination of such views constituted a danger to society." They *were* a danger to society. Ferenczi's belief that children were often sexually abused, like Freud's in 1896, endangered a society that wanted to pretend that parents were benevolent beings who transformed bad children into good citizens. Freudians reacted to Ferenczi the way the public reacted to the nineteenth-century women who accused their fathers of rape. Ferenczi was accused of being crazy and the women of "moral insanity," women who were sometimes sent to insane asylums, for everyone in their right mind knew that fathers didn't commit such vile acts. Therefore, those who spread such lies had to be isolated. Otherwise, people might discover that society's alleged mental health depended on maintaining certain lies about the family.

Denial does make us feel better, but the effects of abuse of any kind (not just sexual abuse) don't go away; we don't rest in peaceful ignorance. Though denial seems to keep us sane, our inability to face the truth makes a part of us crazy, like Freud.

VIII   Freud As An Ambulatory Psychotic

"Ambulatory psychotic" was a phrase Robert Fliess devised to try to understand the phenomenon of a man like his father, Freud's beloved Wilhelm, who seemed normal, was a respected physician, and yet was psychotic in his sexual life.   Robert thought that his father's sexual assaults and brutal beatings were signs of psychosis. They were. Many who walk among us, seemingly normal, respectable, even distinguished in their profession, are psychotics when they brutally beat or molest their children.   But many who don't beat or molest children are ambulatory psychotics.   Most of us in certain areas of our lives that have nothing to do with sex are psychotics, having been driven crazy in childhood.

Craziness by Merger

Children are driven crazy in many ways.   One of Ferenczi's most important insights was that when children are sexually abused, they escape from their fear by merging with their "uninhibited and therefore as good as crazy" molesters.   When he was a child, Freud was the victim of uninhibited molesters and it made him an ambulatory psychotic, "as good as crazy" in certain areas of his mind.

When Sigi was a helpless child and his body felt ripped apart as his father anally raped him, and his mind dissolved as his mother sucked on his penis, crazy with fear, unable to get away, he did what many children do: he stopped being a victim by literally going out of his mind into the feelings and thoughts of his powerful abusers.

Freud was certain that babies were born lustful because he'd felt the lust of his abusers and thought it was his own. Freud accused children of being sexual aggressors because Sigi had absorbed the sexual aggression of his molesters. He'd also absorbed their rationalization that children want sex, and their delusion that children make the first moves. Freud saw babies as sexy because Sigi saw them the way his abusers did. Freud's idea that babies fall narcissistically in love with their genitals wasn't his own. Narcissus was beautiful; penises are not. Freud compared penises to Narcissus because his penis had been the cynosure of his molesters' eyes, which made little Sigi decide it was the most lovable part of him, and the adult Freud overrate penises.

Adults who were molested in childhood are often so appalled by their sexual fantasies, they're certain they were born bad. They don't realize that their fantasies are repetitions and variations of what their molesters felt and thought when they were abusing them, thoughts and feelings that become imprinted on children's brain cells and which they think are their own. Freud said that infants had perverse sexual fantasies because when he was a child he was submerged in the perverse feelings and thoughts of his mother and father and nurse when they were molesting him.

Because sexual abuse violates children at the site of their life force, it has a powerful effect, which Freud blamed on his old reliable, heredity. But if fear hadn't shut down his mind to his own abuse, he might have observed, as Ferenczi did, the transmission of this effect by merger with the abuser, and not devised his theory that human infants are born already highly sexual, as if infantile sexuality were the necessary prelude to adult sex.

Some of Freud's ideas originated, not from merger, but from the effects of sexual abuse. If Sigi's orifices hadn't been used at will by his abusers, Freud wouldn't have said that babies were born polymorphous perverse. Freud felt he could compare prostitutes to children because they retain the "infantile disposition" to be polymorphous perverse, a comparison he wouldn't have made if he'd known that most prostitutes were sexually abused, that the johns they let use their orifices at will are stand-ins for daddy. Prostitution is a memorial to incest, just as babies who masturbate are memorializing incest.

Much of what Freud said about babies makes sense only when seen through Sigi's eyes. When I first read that "innocent caresses" of "affectionate fathers" sexually aroused their infants, I thought Freud was out of his mind. Not till much later did I understand that Freud had slipped out of his mind into the mind of Sigi, who'd been caressed as a prelude to sexual abuse, a childhood experience which made Freud believe that too much cuddling was harmful to children.

Freud was supremely confident that, without observing babies, he'd discovered the truth about their sexual nature because the 'truth' largely consisted of unconscious memories of his abuse. Many of Freud's alleged scientific theories had their origins in the perverse sexual feelings and ideas transmitted to Sigi when he merged with his abusers and from the experiences of sexual abuse stored in his mouth, anus and penis. Psychoanalysis thus sanctified as holy writ much of the crazy psychology of pedophiles and abused children.

Paranoia

When Serge, a son who'd been sodomized by his father, told Freud at his first session, "I'd like to use you from behind and shit on your head," I wondered if being put in the analytic position—lying on a sofa with a father figure behind him—had triggered his old fear that his father would come up from behind and bugger him. Serge had paranoia; in the 1920s he got so severe an attack he went back to Freud who, fortunately, sent him to another analyst who, despite her Freudian indoctrination but without Freud's personal history, saw the obvious, that Serge had been anally raped by his father. The 'paranoid' position in which Freud put

Serge when he started analysis made Serge so afraid that he merged with his powerful father and turned Freud into the victim he was going to use "from behind." Freud said he sat behind his patients so it would be easier for them to freely associate. That's a valid reason, and may be all there was to it. But a man who'd been buggered by his father might feel safe in his office only when no one could come up from behind him, when he was the father figure who could stick it to his patients.

And Freud did stick it to his patients when they refused to receive his theories as if God were talking. He was cruel to Dora because she dared to argue with him. He also falsely accused her of homosexuality, as he later would rebellious colleagues. He did by diagnosing them as paranoiacs, which Freud believed was caused by repressed homosexuality, a crazy theory that wasn't questioned by his followers. In Freudian circles to call someone paranoid was the equivalent of calling him a "homo." But, though Freud frankly admitted his own suppressed homosexuality and had Fliess-like relationships with Adler, Jung and others, he was exempt from ridicule. The King's madness isn't madness. The King, however, had diagnosed his own madness when he accused defiant colleagues of what he most feared in himself. Paranoiacs think someone's after them. Freud feared that the homosexual feelings his father had aroused, feelings he didn't act out but that pursued him like Furies, would suddenly come up from behind and drive him mad.

Sexual Obsession

Women who become promiscuous or prostitutes have a compulsion to return to the scene of the crime committed against them: their rape by Daddy. Freud's rape by his Daddy and seduction by his Mummy didn't make him promiscuous. He became sexually obsessed in another way. Freud reminded me of the mad Mr Dick in *David Copperfield*, who was writing a Memorial about his or some Lord's affairs (he wasn't sure which) and couldn't finish it because the severed head of King Charles the First "always strayed into it," and he felt he had to start over. Freud's King Charles's head was sex, sex, sex, which strayed into his work and which Freud, crazier than Mr Dick, didn't know shouldn't be there.

Freud had a severe case of sex on the brain. For him, children's delight in being "thrown up in the air" was a sexual delight, and when they ran around, arms out, pretending to fly, they weren't wishing they could soar through the air like birds. Children, he announced, were revealing their desire to soar to the sexual heights, "be capable of sexual performance." Freud delivered that insight in his study of Leonardo, whose interest in the flight of birds and the possibility of human flight was, he said, a sublimation of baby Leonardo's desire to "fly" when his mother passionately caressed him, that is, to fuck her.

When Freud said that adult dreams were sexual wish-fulfillments, he said what one would expect him to, but to say that the shell shock thousands of soldiers suffered from in the first World War had a sexual cause is shocking. Now called post-traumatic stress disorder, the soldiers had nightmares, flashbacks, fits of crying and trembling, paralysis, guilt for being alive, total breakdowns. Some physicians said the obvious, that their symptoms had been caused by their constant fear of death, the sight and stench of dead bodies, having to live in mud trenches infested with rats, and bombs perpetually exploding. Not so Freud, who fled from facing the hideous realities of war by hiding behind his obsession; he madly declared that shell shock didn't have an external cause but an internal, sexual cause (*Psychoanalysis and War Neuroses*, 1919).

"All seems infected that th'infected spy, As all looks yellow to the jaundiced eye," said Pope, and Freud's "eye" had been indelibly infected by sexual abuse.

Oedipal Follies

The Oedipus complex is not considered one of Freud's follies. Freudians still accept as a fact that Oedipus "represents every boy's sexual desire for his mother," to quote a reviewer in *The Times Literary Supplement* (8-9-2002). In the popular mind, though, the Oedipus complex has been desexed and means that little girls' hearts belong to Daddy and that when little boys grow up, they want to marry a girl just like Mom. Since few people read Freud, they don't know what he actually said: that children are born eager to commit incest with Mummy/Daddy and kill the parent of the opposite sex so Mummy/Daddy will be theirs alone; that when children's sexual overtures are rejected by their virtuous parents, they resort to masturbation while pretending Mummy/Daddy is having sex with them; and that these fantasies, when recollected at puberty, can make people neurotics, even hysterics.

That infants have fantasies about sex they never experienced is absurd, and that such impossible fantasies could eventually make them neurotic or crazy is more absurd. Equally irrational was Freud's belief that incest is an innate drive. The male infant is "biologically ... driven toward a prohibited union with his mother," said a twenty-first century reviewer in *The Times Literary Supplement* (8-11-2000), repeating Freud's delusion. Freud, though a great admirer of Darwin, didn't comprehend that incest couldn't be instinctive, for instead of advancing the evolution of Homo sapiens, it would ultimately have destroyed the species. But Freud's need to establish the sexual perversity of infants clouded his reason, which he wanted to stay cloudy. The Oedipus complex didn't result from Freud observing children, but from his inability to see that he'd been sexually abused in childhood.

Madness is often defined as an inability to see reality, and in the area of sexual abuse Freud couldn't see reality. Children do not desire to have sex with a parent, even unconsciously, unless the parent has made sexual advances. They may dream of snuggling with Mummy or Daddy; they don't dream of having sex. Even when a parent forces sex on a child, the results are not necessarily Freudian. A son who's having a liaison with Mummy does not invariably want to kill Daddy so he can have Mummy all to himself. Little Hans's "love of his mother" did not, as Freud said, make "him hate his father." He was very fond of his father even though Mummy was probably fooling around with his penis. Freud had to say that love of Mummy made boys hate Daddy because he'd hidden from himself why he hated his father. Boys sodomized by their Daddies want to kill them, and may think Daddy wants to cut off their penis because they want to cut off Daddy's offensive penis, a wish girls who are raped by Daddy may also have. Girls who were raped by Mummy—who were masturbated and had fingers, pencils and knives pushed into their vaginas—want to kill her, and so do boys whose Mummy seduced them, no matter how much they also 'love' her.

Freeing ourselves from the Freudian paradigm opens our eyes to the great variety of sexual abuse that occurs in families, and also to the morbid bond that can be created between parents and children though no sex is involved. Many parents commit emotional incest when they make a daughter or son their special darling. To insure that his work would not die after him, Freud took over his daughter Anna's life. A common common-law marriage is that between a possessive parent and a child, who soon feels he or she exists to satisfy Mummy's or Daddy's need to be loved or to live through a child. It's not just the hearts of many husbands that still belong to Mummy, so do the hearts of many wives. It's not just the hearts of many wives that still belong to Daddy, so do the hearts of many husbands.

Freud said Ferenczi was crazy because he imagined he lived in a world in which children were victims of cruel parents. Freud was the one who lived in Fantasyland when he imagined that innocent parents were the intended victims of oversexed children, a crazy belief Freud held so he could deny the sexual assaults of his childhood.

"The Body Electric"

Freud advocated a greater acceptance of sex as natural and healthy, but the baby he described in "Infantile Sexuality," the baby whose chief delights were varieties of masturbation, was incapable of healthy sex. His body had already been contaminated by abuse. "I Sing the Body Electric," Walt Whitman's celebration of the human body, makes clear how sexually sick Freud was.

"If anything is sacred the human body is sacred," said Whitman. The bodies of everyone—men, women, babies, the young, the old, the sick, the crippled—and every single part of every body is sacred. "I believe in the flesh and the appetites. Seeing, hearing, feeling, are miracles, and each part and tag of me is a miracle" (*Song of Myself*). In the presence of a newborn baby, Whitman, like some obstetricians, felt in the presence of a miracle, but for Freud every new birth was delivering a bundle of perverse sex into the world. After reading Freud on infantile sexuality, to read Whitman's celebrations of being alive in a body is to escape from a strip joint into the fresh air.

Whitman wanted to help humans escape from the ancient, religious division between the disgusting, lustful, decaying flesh and the ethereal, pure, eternal soul. He wanted to "discorrupt" bodies. He imagined himself sitting with an arm around men, women, children, simply being close to "the armies of those I love." He delighted in seeing bodies rowing, wrestling, swimming naked, running, dancing, the long lists of individual bodies Whitman gloried in enumerating, and always without prurience. Freud, in contrast, could have been a Christian preaching about the devil in the flesh. Whitman declared that old belief nonsense because body and soul were inseparable. The first edition of *Leaves of Grass* was published in 1855, the year before Freud was born, but it was light-years ahead of Freud in its appreciation and love of the marvelous human body.

Freud couldn't sing the body electric; his infantile delight in his body had been destroyed when Sigi was used as if he were a doll specially created for adults' pleasure. The plight of Freud as a child made me wonder if the phrase, "the devil in the flesh," would have come into existence if children's bodies hadn't been routinely abused, and not just sexually. "No one ever hated his own flesh," Augustine stupidly said (*Of Continence*, circa 425), stupidly, because hatred of one's body has been virtually universal in a world in which babies' were smacked on the butt at birth, tied in swaddling bands to stew in their pee and shit, given frequent enemas that proved they were shit on the inside too, routinely beaten and sexually used, varieties of physical abuse that could easily make babies' feel that devils possessed their flesh.

Unable to acknowledge the sexual abuse of his childhood, Freud projected a perverse sexuality onto infants and ultimately saw all intellectual and creative acts as the sublimation of the sex drive. Dante declared that love was the energy that "moves the sun and the other stars," but Freud, having been sexually used by his mother, father and nurse, was sure that the prime mover of the universe was sex.

Sex Is Love

The most significant difference between Freud and Ferenczi was that Ferenczi knew the difference between sex and love. Bits and pieces of Sigi's sexual abuse pop up in Freud's work because we all have a strong inner force that wants us to heal and knows that truth is the healer, the way back to the love that's part of our original nature. When Freud heard Ferenczi's 1932 paper, Sigi knew that what he said had once been true of him, that he'd wanted love and tenderness and had felt hatred and disgust when the sex began, and was surprised and terrified by the "hatred" he felt coming from his abusers.

The shock of that hatred and children's reactive hate are too great for them to bear. Their need to love and be loved is so powerful they quickly decide, even when the sexual abuse is severe, that "Mummy does love me, and I love Mummy, too," a conversion of sex into love that's confirmed when children merge with molesters who, when they were molested as children, also converted sex into love. Thus is passed down from generation to generation an emotional deformity as real as genital mutilation.

Freud's acquisition of that emotional deformity skewed his thinking. He told Dora that the lecher, Herr K, loved her because in childhood he'd decided that when an adult had sex with you, it was love. Freud said that "the first trace of [Hans's] homosexuality" was hugging his five-year-old cousin because, when Freud was a child, his father's affection turned into sex. Freud argued that Dr Schreber's homosexuality was love of his father "intensified to an erotic pitch" because as a child Freud had transmuted his father's sodomy into love. The child Schreber and his father had not been a romantic couple whose love became sexual. Love of a father becomes erotic only after Daddy sexually abuses a child, abuse the child interprets as love in order to feel loved, to escape from the most devastating feeling children can have, that they're not loved.

If Freud hadn't felt the hate exuding from his mother, father and nurse as they used his body to sexually gratify themselves, he wouldn't have said that hate is mankind's primary emotion, or defined love as a sublimation of our predatory, sexual drive, beliefs that so warped his values he thought children who wanted sex were good, "perfect paragons of all the vices" (as he happily described Hans), and that children who wanted love were bad. "A child in its greed for love," he remarked in the case history of Dora, sounding like a parent who didn't want to be pestered by children clamoring for affection. Freud hadn't always been like that. He told Ferenczi that in his "seduction theory" days, he would sometimes sit on the floor for hours with a distraught patient.

Ferenczi tried to convince Freud "how lovingly one must treat one's patients in order to help them," advice Freud scorned. He told Ernest Jones that Ferenczi had regressed to his childhood, a time when he imagined "his mother had not loved him ... passionately or exclusively enough." But it was his own mother whom Freud thought hadn't loved him passionately and exclusively enough, for all too soon, she had another baby and kept on having them. To keep unconscious his frustrated longing for her exclusive love, and unable to do for others what had been taken away from him, Freud couldn't respond to the silent pleas for love rising like heat waves from the child in his patients.

The deepest source of Freud's craziness was Sigi's need to interpret sex as love, and, because of the "erotic bliss" he'd once enjoyed with Mummy, he never wanted to stop confusing sex with love.

Passing on Hate

After Freud decided that children were not molested, he despised his patients. He shamelessly confessed to Ferenczi that he thought of them as "rabble." Freud despised his patients because the love he got from his mother wasn't love. Freud's self-confidence is attributed to his mother's 'love,' but a child who's forced to have sex is used, not loved. Freud was arrogant, not self-confident. Ferenczi said that the love sexually abused children get is "saturated with hatred." I disagree. To use a child for sex is pure hatred, the hatred Freud couldn't help passing on to his patients by despising them.

When compassion was called for, Freud, like a frightened snail, withdrew into callousness. Reading the memoirs of Dr Schreber (the man whose homosexual involvement with his father drove him mad), Freud came across the phrase, "soul murder," which, strangely, made him laugh. Schreber had used "soul murder" because of Anselm von Feuerbach's popular book about Kaspar Hauser, a child who'd been kept isolated in a dark cellar and whose soul, according to Feuerbach, had thus been murdered. "Soul murder" resonated with Schreber because he felt he was the victim of a "plot whereby my soul was to be murdered and my body used like a strumpet" by his physician. Freud knew his physician was a stand-in for Schreber's father, but his denial of his own abuse prevented him from registering that Schreber's father had long ago possessed his son's body and thus murdered his soul. Instead of feeling for Schreber, Freud singled out "soul murder" and other "Schreberisms" to laugh at, in-jokes he shared with his colleagues who, being Freud's yes-men, also laughed. Freud didn't know he laughed at "soul murder" to cover up that his soul had been partly murdered when he was a child, and in a way similar to Schreber.

Sigi learned early that he existed to satisfy his abusers' sexual needs. When Freud's colleagues defected, he treated them as if they'd existed to satisfy his need to have his sexual theories confirmed. Abusers molest children when the pain of their own abuse threatens to surface. Freud, his defense threatened when colleagues disagreed with him, could have no mercy. Max Graf (Hans's father) was at the meetings in which Freud ousted Alfred Adler and was so appalled by Freud's ruthlessness he broke with him.

Freud provided us with an example of his cruelty in the case history of Dora, the young woman who'd often disagreed with Freud and who, on December 31, 1900, abruptly left analysis. She returned about two years later, giving Freud an opportunity for revenge he didn't resist. Dora returned because she'd developed a painful neuralgia on the right side of her face. Freud asked her how long she'd had it and, as soon as she said "a fortnight," Freud "could not help smiling." He knew the cause. Exactly a fortnight before, the newspaper had announced his appointment to a Professorship, an item Dora confirmed she'd read, whereupon, said Freud, she'd inflicted the neuralgia on herself as a punishment. Why? Because when she'd seen him before, she'd transferred "her feelings of revenge" from her would-be seducer Herr K "onto me." Freud apparently thought that abruptly leaving analysis was the equivalent of Dora having on one occasion slapped Herr K on the face and walked away. Therefore, when Dora learned that the man she'd scorned by leaving analysis had been raised to the rank of a Professor, she felt sorry for treating him badly and punished herself with a facial neuralgia.

But it was Freud who punished Dora: when he told her that reading about his professorship had caused her painful neuralgia, he psychologically slapped her in the face. Dora's facial neuralgia could have been another symptom of having to fellate her father, but whatever the cause, it wasn't Freud's elevation in status. But having got his revenge, Freud professed not to "know what kind of help she wanted from me." He called Dora's neuralgia "alleged" and summarily dismissed her, pompously saying he forgave her for having deprived him of "the satisfaction" of curing her hysteria. He never could have cured her hysteria, and he never forgave her. He bad-mouthed her as a homosexual, a lie that continues to be repeated.

Freud's Me-Me-meanness, his arrogance and lust for revenge may have been made worse by something Dora told him. Her father had continued to deny that he and Frau K had had an affair and that Herr K had tried to have sex with her. Determined to expose the truth, Dora visited them when one of their children died and used the occasion to get Frau K to admit she *had* had an affair with her father, and to get Herr K to admit he *had* made sexual advances, confessions she triumphantly announced to her lying father. When Dora told Freud, though he'd always known Herr and Frau K and her father had lied, he accused Dora of exacting revenge, that is, of doing what he'd just done to her.

Freud never shared Dora's moral outrage at her father's deceit and dishonesty, and he now called Dora's quest for the truth revenge when he should have praised her courage; few young women (or men) would

have been capable of confronting the K's. Freud may have been especially cruel to Dora because she reminded him of the time when he'd had
greater courage than she had, when he'd boldly confronted his colleagues
with proof that parents *did* sexually abuse children.

Postmortem

Freud's passionate desire to make the truth known had already died
when he analyzed Dora. It died first when he was a child and decided
that sexual abuse was love. He tried to wake up to the truth when he
stopped being a neurologist and developed his theory that hysteria was
caused by sexual abuse. He hadn't consciously known why he'd got
interested in the subject, and when self-analysis began to stir up memories of his father's abuse, Freud died to the truth again. Worse, he created
an organization whose purpose was to prove to patients and the world
that, except for a few exceptional cases, sexual abuse was a fantasy created by the sexually obsessed minds children are born with.

And yet, a part of Freud wanted to be released from the lie about his
childhood, which needed constant will power to keep repressed. "How
sweet it must be to die," he'd sighed in 1912 after fainting when Jung
was telling a story about a son's hatred of his father. However, when
Freud was actually dying, the experience wasn't sweet. The cigar he'd
constantly had in his mouth had turned the agony of oral sodomy into
a pleasure, but it caused a cancer that was eating up his jaw. The pain
became so intense that on September 21, 1939, he asked his doctor, Max
Schur, to end his torture, as he'd promised he would. Shur injected him
with a strong dose of morphine, which he repeated during the day and a
half before Freud died.

That Freud started his journey into oblivion on September 21st
wasn't, for me, a meaningless coincidence. For that was the date when, in
emotional agony because memories of his father's rapes were threatening
to become conscious, Freud wrote the letter in which he said that "widespread perversions against children are not very probable," a first giant
step in his denial of child sexual abuse. I hope, on the forty-second anniversary of denying the truth, that Freud, having blissed out on a stronger,
sweeter pain killer than cigars, let go of his defenses and finally understood the personal reasons why he'd said that all sons wanted to marry
Mummy and kill Daddy, and thus had compassion for the suffering child
he'd abandoned. I hope that freedom from the lie that had disfigured his
work and character enabled him to feel remorse. He needed to. Freud
died on the Jewish Day of Atonement, and he had much to atone for.

I make that charge although Freud is justly honored for helping
make sex a more respectable area of psychological inquiry, and a less
shameful part of our lives. Freud also greatly increased our awareness of
the unconscious, where we often consign traumatic events. Repression

is a Freudian insight, as were other defense mechanisms, like denial, displacement and projection. Taboo feelings that unconsciously escape are now called Freudian slips. Free association and studying dreams can also access the unconscious, which Freud rightly thought needed to become conscious since it was the path to psychological freedom.

Freud, however, is best known for dividing the mind into the ego, the super-ego, and the id, and for discovering the Oedipus complex, castration anxiety, penis envy and infantile sexuality. I regard his division of the mind as not proved and grossly oversimplified, and the Oedipus complex and its adjuncts as a defense Freud constructed so as not to face that he was sexually abused, a defense that, based as it was on a lie, necessitated lengthy far-fetched reasoning.

Lies sometimes have serious consequences. Freud's lie that parents rarely molest children made it easier for almost a century for families to continue to remain secret dens of incest. And yet, Freud, like the rest of us, couldn't help constructing the lie that made his life bearable, nor could he, like the rest of us, help believing that his lie was the truth. In 1932 he boasted to Einstein: "I always tell the truth as much as possible. It has become my métier." Previously, he'd told the American psychologist, James Jackson Putnam, that he was "a very moral human being [who has] never done anything shameful or malicious." That was in 1915 when he'd already been egregiously cruel to Dora and ruthlessly ousted Adler, Stekel and Jung. The truth is that no one can live long without doing things that are shameful and malicious. Nor can anyone live long without lying. But the psychological necessity of lying made Freud incapable of knowing he was lying.

Freud thought he knew himself, thought he'd probed his unconscious, self-analyzed away his childhood difficulties and gone on to lead a successful life. He had a wife and children, many devoted followers and, proof positive, he'd become internationally famous. But he was incapable of knowing himself because he hadn't opened his heart to the child within him who'd been sexually abused. He therefore thought that his definition of love as a sublimation of the sex drive was a general truth, not the transformation of sex into love forced on him in his loveless childhood. Freud's work and his life can't be fully understood unless his sexual abuse is factored in.

The Mexican sorcerers (as I discussed in Chapter 26) thought that "the topic of topics," the most important one in the world, was solving the problem of the fall of man, of why we lose the great awareness we're born with and become "trite, conventional, imbecilic," "obedient," and yet "egomaniacal." They were right; it is "the topic of topics," but their theory that the fall of man was caused by predators who flew up from an alien world and ate babies' coats of awareness was as far-fetched as the

Christian myth that Satan flew up from hell and got Eve and Adam to eat a God-forbidden apple, an act that forever polluted their offspring.

Freud's life demonstrates what caused the fall of a particular man. It shows how sexual abuse in his childhood drove him out of his right mind into the minds of his abusers, made him so sexually obsessed he saw sex where it wasn't, thought sex was love, and madly accused babies, not parents, of being sexual aggressors.

Sexual abuse chanced to be the cause of Freud's fall. But the fall of man occurs whenever the love we're born with is contaminated by beatings, blows, too much control, rejection, possessiveness ... whatever. Babies accept the treatment they get as love because they have to feel loved. Besides, ersatz love makes them normal, makes them like everyone else, the other ambulatory psychotics who live in the crazy, destructive world that warped love creates.

Chapter 28   The Family Legacy

"They fuck you up"

When Freud said that babies, not parents, were sexual aggressors, he was continuing the old tradition of blaming newborns for bringing evil into the world. Those limbs of Satan!, those original sinners! were replaced by "positive paragons of all the [sexual] vices" (as Freud described five-year-old Hans). The usual phrase is a "paragon of virtue," but "sexiness," from which the public had previously exempted babies, became an infantile virtue for Freud. It did for a personal reason: in a Shangri-la in his unconscious, baby Freud was still basking in "the highest erotic bliss" with Mummy.

The Oedipus complex belied the deepest personal truth of Freud's infancy. He hadn't, as he said, been born with an innate sexual drive that made him, like all male children, long to have sex with his mother; his mother had used him for sex (as had his father). In his 1896 paper, "The Aetiology of Hysteria," Freud told the truth when he'd said, to quote the first line of a Philip Larkin poem, "They fuck you up, your mum and dad," except that Freud had said mum and dad literally fucked you (however they could), whereas Larkin meant that they messed up the job of parenting.

Larkin's poem (published in 1974) hit the nail directly into the heads of the household, putting the blame for the fall of man where it belonged — on the family. That's why I thought the title, "This Be The Verse," was tame, meaningless. "Family Legacy" seemed better since the poem says that, though mum and dad may not mean to, they fuck up their children because they were fucked up themselves, that the family is the ancient site where "man hands on misery to man," so it's wise to leave home "as early as you can" and not "have any kids yourself."

But "This Be The Verse" may have been a better title than I thought if Larkin meant that "This" was the verse of all verses because its truth was a trumpet blast proclaiming a new era. That a distinguished poet, one asked to be Poet Laureate of England, used "fuck," *the* obscene word in English, to dishonor parents, was a milestone in human history. In religious times, Larkin would have been excommunicated and, if not burned at the stake, put under house arrest like Galileo, who merely wanted the world to understand that the Earth was not the center of the universe. Larkin, far more radically, wanted the world to understand that the center of the universe in which children grow up is not a life-giving sun, but a mum and dad who fuck them up, a fact more important to face because mums and dads have created so much hate in children that the adults they become are on the verge of destroying the planet. Freud got it backward when he said that children, without parents to suppress their aggressive, lustful, incestuous drives, would fuck up the world. Children fuck up the world because they were fucked up at home.

To say straight out, "They fuck you up, your mum and dad," was a three-thousand year overdue revolution. It was a jackhammer drilling "Honor thy father and thy mother" out of the stone tablets that allegedly contained the Ten Commandments, a 'thou shalt' that should have been reduced to rubble long ago. Parents who dishonor children should not be honored. We continue to honor them because, even in the twenty-first century, not to honor them, is taboo. Social workers don't honor the bad parents they deal with, but they assume they're exceptions to the rule of good parents.

The very way we use language protects parents. For example, when I was writing Chapter 15, a summary of the most common ways children have been abused … !! Exclamation marks, because here I am, doing it again. I said that children *were* abused, not that parents abuse children. By using the passive voice, I vanished the parents. I was like an artist who drew an infant's face, its cheeks ballooned out of shape by something jammed into its mouth, which you had to figure out was a penis because the man fucking the baby's mouth wasn't in the picture. I too, in Chapter 15, often left parents out of the picture. When discussing the custom of killing babies, I said that in a certain part of India they were drowned in milk, omitting the mother who pushed the baby's head into a bucket of milk and kept it there until the baby stopped thrashing. I said that little girls were raped, which omitted the men who forced their penises into tiny, bleeding vaginas. The subject of one of Freud's cases, a Russian named Serge, is known as the Wolf Man, but not his father, the big bad wolf who sodomized him.

The culture demands that parents be protected. I used to tell people in some detail how my mother physically tortured me. I've learned to say, if I say anything, the passive, "I was abused by my mother," thus avoiding the response I used to get most of the time when I spelled out the truth: an uncomfortable silence, followed by a change of subject, or the damning, "What a terrible thing to say about your own mother!" The fingers of one hand would be enough to count the times someone said, "How terrible for *you*!" We live in an "Honor your mother and father" society. To speak harshly of mum and dad, no matter how much they deserve it, is considered in very bad taste.

I Made It All Up!

When Freud was helping patients whose parents had sexually abused them, he was surprised that after they'd dredged up the memories and relived their feelings, they would "emphatically" insist that they didn't believe what they'd remembered. They refused to although Freud assured them *he* believed them. That was one reason he repudiated his "seduction" theory. For no matter how hard he tried, the "complete successes on which [he'd] counted" were absent; even patients who'd "been most gripped" by their analysis ran away.

Freud's patients were reacting to breaking the taboo against dishonoring mum and dad. And when memories of his own sexual abuse began to surface, he too honored the taboo by declaring that little children, not their parents, were the ones who wanted sex.

To believe that children want sex before hormones make them capable of reproduction doesn't make common sense. So Freud claimed that the period of infantile sexuality ends with a long 'latency period' that precedes puberty. The child in Freud, like the child in his patients, couldn't bear to believe that "My Mummy and Daddy did bad things down there" — they just imagined they did. Children blame themselves so they can receive the benefits of what in Chapter 23 I called the "balm of guilt."

To sum up the personal experience that taught me about that strange phenomenon: one night I was waked from a doze by my husband chatting away on the answering machine about yet another exotic place he'd seen on the travels from which he'd rejected me. A shooting pain gripped my chest, so intense I was sure I was having a heart attack. I wasn't. I'd been catapulted back in time to the heartbreak of infancy when my mother rejected me by isolating me from the rest of the family. I'd then dealt with the heartbreak by deciding my mother was right to reject me, and as soon as I decided that my husband was right to reject me, my 'heart attack' vanished. No shot of morphine could have taken away my pain faster than taking on blame. A magic poultice had calmed my anguished breast, the blessed balm of guilt. Children learn that form of self-soothing early.

When Freud denied that parents molested children, he said he was "proud" he'd been capable of self-criticism and had "more the feeling of a victory than a defeat (which is surely not right)." But pride in our ability to see our faults is a perk of the balm of guilt, and the sense of victory comes from our relief at not having to face the grim facts.

Freud wanted to give his patients the same relief, so when they accused parents of sexual abuse, the job of the analyst was to make them admit that they'd falsely accused their honorable parents. That was easier to do in Freud's time, when most adults agreed that children were natural liars, especially when they claimed to be sexually molested. In 1863, when Freud was seven, Johann Ludwig Casper, on the very first page of *Clinical Stories from Forensic Medicine* said that when children accused adults of rape, they were telling "outright lies." Freud differed from Casper by giving such lies the polite name of "fantasies," for children could hardly be responsible for what arose from their innate sexiness.

The Oedipus complex was accepted not because babies are born sexy but because it expressed the psychology of children, whose sense of well-being depends on believing that they, not their parents, are the bad ones. Patients were eager to believe they were liars because it preserved their domestic tranquility and gave them peace of mind. If you think you made it all up, you can "pack up your troubles in your old kit-bag and smile, smile, smile" and enter the mythic land of Happy Childhood.

Lama Yeshe, a mid-twentieth century Tibetan Buddhist, often said that "true peace of mind can only come about through staring reality fully in the face," a process that's not as simple as it seems. I was sure I'd stared my abuse fully in the face, but I didn't get peace of mind. I then wondered if my brain, having been hard-wired by abuse at an early age, could ever be unwired. When Prozac and other emotional pain-killers became available, some of my friends took them, and most were able to function much more effectively. From time to time, though, they'd go through bouts of depression as bad as they once were, and often the old horrors would haunt their dreams. Was there no end to it? Why couldn't we put our abuse behind us and do what we were often told to do — go on with our lives? I often puzzled about it. I pictured myself sitting facing a wall, the way some Buddhists meditate, except that the wall was within me, a wall that was hiding I knew not what and that I couldn't break through. But as I remembered my abuse, my life did become better than it had been, in important ways much better, but I didn't find the "peace of mind" that Lama Yeshe said would come from "staring reality fully in the face." I then thought I had more horrors to remember. I did, but remembering them didn't bring me peace of mind.

I finally figured out why. Only my intellect believed what I'd remembered; the child who'd endured the abuse didn't. Somewhere in my psyche, she was pretending that nothing had happened, or had happened to another child in an alien land far away, not to her. "I don't believe it. I made it all up," the typical reaction to first memories of abuse, was the mantra she endlessly repeated. She feared that believing would destroy her. She didn't know, nor did I, that child-me repeated "I made it all up" to cover up something far more devastating than sexual abuse.

The Unmentionable of Unmentionables

"Unmentionables" was the name given to the tight breeches men wore in the late eighteenth and early nineteenth centuries. Made of a jersey-like fabric that clung to the body, outlining what used to be concealed in public. Hence the name "unmentionables." The sexual abuse of children used to be an unmentionable, hidden behind the closed doors of home, where it was taken for granted or covered up. In the twenty-first century, it has (though not in polite society) become mentionable.

What remains unmentionable is to suggest that the love parents feel for their children is tainted.

Parents, of course, say they love their children, and a part of them does, but it's not the unconditional acceptance that mothers nowadays are alleged to express as naturally as breast milk. A woman, whose parents cared for her more than most do, didn't feel loved until she was three years old and taken to see her dying godfather, who'd never met her. When he did, he smiled and his eyes filled with "great love and appreciation" as he said, "I've been waiting for you," and for the first time in her life, she felt "a deep sense of being welcome, of mattering to someone" (Rachel Naomi Remen, MD *Kitchen Table Wisdom*, 1996).

Most of us never feel that love, but we're not aware of our loss. Freud, to repress his own abuse, interpreted sex as love because his child-self couldn't bear to admit that he hadn't been loved. Few of us can admit, even to ourselves, that our parents didn't love us, especially "my Mummy," and woe to anyone who even hints otherwise, as I've learned to my chagrin.

At lunch in the garden of a restaurant, a young friend told me that during a massage to release a severe pain in her back, she began to cry, which surprised her. An athlete, her motto was, "No pain, no gain." But, even after the pain in her back was released, the crying continued, and for days. "Do you know why?" I asked. She shrugged. "Does that mean, you don't know?" She shrugged again, and I told her she should find out. "No!" she burst out so loudly that people near us looked at our table. Her "No!" could only mean she was dangerously close to facing her severe rejection by her mother. But the chances were high she never would. Much better to have a back pain than the worst emotional pain a child can feel.

She was like the aging hippie (almost sixty) who complained to me that, although he was on an anti-depressant, the feeling that he didn't want to be in the world dragged him down. He'd told me years before that when he was a child, his mother had treated him like her "little husband," so I suggested that his depression went back to that. No sooner were the words out of my mouth than venom shot from his eyes. "Don't you dare say that about my mother!" he yelled. I shut up.

My friend was almost as scary as Tony in the TV series *The Sopranos* when Tony, the head of a gang, upset because he'd learned that his beloved mother had ordered his uncle to have him killed, tells his therapist. She, thinking that at long last he was ready to face the truth, said that his mother hadn't loved him. She was quoting a definition of border-line personality from a diagnostic manual when Tony jumped up from his chair, put his distorted face into her frightened one and screamed, "You filthy bitch. It's my mother you're talking about. We're through, you and I. It's lucky I don't break your face into 50,000 pieces." He flung out of the room, and she rushed to the door and locked it.

Tony's therapist was right to lock the door. Hell hath no fury like the child in us who doesn't want to hear anything bad about Mummy. Tony was like Chris, a thirteen-year-old in a *Law & Order* episode whose friend called his mother a whore. Chris beat him up with such ferocity he died. But Chris knew his mother was a whore, and worse; to get money for drugs, she'd handed him around to be sexually used. Chris killed because someone said out loud what he most didn't want to hear, that Mama hadn't loved him. Tony and Chris went ballistic when someone cast aspersions on their mummy. They were more honest than Freud who, to let the world know how much his mummy had loved him had to let his unconscious project his great romance onto Leonardo da Vinci.

"Mama, why didn't you love me?" asked Ingemar, the child in a 1985 Swedish film when he finally faced that his dead mother hadn't loved him. At the beginning we see Ingemar at the beach doing somersaults in front of his mother, wanting to entertain her, to please her, to make her like him, a scene often repeated in the film, which is called, *My Life As A Dog* because sometimes Ingemar got on his hands and knees and barked like a dog, so willing was he to be his mother's dog, if only she'd love him.

Newborn animals naturally trust that their mother will love them, in the sense that she'll feed and protect them. Nowadays, children generally get at least a bare minimum of that kind of love. They rarely get what human babies need as much, what Rachel Remen didn't get until she was three, the feeling that she was welcome, that she mattered, that she was worthy of being loved. In his *Divine Comedy*, Dante said that the worst circle of hell was being denied God's loving presence because the worst hell for children is being judged unworthy of love.

Children go on with their lives by clinging to the belief that Mummy or Daddy loves them, which each generation is able to do by finding scapegoats, by forming what I call love-hate knots, and by becoming self-haters.

Chapter 29   **I Need Somebody To Hate**

"I Need Somebody To Love," a once popular song, expressed our yearning to love and be loved. We're born with that need, but it's warped in childhood when we get what passes for love in the average family. Though we go on loving mom and dad, an anger grows in us that needs to find somebody to hate.

The Necessity of Scapegoats

The ancient Hindus catered to this effect of human nurture when it divided people into four castes, plus the Untouchables—the rest of the population whom the castes segregated, despised, overworked, beat and killed without the law interfering. Their reason for mistreating them—that they'd committed great sins in a past life—was a religious rationalization. That social system lasted thousands of years and has been difficult to eliminate because it supplied the castes not only with cheap labor but with a mass of readily available scapegoats.

The word scapegoat comes from the Old Testament, where it had a somewhat different meaning. As part of a ritual for what became the Day of Atonement, God told Aaron, the first high priest of the Israelites, to put his hands on the head of a live goat "and confess over it all the iniquities of the Israelites and all their acts of rebellion." The goat was then led to a "barren waste" in the wilderness and left to die, thus expiating the sins of the Israelites (Leviticus 16: 20-22).

Scapegoating in the Old Testament is like Christianity's purifying rituals of confession and baptism, except that a man not a goat, had to die for human sins. But, and in this way scapegoating in the Old and New Testament is worse than the scapegoating that results from the way we bring up children: innocent animals or people don't always have to die for others' misdeeds; usually they only have to suffer.

Scapegoating begins when we're young. A two-year-old, visiting with his mother, toddled over to me, someone he hardly knew, and up and bit me on the arm, not the mother who'd been telling me she was finally weaning him. He was like Lily, who, when her mother started yelling at her, whomped smaller kids at nursery school. Neither child attacked the Mom who'd made them angry.

Children find it unbearable to hate those they love. To keep sane they go on loving mom and take out their hate on someone else. For how can we hate the person we first loved, and on whom we depend for protection and food? Just as many a dog has borne a kick that belonged to a boss, scapegoats are substitutes for the person we hate.

Dictators provide their subjects with scapegoats. God, who regularly punished the Israelites, encouraged them to hate and kill Baal worshipers. After Ayatollah Khomeini took over Iran in 1979, he executed thousands and imposed strict Islamic law. To deflect hate away from him, his motto became "Death to America." His frenzied followers seized the American embassy and children were taught to chant "Death to America" in school. In 2002 Palestinian kindergartners had to learn the litany: "Who are the Jews? The enemy. What should we do to them? Kill them!"

I'm sure they enjoyed it. What a relief to feel free to hate! In December 1960, *Time* magazine used the phrase, "an ecstasy of hatred" to describe the New Orleans women who "cursed, kicked and clawed" the few black students who tried to integrate white schools. One reason the Germans loved Hitler was that he let them openly hate an ancient scapegoat, the Jews. Big Brother in Orwell's *1984* had mass hate-fests against an imaginary "Goldstein" to achieve the same release of hate. At the time of Jesus, Jews looked down on Jews who were Samaritans, and some sects of Jews still passionately hate other sects. But, as Tom Lehrer said in his song, "Toleration," "everyone hates the Jews." In America, though, Blacks have been the chief Untouchables.

Freud got it wrong in *Totem and Taboo* when he imagined sons in a primitive tribe beating to death their dictatorial father. More likely, they would have found a scapegoat. Wade Davis, when exploring the Amazon rain forest, discovered a tribe in which fathers, after they'd killed the enemy in battle, came home and beat up their sons so that they too would become powerful warriors (*One River*, 1996). The fathers were carrying on a tribal tradition guaranteed to make sons go on the war path. Without the phenomenon of scapegoating, we would have had fewer wars.

Wild Injustice

Francis Bacon said that revenge is a kind of wild justice; scapegoating is a kind of wild injustice.

Our first God is often the first one who scapegoats us. I knew a mother who treated her older daughter like a queen and threw verbal stones at the younger one, the family scapeghost. I say scapeghost because her unusual beauty was a ghost from Mom's past—her own younger sister had been beautiful and she hadn't been.

Mothers sometimes select one child to become the deadgoat. A four-year old, who was found starved to death in 1996, had been kept in a back room and wasn't fed regularly for a year. So said her mother, who fed the other children but admitted that she hadn't wanted and didn't love Nadine. This mother was extraordinary, for usually mothers who use children to discharge their hate swear they love them. Nadine's mother may have blurted out the truth because she was on drugs (*San Francisco Chronicle* September 2, 1996).

Chapter 30 *Amo Et Odi*

The Roman poet, Catullus, long ago confessed, "Odi et amo," I hate and I love. He got it the wrong way around. First we love, then we hate. Catullus wouldn't have hated his mistress if he hadn't first loved her, and then she was unfaithful. Catullus said he was tortured by his conflicting emotions. So are children, who start out loving the first woman in their lives, then she makes them afraid, fear that turns into a lasting hate, for, unlike Catullus, they can't leave their mistress. They can't even show their hate. Instead, they love Mummy and put their hate, like the ancient Israelites, on a scapegoat.

Scapegoating wouldn't exist if children didn't love Mummy and want to go on loving her 'purely'. Norman Mailer almost stabbed his wife to death because he couldn't emotionally separate from the domineering mother who'd idolized him and whom he idolized, but from whom he wanted to be free. (Adele Mailer, *The Last Party: Scenes from My Life with Norman Mailer*, 1997).

The One We Love Most of All

A thirteen-year-old, who'd been flogged by his psychotic mother, set fire to a wastebasket, which he quickly put out. Nevertheless, his mother called the police and had him taken to court. He was glad, assuming the judge would separate him from his crazy Mom. But the judge roared, "Don't you love your mother?" (Dorothy Lewis, *Guilty by Reason of Insanity*, 1998). The trouble with that truism is it's true. Underneath the boy's hatred of his mother was the baby who'd once loved her, love that lives on despite justified hate. "You always hurt the one you love," sang a 1944 ballad, whose last line was: "So if I broke your heart last night, It's because I love you most of all." But the one we love "most of all" is the Mom who also hurts us. She creates a tie that binds no matter how monstrous she is.

Marcia Cameron, in *Broken Child* (1995), listed her mother's tortures, which started when she was three: she sewed up her labia with black thread; shoved a wooden spoon and knives into her vagina; hit her head against walls; poked her with an ice pick, threatening her eyes; pretended she was going to cut off her fingers and broke some with a nutcracker, gave her huge enemas to wash the wickedness out of her; put out cigarettes on her thighs; hung her up by her braids; locked her for hours in a foul-smelling hidden closet; broke her nose, and on and on. And yet, said Marcia, "In spite of all the abuse, I still loved her. I wanted desperately to see her eyes glow with love for me."

To keep her dream of love alive Marcia learned to trance out during the torture, but when she was eleven, she began to remember and got so angry she stood over her sleeping mother with the knife she'd cut her with. But she tiptoed away, and only fantasized stabbing her. The other times that she got into a fury, she wasn't there. 'Emily' slammed her mother against a wall, jammed a shotgun into her stomach while her mother begged for mercy. Like some severely-abused people, Marcia developed an angry alternate personality. Acquiring an 'alter' was more efficient than scapegoating; Marcia could act out her hate, yet be a good girl.

For a long time Emily kept Marcia dissociated from her rage. But slowly she did remember the atrocities and wondered how she could have forgotten, one especially. When she was nine, her mother tied her up, duct-taped her head to the floor, and hammered out her three front teeth. She asked herself, "How could I for thirty years take my false teeth out to brush them and never think about how I lost them!" She said it wasn't that she forgot; "I just couldn't acknowledge it in my conscious mind." But that's what forgetting is about. The unconscious mind comes into existence partly to 'forget' unbearable events. When the adult Marcia, wanting to die, drove over an embankment, her doctor was amazed to see in her X-rays "many old calcified fractures" of her "right shoulder, clavicle, left arm, fingers, nose and ... skull."

If X-rays could reveal emotional trauma, Marcia's worst one would have been that even into her fifties, she still craved her mother's love. When her mother took an overdose of sleeping pills and died, Marcia, instead of shouting "Hallelujah!" cried, wishing that Mom had "taken me in her arms before her death to say, I'm sorry for all that I did to you." Her "heart ached leadenly" knowing that now her mother never would. "Selfishly, I lay there weeping for myself not her."

Selfishly! It took Marcia years to untwist her warped emotions and feel what her psychotherapist assured her was "healthy anger." And at times a "volcano of anger" would erupt and she could've carved her mother into "chunks." Yet "to be assertive and angry" was far more difficult than to be "the pale, frightened child ... waiting to be hurt one more time." She said she wasted many days being that frightened child.

So did I. Long after I remembered my sister's verbal, physical and sexual torture, I couldn't hate her. I tried to; I yelled and screamed out loud at invisible her (I'd stopped speaking to her), but the hate came from my intellect not my guts. In mid hate-fest, I'd find myself raging at some one else. Once driving, wrath percolating, I saw a few children on the sidewalk and my head flashed, "What if I mowed them down?" Scapegoating again! Instead of hating my sister, I'd imagined my car hitting children. The children were child-me, who'd rather die than stop loving her. My hate, my "God damn you, why didn't you love me?" bound me to her.

You Must Love Me!

My hatred of my sister reeked of the "Love me! Oh, please someone love me" that's the driving force behind many popular songs. We all hope that "One enchanted evening across a crowded room," there he or she will be, the one I love who'll love me too. Despite rap lyrics that snarl, "Kill the bitch!," old romantic ballads don't lose their popularity, and new ones are written.

"You must love me," a song from the Madonna movie *Evita*, won a Golden Globe Award in 1997. Like many romantic songs, it's about love gone wrong. "What happened?" Evita asks. We believed in each other, but our dream is disappearing and "I'm frightened you'll slip away." Oh, how can we keep the "passions alive?" The answer is the refrain, "You must love me," that repeats until it seems like a threat: "You must love me," or else. The Old Testament God also told the people he'd chosen to love that they had to love him with all their "heart, soul and strength," or else, he'd pursue them "with the naked sword." A you-must-love-me lover may also be like the nymph Echo, who, in one version of the Greek myth, when her love isn't returned, repeated, "Love me, love me" until all that was left of her was an echo, in other words, "I'm nothing without you," a common romantic bludgeon.

"I'm nothing without you," and "You must love me" are the frightened, angry cries of the child in us who feels unloved. They're symptoms of a family disease, though nowadays many parents try hard to do their best. But the best will in the world helps only a little if parents carry unprocessed hate in their veins because they weren't loved by their parents. Unaware of their own hate, they can't help taking it out on their children, who in their turn feel unloved.

The result is that adults write songs insisting "You must love me." Emotionally they stay babies. When they fall in love, they fall into baby talk and get high on songs laced with "baby, baby." To become someone's "baby lamb," was the goal of a successful professional woman I knew. Men who flex their muscles and insist on being the boss are needy babies underneath. For both sexes romantic love is a dream of being made much of and assured we're loved by a mother.

At certain times of the year, hurricanes blast through parts of the world. You-must-love-me is a hurricane that blasts all over the world, all the time, that mixture of longing and rage that brews in babies when they're not loved. An unmet need to be loved can make us cling to a partner who mistreats us and deny we're mistreated. We put up with everything so we can go on believing that someone loves us. As long as we demand, hope, search for love, we don't have to deal with the damnation of not having been loved.

Chapter 31   A Clutch Of Love-Hate Knots

Mankind worshiped a God of Wrath yet thought he was a loving God because we were once children who had contradictory feelings about our parents. Picture a young child clinging to the Mama who's just yelled at or spanked her, and you're in at the creation of what I call love-hate knots. The hate loops with the already present love and becomes the coat of arms, the heraldic emblem of the parent-child relationship.

A man drunkenly cursing his dead father for always cheating on his mom and abandoning the family for years, breaks down and cries because "In spite of it all, I loved him." He's expressing one of the most familiar love-hate knots.

At a workshop I heard a woman explain, "My mother always hit me, but it was my fault because I did everything wrong, so I have to keep bringing her presents." She's one of many children who had to appease a fearful God. Children, like dogs, lick the hand that beats them. Women who say, "I could be a slave to the man I loved," say it because in child-hood they got hooked on abject love. Mothers and fathers can be as jeal-ous as the biblical God, demanding that a son or daughter love only them and show it often. That home-bred slavery is mirrored in their adult rela-tionships by not only playing the role of abject child but domineering parent.

In 2001 when America was in Afghanistan fighting the despotic Taliban, a friend said we should treat them with love, that only love would transform them, and she went on and on, with great passion. She was advocating that America do what she'd done. For decades she'd been kind to the mother who beat her when she was a child, but who'd become merely sharp-tongued and demanding, though she'd periodically stop taking Prozac the better to spew out hate. Daughters and sons will often continue to be kind to mothers who treated them badly in child-hood and still continue to wield snide remarks and guilt trips. It doesn't matter that the children phone regularly, never forget a birthday, take mom to movies, even on vacations. Since their mothers don't change, why don't their children give up a lost cause? Their love-hate knot is all they know of love.

An artist told me that she'd had an affair with her father from as far back as she could remember, and if the world didn't think it was wrong, it wouldn't be wrong. "We loved each other." Yet, in a series of paint-ings of her child-self, she made her head square, a blockhead; her skin a dank yellow; her mouth a slit. Her artist's hand had revealed that her father having sex with her had made her feel like a little monster, which meant she hadn't loved him, and he hadn't loved her. Theirs was a love-hate knot.

Children used as prostitutes by Daddy, often refuse to condemn him. "He's my father and I love him," they say as if fathers are automatically loved no matter what they do. But what about the hate that automatically arose when he ejaculated into her mouth, vagina or rectum? "I knew it was horrible," said Eileen Franklin, "but I forgave my father in my heart all along. Hating only hurts the hater. He did love me. He said he did. That I was special to him" (*The Sins of the Father*, 1991).

Jesus said that we must forgive our brother "seventy times seven." Children forgive their parents' mistreatment seventy-thousand times seven and often 'forget' what their parents did and loyally love them so they can go on feeling loved. Children, not parents, love unconditionally; they invented the precept that forgiveness gives us peace. Yet children at first registered that mistreatment wasn't love and their suppressed hate keeps disturbing their peace and the peace of others. Some people who were rejected in childhood become addicted to a romantic love that requires them to break up with one 'true love' after another. They're driven to pass on their rejection pain, to cut notch after notch into what's become their love-hate knout.

In some native tribes physical cruelty to women is a standard expression of love. An anthropologist overheard two young Yanomamo wives discussing their scalp scars. Said one to the other with envy, "You're husband must really care for you since he's beaten you on the head so frequently" (Napoleon Chagnon, *Yanomamo*, 1983). Civilized wives are hardly different when they say they love the husbands who beat them. Some wives, though sure their husbands will kill them, don't leave because "he really loves me," and many a husband, after he beats his wife, swears he does love her. If such couples break up, there's an almost 100 percent chance they'll exchange the same love-hate knot with their new spouse.

Freud called that phenomenon the repetition compulsion, an attempt to repeat old wounds and this time get it right. A battering husband would like to think that's his motivation. It would be more comfortable than remembering his mother's beatings when he was a scared little boy, or registering that when he beats his wife, he's repeating the past but now getting it right; he is now his powerful mother and his wife a scared little boy.

For years a man had a dream in which his body was torn in half down the middle. He thought of Plato, who said that love was finding one's 'other half' and feeling whole again. That didn't seem right. Only when he remembered that his mother had made him her sexual playmate, did he understand that he was torn apart by love and hate for her. As he put it, "You want to stab them in the chest, right where you want them to hold you." His love-hate knot is as common as child molestation.

Marriages may break up when a love-hate knot doesn't fit the past. A husband became mysteriously dissatisfied when he married a woman who was much kinder than his cruel mother. Hardly aware of what he was doing, he became mean to her, yet was amazed when she got angry the way Mummy used to. But he sighed with relief; he'd got his child-hood love-hate knot back, and now that he hated his wife, he could be loyal again to his darling, cruel Mummy. His wife will stay with him only if she was demeaned as a child and learned to love the one who demeaned her. They then may live happily ever after, reaffirming their old love-hate vows.

My husband and I took an old friend to dinner. We were celebrating his return from a long visit to his mother, and he was a changed man. He told us that after he left her, he cried for two days because he realized he loved her as much as a girlfriend. Gone was his old fury at her for trying to rip off his testicles when he was two-months old and for breaking his arm when he was a year old. And gone was his fury at his dead Dad. He informed us that he'd known even when he was buggered at the age of two, that it was his father's way of loving him. "Dad did kind things and he helped me in many ways; he really loved me." The ability of the child in us to turn parental hate into love would be true alchemy if the hate didn't re-emerge. Violence builds up when we love someone we ought to hate. That very night, when the waitress forgot to bring the dessert menu, our friend let her have it with his old fury. And a few years later when he went home to care for his mother who'd developed Alzheimer's disease, he found himself yelling at her and slapping her around. Afraid he'd kill her, he put her in a home.

An adult daughter was appalled to realize that her father was being destroyed by his dependence on the wife who "had become his habit to love." He couldn't break with her, said Maria Riva, though "an impotent fury" "damaged his kidneys, destroyed three-quarters of his stomach" and finally gave him a fatal heart attack (*Marlene Dietrich*, 1993). Love-hating the one we should purely hate can eat up our bodies.

Perfectionism often starts from thinking that Mom/Dad doesn't love bad me but will when I become perfect. Winning first prize, proving we're the best in our field becomes a way of saying, "Look, the one you scorned is now loved by the whole world." Perhaps because we're partly getting revenge, we still don't feel loved, so we try harder. We would anyway. Perpetually striving to be perfect has become our love-hate knot, an addiction no more moral than compulsive sex.

Every year fraternities acquire new members by a ritual called hazing in which the older 'brothers' initiate the new ones by hurting and humil-iating them in a variety of ways. The new brothers endure it because they've already learned the game of love-hate knotmanship in the family, where subordinates, in order to be accepted, have to endure pain and humiliation from those in power.

In his *Confessions* (1781-1783), Rousseau wrote about the pleasures of pain and humiliation. Like children at that time, he was beaten regularly on his bare bottom. At the age of eleven he began to experience a growing sexual excitement when a woman spanked him. "I had found in pain, even in shame, an admixture of sensuality, which left me with more desire for, than fear of, a repetition by the same hand."

When T E Lawrence (1888-1935) was captured in Arabia, he was beaten savagely and raped. But though he was terrified of pain, he found himself seeking out beatings. So he said in The Seven Pillars of Wisdom. But some of his biographers think his accounts are fantasies; they note that he wrote about beatings and rape only after a military failure. When he was a child, his fearsome, beautiful mother would thrash him on his bare buttocks for every failure of her high standards. They sent "a delicious warmth, probably sexual, swelling through me," he wrote of the beatings in Arabia, which may be what he felt when his mother beat him. At any rate, being beaten became his sexual love-hate knot. Later in life, he paid men to flog him on his buttocks, and one flogger disclosed that Lawrence would sometimes have orgasms (Michael Asher, *Lawrence*, 1989).

If these tidbits about Lawrence or Rousseau turned you on even a little, you should have sympathy for the multitude of men and women, straight and gay, who search the ads in the back pages of newspapers for partners in a variety of sado-masochistic acts. Successful brothels have specialists in spanking to accommodate their customers, particularly nowadays when anything goes. Doing your own thing may have come out of the closet because of the influence of Michel Foucault, who in the 1970s used to lecture that what we prefer sexually comes from the culture not the body. Being one type of homosexual, he used to have himself strapped to a barrel in a gay bar and let all and sundry bugger him. The sexual desire to have a penis shoved into his rectum did come from the gay culture, not from his body. Babies and children scream with pain when a penis invades their rectum. Pleasure from buggery first arises as a defense, the body's way of enduring pain by forming a love-hate knot at the wound.

A book subtitled *An Exploration of the World of Sexual Domination and Submission* (Gloria G Brame et al, 1993), had the title *Different Loving* because its purpose was to inform the world that sado-masochists are not sexually immature, but "loving and compassionate individuals" for whom pain happens to be pleasure. They find it emotionally and physically liberating to be tied in chains and whipped till they come, to take golden showers (be peed on), brown showers (be shat upon), be sat on as if they were chairs, have their genitals and nipples pierced, and so on. They think they have special genes that compel them to think love is painful or humiliating, not that Mummy or Daddy molested them when they were little.

Emily, the alternate personality who acted out Marcia Cameron's rage, needed pain to get sexual pleasure. She'd ask the men she picked up to tie her tight with a belt, pull her hair hard. "Hurt me!" she'd order. The sex had to be rough before she could come, but when she occasionally did, Marcia would reappear, and making love-hate was over. Marcia wasn't a sexual masochist; she was a mama masochist. If the mother who'd tortured her asked her for anything, "I did it like an obedient slave," she said. "When Mom commanded, I jumped."

When a parent hurts a child, a mutual bond is created between them — the parent's pleasure-guilt at loving to hurt a child, and the child's guilt at its surge of hatred for the parent it loves. The chains sado-masochists use are visible symbols of that bond. But we're all on a sado-masochist continuum. We endure mistreatment from loved ones and inflict it on loved ones. That tit-for-tat seesaw is standard equipment in the family playground.

When he was dying in agony on the cross, Jesus asked the God he'd been sure loved and protected him, why he'd forsaken him. He didn't quote what might be expected from a good Jew who'd studied scripture: "How good it is for me to be punished" (Psalm 119:71). Christians later decided that God hadn't forsaken him, that God had planned all along that Jesus who was now called Christ would suffer and die for human sins so that everyone who stopped being bad and became good could go to heaven and be with God. Except there was a hitch. Humans couldn't go straight there. Some were so bad they had to suffer in hell forever, the rest had to endure punishment in purgatory before God could love them in heaven.

Christians had to believe in physical immortality because they needed flesh to endure the requisite pain in the after life. On planet earth, they'd already learned that love-hate system: they'd been punished to make them good by parents who said that the pain they caused them was love. When a Voice told Abraham that the One True God was informing him that he'd chosen the Israelites to be his one true love, they believed him even when he proved to be a God of Wrath. He was like their punishing parents.

When religion requires children to submit to punishment from a God in heaven as they did on earth, religion is a celestial love-hate knot. The sanctification of sado-masochism took center stage in fourteenth-century Germany, where crucifixes displayed Christ's bloody body writhing in exquisite curves of pain. Holy sado-masochism continues to make Christians flog their backs bloody for the love of Christ, as do Shiites for the love of Allah, which doesn't prove that God is one, but that Muslim children suffer at the hands of their loving parents too.

Whatever love parents have for their children, they also pass on hate. Proof of that transmission is found in our inner world, where children embed a mummy and daddy who continue to criticize and judge them. The child in us thinks it needs to be corrected, for they were taught corrections were love, just as they learned fear was love. Scapegoating keeps them unaware of their hate, and should it begin to raise its scary head, they embrace forgiveness like a savior.

The mess of our emotions can't be fixed; it is a fix. Our heads spin. Our ability to pick up bad vibes is skewed; we may think a local thug is really a nice man, that a boyfriend who slaps us really loves us. It's as if children drank attar of roses in vodka, a cocktail that lets them keep their hate disguised and their love smelling sweet. Many go on drinking that drug until they're reborn into fundamentalists who glorify family values. Love-hate knots is an addiction hard to break because loving our abusers makes hate sexy and cripples our authentic hate.

An oracle said that whoever untied the Gordian knot would rule all Asia. Alexander the Great impatiently cut it with his sword because he wanted to rule the whole world "Now!" and he did. If the Gordian knot had been his personal love-hate knot, it's a good thing he cut it; if he'd waited and tried to untie his tangled emotions, he would have lost his lust for power. Most of us opt for power, to rule a world where might is right like Mom/Dad did, or to climb the corporate or professional ladder and control the lives of those below. To go to war and fight, to kill, rape, loot and riot are intoxicating. "Evil be thou my good," what Milton has Lucifer say when he revolts from God, becomes our (secret) rallying cry too. Cutting our love-hate knot by choosing hate is a breath of fresh air. Wanting to blow up the world feels a hell of a lot better than yearning for a love that saps us into helpless babies lying in a mess of fetid, shameful emotions.

"Be kind, for everyone you meet is fighting a great battle." I don't know what Philo of Alexandria (who lived in the first century) meant by "a great battle," but one battle we're all fighting is between our original love and the hate we develop when we're not loved, a tug of war that knocks us off our true center so that we easily fall into a hell of self-hate, our real damnation and the tragedy of human life.

Chapter 32   A Primer Of Self-Hate

How Do I Hate Me? Let Me Count The Ways

Self-hate is more common than the common cold, but we're so used to its symptoms, we don't know we're sick. We think self-hate's manifestations are who we are.

To get a sense of its prevalence, consider the legions who worry a lot. Would they fear the worst will happen if they didn't believe they deserved it? If that seems far-fetched, why, when we hear people laughing nearby, do we stiffen, sure they're laughing at us? Why when we leave a group, do we fear they're gossiping about us? At the slightest slight, many of us feel rejected, and at a small criticism, collapse into self-doubt. Yet a compliment gives us a high, as do the self-compliments called dreams of glory. When I was an adolescent, if a boy liked me, I thought he must have a screw loose, or be one of the inferiors of the world, like me.

A friend won a gold medal at an international rowing contest, and when I congratulated her, she ordered me to "shut up about it." I was astonished until I remembered that her older sister had been the family winner, my friend the family fuck-up, a role that still barred her from triumphing over her, at least not openly. Women who insist "I'm ugly" and can't comprehend it's a metaphor about how they feel about themselves; those who have frequent accidents and think they were born clumsy; those who have voices that can hardly be heard, who walk slumped over, make a vice of assertiveness and a virtue of meekness; those who brood over minor mistakes, and beat themselves up for failures; those who aim to please, and can't say "No" — have the pustules of self-hate. Their inner sense of unworthiness pops up everywhere in their lives.

If ads didn't press our self-hate buttons, we wouldn't be suckers for sleek new cars that will advertise our high status, or wear the most expensive cosmetics because "I'm worth it." We like feathers in our cap because self-hate has made our outer lives a fight for status, a necessity when self-hate has laid us low in our inner lives.

If, at the top of a flight of stairs, we see ourselves falling down; if we imagine a car running into us, a sniper shooting at us, self-hate is delivering the old news that we're so bad we ought to be hurt, killed. We take insults personally, sure the insulter is telling us the truth, because we've already insulted ourselves. If we hadn't suffered early rejection, current rejection wouldn't make our unhealed wound bleed. Outside affirmation feels so good because it takes away the pain of self-rejection … for a short while. Our opinion of ourselves rises and falls depending upon how we're judged, and judges are out there, but the harshest judge is in ourselves. Judgment Day is every day for self-haters.

When we look in a mirror, we often hear our judge say "Ugly!", but sometimes we imagine a friend, not us, saying it. Self-hate is using the friend for its own needs. Self-hate, sooner or later, doubts friendships and this friendship's time may be up. Or the friend may have appealed to us because he or she has traits of a parent or sibling whose mistreatment we don't want to remember; by imagining a friend being abusive, we can go on loving our actual abuser. Self-hate conjures up people from the past or present to hiss at us because it needs a constant flow of hate to maintain its identity.

Self-haters who suspect they're an evil force that makes bad things happen are creating their hostile world. But they also create their hostile world by thinking this can prevent bad things from happening. Worrying is the black-magic that wards it off. When passengers in a car, they're sure the car will crash and they'll be killed. Fear becomes the rabbit's foot they rub so the accident won't happen. Yet they feel guilty because their self-hate tells them they deserve to die. Nevertheless, they want to live, so they die over and over in their imagination as the price of living. Self-haters are prone to such maneuvers, complex battle plans to get through life. They're unaware they're making their own life scarier than it need be and that their fear and self-loathing affect others. The 'bad' seeds parents plant in children charge the emotional atmosphere and the world reaps the whirlwind.

Part of the whirlwind is caused by the human miseries we've labeled Deadly Sins. Greed tries and tries to fill the pit that opened in us when we weren't loved, a pit we can never fill. Jealousy is a verification of what we learn early: anyone else is better, more lovable, than we are. For the family favorite, the pain of jealousy quickly turns into indignation that a boyfriend dared cheat on ME! Envy is rubbing in the harsh fact that life's golden apples are not for the likes of second-rate me. Big egos are huffing and puffing to keep their deflated selves blown up. Muhammed Ali gave himself shots of the 'greatest' to get the iron to fight. Arrogance raises me far above those inferior beings I never was, and helps me get more and more success, the high that keeps me feeling good. Others' feel-good comes from being humbly needed, indispensable, impossible to abandon. Lust is fast food, a quick meal, which won't remind me of the nurturance I never got. Self-hate becomes Sloth as "The world would be a better place without me" slips into "Nothing matters, I always fail. Besides, I no longer know what I want." That we wanted Mummy to love us becomes a deadly feeling we bury, an early act of self-censorship.

Children have to think Mummy loves them and that when they become good, she'll show it. To make the world just, children transfer the hate they feel toward Mummy to 'bad me', the child's name for self-hate, which later in life makes us continue to take on blame when we shouldn't and, dutifully honor the parents who harmed us, a biblically approved masochism that easily flips into sadism.

Self-hate, by turning us against ourselves, turns us against others. Harshly judging ourselves turns us into a hanging judge. We wish others ill, so we'll have companions in the same leaky boat we're in. Putting ourselves down compels us to give others a taste of our own nasty medicine. Cruelty is the backhand of self-cruelty. The goal of "I must win" is "You must lose," as I did when I was flattened, a baby who lost the high stakes love-match. We think competition builds character because our self-hate became stronger from constantly beating ourselves up. Therefore, my beating you in a game makes you tougher too. Forced in childhood to take a daily dose of "You are bad," we soon dose ourselves, and the venom we store from self-hate automatically injects venom into anyone who threatens our counterfeit self-esteem.

Stretched on invisible racks of self-hate, we become self-rejecters who reject, self-scapegoaters who scapegoat, self-torturers who torture, self-murderers who slap, fight, punch to prove we're tough, not patsies who had to surrender to the powers that be. The acid drip, drip of self-hate won't let us have compassion for ourselves. If we start to, an old physical pain may jab us, or raise the decibel levels of the put-downs in our head. We invented a Jesus to forgive us because we can't forgive ourselves. Self-hate forbids it.

How do I hate me? The effects of self-hate are countless. They're not recognized as self-hate because they're accepted as human traits, the evil side of human nature, which morality and religion try to teach us to overcome. Spiritual teachers tell us we have a higher self and a lower self but don't tell us that not-being-loved is the source of the lower self. The source is rarely recognized because self-hate orchestrates our opera from the pit; it's like the inner critic, who's usually as silent to us as the sounds only animals can hear. The inner critic and self-hate are the mainsprings of our emotional works, the infrastructure that forms when children aren't loved. It's as if ghosts of parents and siblings (dead or alive) are jerking us around. The ghosts are us; we learned to do it to ourselves, but we don't want to know. We only want to get out of our pain.

The Quest To Feel Good

A chimp in an animal sanctuary hits himself over and over. As I watched him on TV, I thought of the monks who'd lash themselves with thorns over and over for their sins. The chimp wasn't hitting himself for his sins; he couldn't get over his childhood anguish at seeing his mother killed by poachers and being torn away from his jungle home. Chimps don't beat up their children. The monks, as a matter of course, were beaten by their parents to make them good, a childhood trauma the monks reenacted so they'd never forget they were sinners. The monks had to remind themselves that *they* were the sinners because, like other human self-mutilators, they had to deny the anguish of having had parents who abused them.

Humans in every society try to forget the catastrophe of not having been loved by using substances that temporarily take away our bad feelings and give us good ones. In the twentieth century, popular drugs were alcohol, marijuana, heroin, cocaine, binge eating and shopping, and the vicarious vengeance of watching the fights and murders on TV's nightly Roman games.

Since 1988 when Prozac came on the market and became a bestseller, millions of people have been using it and similar drugs to help them feel good in what's been described as an era of extreme stress and anxiety. But in 1621 Robert Burton published *The Anatomy of Melancholy*, a long, popular treatise on what he said was a malady "inbred in every one of us." What's now called depression is endemic to man. At its simplest, it's the sadness, the sense of separateness, the suspicion one's own life and life itself has no meaning that haunt us. We can bear that, but not the depression that drags us around not wanting to face another day, hopeless, suicidal, crying, unable to eat or sleep, or sleeping and eating all day, a bump in the road heaving into a twenty-foot hurdle.

When Prozac first came on the market, depression was thought to be a genetic defect that caused low serotonin levels. Serotonin, a chemical that transmits messages to the nervous system, was found to be deficient in rats and monkeys who were atypically aggressive or meek. The cure was to raise their serotonin levels; so the cure for humans must be to raise their serotonin levels — and it worked.

But could billions of people have been born with low serotonin levels? Nature doesn't make that many mistakes. Scientists have since learned that, whereas manic-depression is a genetic brain disorder, depression is not. Situations that make us feel trapped, helpless, inferior can lower serotonin levels. Since body and mind are a team, it would be strange if turning a child into a self-hater didn't damage the bodily matter we call brains.

Hate turned inward causes major depressions. That's made clear by the people who took Prozac and, instead of feeling happier, became violent. Many cases have been recorded, like a woman who, after two years on the drug, began to have temper tantrums and smashed the windshield of her car with a baseball bat. Prozac had made her emotionally strong enough to let out her long imprisoned hate. Some Prozac users got restless, unable to sit still, echoes of the compulsive busyness that keeps humans running from the fumes of their self-damnation. The rising up of hostility may have made other Prozac users catatonics; it felt safer to damp down all their feelings than let hate ignite and explode. Prozac and similar drugs can occasionally cause suicide, as it well might if, instead of bypassing their self-hate, people suddenly became conscious of it overwhelming them, virtually commanding them to die.

Man's Weapon of Mass Self-Destruction

When children can't show their anger, it can grow into a hate that creates a killer. Few children grow up and kill, but little children imagine their hate can kill because they want to be rid of the parents who hurt them. But since parents also protect them and teach them the ways of the world, and since children learn they won't be loved if their hate explodes, children's hate has no way out but in. The monks lashed their skin bloody with thorns; self-hate can also cause internal injuries: backaches, heartburn, headaches, heart trouble, high blood pressure, cancers, and who knows what other disorders develop when we turn our wish to hurt others against ourselves.

We've been reluctant to face how damaging self-hate is. Otherwise, we wouldn't call it 'low self-esteem', as if self-esteem were the norm. The norm is low self-esteem, a genteel euphemism for a destructive force that starts to ravage us when we're not loved as babies. When parents cover up their incapacity to love by accusing children of being bad, they consign them to suffering that's greater than the victims in Dante's Hell. Dante thought he was describing punishments that God would impose on sinners, but no such tortures could have been conceived by a loving God. They sprang into Dante's mind because parental punishments are tortures to children who, unable to retaliate, have fantasies of torturing adults. The weapons of mass destruction that humans invent are the retaliations of those grown-children known as adults, the grown-up toys that embody the rage they felt when they were punished as children.

"The Lord takes vengeance and is quick to anger" says the Bible in the book of Nahum (1:3), which celebrates vengeance but gives no hint of why we want vengeance. We want it for the same reason we want money, which the Bible says (1 Timothy 6:10) is the root of all evil. It isn't. We lust for vengeance, money and the luxuries money can buy to be comforted, to soothe the baby in us who's crying for love and needs many comforts to compensate for the self-hate it inflicts on itself. When parrots are owned by people who lock them in cages and pay no attention to them, they react like chimps and humans; they succumb to self-hate. Parrots attack themselves by pulling out their feathers. Insane, they have to be sent to special homes where they're given lots of attention, but very few get better. Humans are worse off. Having found many ways to comfort themselves, from cream puffs to fights, they guarantee they don't get better. Depression gives them the chance if they delve into the cause, but very few can make their way out of the caged rage of self-hate.

It's hard to get out because self-hate starts so early, when we're most affected by outside influences. Since embryos react to their mother's feelings, if a mother curses the embryo, its creative energy stops in its tracks for a second. In that instant, the mother's "I wish you didn't exist" pierces into what before was wholly positive energy and adds molecules of hate, a negative additive that gives the embryo less efficient fuel to work with. Babies and children continue to pick up negative feelings from parents until numbness gives them a kind of peace.

Self-hate is a bad placebo effect which, like a good placebo effect, proves the power of belief. If a physician says a medication will make us well, the chances are high that it will, though it's a sugar pill. When a shaman tells a native he'll die if he eats a certain food, he dies if he eats it (though the food is wholesome). In terrified obedience, he must die; otherwise, his belief system, the universe he lives in, will collapse. Like Atlas in the Greek myth, who held up the heavens on his shoulders, every child has to do its part to hold up the belief system of planet Earth—the self-hate-based, I-am-a-sinner-religion that assures the salvation of man's psychological universe for another generation.

Another reason our sick psychology survives is that humans have an almost fail-safe escape hatch, the haven of the intellect, where we can cultivate abstract thinking, logic, mathematics, physics, philosophy, engineering and other scientific pursuits that engage our minds. Meanwhile, the child in us sits in a swarm of painful feelings, afraid to experience them, a disability that keeps adults emotionally three-years old, fixated on revenge and longing for love at the same time.

Our emotional retardation goes unnoticed because we identify with power figures, which in childhood is usually a parent. Later, if we're exposed to the power figure in the Bible, the Koran, or the Book of Mormon, God has greater appeal, for he claims his punishments, including killing, are holy. When a murderer says, "God made me do it," he says it with confidence. He's sure he became one with God because killing felt holy; it made him feel good, his power just. By identifying with God, he enjoyed that feeling without knowing he killed a substitute for the parent who turned him into a self-hater, that his child was having a moment of triumph, the thrill, at last, of not being a victim.

Most of us don't kill; we go on with our lives as we're supposed to, with not a clue that love-deprivation controls many of our choices. If they'd been loved, girls' chief goal wouldn't be to get married in a white halo and live happily ever after, having gained a Prince who'll love them forever. No Prince does and neither does the Radiant Bride; the self-hate habits we acquire in childhood poison our human relationships. More and more we're living in a world that's deconstructing. To correct the problem, the Religious Right has been trying for decades to bring America back to a strong belief in a Christian God and Family Values.

Since the God they worship evolved from family values, they want to bring us back to the cause of the problem.

In the sixteenth century Martin Luther mustered an enormous amount of courage and succeeded in curbing the corrupt power of the authoritarian Roman Catholic Church, but he couldn't see the cause of the Church's problem, though his family life had given him every reason to.

Luther's Holy Hate

Young Martin Luther, after visiting his parents, was riding back to school through a forest, when he was caught in such a violent storm he was sure lightning would strike him dead. Terrified, he vowed that if he was spared, he'd devote his life to God. Luther survived the storm. His father, who'd ordered him to study law, raged when Luther told him he'd become a monk. Luther withstood the wrath of his father, who used to beat him as if he were made of stone not flesh. For God, who could have killed him, had saved his life, and could save him eternally.

Luther, alas, had trouble with his heavenly Father, too. The monastery was a lot like home. He had to obey many rigid rules, and he himself had to whip his bare back. He was supposed to suffer like Christ, so he slept without blankets, and once in a fit of religious masochism slept in the snow until his fellow monks dragged him inside to save his life. He spent six hours a day doing penance and confessing. To no avail; his heart told him he wasn't sorry for his sins. That meant God, who knew all, would never forgive him and grant him salvation but damn him forever. Despairing of pleasing God and winning his love, he wanted to kill himself.

When he was a boy, Luther despaired of his father's love and his mother's, whose beatings were worse than his father's; she once beat little Martin bloody for stealing one nut. He must have raged at the injustice of his beatings. That the boy Luther had not felt sorry for his sins may explain why the monk Luther couldn't feel sorry for his sins. His rage at his parents was still in his heart. Precepts about forgiveness and honoring parents don't change the heart.

The boy Luther's longing for a loving God was so strong that the monk Luther studied scripture and found what he needed, a God who didn't want his children to suffer like Christ. God required only that his children have faith in him and he would gladly save them. He turned God into the loving father he wished his father had been, one who didn't impose excruciating punishments for small sins.

Finding God's love freed Luther from needing to perform rituals. When studying scripture, he discovered that God hadn't ordained seven sacraments but only two, and, of course, hadn't imposed an abomination like having to pay money (indulgences) to get into heaven. When salvation is a simple bond between God's love and man's faith, the Church's power as the only pathway to heaven was threatened. The Pope excommunicated Luther and would have had him burned alive if the head of the state where Luther lived hadn't refused to hand him over. Other heads of German states felt the same way. They wanted more power for themselves and more of their subjects' money to stay in the state, not be handed over to the Church. Inspired by Luther's revolutionary ideas, the peasants revolted too, demanding social and economic rights from their masters.

Luther was appalled by their presumption and called them demons who should be "stabbed," "slain," "smitten," using the God of Wrath's favorite kill-words. Luther wanted to curb only the autocratic power of the Church. He wasn't interested in what we now call human rights, equal rights, or, that outlandish notion, children's rights. When he married and had children, he demanded total power as a father. Like his rageful parents about to beat him, or the Pope about to have a poor soul tortured, he declared, "I would rather have a dead son than a disobedient one."

Luther unjustly beat his children, but he justly raged against the Church, which sorely needed its corruptions stopped. Luther was able to defy the Church because he'd harvested some of the healthy rage he'd felt when he was beaten in childhood. He valued anger. "In anger," he said, "I feel the full might of my being," and he was doing more than identify with the God of Wrath. He'd got back a power he'd lost in childhood and felt whole again. Fortunately for the world, the anger Luther released from his childhood gave him enough positive energy to make the world a better place. Luther was like Richard Wright, who'd also been cruelly beaten when he was a child, and also carried a grenade of hate in his heart and brain, which mangled his human relationships and much of his fiction. Despite that, Wright's wrath shook the complacent racism of many Americans. Luther's wrath shook the institution of the Church, so much so that a Protestant Church developed in protest against the Roman Catholic Church. Luther's successful challenge of the Church's authority became part of a movement that, having started in the Renaissance, slowly led to America's revolt against the autocratic British government.

The Full Might of Our Being

Democracies have always been shaky because we underestimate the lifelong effects on children of the autocracy they grow up in. Luther should have nailed 95 indictments on the family door; but he would have got nowhere. The family remains sacred and continues to be the model for Churches, Schools, Governments, Businesses, and institutions in which authority figures rule underlings who are afraid to speak up.

Luther said he felt the full might of his being when he got angry, but adults would rarely have to get angry if as children they'd been allowed to speak up, to disagree, not have to obey or be punished. If children were given some power, they'd know how to use power, to calmly stand up for themselves, be able to compromise, not have to always be right. Democracies will ultimately fail until parents stop being God Almighties who rule over 'bad' children, a method of child-rearing guaranteed to produce vengeful self-haters.

We've only begun to reform the institution of the family because the red flag—"HONOR THY FATHER AND THY MOTHER"—stops us in our frightened tracks. The child in us upholds that commandment because it needs to love Mom/Dad no matter what, though virtually every child has killed them in fantasy, and for a good reason. The pull between our rage at injustice and our love would rip us apart if humans hadn't devised coping techniques: scapegoating so we can act out our hate without recognizing its source; love-hate knots, which keep us trapped in a labyrinth that has no exit; media that inundates us with images of happy children and understanding moms and dads who don't scream, yell "stupid!" or smack them. Meanwhile, wars and personal acts of violence continue to break out all over the globe.

Humans have given the same answer to life's mysteries for thousands of years. To the fundamental questions—What is the meaning of life? Why am I here?—we've given the answer we were taught in the family: the purpose of my life is to stop being bad and become good so my Gods will love me, the same purpose that was translated into religion as: to stop being a sinner and become good so I can get to heaven and bask in God's love. Mankind's main religions wouldn't exist if children weren't trained to be self-haters and want to find love. Whatever the purpose of life, it's not the familiar religious one. Nor is it the materialistic substitute—to be rich and get power. We may never know the answer, but we'll have a better chance to find out when parents stop telling children they're bad, a lie that eventually numbs us, drastically reducing human consciousness.

At the beginning of the new millennium, the physicist Stephen Hawking said that the twenty-first century must do something about human aggression. Early man needed it to survive but now it was destroying the world. He thought genetic engineering might be the way to modify it. But we can't make better babies the way we breed cattle, or by tinkering with genes. Hawking left out the after birth cause of aggression. If I could modify babies, I'd make them immune to the physical and emotional condemnations their parents batter them with. To transform society, we need a few generations without families that manufacture self-haters. Who knows what the world would be like if children were respected and admired, treated not as inferiors or superiors but as unique, worthwhile human beings with a vast potential. A population that could realize the full might of their humanity would have to be different from the generations who, having picked up a load of self-hate early in life, drag a heavy insecurity blanket after them until they die. Far from realizing our full potential, most of us become child sacrifices.

Chapter 33   **Child Sacrifice**

In ancient times, children were sacrificed to Gods. The second book of Kings in the Bible records the common practice of fathers throwing children into the fire to propitiate Baal, one of the fertility and nature Gods. Even the biblical God that millions of people still worship used to demand the sacrifice of "your first-born sons" (Exodus 22:29). Gods apparently liked babies and children best. Archeologists have dug up thousands of bones of sacrificed children and they continue to find them. In the late twentieth century they found another burial site in Carthage, and in Zoque in Chiapas, Mexico, they found many skeletons of children between one and five who'd been sacrificed about 900 years before.

Eventually, most cultures substituted animals for children. At present, old-fashioned child sacrifice lingers on chiefly in underground satanic cults. In the late 1980s at my incest survivor group, I met a dozen or more people whose parents had taken them to satanic cults where they saw children killed. The San Francisco Chronicle on August 4, 1997 reported that a General in the Liberian civil war, Joshua Milton Blahyi, confessed that when he was eleven he'd been "initiated into a satanic society" where he'd made a contract with a devil who craved "fresh blood." Before each battle Blahyi had to "make a human sacrifice." Usually he chose "a small child": he'd dive under water where children were playing, pull one down and break its neck.

Parents now rarely feel compelled to give their Gods "fresh blood" but they don't object to handing over their young sons (and now their daughters) to become bloody cannon fodder in the endless wars on this planet. "Sweet and right is it to die for one's country," said Horace (65-8 B.C.) and young men have been eager to slaughter and be slaughtered for their fatherland. Patriotism reached an extreme in World War II when many young Japanese became kamikaze pilots, ones who crashed their planes into enemy targets. As their planes went down, they'd call out the name of their Sun-God Emperor. One man who wasn't allowed to be a kamikazi because he had a wife and three daughters, luckily had a patriotic wife, who killed herself and the children, leaving her husband free to die for the emperor.

Many parents have sacrificed their children to mortal Gods. When Germany was defeated in World War II, Joseph Goebbels, before he killed himself, sacrificed his six children to his God—Hitler. In Jonestown in 1986 parents forced their children to drink cyanide-laced Kool-Aid at the behest of their God, Jim Jones. In 1995 in Waco Texas, parents let their children die a fiery death to be one with their Messiah, David Koresh.

Parents often practiced child sacrifice for a community good. Natives in Zoque, Mexico sacrificed their children to the local rain God. They reasoned that since babies cried when they were taken away from their mothers, the rain to grow crops would surely flow. The drama central to Christianity was also child sacrifice for a community good. God said that if his son, Christ, took on man's sins and then was crucified, mankind's sins would be forgiven. He'd had a similar solution for the Israelites' sins, which would be forgiven if they were recited over the head of a goat that was sent to a desert to die.

It's hard to believe that a good, loving and omnipotent God would let his son be killed when he had the power to save him (and forgive mankind too). But billions did and still do believe it. They do because children are routinely sacrificed by parents. We fail to see that God flaw for the same reason clients often don't hear a therapist's insight when they're not ready to take it in. Cultures develop the idea that love is blind because the child in us isn't ready to see the blinding truth that our parents were not particularly good, were in fact often cruel, that their love was hardly unconditional. To see that truth early can be lethal.

"Bad Report Card Caused Boy's Suicide, Police Say"

In October 1998 on the back pages of a newspaper the above headline caught my eye. The brief item (with names changed and the place omitted) read: "An 8-year-old boy fatally shot himself at home this week while his mother was outside getting a switch to whip him because of a bad report card, the police of [city] said today. On Wednesday afternoon, the boy, Keith Parsons, apparently climbed onto a dresser to get a gun that was hanging on a nail on the wall, straightened a doily he had wrinkled, then shot himself in the head, Detective Truman Cobb said. Keith, who was in the third grade, died on Thursday."

The headline was wrong. Keith didn't kill himself because of a bad report card. Why he killed himself is partly revealed by what puzzled Detective Cobb: — if Keith had climbed onto the dresser to get the gun, why was the doily unwrinkled? It's hard to imagine an eight-year-old boy straightening a doily, especially before he kills himself. The detective must have asked his mother about the neat doily and was still skeptical. Otherwise, the news item wouldn't have read "apparently" Keith climbed onto the dresser to get the gun, then straightened the doily. That Keith would do that before he shot himself makes sense only if his mother was a drill-sergeant who'd taught him that in her home things were kept neat and tidy. Fearful obedience may not have been the only reason he straightened the doily. Keith may have been leaving his mother a message: "See, I really have tried to be a good boy."

I'm sure Keith wanted to be good boy at school too, that he was more upset than his mother by his bad report card. How smart Keith was, I don't know, but fear can shut down a child's ability to think, and Keith must have waited in fear and trembling many times while his mother cut a switch to give him one of her "good beatings," which the Bible said would whip him into shape (Proverbs 20:30). It didn't work, and his mother's constant dissatisfaction with him may have made Keith feel Mama didn't love him. Like all children, he wanted to please his mother. By shooting himself, he may have thought he was doing what she wanted, getting rid of bad rubbish.

When children aren't loved by their first God, a part of them wants to die, but a child, who's still teeming with primal energy, has to be in hell before he kills himself. For years Keith had lived in fear and also with the shame that he was bad. For eight long years he'd tried to be good to please Mama and failed. He may have thought of running away but was sure they'd bring him back, and he was too ashamed to tell a teacher. Besides, Mama would find out and beat him more. Keith may have caught himself daydreaming about having a nice mother, then felt disloyal. "How bad he was to wish her dead! Better to blow out his own stupid brains." Being a child, Keith could see no end to his misery. It was logical to conclude, like Hamlet, that the only way he could "take arms against [his] sea of troubles" was by self-murder. And there was the gun, in plain sight, as if God wanted him to kill himself.

The majority of young boys would have released their hate by taking up a competitive sport, bullying smaller kids, taunting 'niggers', identifying with killers on TV and in video games — availed themselves of the many outlets the culture provides to discharge hate. A Darwinian might say it was right that Keith didn't survive to reproduce, that only the fittest ought to survive and Keith didn't fit into our tough, callous society. Keith was culturally retarded, too vulnerable, too sensitive. Unable to become tough or numb, Keith sensibly got out of here. I hope that during the many hours he was dying (he didn't die till the next day), he had a near-death experience and found himself surrounded by a light that saturated his being with the love he'd never got when he was alive.

Keith's mother would have been sure that God had sent him straight to Hell, where suicides belonged. But she'd done her best, everything she could think of to turn him into a good Christian, and she'd failed. She'd been right all along; Keith was a bad apple.

If Keith had waited until he was an adolescent and less afraid of his mother, he, like the young parricides Paul Mones defended, might have shot her instead of himself. If anyone died, it should not have been Keith. But his mother, by taking her hate out on him, trained Keith to take out his hate on himself. By disrespecting him, she taught him to disrespect himself, to get rid of his despised being. Perhaps it was best he died at eight; to heal a heart that's broken in childhood is almost impossible, though most children carry on.

Keith's blood, splattered in the room where he shot himself, was sacrificed on the altar of his mother's values, which he'd accepted. If he hadn't believed he was a bad boy, he wouldn't have killed himself. He would have endured his mother's beatings, hoping they'd make him good, like Mama said, who beat him because she loved him. A good boy to the end, he didn't let his anger show; nor did he scapegoat, nor do what an unhappy six-year-old boy did in Michigan in March 2000 — shoot a happy six-year-old girl at school.

That murder made the national news; Keith's suicide rated a column inch in the newspaper because he'd been a good boy and shot himself. The boy in Michigan, however, proved what the culture still wants to hear, that children who kill are bad seeds, and that the Mom/Dad from whom they inherited their 'seeds' loved their children and treated them well. We're comfortable with that contradiction because we don't have to see that the same parents who give children life, can take the juice of life out of them. Eight-year-old Keith killed himself because his will to live dried up; his mother squeezed him too hard. She failed as a parent because she was unable to make Keith over into the species that's able to play the cruel family game our planet has developed.

Earth's Cruel Legacy

In 1866 Hannah Smith beat her four-month-old son till he was black and blue because a mother's first religious duty was to break a child's will, which meant making his will bend to hers, which she assumed was God's will. Her son, Logan Pearsall Smith, became a good writer, despite his damaged spirit. Despite coming from a family of peace-loving Quakers, Hannah Smith was no different from parents in an African tribe who thought they had to get rid of the "evil spirit" in children by ritual beatings. In Britain in 2002 some Africans were still practicing the ritual, which wouldn't have been found out except that a couple beat the life out of their wayward child, along with its "evil spirit."

Parents seem to have to believe that evil spirits, original sin or what Freud called dangerous drives require strong measures to be tamed. It was inevitable that the Good Old Boys of Christianity made cruelty a virtue. Aquinas was raised to sainthood in record time because he proved that the Church's doctrines were true, which meant, he said, that not believing in them was heresy and deserved death. Dante in his *Divine Comedy* lets us rubberneck the damned as they're tortured in Hell and, depending which side we're on, sadist or masochist, get our jollies. Milton wrote *Paradise Lost*, an epic poem about Adam and Eve disobeying an order, for which childish failing God punished them and all humankind with death. Milton said he wanted to "justify the ways of God to man," but he was justifying the parental custom of punishing children to make them good.

Keith was sacrificed to his mother's cruel Christian values, according to which, he will not be buried in consecrated ground, but she will. It didn't matter that she made a child's home so harsh and unloving he preferred death to living there. That sort of parental cruelty is not a punishable crime, nor is treating a child as if he should be an extension of a parent. Gandhi was guilty of that crime, and worse.

Gandhi gave his two elder sons no affection when they were young, and when they were older he was actively cruel. Gandhi, following Indian custom, had been married at thirteen, which he thought had made him a slave to sex, so that when his oldest son, eighteen-year-old Harilal, asked permission to marry, Gandhi coldly told him he'd ceased to think of him as a son. Harilal did marry, but when his wife died, Gandhi wouldn't let him remarry. He became a drunk, a womanizer, a swindler, wrote articles attacking his father and, to spite him, became a Muslim. He died a derelict in a TB hospital in Bombay. When Gandhi found out that his second son, Manilal, who was living in South Africa, had slept with a married woman, he made it public, fasted, and persuaded the woman to shave off her hair. He said he'd never allow his son to marry and didn't relent until he was thirty-five, and then because his wife pressured him. Gandhi, who had trouble taming the sexual urges he thought defiled body and spirit, insanely wanted his sons to be celibate like him (Louis Fischer, *The Life of Mahatma Gandhi*, 1950).

Gandhi and Keith's mother wanted their sons to be good. Her cruelty was understandable because she believed in original sin, but Gandhi wrote to the boys and girls in his ashram that "Children are innocent, loving and benevolent by nature. Evil comes in only when they become older." How does it come in? Does it grow in like teeth? Gandhi didn't comprehend that his lack of love and benevolence toward his children changed their loving nature into hurt, resentment and hate.

That the great Gandhi mistreated his children only proves that parents don't know how to bring up children, or rather, that they don't know that becoming a parent can bring out the worst in them. As the authors of *Raising Cain* (1999), Dan Kindlon and Michael Thompson, put it, "If you want a tour of your own dark impulses, have children."

Misconceptions

When parents used to sacrifice babies to Gods, I doubt they reasoned that being sacrificed spared them the suffering of becoming good Mayans or Hutus. If Keith had lived and become the good boy his mother wanted, he too wouldn't have got over the suffering that turned him into a Christian. Nor do children of any religion or non-religion get over their indoctrination into goodness.

Buddhists profess that babies don't have to be taught to be good, that they're already there. Lawrence Shainberg, who was a student of Zen for many years, disagreed. He said Zen was "closet Catholicism" because it too had a goal we had to attain—equanimity. He could feel the calm and contentment radiating from his Zen master, but it didn't encourage him; it filled him with despair. For when he and the other students meditated, they found their thoughts focusing on "self-criticism, self-loathing, desire for self-improvement." Shainberg thought he was feeling the agony of having an ego, but he couldn't "conceive of life without" it (*Ambivalent Zen*, 1995).

Family life filled children with self-criticism, self-loathing, and a desire for self-improvement long before Buddhism or religions developed. But Shainberg's Zen master said we could learn nothing from examining our biography. He compared it to examining the shit that drops from your anus into a toilet, or to "saving toilet paper after you've used it." But to attain equanimity we have to examine our shit, the shit in our head. Until we do, we unconsciously carry around our soiled toilet paper.

We have shit in our head because it was put there, first by Mom, then Dad. They didn't think they were doing it. Keith's mother thought she was making Keith a good boy, not harming him. Baby birds trigger their parents to regurgitate food into their open mouths. Children trigger their parents to pass on a human virus. In the nineteenth century some men thought they could be cured of syphilis by ejaculating into a child's vagina, that their sexually-transmitted disease would be cured at an innocent sex-site. Starting in the late twentieth century many men tried that cure for AIDS. They didn't get cured; they passed on their disease. On the same principle, parents may think they can be released from their self-hate when they slap, beat, and yell at children. They too feel a pleasurable release but don't get cured. They give children's innocent bodies and minds an auto-immune disease specifically designed to attack self-love cells and break them down into self-hate. Parents are the vector of an infection essential for life in the societies human beings have created.

I said that Keith was too vulnerable and sensitive to live in this cruel world, and so are an enormous number of children who don't kill themselves. Yet everyone kills the best in them when they become self-haters, and virtually all of us do. In the process of becoming good boys and girls we learn to think of ourselves as our parents do. If Mama says I'm bad, I'm bad; I'm stupid if she says so. It never occurred to Keith that Mama was bad, that Mama was stupid.

Every child becomes a victim of its parents' misconceptions, prejudices, numbness, cruelty, its mind partly misshapen, with the result that the vast potential of humans is lost. Not only does our capacity to feel for others become minimal, the innate ability of babies and young children to sense danger pretty much stops functioning, as does our sense of fairness and access to our inner guidance. We also lose mysterious powers, like knowing what others are thinking, and seeing the future, which are labeled psychic because so few of us retain them. Our powers are suppressed because they challenge the way our group has been trained to see, think and feel.

"The essence of humanity" said Charles Pasternak is our pleasure in searching, analyzing, exploring, seeking, the sole advantage we have over other species, the advantage which created civilization (*Quest*, 2003). Yet the parental custom of teaching children to be good by telling them their essence is bad puts civilization in jeopardy. That false belief makes us seekers, but not so much of knowledge, as salvation. We strive to be judged good by parents, the Great Superparent, and by that greatest authority, Public Opinion, whose approval we seek by getting status, success, wealth, celebrity, the grown-up way of boasting, "Look Ma, look what I did."

Man has made the most use of his technological capacities because it's safe to explore the area of our mind that can deal with abstractions. But our capacity for scientific inquiry would be greatly increased if we didn't waste a huge amount of energy proving what we shouldn't have had to prove, that we're good not bad, a quest that wastes even more energy because of the restrictions, fears and self-doubts we acquire from believing we're bad. Socrates said that "the unexamined life is not worth living," Few can follow his advice because it's not safe to explore our emotions lest we find feelings that reveal we're bad, feelings we're ashamed to have, and don't want to know we have.

To be sacrificed to a God when we're babies has an advantage; it spares us the misery of a lifetime of self-hate. We try to avoid the misery by leading an unexamined life. When Eve was in Eden she disobeyed God by seeking knowledge. After God chased her and her mate out of Eden, humans, like animals chased by predators, have run from knowledge — not of how to do things, but from inner knowledge, particularly knowledge of their own self-hate. Though self-hate damages us in endless, painful, self-defeating ways, it becomes the air we breathe; the air we think sustains us. It does sustain us. It keeps us safe from the truth that almost knocked us out when we were children, a truth that, no matter how old we get, we're still sure will kill us.

Chapter 34   The Lethal Truth

Ancient warriors tried to protect themselves by wearing full-body armor. It's a better defense than self-hate, which has the power to attack our bodies from the inside, never mind its power to make us deliberately self-mutilate or 'accidentally' hurt ourselves, even to walk the plank willingly to our death, forsaking the marvel of consciousness to get out of the Hell humans have made on Earth.

We're willing to forsake consciousness to stay unconscious of the greatest unsatisfied need of human beings. "All children, including boys, are born loving and wanting to be loved," said Dan Kindlon and Michael Thompson in *Raising Cain* (1999). They said "including boys," because their purpose was to break down the stereotype that boys are born little tough guys. The loving "emotional life of boys" does have to be protected if our cruel culture is to change. The loving emotional life of girls also has to be protected from the stereotype that they're made of sugar and spice and everything nice if our cruel culture is to change. Girls who haven't been loved can be as cruel as boys who haven't been loved.

Our cruel culture has rarely satisfied the need of any child to love and be loved, and not because children are insatiable. Planet Earth has become an emotional Hell because homo sapiens hasn't been sapient, our species has had a few foggy ideas about love, most of them wrong, and stereotypes meant to fix sex-roles. We would never have believed that girls are born kind and compassionate mothers-in-little, if the baby in us didn't want to stay in a magic Mama's arms forever. "If we can't get mummy's love, we might as well blow up the whole world because without mummy's love, life is not worth living," said a man who was going into his childhood feelings. He put the plight of the world in a nutshell. The mass outbreaks of hate we call war go on and on because babies don't get mummy's love, as mummy herself didn't.

Robert E Lee in a letter to his wife during the Civil War said that war "fills our hearts with hatred instead of love for our neighbors." As if we loved our neighbors. Our love is phony unless we love ourselves, and few of us do, having learned self-hate at home.

I've said over and over that babies want to love and be loved and that they're damaged in mind and body when they're not. Parents hotly insist that their feelings for their children are love. The culture says parents love children; the culture says so because parents were once children who couldn't face a truth they felt would destroy them. Our need not to know is revealed in all the happy endings the public demands, including mystery stories, which also have phony happy endings.

Whodunit?

Murder mysteries became so popular they got the pet name 'whodunits'. We eagerly turn page after page until we find out who did it, who committed the murder. To entertain the reader en route, authors give us more information than we want to know about bell ringing or whatever interests them. "The butler did it" has become a cliché for the denouement, when the killer turns out to be the person we least suspected. The emphasis of murder mysteries on extraneous information, contrived plots, and false leads keep us distracted until the last pages reveal the killer, an ending that's hardly more than a toe tag, as if the killer were already a corpse in a morgue. He (or she) *is* dead. His job as killer is over. He no longer has to delude us into thinking the murder is solved. I rarely think it has been. Murder mysteries usually turn out to be like murder trials, where judges and lawyers also think the important question is whodunit, not *why* whoever dunit did it.

America bans drugs like Ecstasy and LSD because, if taken in the right way, they can jet people into the traumas of their childhood, and reveal who dun them in, facts the government rightly thinks would undermine the institution of the family. No need to worry. Mankind has mostly used drugs to get high, to fly far away from old traumas. Besides, the nineteenth century's decades-long idealization of children, has supplied us with a legal psychedelic. Called "Happy Childhood," it keeps unhappy childhoods in the black hole where we abandon them.

"People seek to forget, seek not to know. They need consolation," said Maxim Gorky. Many others, like T S Eliot, have said that "humankind cannot bear very much reality." Why can't we? Why do we need consolation? Why did we invent a Jesus who walks with us and talks with us and tells us he is our own? I'll say it again: because our parents didn't love us. The world is packed solid with people who "seek not to know," who never want to know.

Our passion for murder mysteries satisfies our need both not to know who did the foul deed and the part of us that sort of does. We enjoy the thrill of being assured again and again that the killer is the person we least suspected, the person whose motivation almost always remains a psychological mystery, just as children at first are puzzled at being judged bad by their parents. Murder mysteries also let the child in us enjoy the pleasures of scapegoating, of killing and getting away with it.

Pop Psychology

After the author Richard Condon (1915-1996) died, Scott Simon on National Public Radio played an old interview in which Condon explained his stutter as a reaction to his father's incessant shouting at him when he was a child, which he suspected was why he expressed himself by the silent act of writing. Simon dismissed his theory as "pop psychology," a popular pooh-pooh tossed at those who dare to blame Pop or Mom for their own defects.

Another mud pie we throw at people who blame parents is "psychobabble." When people in the Bible tried to build a tower that would reach to heaven, God was so outraged he deprived them of the ability to speak intelligibly; they could only babble like babies. The public gets outraged at those who dishonor our first Gods, and pretends that what these psychobabbelists say is Greek to them.

Our need to preserve the idealized image of parents is one reason that, until late in the twentieth century, lawyers defending children who killed their parents were not allowed to mention the parents' abuse. Even when the law changed, judges and juries felt that no matter how badly parents made children suffer, children shouldn't kill them. A child should behave like a *mensch*, a Yiddish word for an upright, responsible person, and courageously take their blows and keep a stiff upper lip, no matter how many times that lip was split. Children are supposed to bear assaults that few adults could bear and be good boys and girls and honor their parents as God says they must, and forgive them as Jesus said they should, and go on with their lives, doing what they're told, forever grateful to their parents for giving them the gift of life.

Alcoholics Anonymous endorsed the same code of behavior. Drunks were told to chuck the bottle, pull up their socks, get into clean clothes, find a job and be respectable. To reach that goal, drunks had to pray to a higher power, focus on hope and recovery, and above all, "keep coming back," go to meetings as often as possible. Drunks needed outside support to counteract a physical disease that attracted them to a substance which made them lose control of their lives.

Part of pulling up your socks was to "Get off the pity pot," a slogan I first heard at Incest Survivors Anonymous where an AA-er would often show up complaining, "Did I get sober for this?" They usually didn't stay long because when an incest survivor would break down and cry, the guy from AA would bellow, "Get off the pity pot!" and be shocked when he was informed that at ISA you were encouraged to cry.

At AA you were supposed to stop sniveling, and get your act together, not weep on the pity pot, which, when you say it fast enough—pity pot, pity pot, pity pot—turns into pity potty and you can practically hear a baby, its bare bottom exposed, tinkling into a chamber pot. For AA-ers, tears were as disgraceful as wetting your pants. A successful AA-er went on with his life. The program worked for billions of people.

It worked for Preppy, the nickname Dr Dorothy Lewis (*Guilty By Reason of Insanity*, 1998) gave a man who wore the adult prep-school uniform: gray slacks, striped tie and blazer. A former drunk, he'd been sober for six years and not only looked respectable, but had a white-collar job. Lewis had brought him and his brothers together in a hotel room to get information about their brother Roger, who'd hacked a woman, her child and sheepdog to death and didn't remember the murder and, what's stranger, that his back was covered with scars. Lewis hoped to find out about Roger's childhood. At first no brother remembered, then the oldest told Lewis that their parents had been so cruel they'd been sent to a home in the country, where their foster mother hailed down god-of-wrath beatings on their bare backs, and her lout of a son had, among other atrocities, forced his penis into their rectums.

Preppy had remembered nothing. The scars on his back were the most severe, but he had no idea they were there. He reminded me of Marcia Cameron, who for decades took out her three false teeth to brush them and didn't remember that her mother had knocked out the real ones. Forced to remember, Preppy took Valium that night, washed down with glasses of bourbon and soda. I don't know if he became a drunk again but I hope he forgot again and got sober. T S Eliot could say that "humankind cannot bear very much reality" because reality is often too much to bear. Preppy would have been better off if he'd kept his childhood in the deep freeze. AA had been the right program for him. Incest Survivors Anonymous's theory that the cure is remembering your abusive past and feeling the hate, grief and fear, may not be right. But not many people attempt it, and few of those are able to stick it out. The truth hurts so much it feels like your heart is exploding in your chest.

Man's inability to bear the pain of not being loved made Preppy and millions of other people become drunks. They have to keep going to AA meetings to go on with their lives, like people who've had heart attacks have to keep taking medications so their new heart won't be rejected. To get a new heart, in the sense of acquiring a new heart for life, is almost impossible. "Till death do us part" is the usual lot for those whose heart was broken in childhood.

I can never get rid of the me who was created in childhood.

Murdering the Past
Some people think they can get a new heart by killing the guilty party in effigy. Harold Shipman, a British doctor, after his addiction to illegal drugs was discovered by his peers and he had to give it up, found him- self killing his patients. In 2000 he was convicted of murdering fifteen of them, which turned out to be at least 300, almost all elderly women, whom he injected with diamorphine (now called heroin). Since Shipman claimed he was innocent, others wondered why he killed. Some thought that just as he'd earlier been addicted to drugs, he later became addict- ed to death because, as he'd once admitted, he got "a buzz" from seeing people die. Others speculated that "his killing might have stemmed from the fact that, at age 17, he witnessed his 43-year-old mother's death from lung cancer and saw her given doses of diamorphine to ease her agony,"

the same drug he'd used to kill his victims. (*Los Angeles Times*, January 6, 2001).

To commit my own "pop psychology": the buzz Shipman felt when he saw patients die may have echoed the high he'd felt when he saw his mother die. If that's true, his high was a sign he had a severe mother problem. Becoming a drug addict kept it repressed. When he had to get off drugs, his hatred of Mom began surfacing and, instead of feeling it and discovering the cause, he killed women. An addiction to killing women is a sign to *cherchez la mère*. Shipman was a friendly, kind man, beloved by his patients, so he may have reasoned that, since they were old and going to die soon, he was saving them from a painful death; he disguised his hatred of his mother as love, and again and again was glad she was out of her misery.

Early in January 2004, Shipman got out of his misery by hanging himself in his jail cell. A man whose mother Shipman killed felt cheated; he'd hoped that one day he could "confront him and ask him why." I've often thought that murderers, instead of being executed or sitting in jail would benefit society by being required to take a truth serum that made them reexperience their childhood and find out why they killed. But would they want to reexperience what Dr James Gilligan in *Violence* said was beneath murderers' tough or numb exterior—a baby crying because he wasn't loved? Could they admit their shameful, secret wish to be a helpless, totally taken care of infant?, that their need to kill was a reaction to not having a universal need satisfied? Since that baby-agony is devastating, I'm sure they'd rather die than feel it. Killing makes them feel powerful, which they have to feel over and over to fight off their desire to be a helpless but cared for baby.

On August 1, 1966 Charles Whitman went to the top of the tower at the University of Texas at Austin and shot at people, killing fourteen and wounding thirty-one. Before he went to the tower, he shot his mother and wife. He may not have wanted them to know what he was about to do, or his mother may have been the real target and his wife a stand-in for mom. If that's true, the people he shot at the university were overkill. Whitman was like many murderers who stab and stab or shoot and shoot the dead body, compelled to release their hate many times. That's a sign that the killer in them is young, that they have to make sure powerful Mom/Dad is really, really dead. The police killed Whitman in the tower, so we'll never know why he killed, which is how we like it.

Index

Index-5

L

M

Index-16

young children all play the same way 203

Z

Zapatistas 44
Zephaniah 17, 18
Zorba the Greek 106